Fifth Edition

BARRON'S

JAPANESE

AT A GLANCE

NOBUO AKIYAMA
Former Adjunct Professor, Japanese Language
Johns Hopkins School of Advanced International Studies (SAIS)
Washington, DC

CAROL AKIYAMA
Language Training Consultant
Washington, DC

PHRASE BOOK · DICTIONARY
TRAVELER'S AID

Published by Barron's Educational Series, Inc.
750 Third Avenue
New York, NY 10017
www.barronseduc.com

Library of Congress Catalog Card Number 2016054341

ISBN: 978-1-4380-0879-0

Library of Congress Cataloging-in-Publication Data

Names: Akiyama, Nobuo, author. | Akiyama, Carol, author.
Title: Japanese at a glance : phrase book & dictionary for travelers / by
    Nobuo Akiyama, Carol Akiyama.
Description: Fifth edition. | Hauppauge, New York : Barron's, 2017. |
    Includes bibliographical references and index. | In English and Japanese.
Identifiers: LCCN 2016054341 | ISBN 9781438008790 (alk. paper)
Subjects: LCSH: Japanese language—Conversation and phrase books—
    English. | Japanese language—Conversation and phrase books (for
    businesspeople)—English.
Classification: LCC PL539 .A649 2017 | DDC 495.6/83421—dc23
    LC record available at *https://lccn.loc.gov/2016054341*

9 8 7 6 5 4 3

Barron's Educational Series, Inc. print books are available at special
quantity discounts to use for sales promotions, employee premiums, or
educational purposes. For more information or to purchase books, please
call the Simon & Schuster special sales department at 866-506-1949.

CONTENTS

PREFACE

So you're taking a trip to one of the many fascinating countries of the world. That's exciting! This phrase book, part of Barron's popular *At a Glance* series, will prove an invaluable companion.

In these books we present the phrases and words that a traveler most often needs for a brief visit to a foreign country where the customs and language are often different. Each phrase book highlights the terms particular to that country, in situations that the tourist is most likely to encounter. This book includes dialogues using words and expressions for each situation. With English, Japanese characters, and romaji (the romanized transcription) for all entries, this book will enable you to communicate quickly and confidently in colloquial terms. It is intended not only for beginners with no knowledge of the language, but also for those who have already studied it and have some familiarity with it.

Some of the unique features and highlights of the Barron's series are:

■ Easy-to-follow *pronunciation* guide and complete phonetic transcriptions (in this book, romaji) for all words and phrases in the book.

■ Compact dictionary of commonly used words and phrases— built right into this phrase book so there's no need to carry a separate dictionary.

■ Useful phrases for the *tourist*, grouped together by subject matter in a logical way so that the appropriate phrase is easy to locate when you need it.

■ Special phrases for the *business traveler*, including banking terms.

■ Thorough section on *food and drink*, with comprehensive food terms you will find on menus.

■ *Emergency phrases* and terms you hope you won't need such medical problems, theft, or loss of valuables.

■ *Sightseeing itineraries*, shopping tips, practical travel tips to help you get off the beaten path and into the countryside, to the small towns and cities, and to the neighboring areas.

■ A *reference section* providing: important signs, conversion tables, holidays, telling time, days of week and months of year.

■ A brief *grammar section*, with the basic elements of the language quickly explained.

■ Dialogues coordinated with the numerous situations covered in this book.

Enjoy your vacation and travel with confidence. You have a friend by your side.

INTRODUCTION TO THE JAPANESE LANGUAGE

Speaking some Japanese will make your trip to Japan a more pleasurable experience. The Japanese people appreciate any efforts foreigners make to communicate in their language. Even a few words or phrases elicit an encouraging response.

You'll probably find Japanese unlike any language you are familiar with. It's not like English, French, Spanish, German, or any other Indo-European language. It's not like most other Asian languages either. Although it borrows some vocabulary and much of its writing system from China, spoken Japanese is completely different from Chinese.

Some linguists think Japanese may have originated in the Altaic language family of Central Asia, but its relationship to any existing language hasn't been proved.

Japanese is rich in the intricacies and sophistication of a 2,000-year-old culture. You will find that in many ways it is complex and subtle, in other ways simple and direct. It reflects how the Japanese people think and reason, and their deeply held values, many quite different from western ones. As you use the phrases in this book, you may begin to perceive how the Japanese look at life, and your interactions will become easier and more natural.

Although there are many regional dialects in Japan, the people in the regions know standard Japanese. No matter where you go, you can communicate with the people and enjoy your visits.

QUICK PRONUNCIATION GUIDE

Japanese isn't difficult to pronounce if you follow a few simple guidelines. Take the time to read this section, and try out each sound presented.

Each English entry is followed by the Japanese, and then the romanization, or romaji.

Good morning.　　おはようございます。Ohayō gozaimasu.

VOWELS

If you have studied Spanish, it may help you to know that Japanese vowels are more like those of Spanish than English. The following vowels are short and pure, with no glide—that is, they are not diphthongs.

Japanese Vowel	English Equivalent	Example
a	as in **fa**ther	*akai (ah-kah-ee)* red
e	as in m**e**n	*ebi (eh-bee)* shrimp
i	as in s**ee**	*imi (ee-mee)* meaning
o	as in b**oa**t	*otoko (oh-toh-koh)* male
u	as in f**oo**d	*uma (oo-mah)* horse

The following vowels are like the ones on the previous page, but lengthened.

Japanese Vowel	English Equivalent	Example
ā	as in f**a**ther, but lengthened	bat**ā** (*bah-tāh*) butter
ei	as in m**e**n, but lengthened	**ei**go (*ēh-goh*) English
ii	as in s**ee**, but lengthened	**ii**haru (*ēe-hah-roo*) insist
ō	as in b**oa**t, but lengthened	**ō**sama (*ōh-sah-mah*) king
ū	as in f**oo**d, but lengthened	y**ū**bin (*yōo-been*) mail

MACRONS

A macron, or bar, above a vowel means it should be lengthened.

EXAMPLE:

butter	batā	*bah-tāh*

In the above word, the macron above the second vowel means you should hold the sound twice as long as you normally would.

And keep in mind these points:

▋ Long vowels are important. Pronouncing a long vowel incorrectly can result in a different word or even an unintelligible one.

EXAMPLE:

ob**a**san (*oh-bah-sahn*) means **aunt**
ob**ā**san (*oh-bāh-sahn*) means **grandmother**

oj**i**san (*oh-jee-sahn*) means **uncle**
oj**ii**san (*oh-jēe-sahn*) means **grandfather**

seki (*seh-kee*) means **seat**
seiki (*seh-kee*) means **century**

▨ Sometimes the **i** and the **u** aren't pronounced. This usually occurs between voiceless consonants (**p, t, k, ch, f, h, s, sh**), or at the end of a word following a voiceless consonant.

EXAMPLE:

sukiyaki (*skee-yah-kee*)
This word for a popular Japanese dish begins with **skee**, not **soo**. The **u** is not pronounced.

tabemashita (*tah-beh-mahsh-tah*) **I ate**.
The **i** is not pronounced.

CONSONANTS

With a few exceptions, Japanese consonants are similar to those of English. Note those that are different:

f   To make the Japanese **f**, blow air lightly between the lips as if you were just beginning a whistle. (The English **f** is pronounced with a passage of air between the upper teeth and the lower lip.)

g   Always pronounce this as in **go**, never as in a**ge**. You may also hear it pronounced as the **ng** sound in ri**ng**, but not at the beginning of a word.

r   To make the Japanese **r**, lightly touch the tip of your tongue to the bony ridge behind the upper teeth, almost in the English **d** position. This is different from the English **r**. It's more like the Spanish **r**, but it's not trilled.

s   Always hiss this as in **so**; never voice it as in hi**s** or plea**s**ure.

And note the following points as well:
▨ If you have trouble making a consonant the Japanese way, your English pronunciation will be intelligible.

■ Some Japanese consonants are doubled. In English, this is just a feature of spelling and often doesn't affect pronunciation. In Japanese, the doubling is important and may change the meaning of a word.

EXAMPLE:

ki**t**e kudasai (*kee-teh koo-dah-sah-ee*) means **Please put it (clothing) on.**

Ki**tt**e kudasai (*keet-teh koo-dah-sah-ee*) means **Please cut it.**

In a word with a doubled consonant, don't say the consonant twice—simply hold the sound longer.

LOAN WORDS

If you know English, you may already know more Japanese than you think. There are thousands of English loan words in everyday use in Japan. Most of these common words have been borrowed with no change in meaning. But there is a change in pronunciation. This can be tricky: On the one hand you're secure with the familiar words; on the other, if you pronounce them as you're used to doing, you won't be understood and you won't understand **t**he words when Japanese use them. For example, baseball won't work; **bēsubōru** (bē̄h-soo-boh̄-roo) will! If you order a beer, you might not get one; say **bīru** (bē̄e-roo) and you will. (Note the long vowel: **biru** with a short vowel means "building.")

Here are a few more examples of familiar words with somewhat different pronunciations in Japanese:

gasoline	ガソリン	*gasorin*
pocket	ポケット	*poketto*
pink	ピンク	*pinku*
ballpoint pen	ボールペン	*bōru pen*
supermarket	スーパー	*sūpā*
milk	ミルク	*miruku*
ticket	チケット	*chiketto*

THE BASICS FOR GETTING BY

MOST FREQUENTLY USED EXPRESSIONS

The expressions in this section are the ones you'll use again and again—the fundamental building blocks of conversation, the way to express your wants or needs, and some simple forms you can use to construct all sorts of questions. It's a good idea to practice these phrases until you know them by heart.

GREETINGS

Good morning.	おはよう ございます。	*Ohayō gozaimasu.*
Good afternoon.	こんにちは。	*Konnichiwa.*
Good evening.	こんばんは。	*Konbanwa.*
Good night.	おやすみなさい。	*Oyasuminasai.*
Pleased to meet you.	おめにかかれて うれしいです。	*Ome ni kakarete ureshii desu.*
How do you do?	はじめまして。 どうぞ、よろしく。	*Hajimemashite. Dōzo, yoroshiku.*
How do you do? (reply)	はじめまして。 こちらこそ、 よろしく。	*Hajimemashite. Kochira koso, yoroshiku.*
How are you?	お元気ですか。	*Ogenki desu ka.*
Fine, thank you.	はい、おかげさ まで。	*Hai, okagesama de.*
Goodbye.	さようなら。	*Sayōnara.*

COMMON EXPRESSIONS

Yes.	はい。／ええ。	*Hai./Ee.*
No.	いいえ。	*Iie.*
Mr./Mrs./Miss/Ms. ____	____さん	(name) *san*
Thanks (casual).	どうも。	*Dōmo.*
Thank you.	どうも、ありがとう。	*Dōmo, arigatō.*
Thank you very much (coming or ongoing favor, kindness, etc.).	どうも、ありがとうございます。	*Dōmo, arigatō gozaimasu.*
Thank you very much (just finished or past favor, kindness, etc.).	どうも、ありがとうございました。	*Dōmo arigatō gozaimashita.*
You're welcome.	いいえ、どういたしまして。	*Iie, dō itashimashite.*
I'm sorry (apology).	ごめんなさい。／すみません。	*Gomennasai./Sumimasen.*
Excuse me (forgiveness).	ご免なさい。／失礼します。	*Gomennasai./Shitsurei shimasu.*
Excuse me, but . . . (attention getter).	すみませんが、、、	*Sumimasen ga, . . .*
Please (permission).	どうぞ。	*Dōzo.*
Please (request).	お願いします。	*Onegai shimasu.*
Hello (for telephone calls, for getting someone's attention).	もしもし。	*Moshimoshi.*
Of course.	もちろん (です)。	*Mochiron (desu).*
Maybe.	たぶん。	*Tabun.*
Pardon me, but . . .	すみませんが、、、	*Sumimasen ga, . . .*
It's all right (condition).	大丈夫です。	*Daijōbu desu.*
It's all right (permission).	はい、結構です。	*Hai, kekkō desu.*

It doesn't matter.	構いません。	*Kamaimasen.*
With pleasure.	喜んで。	*Yorokonde.*
I don't mind.	どうぞ。／ 構いません。	*Dōzo./ Kamaimasen.*
I don't mind (willingness).	いいですよ。	*Ii desu yo.*
Oh, I see.	ああ、なるほど。	*Ā, naruhodo.*
Is that so?	そうなんですか。	*Sō nan desu ka.*
Really?	本当ですか。	*Hontō desu ka.*
Let's go.	さあ、 行きましょう。	*Sā, ikimashō.*
Shall we go?	行きましょうか。	*Ikimashō ka.*
Let's (go/eat/etc.).	さあ、...	*Sā, ...*
No thank you.	いいえ、結構です。	*Iie, kekkō desu.*
I don't want it.	いりません。／ 結構です。	*Irimasen./ Kekkō desu.*
I think so.	そうだと、 思います。	*Sō da to, omoimasu.*
I don't think so.	そうとは、 思いません。	*Sō to wa, omoimasen.*
It's interesting/fun.	面白いです。	*Omoshiroi desu.*
It's over/I'm finished.	終わりました。	*Owarimashita.*
Yes, it is.	はい、そうです。	*Hai, sō desu.*
No, it isn't.	いいえ、 違います。	*Iie, chigaimasu.*
Just a moment, please.	ちょっと待って 下さい。	*Chotto matte kudasai.*
Just a moment, please (polite).	少々お待ち下 さい。	*Shōshō omachi kudasai.*
Not yet.	まだです。	*Mada desu.*
Soon.	もうすぐです。	*Mō sugu desu.*

Right away (request).	すぐ、お願いします。	*Sugu, onegai shimasu.*
Right away (response).	ただいま。	*Tadaima.*
Now (request).	すぐ、お願いします。	*Sugu, onegai shimasu.*
Later (request).	後で、お願いします。	*Ato de, onegai shimasu.*

SOME QUESTIONS AND QUESTION WORDS

What's the matter?	どうか、しましたか。	*Dō ka, shimashita ka.*
What's this?	これは、何ですか。	*Kore wa, nan desu ka.*
Where's the _____?	_____は、どこですか。	_____ *wa, doko desu ka.*
bathroom	お手洗い／トイレ	*otearai/toire*
dining room	食堂	*shokudō*
entrance	入り口	*iriguchi*
exit	出口	*deguchi*
telephone	電話	*denwa*
When?	いつですか。	*Itsu desu ka.*
Where?	どこですか。	*Doko desu ka.*
Where? (polite)	どちらですか。	*Dochira desu ka.*
Why?	なぜですか。／どうしてですか。	*Naze desu ka./Dō shite desu ka.*
Who?	だれですか。	*Dare desu ka.*
Who? (polite)	どなたですか。	*Donata desu ka.*
Which?	どれですか。	*Dore desu ka.*
Which? (polite)	どちらですか。	*Dochira desu ka.*
What?	何ですか。	*Nan desu ka.*

How?	どうやって。／ どのように。	*Dō yatte./* *Dono yō ni.*
How much?	どのくらいですか。	*Dono kurai desu ka.*
How much (money)?	いくらですか。	*Ikura desu ka.*

NEEDS

Could you tell me where the _____ is?	_____ がどこか、教えて下さい。 _____ *ga doko ka, oshiete kudasai.*
Could you give me _____ ?	_____ を、下さい。 _____ *o, kudasai.*
I need _____ .	_____ が、いります。 _____ *ga,* *irimasu.*
I want _____ .	_____ が、欲しいです。 _____ *ga,* *hoshii desu.*
I want to go to _____ .	_____ に、行きたいです。 _____ *ni, ikitai desu.*
I want to see _____ .	_____ が、見たいです。 _____ *ga,* *mitai desu.*
I want to buy _____ .	_____ が、買いたいです。 _____ *ga,* *kaitai desu.*
I want to eat _____ .	_____ が、食べたいです。 _____ *ga,* *tabetai desu.*
I want to drink _____ .	_____ が、飲みたいです。 _____ *ga,* *nomitai desu.*

YOUR PERSONAL CONDITION

I'm thirsty.	のどが、かわいています。 *Nodo ga,* *kawaite imasu.*
I'm hungry.	おなかが、すいています。 *Onaka* *ga, suite imasu.*
I'm full.	おなかが、いっぱいです。 *Onaka* *ga, ippai desu.*
I'm tired.	疲れています。 *Tsukarete imasu.*

I'm sleepy.	眠たいです。	*Nemutai desu.*
I'm sick.	病気です。	*Byōki desu.*
I'm fine.	元気です。／何ともありません。	*Genki desu./Nan tomo arimasen.*
I'm all right.	大丈夫です。	*Daijōbu desu.*

SOME ADJECTIVES

It's cold (weather).	寒いです。	*Samui desu.*
It's hot (weather).	暑いです。	*Atsui desu.*
It's hot and humid.	蒸し暑いです。	*Mushiatsui desu.*
warm/cool (weather)	暖かい／涼しい	*atatakai/suzushii*
pretty, beautiful/ugly	きれい／みにくい	*kirei/minikui*
delicious/awful-tasting	おいしい／まずい	*oishii/mazui*
good, fine/bad	いい／悪い	*ii/warui*
fast, quick/slow	速い／遅い	*hayai/osoi*
high/low (height)	高い／低い	*takai/hikui*
expensive/cheap	高い／安い	*takai/yasui*
hot/cold	熱い／冷たい	*atsui/tsumetai*
same	同じ	*onaji*
big/small	大きい／小さい	*ōkii/chiisai*
long/short	長い／短い	*nagai/mijikai*
strong/weak	強い／弱い	*tsuyoi/yowai*
far/near	遠い／近い	*tōi/chikai*
wide/narrow	広い／狭い	*hiroi/semai*
heavy/light	重い／軽い	*omoi/karui*
new/old	新しい／古い	*atarashii/furui*
young (person)	若い	*wakai*
dark/light	暗い／明るい	*kurai/akarui*
quiet/noisy	静か／うるさい	*shizuka/urusai*

a lot, many/a little, few	たくさん／少し	*takusan/sukoshi*
intelligent/stupid	頭がいい／ 頭が悪い	*atama ga ii/ atama ga warui*
right/wrong (judgment)	正しい／悪い	*tadashii/warui*
right/wrong (accuracy)	正しい／間違い	*tadashii/machigai*
easy/difficult	易しい／難しい	*yasashii/ muzukashii*
early/late	早い／遅い	*hayai/osoi*

PRONOUNS

I	私	*watakushi*
I (informal)	わたし	*watashi*
I (very informal, for men only)	僕	*boku*
I (very informal, mostly for women)	あたし	*atashi*
you (singular)	あなた	*anata*
he/she	彼／彼女	*kare/kanojo*
we	私達	*wakakushitachi*
you (plural)	あなた達	*anatatachi*
they	彼ら	*karera*

■ For the word "I," the safe usage for a beginner is *watakushi*.

■ In Japanese, "you" has limited usage, unlike the convenient English "you." The preference is a person's last name plus *san*.

Possessives: To form the possessives, simply add the particle *no* to the above pronouns:

my	私の	*watakushi no*
his	彼の	*kare no*

MORE BASIC WORDS

here/there/over there	ここ/そこ/あそこ	koko/soko/asoko
this/that/that over there (nouns)	これ/それ/あれ	kore/sore/are
this/that/that over there (adjectives)	この/その/あの	kono/sono/ano
and (between nouns)	と	to
and (between sentences)	そして	soshite
then	それから	sore kara
but	けれども/でも/しかし	keredomo/demo /shikashi
or	それとも/または/あるいは	soretomo/mata wa/aruiwa
also	も/また	mo/mata
before	_____の前に	_____ no mae ni
during	_____の間に	_____ no aida ni
after	_____の後で	_____ no ato de
to	_____へ/	_____ e/
	_____に	_____ ni
from	_____から	_____ kara
at	_____で	_____ de
in	_____に	_____ ni
up	_____の上に	_____ no ue ni
down	_____の下に	_____ no shita ni
inside	_____の中に	_____ no naka ni
outside	_____の外に	_____ no soto ni
on	_____の上に	_____ no ue ni
near	_____の近くに	_____ no chikaku ni
above	_____の上に	_____ no ue ni

below	_____の下に	_____ *no shita ni*
between	_____の間に	_____ *no aida ni*
through	_____を通して	_____ *o tōshite*

COMMUNICATING

Do you understand?	わかりますか。*Wakarimasu ka.*
Yes, I understand.	はい、わかります。*Hai, wakarimasu.*
No, I don't understand.	いいえ、わかりません。*Iie, wakarimasen.*
Did you understand?	わかりましたか。*Wakarimashita ka.*
Yes, I understood.	はい、わかりました。*Hai, wakarimashita.*
No, I didn't understand.	いいえ、わかりませんでした。*Iie, wakarimasen deshita.*
Do you understand English?	英語がわかりますか。*Eigo ga wakarimasu ka.*
Can you speak English?	英語が話せますか。*Eigo ga hanasemasu ka.*
I can speak a little Japanese.	日本語が少し話せます。*Nihongo ga sukoshi hanasemasu.*
I know very little Japanese.	日本語は殆ど知りません。*Nihongo wa hotondo shirimasen.*
I don't understand Japanese.	日本語はわかりません。*Nihongo wa wakarimasen.*
Could you repeat it, please?	もう一度、お願いします。*Mō ichido, onegai shimasu.*
Please speak slowly.	もっと、ゆっくり話して下さい。*Motto, yukkuri hanashite kudasai.*
Write it down on the paper, please.	紙に書いて下さい。*Kami ni kaite kudasai.*
Is there anyone who understands English?	誰か、英語がわかる人がいますか。*Dareka, eigo ga wakaru hito ga imasu ka.*

Do you speak English?	英語を話しますか。*Eigo o hanashimasu ka.*
Can you speak English?	英語が話せますか。*Eigo ga hanasemasu ka.*
What do you call this?	これは、何といいますか。*Kore wa, nan to iimasu ka.*
What's this called in Japanese?	これは、日本語で何といいますか。*Kore wa, Nihongo de, nan to iimasu ka.*
What's this called in English?	これは、英語で何といいますか。*Kore wa, eigo de nan to iimasu ka.*
What is this?	これは何ですか。*Kore wa, nan desu ka.*
Excuse me, could you help me, please?	すみませんが、助けていただけますか。*Sumimasen ga, tasukete itadakemasu ka.*
Please point to the suitable phrase in this book.	この本にある、適切な文を指さして下さい。*Kono hon ni aru, tekisetsu na bun o yubisashite kudasai.*

POLICE

Japan is a safe country; the crime rate is one of the lowest in the world. It's unlikely that you'll ever need to talk to the police for anything but directions. Nevertheless, here are a few "just in case" phrases.

Excuse me.	すみませんが。*Sumimasen ga.*
Would you call the police for me please?	警官を呼んでもらえますか。*Keikan o yonde moraemasu ka.*
What's the telephone number for the police?	警察の電話は、何番ですか。*Keisatsu no denwa wa, nan ban desu ka.*
I lost <u>my wallet</u>.	<u>財布</u>を無くしてしまいました。<u>*Saifu*</u> *o nakushite shimaimashita.*
passport	パスポート *pasupōto*

plane tickets	飛行機の券	*hikōki no ken*
My <u>luggage</u> has been stolen.	スーツケースを盗まれて しまいました。 *<u>Sūtsukēsu</u> o nusumarete shimaimashita.*	
cash	現金	*genkin*
What shall I do?	どうしたらいいですか。 *Dō shitara ii desu ka.*	
I want to report <u>a theft</u>.	盗難を、報告したいのですが。 *<u>Tōnan</u> o, hōkokushitai no desu ga.*	
an accident	事故	*jiko*
I think my money has been stolen.	お金を盗まれてしまったみたいです。 *Okane o nusumarete shimatta mitai desu.*	
Someone just grabbed my <u>camera</u>.	たった今、<u>カメラ</u>をひったくられてしまいました。 *Tatta ima, <u>kamera</u> o hittakurarete shimaimashita.*	
purse	ハンドバッグ	*handobaggu*
Can you help me?	助けてもらえますか。 *Tasukete moraemasu ka.*	
My name is _____.	私の名前は _____ です。 *Watakushi no namae wa _____ desu.*	
I'm <u>an American</u>.	私は <u>アメリカ人</u>です。 *Watakushi wa <u>Amerika jin</u> desu.*	
I'm in Japan <u>on business</u>.	日本には <u>仕事</u>で来ています。 *Nihon niwa <u>shigoto</u> de kite imasu.*	
as a tourist	観光	*kankō*
I'm staying at _____.	_____に 泊まっています。 *____ ni, tomatte imasu.*	
My telephone number is _____.	私の電話番号は _____番です。 *Watakushi no denwa bangō wa _____ ban desu.*	

I've lost my way.	道に迷ってしまいました。*Michi ni mayotte shimaimashita.*
Can you direct me to _____?	_____への行き方を 教えて下さい。__ _____*e no ikikata o oshiete kudasai.*

SPECIAL NEEDS

I'm blind.	目が見えません。*Me ga miemasen.*
I'm deaf.	耳が聞こえません。*Mimi ga kioemasen.*
I'm hearing/visually impaired.	難聴／難視です。*Nanchō/nanshi desu.*
I'm disabled.	手足が不自由です。*Teashi ga fujiyū desu.*
I can't walk.	歩けません。*Arukemasen.*
I can't go up and down stairs.	階段の上り下りができません。*Kaidan no noboriori ga dekimasen.*
I'm using <u>a wheelchair</u>.	<u>車椅子</u>を使っています。<u>*Kuruma isu*</u> *o tsukatte imasu.*
a walker	歩行器　　*hokōki*
a crutch/crutches	松葉杖　　*matsubazue*
a cane	杖　　*tsue*
Is it wheelchair accessible?	車椅子で行けますか。*Kuruma isu de ikemasu ka.*
Are there <u>stairs</u>?	<u>階段</u>がありますか。<u>*Kaidan ga arimasu ka.*</u>
steps	段差　　*dansa*
Is there <u>an elevator</u>?	<u>エレベーター</u>がありますか。<u>*Erebētā ga arimasu ka.*</u>
a ramp	スロープ　　*surōpu*
Is there a place for a wheelchair?	車椅子の置き場がありますか。*Kuruma isu no okiba ga arimasu ka.*

Is there a toilet for the disabled?	障害者用トイレがありますか。 *Shōgaisha yō toire ga arimasu ka.*
Are there handrails?	手すりがついていますか。*Tesuri ga suite imasu ka.*
I need assistance.	助けてください。*Tasukete kudasai.*
Is there a brochure in braille?	点字のパンフレットがありますか。 *Tenji no panfuretto ga arimasu ka.*
Are there special seats for the disabled?	障害者の優先席がありますか。 *Shōgaisha no yūsen seki ga arimasu ka.*
Can you please help me?	手を貸してもらえますか。*Te o kashite moraemasu ka.*

BABIES AND CHILDREN

Where can I buy some <u>diapers</u>?	どこで<u>紙おむつ</u>が買えますか。*Doko de kamiomutsu ga kaemasu ka.*
baby wipes	おしりふき *oshiri fuki*
baby bottles	哺乳ビン *honyū bin*
pacifiers	おしゃぶり *oshaburi*
nipples	乳首 *chikubi*
Are <u>babies</u> allowed here?	<u>赤ん坊</u>も構いませんか。*Akanbō mo kamaimasen ka.*
toddlers	幼児 *yōji*
children	子供 *kodomo*
Is it stroller accessible?	ベビーカーは入れますか？*Bebī kā wa hairemasu ka.*
Is there a place to put a stroller?	ベビーカーの置き場所がありますか。 *Bebī kā no okibasho ga arimasu ka.*
Is there a place for <u>nursing</u>?	授乳の場所がありますか？*Ju-nyū no basho ga arimasu ka.*
changing diapers	オムツ交換 *omutsu kōkan*

Is there a <u>highchair</u>?	子供用の椅子がありますか。	*Kodomo yō no isu ga arimasu ka.*
crib	ベビーベッド	*bebī beddo*
children's fare	子供料金	*kodomo ryōkin*
children's discount	子供割引	*kodomo waribiki*
children's menu	お子様メニュー	*okosama menyū*
Is there a playground nearby?	近くに子供の遊び場がありますか、	*Chikaku ni kodomo no asobiba ga arimasu ka.*
Is there a pediatrician nearby?	近くに小児科医がいますか？	*Chikaku ni shōnika i ga imasu ka.*

NUMBERS

CARDINAL NUMBERS

0	ゼロ／零	*zero/rei*
1	一	*ichi*
2	二	*ni*
3	三	*san*
4	四	*shi/yon*
5	五	*go*
6	六	*roku*
7	七	*shichi/nana*
8	八	*hachi*
9	九	*kyū/ku*
10	十	*jū*
11	十一	*jū ichi*
12	十二	*jū ni*
13	十三	*jū san*

14	十四	*jū shi/jū yon*
15	十五	*jū go*
16	十六	*jū roku*
17	十七	*jū shichi/jū nana*
18	十八	*jū hachi*
19	十九	*jū ku/jū kyū*
20	二十	*ni jū*
30	三十	*san jū*
40	四十	*yon jū*
50	五十	*go jū*
60	六十	*roku jū*
70	七十	*nana jū*
80	八十	*hachi jū*
90	九十	*kyū jū*
100	百	*hyaku*
200	二百	*ni hyaku*
300	三百	*san byaku*
400	四百	*yon hyaku*
500	五百	*go hyaku*
600	六百	*roppyaku*
700	七百	*nana hyaku*
800	八百	*happyaku*
900	九百	*kyū hyaku*
1,000	千	*sen*
2,000	二千	*ni sen*
3,000	三千	*san zen*
8,000	八千	*hassen*
10,000	一万	*ichi man*

20,000	二万	*ni man*
100,000	十万	*jū man*
200,000	二十万	*ni jū man*
1,000,000	百万	*hyaku man*
2,000,000	二百万	*ni hyaku man*
3,000,000	三百万	*san byaku man*
4,000,000	四百万	*yon hyaku man*
5,000,000	五百万	*go hyaku man*
6,000,000	六百万	*roppyaku man*
7,000,000	七百万	*nana hyaku man*
8,000,000	八百万	*happyaku man*
9,000,000	九百万	*kyū hyaku man*
10,000,000	千万	*sen man*
20,000,000	二千万	*ni sen man*
30,000,000	三千万	*san zen man*
80,000,000	八千万	*hassen man*
100,000,000	一億	*ichi oku*

CARDINAL NUMBERS (ANOTHER SYSTEM)

1	一つ	*hitotsu*
2	二つ	*futatsu*
3	三つ	*mittsu*
4	四つ	*yottsu*
5	五つ	*itsutsu*
6	六つ	*muttsu*
7	七つ	*nanatsu*
8	八つ	*yattsu*
9	九つ	*kokonotsu*
10	十	*tō*

| 11 | 十一 | *jū ichi* |
| 12 | 十二 | *jū ni* |

Note: This is the traditional Japanese cardinal number system. It covers up to ten, but the rest is the same as the first set of cardinal numbers.

ORDINAL NUMBERS

first	一番目(の)／第一(の)	*ichi ban me (no)/ dai ichi (no)*
second	二番目(の)／第二(の)	*ni ban me (no)/ dai ni (no)*
third	三番目(の)／第三(の)	*san ban me (no)/ dai san (no)*
fourth	四番目(の)／第四(の)	*yo(n) ban me (no)/ dai yon (no)*
fifth	五番目(の)／第五(の)	*go ban me (no)/ dai go (no)*
sixth	六番目(の)／第六(の)	*roku ban me (no)/ dai roku (no)*
seventh	七番目(の)／第七(の)	*nana ban me (no)/ dai nana (no)*
eighth	八番目(の)／第八(の)	*hachi ban me (no)/ dai hachi (no)*
ninth	九番目(の)／第九(の)	*ku ban me (no) or kyū ban me (no)/ dai ku (no) or dai kyū (no)*
tenth	十番目(の)／第十(の)	*jū ban me (no)/ dai jū (no)*

THE LAND AND PEOPLE

GEOGRAPHY

Japan is an island nation in the North Pacific, off the eastern coast of Asia. Its four major islands are:

Honshu (main)	本州	*Honshū*
Hokkaido (northernmost)	北海道	*Hokkaidō*
Kyushu (southernmost)	九州	*Kyūshū*
Shikoku (smallest)	四国	*Shikoku*

The major cities, in order of population size, are:

Tokyo	東京	*Tōkyō*
Yokohama	横浜	*Yokohama*
Osaka	大阪	*Ōsaka*
Nagoya	名古屋	*Nagoya*
Sapporo	札幌	*Sapporo*
Kobe	神戸	*Kōbe*
Kyoto	京都	*Kyōto*
Fukuoka	福岡	*Fukuoka*
Kawasaki	川崎	*Kawasaki*

TALKING ABOUT THE COUNTRY

Japan	日本	*Nihon/Nippon*
island nation	島国	*shimaguni*
population	人口	*jinkō*

land area	面積	*menseki*
Pacific Ocean	太平洋	*Taiheiyō*
Sea of Japan	日本海	*Nihonkai*
Pacific side	表日本	*Omote Nihon*
Sea of Japan side	裏日本	*Ura Nihon*
Inland Sea	瀬戸内海	*Setonaikai*
volcano	火山	*kazan*
hot springs	温泉	*onsen*
earthquake	地震	*jishin*
tsunami	津波	*tsunami*
ocean	海	*umi*
coast	海岸	*kaigan*
bay	湾	*wan*
peninsula	半島	*hantō*
island	島	*shima*
mountain range	山脈	*sanmyaku*
mountain	山	*yama*
hill	丘	*oka*
river	川	*kawa*
lake	湖	*mizuumi*
marsh	沼	*numa*
waterfall	滝	*taki*
capital	首都	*shuto*
city	市	*shi*
big city	都会	*tokai*
suburb	郊外	*kōgai*
countryside	地方／田舎	*chihō/inaka*
town	町	*machi*

village	村	*mura*
prefecture	県	*ken*
prefectural capital	県庁所在地	*kenchō shozaichi*
map	地図	*chizu*
national park	国立公園	*kokuritsu kōen*
World Heritage Site	世界遺産指定地	*sekai isan shiteichi*

SEASONS AND WEATHER

season	季節	*kisetsu*
four seasons	四季	*shiki*
spring	春	*haru*
March/April/May	三月／四月／五月	*sangatsu/ shigatsu/gogatsu*
summer	夏	*natsu*
June/July/August	六月／七月／八月	*rokugatsu / shichigatsu / hachigatsu*
fall	秋	*aki*
September/October/ November	九月／十月／ 十一月	*kugatsu/jūgatsu/ jūichigatsu*
winter	冬	*fuyu*
December/January/ February	十二月／一月／ 二月	*jūnigatsu/ ichigatsu/nigatsu*
warm	暖かい	*atatakai*
hot	暑い	*atsui*
hot and humid	蒸し暑い	*mushiatsui*
cool	涼しい	*suzushii*
cold	寒い	*samui*

dry	乾燥している	*kansō shite iru*
humid	湿気が高い	*shikke ga takai*
climate	気候	*kikō*
weather	天気	*tenki*
clear (sky)	晴れ	*hare*
cloudy	曇り	*kumori*
wind	風	*kaze*
windy	風が強い	*kaze ga tsuyoi*
rain	雨	*ame*
heavy rain	豪雨	*gōu*
thundershower	雷雨	*raiu*
shower	夕立	*yūdachi*
drizzle	霧雨	*kirisame*
rainy season	梅雨	*tsuyu*
snow	雪	*yuki*
sleet	みぞれ	*mizore*
hail	あられ	*arare*
ice	氷	*kōri*
frost	霜	*shimo*
typhoon	台風	*taifū*
When does the rainy season begin?	梅雨は、いつ始まりますか。	*Tsuyu wa, itsu hajimarimasu ka.*
When does the rainy season end?	梅雨は、いつ終わりますか。	*Tsuyu wa, itsu owarimasu ka.*
When do the cherry blossoms bloom?	桜は、いつ咲きますか。	*Sakura wa, itsu sakimasu ka.*
When do the autumn leaves begin?	紅葉は、いつ頃ですか。	*Kōyō wa, itsu goro desu ka.*
It's a nice day, isn't it?	いい(お)天気ですねえ。	*Ii (o)tenki desu nē.*

It's terrible weather isn't it?	いやな(お)天気ですねえ。 *Iya na (o)tenki desu nē.*
It's <u>hot</u> today, isn't it?	今日は、<u>暑い</u>ですねえ。 *Kyō wa, <u>atsui</u> desu nē.*
cool	涼しい *suzushii*
cold	寒い *samui*
warm	暖かい *atatakai*
It's <u>fine</u>.	<u>晴れ</u>です。 *<u>Hare</u> desu.*
cloudy	曇り *kumori*
raining	雨 *ame*
snowing	雪 *yuki*
windy	風が強い *kaze ga tsuyoi*
Will it stop raining/ snowing soon?	もうじき、止むでしょうか。 *Mōjiki, yamu deshō ka.*
I hope it will clear up.	晴れるといいのですが。 *Hareru to ii no desu ga.*
What's tomorrow's weather forecast?	明日の天気予報はどうですか。 *Ashita no tenki yohō wa dō desu ka.*
When is the typhoon season?	台風シーズンはいつですか。 *Taifū shīzun wa itsu desu ka.*
Do you think a typhoon is coming?	台風は、来そうですか。 *Taifū wa, kisō desu ka.*

GETTING TO KNOW THE JAPANESE

Japanese culture is not only very old, it's also remarkably intact. Perhaps geography played a role, perhaps history—Japan was virtually isolated from the rest of the world for two and a half centuries, ending in 1868. Because the Japanese people were free from outside contacts for so long, their own traditions became stronger. Even today, with the influence of the West so visible, the Japanese adhere to their unique customs and values. Some Japanese cultural requirements may differ from your own. No one expects foreign visitors to act like Japanese. But a few insights into new and different customs can help you speak Japanese more easily.

INTRODUCTIONS

In general, the Japanese prefer "proper" introductions. Some people will be glad to strike up a conversation with a stranger under casual circumstances. You can introduce yourself if you like. But formal introductions are preferable; they can set the tone of the ongoing relationship. Whenever possible, have a mutual friend, acquaintance, or colleague introduce you to someone he or she already knows.

Who is that?	あの人は、だれですか。*Ano hito wa, dare desu ka.*
Who is that? (polite)	あの方は、どなたですか。*Ano kata wa, donata desu ka.*
Do you know who that is?	あの人がだれか、知っていますか。 *Ano hito ga dare ka, shitte imasu ka.*
Do you know who that is? (polite)	あの方がどなたか、ご存じですか。 *Ano kata ga donata ka, gozonji desu ka.*
I would like to meet him/her (literally, that person).	あの人に、会いたいのですが。*Ano hito ni, aitai no desu ga.*
I would like to meet him/her (literally, that person). (polite)	あの方に、会いたいのですが。*Ano kata ni, aitai no desu ga.*
Would you introduce me to him/her (that person)?	あの人に、紹介してもらえますか。 *Ano hito ni, shōkai shite moraemasu ka.*
Would you introduce me to him/her (that person)? (polite)	あの方に、紹介していただけますか。 *Ano kata ni, shōkai shite itadakemasu ka.*
Mr./Ms. A, may I introduce Mr./Ms. B?	Aさん、Bさんをご紹介したいのですが。 *A san, B san o goshōkai shitai no desu ga.*

I would like you to meet Mr./Mrs./Ms. C.	Cさんを、ご紹介します。 *C san o, goshōkai shimasu.*
Have you met Mr./Mrs./Ms. D?	Dさんを、ご存知ですか。 *D san o, gozonji desu ka.*
Mr./Mrs./Ms. F, this is Mr./Mrs./Ms. G.	Fさん、こちらはGさんです。 *F san, kochira wa G san desu.*
Pardon me, may I introduce myself?	突然ですが、自己紹介させてください。 *Totsuzen desu ga, jiko shōkai sasete kudasai.*
This is my <u>friend</u>.	ここにいるのは、私の<u>友人</u>です。 *Koko ni iru no wa, watakushi no <u>yūjin</u> desu.*
husband	夫／主人　*otto/shujin*
wife	妻／家内　*tsuma/kanai*
son	息子　*musuko*
daughter	娘　*musume*
father	父　*chichi*
mother	母　*haha*
How do you do?	初めまして。どうぞよろしく。 *Hajimemashite. Dōzo yoroshiku.*
How do you do? (reply)	初めまして。こちらこそよろしく。 *Hajimemashite. Kochira koso yoroshiku.*
I'm glad to meet you.	お目にかかれて、うれしいです。 *Ome ni kakarete, ureshii desu.*
I'm <u>Joe Smith</u>.	ジョー・スミスです。 *<u>Jō Sumisu</u> desu.*
My name is <u>Jean Hall</u>.	私の名前は、<u>ジーン・ホール</u>です。 *Watakushi no namae wa, <u>Jīn Hōru</u> desu.*

CARDS

Japanese routinely exchange business cards during introductions. Japan has been called a vertical society; people deal with each other according to their relative positions on that vertical ladder. Knowing a person's profession or business affiliation, including the position within a company, is important. It helps in choosing the right level of language, the right gestures, and in other, more subtle interactions. It's also convenient to have the card to refer to later. You'll be given a lot of cards in Japan, and you'll find it useful to have your own to offer in exchange. You can have them made once you arrive, or you can just take your own cards with you, since many Japanese can read English.

card	名刺　*meishi*
Here's my card.	名刺をどうぞ。*Meishi o dōzo.*
Thank you very much.	ありがとうございます。*Arigatō gozaimasu.*
Here's mine.	私のもどうぞ。*Watakushi no mo dōzo.*
May I have your card?	名刺をいただけますか。 *Meishi o itadakemasu ka.*

NAMES

Japanese rarely use first names with people they've just met. They use the last name followed by the respectful *san.* Even among themselves, most friends of long standing use last names. When friends or family members do use first names, they too are followed by *san.* In the case of children, the first names are followed by *chan.* Because few Japanese are comfortable with the use of their own or others' first names, it's safer for foreigners to use last names plus *san* when addressing Japanese unless specifically asked to do otherwise. Note that when referring to oneself, the *san* is dropped. Also keep in mind that Japanese use the family name first: it's Jones Mary, not Mary Jones.

What's your name?	お名前は。*Onamae wa.*

My name is (last name).	(苗字) です。(last name) *desu.*/ (苗字) と申します。(humble) (last name) *to mōshimasu.*

PERSONAL INFORMATION

Where are you from?	どちらから、いらっしゃいましたか。 *Dochira kara, irasshaimashita ka.*
I'm from <u>America</u>.	<u>アメリカ</u>から来ました。<u>*Amerika*</u> *kara kimashita.*
England	イギリス *Igirisu*
Canada	カナダ *Kanada*
Australia	オーストラリア *Ōsutoraria*
Which country are you from?	お国はどちらですか。*Okuni wa dochira desu ka.*
I'm from <u>the United States</u>.	<u>アメリカ</u>です。<u>*Amerika*</u> *desu.*
Where were you born?	お生まれはどちらですか。*Oumare wa dochira desu ka.*
I was born in <u>Rome</u>.	<u>ローマ</u>で生まれました。<u>*Rōma*</u> *de umaremashita.*
Where do you live?	お住まいはどちらですか。*Osumai wa dochira desu ka.*
I live in <u>Paris</u>.	<u>パリ</u>です。<u>*Pari*</u> *desu.*
Are you married?	結婚していらっしゃいますか。 *Kekkon shite irasshaimasu ka.*
I'm married.	結婚しています。*Kekkon shite imasu.*
I'm single.	独身です。*Dokushin desu.*
Do you have any children?	お子さんがいらっしゃいますか。 *Okosan ga irasshaimasu ka.*
How old are you?	おいくつですか。*Oikutsu desu ka.*
I'm over 20.	二十歳は過ぎています。*Hatachi wa sugite imasu.*

I'm <u>16</u> years old.	十六歳です。	<u>*Jūroku sai desu*</u>.
18	十八歳	*jūhassai*
20	二十歳	*hatachi*
22	二十二歳	*nijūni sai*
25	二十五歳	*nijūgo sai*
30	三十歳	*sanjussai*
35	三十五歳	*sanjūgo sai*
40	四十歳	*yonjussai*
45	四十五歳	*yonjūgo sai*
50	五十歳	*gojussai*
55	五十五歳	*gojūgo sai*
60	六十歳	*rokujussai*
65	六十五歳	*rokujūgo sai*
70	七十歳	*nanajussai*
75	七十五歳	*nanajūgo sai*
80	八十歳	*hachijussai*
85	八十五歳	*hachijūgo sai*
What work do you do?	お仕事は。	*Oshigoto wa*.
I'm a <u>student</u>.	<u>学生</u>です。	<u>*Gakusei*</u> *desu*.
a teacher	教師	*kyōshi*
a professor	教授	*kyōju*
a housewife	主婦	*shufu*
an office worker	会社員	*kaishain*
an office worker (for men only)	サラリーマン	*sararīman*
a secretary	秘書	*hisho*
an engineer	技術者	*gijutsusha*
in the military	軍人	*gunjin*

a company president	会社の社長	*kaisha no shachō*
a company executive	会社の重役	*kaisha no jūyaku*
an industrialist	実業家	*jitsugyōka*
a doctor	医者	*isha*
a dentist	歯医者	*haisha*
a nurse	看護師	*kangoshi*
a pharmacist	薬剤師	*yakuzaishi*
a lawyer	弁護士	*bengoshi*
an accountant	会計士	*kaikeishi*
an architect	建築家	*kenchikuka*
a musician	音楽家	*ongakuka*
an artist	芸術家	*geijutsuka*
a writer	作家	*sakka*
a politician	政治家	*seijika*
a government official	役人	*yakunin*
a government office worker	公務員	*kōmuin*
a journalist	ジャーナリスト	*jānarisuto*

DAILY GREETINGS AND LEAVETAKINGS

Japanese ritual greetings and leavetakings differ somewhat from those of English. There are some phrases that you might not think of saying yourself, but that you will need for daily ritual exchanges. There's no real equivalent for the English "Hi" or "Hello." In Japanese, the initial greeting is based on the time of day:

Good morning	おはようございます。*Ohayō gozaimasu.*
Good afternoon.	こんにちは。*Konnichiwa.*
Good evening.	こんばんは。*Konbanwa.*

This is said by both people, and the exchange is not usually followed by anything like the English "How are you?" There is, however, a phrase that Japanese say when they meet after not having seen each other for a while (several weeks or longer):

It's been a long time.	お久しぶりです。 *Ohisashiburi desu.*

Next comes a statement of gratitude for any kindness or favor the other person may have done for the speaker during their previous meeting or since. The translation seems a bit awkward in English, but knowing what it means will help you to understand why Japanese keep saying to you in English, "Thank you for last time."

Thank you for last time.	この間は、ありがとうございました。 *Kono aida wa, arigatō gozaimashita.*

Another greeting is the ubiquitous "welcome," spoken with a smile and a lilt. Friends will welcome you to their homes or offices that way, and shopkeepers, especially in restaurants, will sing it out to anyone entering the door.

Welcome.	いらっしゃい。 *Irasshai.*
Welcome. (polite)	いらっしゃいませ。 *Irasshaimase.*

There is an exchange that translates as the equivalent of the English "How are you?" / "Fine thank you," but it is not used among people who see each other daily. Save this for when you haven't seen someone in a while—several weeks or longer:

How are you?	お元気ですか。 *Ogenki desu ka.*
Fine, thanks, and you?	はい、おかげさまで。(名前)さんは。 *Hai, okagesama de.* (Name) *san wa.*

Japanese has many ways to say goodbye. Here are some. There are more choices here than for the greetings!

Good night.	おやすみなさい。 *Oyasuminasai.*
Goodbye.	さようなら。 *Sayōnara.*
Well, goodbye.	それでは、さようなら。 *Soredewa, sayōnara.*

Bye (casual).	じゃあ。／じゃあね。 *Jā./Jā ne.*
See you again.	では、また。 *Dewa, mata.*
See you tomorrow.	また、あした。 *Mata, ashita.*
See you soon.	では、また近いうちに。 *Dewa, mata chikai uchi ni.*
See you later.	では、のちほど。 *Dewa, nochi hodo.*
So long.	ごきげんよう。 *Gokigenyō.*
Take care.	気をつけて。 *Ki o tsukete.*
I must go.	おいとまします。 *Oitoma shimasu.*
I'm afraid I'll have to go soon.	そろそろ、失礼します。 *Sorosoro, shitsurei shimasu.*
Sorry for taking your time.	おじゃましました。 *Ojama shimashita.*
Thank you for the delicious food.	ごちそうさまでした。 *Gochisō sama deshita.*

If you're not going to see someone for a long time, there's no equivalent of "I'll miss you." It's a natural thing for English speakers to express, but Japanese feel that some things are better left unsaid!

GESTURES

THE HANDSHAKE AND THE BOW

Although it's not common practice, some Japanese do shake hands with one another, so you can extend your hand for a handshake. Some might even offer theirs first. But anything more, like a greeting hug or kiss, could be offensive unless you know the person very well. Open displays of affection are not common.

bow	おじぎ *ojigi*
to bow	おじぎする *ojigi suru*

When meeting or greeting people, Japanese bow. It's an old and important custom. They bow according to prescribed rules of etiquette and respect that have become second nature to them. The kind and degree of the bow depends on the relationship between the two people, the relative status, age, obligation, and feeling of respect. There are even rules for who bows lower to whom. This custom is so instinctive that Japanese often bow when they're talking on the telephone! They say it helps them to convey verbally the proper nuances.

What should *you* do? To bow or not to bow, indeed, *how* to bow will be up to you. Remember, non-Japanese are not expected to bow. But people *will* bow to you, and you're free to follow suit if you feel comfortable. Just lean forward from the waist, keep your head down, and you'll do just fine.

GIFT GIVING AND RECEIVING

Japan is a country of gift giving and receiving. If you have Japanese friends or acquaintances, you'll probably receive some gifts yourself while you're in Japan. They may be token souvenirs, or much more. These phrases will help!

gift	贈り物／おみやげ *okurimono/omiyage*
return gift	おかえし　*okaeshi*

Although Japanese will give you gifts, they don't expect anything in return. Whether you participate in the exchange or not is up to you; either way is fine.

A special note on gift giving: When visiting a Japanese home, it's customary and polite to bring a gift. It doesn't have to be elaborate: a box of candy or cookies, some fruit or other food item, a bouquet of flowers, or something like that will be welcome, as will something from your country.

GIVING

Here's something for you.	これを、どうぞ。*Kore o, dōzo.*

It's from <u>Virginia</u>.	バージニアからのものです。 _Bājinia_ kara no mono desu.
It's just a token.	これは、ほんのおしるしです。 Kore wa, hon no oshirushi desu.
I hope you like it.	お気にめせば、いいのですが。 Oki ni meseba, ii no desu ga.
This is a small present for you.	ささやかなものですが。_Sasayaka na mono desu ga._
It's not anything special, but . . .	大したものではありませんが。 Taishita mono dewa arimasen ga.

AND RECEIVING

Thank you very much.	どうも、ありがとうございます。 Dōmo, arigatō gozaimasu.
Thank you very much for such a wonderful gift.	大変けっこうなものをちょうだいして。 Taihen, kekkō na mono o chōdai shite.
It's very kind of you.	本当に、ご親切に。_Hontō ni,_ _goshinsetsu ni._
How nice of you!	わざわざ、ご親切に。_Wazawaza,_ _goshinsetsu ni._

When you give or receive a gift, it's good manners to use _both_ hands. Don't be surprised if, when you give a Japanese a gift, he or she doesn't open it in front of you, but waits until after you leave. If _you_ want to open a gift you've received, it's quite all right. Japanese know that Westerners do this. Just say:

May I open it?	開けてもいいですか。 Aketemo, ii desu ka.

Now you can open your gift, and make the appropriate responses; it's hard to thank someone for a beautifully wrapped package when you don't know what's inside!

If you do decide to take some gifts to Japan with you to give to hosts, friends, or new acquaintances, they don't need to be expensive. Something from your country will be most appreciated. When you're gift shopping before you leave home, you may want to check the country of origin of the item. Avoid the things that are made in Japan!

WHEN YOU ARRIVE

ENTRANCE REQUIREMENTS

Entrance formalities for foreigners arriving in Japan are handled quickly and efficiently. If you come by air, you'll probably arrive at one of the following:

- Tokyo International Airport at Haneda (Haneda Airport)
- Narita International Airport at Narita
- Osaka International Airport at Itami
- Kansai International airport at Osaka Bay

If you come by sea, you'll probably arrive at Yokohama or Kobe.

No matter where you arrive, you'll find English-speaking personnel and well-organized procedures to help speed you on your way to your hotel or other destination.

airport	空港	*kūkō*
airplane	飛行機	*hikōki*
passenger	乗客／旅客	*jōkyaku/ryokyaku*
Disembarkation/ Embarkation Card for Foreigner	外国人出入国記録	*gaikokujin shutsunyūkoku kiroku*
name	氏名	*shimei*
nationality	国籍	*kokuseki*
date of birth	生年月日	*seinen gappi*
male/female	男／女	*otoko/onna*
home address/address	住所	*jūsho*
occupation	職業	*shokugyō*
passport number	旅券番号	*ryoken bangō*
flight number	(航空機) 便名	*(kōkūki) binmei*
AA27	アメリカン２７便	*Amerikan nijū nana bin*

ANA 001	全日空1便	*Zennikkū ichi bin*
intended length of stay	滞在予定期間	*taizai yotei kikan*
port of embarkation	乗機地	*jōkichi*
port of disembarkation	降機地	*kōkichi*
purpose of visit	渡航目的	*tokō mokuteki*
signature	署名	*shomei*

QUARANTINE

Unless you are arriving in Japan from an infected area, you are not required to show proof of inoculations. If you are coming from such areas, here are a few phrases. If not, you usually pass right through.

quarantine	検疫	*ken-eki*
vaccination certificate	種痘証明書	*shutō shōmei sho*
Do you need to see my vaccination certificate?	種痘証明書は必要ですか。	*Shutō shōmei sho wa hitsuyō desu ka.*

IMMIGRATION

At Immigration, there are separate, clearly marked lines for Japanese and nonresidents. At Immigration, or Passport Control, show your passport and your Embarkation/Disembarkation Card (a small form you receive on the plane). U.S. citizens who hold transit or return trip tickets may enter Japan for up to 90 days with no visa.

My name is _____.	私の名前は、_____です。	*Watakushi no namae wa, _____ desu.*
I'm <u>American</u>.	<u>アメリカ人</u>です。	*<u>Amerika jin</u> desu.*
British	イギリス人	*Igirisu jin*
Dutch	オランダ人	*Oranda jin*
I'm staying at _____.	_____に、泊まります。	*_____ ni, tomarimasu.*

Here's my <u>passport</u>.	これが、私のパスポートです。 *Kore ga, watakushi no <u>pasupōto</u> desu.*
documents	書類　*shorui*
Embarkation/ Disembarkation Card	出入国記録　*shutsunyūkoku kiroku*
customs declaration form	税関の申告書　*zeikan no shinkokusho*
I'm on <u>vacation</u>.	<u>バケーション</u>です。 *<u>Bakēshon</u> desu.*
a sightseeing tour	観光旅行　*kankō ryokō*
a business trip	仕事の旅行　*shigoto no ryokō*
I'll be staying here <u>a few days</u>.	<u>数日</u>滞在の予定です。 *<u>Sūjitsu</u> taizai no yotei desu.*
a week	一週間　*isshūkan*
two weeks	二週間　*nishūkan*
a month	一月　*hitotsuki*
two months	二月　*futatsuki*
I'm traveling <u>alone</u>.	<u>一人</u>で旅行しています。 *<u>Hitori</u> de ryokō shite imasu.*
with my husband	夫と　*otto to*
with my wife	妻と　*tsuma to*
with my family	家族で　*kazoku de*
with my friend	友達と　*tomodachi to*
with my colleague	同僚と　*dōryō to*

BAGGAGE CLAIM

baggage/luggage	荷物　*nimotsu*
Where is the baggage claim?	荷物の受取所は、どこですか。 *Nimotsu no uketorijo wa, doko desu ka.*

Get that <u>black</u> suitcase for me please.	その黒いスーツケースを取って下さい。 *Sono kuroi sūtsukēsu o totte kudasai.*
white	白い *shiroi*
red	赤い *akai*
blue	青い *aoi*
brown	茶色の *chairo no*
big	大きい *ōkii*
small	小さい *chiisai*
That's mine.	それは、私のです。*Sore wa, watakushi no desu.*
I can't find my luggage.	荷物が、見つかりません。*Nimotsu ga, mitsukarimasen.*
Where's my luggage?	私の荷物は、どこですか。*Watakushi no nimotsu wa, doko desu ka.*
My luggage is lost.	私の荷物がありません。*Watakushi no nimotsu ga, arimasen.*

CUSTOMS

You must present your bags for customs inspection, and they may be opened. You fill out a customs declaration form beforehand and give it to the officer.

Where's customs?	税関は、どこですか。*Zeikan wa, doko desu ka.*
Here's my passport.	これが、私のパスポートです。*Kore ga, watakushi no pasupōto desu.*
Here's my customs declaration form.	これが、私の税関の申告書です。*Kore ga, watakushi no zeikan no shinkokusho desu.*

This is my luggage.	これが、私の荷物です。*Kore ga, watakushi no nimotsu desu.*
This is all I have.	これで、全部です。*Kore de, zenbu desu.*
I have nothing to declare.	特に申告するものはありません。*Toku ni shinkoku suru mono wa arimasen.*
These are my personal effects.	これは、私の手回り品です。*Kore wa, watakushi no temawari hin desu.*
It's not new.	新品ではありません。*Shinpin dewa arimasen.*
These are gifts.	これは、おみやげです。*Kore wa, omiyage desu.*
May I close the bag now?	閉めてもいいですか。*Shimetemo ii desu ka.*
Do I have to pay duty?	閉税を、払わねばなりませんか。*Kanzei o, harawaneba narimasen ka.*
How much do I pay?	いくらですか。*Ikura desu ka.*
Where do I pay?	どこで払いますか。*Doko de haraimasu ka.*
Can I pay with <u>dollars</u>?	<u>ドル</u>で払えますか。*<u>Doru</u> de haraemasu ka.*
a credit card	クレジット・カード *kurejitto kādo*

LUGGAGE

Porters are few and far between in Japan. At airports and train stations they're almost nonexistent. You'll find convenient, plentiful, free luggage carts at airports (although not at train stations). If you have questions or need help, consult your airline's airport staff.

Can you help me put my luggage on the cart please?	私の荷物をカートに乗せてもらえますか。*Watakushi no nimotsu o kāto ni nosete moraemasu ka.*
Thank you so much!	ありがとうございます。*Arigatō gozaimasu.*

TRANSPORTATION, HOTEL RESERVATIONS, AND OTHER QUESTIONS

You've probably made your hotel reservations before arriving in Japan. If not, or if you have questions about transportation to town, or anything else, the following phrases will be helpful. You'll find someone who speaks English at each counter.

Where's the information counter?	案内所はどこですか。*Annai jo wa doko desu ka.*
Where's the hotel reservation counter?	ホテルの予約カウンターは、どこですか。*Hoteru no yoyaku kauntā wa, doko desu ka.*
Where's the Japan Travel Bureau counter?	交通公社のカウンターは、どこですか。*Kōtsū Kōsha no kauntā wa, doko desu ka.*

Note: For information on changing money at the airport, see page 48 in Banking and Money Matters.

NARITA-TOKYO TRANSPORTATION

Narita International Airport is about 40 miles, or 65 kilometers, from downtown Tokyo. The length of the ride can vary depending on the means of transportation, the time of day, and traffic conditions. How can you get to town? Here are several possibilities:

LIMOUSINE BUSES

Limousine bus counters are right outside of the customs areas in the terminals. The buses run frequently.

The limousine buses now go to many major hotels and key train stations all over Tokyo and many suburban areas. You can use the limousine bus service even if you are not staying at the designated hotel or taking a train. Once at the hotel or station, you can take a taxi to your own destination. It's easy and convenient, and it's much cheaper than taking a taxi all the way from the airport.

You can also take a limousine bus to Tokyo City Air Terminal (TCAT, often called "tee-cat"), located at Hakozaki in downtown Tokyo. This takes from 70 to 90 minutes, depending on traffic. Once you arrive at TCAT, you can take a taxi.

I want to go to the <u>limousine bus counter</u>.	<u>リムジンバスのカウンター</u>に、行きたいのですが。<u>*Rimujin basu no kauntā*</u> *ni, ikitai no desu ga.*
JR counter	ジェイアールのカウンター *Jeiāru no kauntā*
Keisei counter	京成のカウンター *Keisei no kauntā*
Is there a bus to the _____ hotel?	_____ ホテルへ行くバスがありますか。 _____ *Hoteru e iku basu ga arimasu ka.*
I want to go to _____ in Tokyo.	東京の _____ へ行きたいのですが。 *Tōkyō no* _____ *e ikitai no desu ga.*
What's <u>the best</u> way to go?	どの行き方が、<u>一番いい</u>ですか。 *Dono ikikata ga, <u>ichiban ii</u> desu ka.*
the fastest	一番速い *ichiban hayai*
the cheapest	一番安い *ichiban yasui*
How long does it take?	時間は、どのくらいかかりますか。 *Jikan wa, dono kurai kakarimasu ka.*
When does the next one leave?	次のは、いつ出ますか。 *Tsugi no wa, itsu demasu ka.*
Where do I get it?	それは、どこで乗れますか。 *Sore wa, doko de noremasu ka.*

TRAINS TO TOKYO

Inquire at the Keisei Line ticket counter and the Japan Railway (JR) ticket counter for schedule and ticket information.

FROM NARITA AIRPORT TO TOKYO

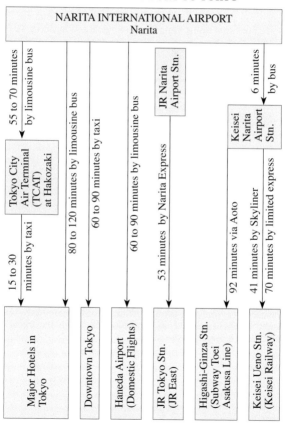

NARITA INTERNATIONAL AIRPORT
Narita

55 to 70 minutes by limousine bus

Tokyo City Air Terminal (TCAT) at Hakozaki

15 to 30 minutes by taxi

80 to 120 minutes by limousine bus

60 to 90 minutes by taxi

60 to 90 minutes by limousine bus

JR Narita Airport Stn.

53 minutes by Narita Express

Keisei Narita Airport Stn.

6 minutes by bus

92 minutes via Aoto

41 minutes by Skyliner

70 minutes by limited express

Major Hotels in Tokyo

Downtown Tokyo

Haneda Airport (Domestic Flights)

JR Tokyo Stn. (JR East)

Higashi-Ginza Stn. (Subway Toei Asakusa Line)

Keisei Ueno Stn. (Keisei Railway)

TAXIS

The taxi ride takes 70 to 100 minutes to Tokyo, depending on traffic and where in Tokyo you're going. Taxis have meters, so it's a very expensive ride. Keep in mind that you should not try to open or close the door yourself. The driver operates the left rear door automatically. It will swing open so you can get in and will close behind you after you leave. Because some hotels have different names in English and Japanese, you might want to have someone write your destination for you in Japanese before you leave the terminal, to show to the taxi driver.

Where can I get a taxi?	タクシーは、どこで乗れますか。 *Takushī wa, doko de noremasu ka.*
How long does it take to Tokyo?	東京まで、どのくらい時間がかかりますか。 *Tōkyō made, dono kurai jikan ga kakarimasu ka.*
How much will it cost?	いくら、かかりますか。 *Ikura, kakarimasu ka.*
Take me to the _____ Hotel, please.	_____ホテルまで、行ってください。 _____ *Hoteru made, itte kudasai.*
Take me to this address please.	この住所まで、行ってください。 *Kono jūsho made, itte kudasai.*

CAR WITH DRIVER

This is the Japanese equivalent of limousine service, but don't expect a limousine! What you can expect is a standard size, immaculate car, with a polite, efficient driver. The Japanese call this "Hire." Be sure to pronounce it in the Japanese way, *haiyā*. It takes about the same time as a taxi and costs about twice as much. It's customary to tip the driver about 7 or 8 percent at the end.

Where can I get a car with driver?	ハイヤーは、どこで雇えますか。 *Haiyā wa, doko de yatoemasu ka.*
How much will it cost to _____ in Tokyo?	東京の_____まで、いくらかかりますか。 *Tōkyō no _____ made, ikura kakarimasu ka.*

Is the rate by <u>meter</u>?	料金は、<u>メートル</u>制ですか。 *Ryōkin wa, <u>mētoru</u> sei desu ka.*
by the hour	時間 *jikan*
by the half-day	半日 *hannichi*
I'd like to get one.	一台お願いします。*Ichidai onegai shimasu.*

RENTAL CARS

You can arrange for a car in the airport terminal. You'll need an International Driving Permit (you can get it through the American Automobile Association or similar organizations in other countries). You'll also need a good knowledge of Japanese road signs and some kanji, or Japanese writing.

If you decide to drive in Japan, you can also find car rental agencies in cities. Some are run directly by major car manufacturers. Some never close. Usually you rent a car with a full tank of gas and return it with a full tank. You should be aware that gasoline prices are extremely expensive in Japan. Highway tolls are, too. Parking in cities is tough, parking meters are hard to find, and parking lots and garages are crowded and expensive. Also, the Japanese keep their cars meticulously clean and scratch-free, so when you're parallel parking, you must be very careful. Even slightly bumping a car in front of or behind you is regarded as a serious offense.

See pages 335–336 for more information on renting a car.

TRANSPORTATION FROM OTHER MAJOR AIRPORTS

Tokyo International Airport at Haneda is conveniently located in the southeast part of Tokyo. So from there it's fast and easy to get to major areas of Tokyo. Limousine buses and taxis are readily available. You can also take a train. The Tokyo Monorail to Hamamatsuchō Station takes 13 minutes. The Keikyu Line to Shinagawa Station also takes 13 minutes

Kansai International Airport at Osaka Bay is located 24 miles southwest of Osaka. Buses, limousine buses, trains, taxis, and ferries are available for easy access to your destination.

BANKING AND MONEY MATTERS

Japanese banks are open weekdays from 9 A.M. to 3 P.M. You can change money at authorized currency exchanges. These are well marked and located at such places as banks, hotels, shops, convenience stores, and airports. You don't need to be concerned about different exchange rates at different places. The rates are almost the same everywhere. You should have your passport with you for all money-exchanging transactions, and you should keep your receipts. The yen is the basic unit of Japanese currency. The symbol for yen is ¥.

Although you'll see many ATM machines, not all of them will give you yen if you use your credit card. You can use your credit card to get yen at ATMs in post offices and at Seven Bank (7 Bank) ATMs in 7-Eleven stores. You can also use VIEW ALTTE ATMs at major train stations of JR-EAST (East Japan Railway Company). Look for the following sign:

| yen | 円 | *en* |

Yen Denominations

COINS	1 yen	*aluminum*
	5 yen	*copper color*
	10 yen	*bronze color*
	50 yen	*silver color*
	100 yen	*silver color*
	500 yen	*silver color*

BILLS   1,000 yen, 2,000 yen,
                         5,000 yen, 10,000 yen

For the yen value of your own currency, check the daily exchange rate with your smart phone or at your hotel front desk, credit card office, bank, or other authorized currency exchange. Some currencies cannot be exchanged for yen and should be converted to a negotiable currency before the bearer arrives in Japan. It's best to check before you leave home. Since exchange rates fluctuate, the following table may be helpful in converting yen into your own currency for easy comparison of prices and values.

Yen	Your Own Currency	Yen	Your Own Currency
50		1,000	
100		5,000	
500		10,000	

EXCHANGING MONEY

Where can I exchange foreign currency?	外貨は、どこで替えられますか。 *Gaika wa, doko de kaeraremasu ka.*
dollars	ドル *doru*
euros	ユーロ *yūro*
traveler's checks	旅行小切手／トラベラーズ・チェック *ryokō kogitte/toraberāzu chekku*
Is there a hotel nearby where I can change my travelers checks to yen?	近くに、旅行小切手を替えられるホテルがありますか。*Chikaku ni, ryokō kogitte o kaerareru hoteru ga arimasu ka.*
Can I change foreign currency into yen at the front desk?	フロントで、外貨を円に替えられますか。*Fronto de, gaika o en ni kaeraremasu ka.*

Where is a <u>bank</u>?	銀行は、どこにありますか。*Ginkō wa, doko ni arimasu ka.*
post office	郵便局　*yūbin kyoku*
7-Eleven	セブンイレブン　*Sebun·Irebun*
VIEW ALTTE ATM	ビュー・アルッテ　*Byū· Arutte ē · tī · emu* エーティーエム
Can I use this credit card at this ATM?	このクレジットカードをこのエーティー*Kono kurejittokādo o kono ē · tī · emu de tsukaemasu ka.*
I'd like to change <u>dollars</u> into yen.	ドルを円に替えたいのですが。*Doru o en ni kaetai no desu ga.*
euros	ユーロ　*yūro*
What's today's <u>dollar</u>-yen exchange rate?	今日のドルと円の交換率は、どのくらいですか。*Kyō no doru to en no kōkan ritsu wa, dono kurai desu ka.*
euro	ユーロ　*yūro*
I'd like to change <u>100</u> dollars to yen.	100ドルを、円に替えたいのですが。*Hyaku doru o, en ni kaetai no desu ga.*
200	*ni hyaku*
300	*sanbyaku*
400	*yon hyaku*
500	*go hyaku*
600	*roppyaku*
700	*nana hyaku*
800	*happyaku*
900	*kyū hyaku*
1,000	*sen*
Do I need to fill out a form?	書式に、記入の必要がありますか。*Shoshiki ni, ki-nyū no hitsuyō ga arimasu ka.*

I'd like the money in <u>large</u> bills.	大きいお札でください。	*Ōkii osatsu de kudasai.*
small	小さい	*chiisai*
I want some change, too.	硬貨もください。	*Kōka mo kudasi.*

AIRPORT MONEY EXCHANGE

If you need to change currency at the airport, these phrases can help.

Where's the money exchange?	両替所は、どこですか。	*Ryōgaesho wa, doko desu ka.*
Is the money exchange open?	両替所は、開いていますか。	*Ryōgaesho wa, aite imasu ka.*
May I cash traveler's checks?	旅行小切手／トラベラーズ・チェック を、現金化できますか。	*Ryokō kogitte/toraberāzu chekku o, genkinka dekimasu ka.*

PERSONAL CHECKS

Personal checks, especially those on foreign banks, are not going to be of much use to you in Japan. Cash, traveler's checks, and major credit cards are all fine.

BANKING TERMS

amount	金額	*kingaku*
banker	銀行員／銀行家	*ginkōin/ginkōka*
bill (money)	紙幣／お札	*shihei/osatsu*
to cash	現金化する	*genkinka suru*
cashier	出納係	*suitōkakari*
check	小切手	*kogitte*
to endorse	裏書きする	*uragaki suru*

I.D.	身分証明書	*mibun shōmei sho*
to make change	こまかくする／ くずす	*komakaku suru/ kuzusu*
processing fee	取扱い料金	*toriatsukai ryokin*
service charge	手数料	*tesūryō*
signature	署名／サイン	*shomei/sain*
teller	窓口係	*madoguchigakari*
window	窓口	*madoguchi*
wire transfer	電信送金	*denshin sōkin*

TIPPING: SOME GENERAL GUIDELINES

Resist the impulse to tip. Hotels and restaurants add a 10 to 15 percent service charge to your bill or check, so individual employees do not usually expect tips. People in service positions take pride in what they do; they consider their wages or salaries sufficient, and they don't look to the customer for something extra.

In some large Western-style hotels, porters, bellhops, and room service staff have been given tips by Westerners so often that they may expect them, and you'll see signs in a few hair salons saying that tips are welcome. The amounts are up to you. It's also customary to tip the room maid in Japanese-style inns.

The general "no tipping" rule does not extend to small gifts (monetary or otherwise) for extra or special service. The Japanese are a gift-giving people, and a token gift is always appreciated, but not expected. In most cases, a smile and a "thank you" will do quite well.

AT THE HOTEL

ACCOMMODATIONS

When you stay in Japan, you have a choice between Western-style and Japanese-style accommodations. The terms "Western-style" and "Japanese-style" categorize both the facilities and the service that each type of lodging offers. In each of the two broad categories, you'll find a wide range of possibilities, from costly and luxurious to inexpensive and simple. You might stay at a Western-style hotel when you first arrive, and then a Japanese-style inn, or *ryokan* for a few nights as you travel around. You might even enjoy staying at a family guest house, or *minshuku*. Sometimes it's possible to have a bit of both worlds: Some Western-style hotels have a few Japanese-style rooms or suites, and some Japanese-style hotels may have a few guest rooms with beds.

The differences between the two styles of accommodations often require different kinds of language. You say certain things at Japanese inns that you would not have to say at Western-style hotels, and you need a slightly more formal or polite level of Japanese, as well. Because of these special language needs, you'll find a section for each category here.

A NOTE ON SLIPPERS AND YUKATA

Most people know that Japanese don't wear shoes inside their homes, but you may not realize how important this is culturally, or how it extends to other places too. Many Japanese-style restaurants, especially traditional ones, require that you remove your shoes before entering. So do temples and shrines and many other places you may visit. In most cases, you do this while standing,

In private homes, and in some restaurants, slippers are offered, especially for wood or carpeted floors. But they're never worn on tatami (woven straw) floors, where you leave the slippers outside before you enter. Special slippers are provided for the toilet area in homes and traditional restaurants.

Slippers are always provided in hotel rooms, although in Western-style hotels, wearing shoes or not is up to you.

You'll also find a yukata, or informal cotton kimono, in your room. This is for your use while there, not a gift from the hotel. Leave it in the room before checking out so it can be freshly laundered for other guests.

WESTERN-STYLE LODGING

HOTELS AND BUSINESS HOTELS

First-class hotels in Japan equal fine hotels anywhere for facilities and quality of service. They may equal them in cost as well. There are options, however. Japan has a great many Western-style hotels of various types and standards. An exceedingly popular one is the business hotel. Some say the name comes from the fact that this category of hotel is popular with Japanese businesspeople. Others maintain it comes from the businesslike competence with which they are run. Whatever the origin of the name, these hotels are convenient, efficient, and usually quite reasonable. They offer clean, comfortable rooms and no-frills service. They're often located near the center of town within easy walking distance of train and subway stations. They're not fancy: The lobbies are plain, the rooms are small, and few have room service. But they're well run, and for many travelers, the price is right.

| hotel | ホテル | *hoteru* |
| business hotel | ビジネス・ホテル | *bijinesu hoteru* |

GETTING TO YOUR HOTEL

| I'd like to go to the _____ Hotel. | _____ ホテルへ行きたいのですが。 _____ *Hoteru e ikitai no desu ga.* |
| Where can I get a taxi? | タクシーは、どこでひろえますか。 *Takushī wa, doko de hiroemasu ka.* |

Which <u>buses</u> go into town?	どの<u>バス</u>に乗れば、市内へ行けますか。 *Dono <u>basu</u> ni noreba, shinai e ikemasu ka.*
train	電車　*densha*
Where is the <u>bus stop</u>?	<u>バス停</u>は、どこですか。 *<u>Basu tei</u> wa, doko desu ka.*
train station	駅　*eki*
How much is the fare?	料金は、いくらですか。 *Ryōkin wa, ikura desu ka.*

CHECKING IN

The registration form you fill out in Western-style hotels has an English translation. Hotels add a 10 percent tax and a 10 to 15 percent service charge to the bill.

My name is _____ .	私の名前は、_____です。*Watakushi no namae wa, _____ desu.*
I have a reservation.	予約がしてあります。 *Yoyaku ga shite arimasu.*
I don't have a reservation, but can I get a room?	予約がないのですが、泊まれますか。 *Yoyaku ga nai no desu ga, tomaremasu ka.*
I'd like <u>a single room</u>.	<u>シングルの部屋</u>が、欲しいのですが。 *<u>Shinguru no heya ga</u>, hoshii no desu ga.*
two single rooms	シングルが二部屋　*shinguru ga futa heya*
a double room	ダブルの部屋が　*daburu no heya ga*
a single room and a double room	シングルを一部屋とダブルを一部屋 *shinguru o hitoheya to daburu o hitoheya*
a suite	スイートが　*suīto ga*

I'd like a room <u>with twin beds.</u>	<u>ツイン・ベッドの部屋が欲しいのですが。</u> *Tsuin beddo no heya ga hoshii no desu ga.*
with bath	浴室付きの　*yokushitsu tsuki no*
with a shower	シャワー付きの　*shawā tsuki no*
with a good view	ながめのいい　*nagame no ii*
facing the mountain	山に面した　*yama ni menshita*
facing the ocean	海に面した　*umi ni menshita*
facing the lake	湖に面した　*mizuumi ni menshita*
facing the street	通りに面した　*tōri ni menshita*
facing the courtyard	中庭に面した　*nakaniwa ni menshita*
I need a baby crib in the room, please.	ベビー・ベッドが欲しいのですが。*Bebī beddo ga hoshii no desu ga.*
What's the rate?	一泊、いかほどですか。*Ippaku, ikahodo desu ka.*
Does the rate include the service charge?	料金には、サービス料も入っていますか。*Ryōkin niwa, sābisu ryō mo haitte imasu ka.*
Does the rate include breakfast?	料金は、朝食込みですか。*Ryōkin wa, chōshoku komi desu ka.*
Is there a discount for children?	子供の割引がありますか。*Kodomo no waribiki ga arimasu ka.*
Is there a charge for the baby?	赤ん坊にも、料金がかかりますか。*Akanbō ni mo, ryōkin ga kakarimasu ka.*
Do you have anything cheaper?	もうちょっと、安い部屋がありますか。*Mō chotto, yasui heya ga arimasu ka.*
I'll be staying <u>just tonight</u>.	<u>今晩だけ</u>、泊まります。<u>*Konban dake*</u>, *tomarimasu.*
a few days	数日　*sūjitsu*
a week	一週間　*isshūkan*

What floor is it on?	部屋は、何階ですか。*Heya wa, nan kai desu ka.*
Can I get the room right now?	部屋は、今すぐとれますか。*Heya wa, ima sugu toremasu ka.*

CHANGING THE ROOM

Could I get a different room?	部屋を、変えてもらえますか。*Heya o, kaete moraemasu ka.*
It's <u>too big</u>.	この部屋は、ちょっと<u>大き過ぎます</u>。*Kono heya wa, chotto <u>ōkisugimasu</u>.*
too small	小さ過ぎます　*chiisasugimasu*
too dark	暗ら過ぎます　*kurasugimasu*
too noisy	うるさ過ぎます　*urusasugimasu*
Do you have a <u>better</u> room?	<u>もっといい</u>部屋がありますか。<u>*Motto ii*</u> *heya ga arimasu ka.*
larger	もっと大きい　*motto ōkii*
smaller	もっと小さい　*motto chiisai*
quieter	もっと静かな　*motto shizuka na*
Do you have a room with a better view?	もっと、ながめのいい部屋がありますか。*Motto, nagame no ii heya ga arimasu ka.*
I'd like a room <u>with more light</u>.	<u>もっと明るい</u>部屋が欲しいのですが。<u>*Motto akarui*</u> *heya ga hoshii no desu ga.*
on a higher floor	もっと上の階の　*motto ue no kai no*
on a lower floor	もっと下の階の　*motto shita no kai no*

HOTEL INFORMATION

Is room service available?	ルームサービスがありますか。*Rūmu sābisu ga arimasu ka.*

Is a masseur/masseuse available?	男のあんまさん／女のあんまさんがよべますか。 *Otoko no anma san/ onna no anma san ga yobemasu ka.*
Is a babysitter available?	子守は、頼めますか。 *Komori wa, tanomemasu ka.*
Is there a <u>restaurant</u> in the hotel?	ホテルには、<u>レストラン</u>がありますか。 *Hoteru niwa, <u>resutoran</u> ga arimasu ka.*

conference room	会議室　*kaigi shitsu*
business center	ビジネス・センター　*bijinesu sentā*
bar	バー　*bā*
coffee shop	コーヒー・ショップ　*kōhī shoppu*
barbershop	床屋　*tokoya*
beauty parlor	美容院　*biyōin*
hair salon	ヘアー・サロン　*heā saron*
pharmacy	薬局　*yakkyoku*
newsstand	新聞売り場　*shinbun uriba*
shopping arcade	ショッピング・アーケード *shoppingu ākēdo*

Where is it?	どこにありますか。*Doko ni arimasu ka.*
<u>Can I send</u> a fax?	ファックスが<u>送れますか</u>。*Fakkusu ga <u>okuremasu ka</u>.*
Can I receive	受け取れますか　*uketoremasu ka*
Is a <u>computer</u> available?	<u>コンピュータ</u>が利用できますか。 *<u>Konpyūta</u> ga riyō dekimasu ka.*
fax machine	ファックス　*fakkusu*
copying machine	コピー機　*kopī ki*

Is there an Internet connection in the room?	部屋でインターネットに繋げますか。 *Heya de intānetto ni tsunagemasu ka.*
Is the Internet connection <u>Ethernet</u>?	インターネット接続は<u>イーサ ネット</u>ですか。*Intānetto setsuzoku wa īsanetto desu ka.*
Wi-Fi	無線LAN／ワイファイ *musenran/waifai*
Is there Wi-Fi in the lobby?	ロビーには 無線LAN／ワイファイがあ りますか。 *Robī niwa musenran/ waifai ga arimasu ka.*
Is an English-language interpreter available?	英語の通訳を頼めますか。*Eigo no tsūyaku o tanomemasu ka.*
Is there a <u>gym</u>?	<u>ジム</u>は、ありますか。*Jimu wa, arimasu ka.*
health club	ヘルスクラブ *herusu kurabu*
sauna	サウナ *sauna*
swimming pool	プール *pūru*
tennis court	テニスコート *tenisukōto*
What time does it open?	何時に開きますか。*Nan ji ni akimasu ka.*
Is there a charge?	料金は。*Ryōkin wa.*
Where's the <u>elevator</u>?	<u>エレベーター</u>は、どこですか。 *Erebētā wa, doko desu ka.*
telephone	電話 *denwa*
dining room	食堂 *shokudō*
tea room/coffee shop	喫茶室 *kissa shitsu*
bathroom	お手洗い／トイレ *otearai/toire*
ladies' room	女子用トイレ *joshi yō toire*
men's room	男子用トイレ *danshi yō toire*

IN THE ROOM

Electrical voltage is 100; American 110-volt small appliances can just be plugged in with no adapter.

Where do I control the <u>air conditioner</u>?	<u>冷房</u>の調節は、どこでしますか。 *<u>Reibō</u> no chōsetsu wa, doko de shimasu ka.*
heater	暖房　*danbō*
Where can I plug in my <u>electric razor</u>?	<u>電気かみそり</u>の差し込みはどこですか。 *<u>Denki kamisori</u> no sashikomi wa doko desu ka.*
hair dryer	ヘアー・ドライヤー　*heā doraiyā*
Do you have an <u>adapter plug</u>?	<u>差し込み用のアダプター</u>がありますか。 *<u>Sashikomi yō no adaputā</u> ga arimasu ka.*
electrical transfomer	変圧器　*hen-atsu ki*
How does the <u>shower</u> work?	<u>シャワー</u>の使い方は。 *<u>Shawā</u> no tsukaikata wa.*
toilet	トイレ　*toire*
I need a <u>bellhop</u>.	<u>ボーイ</u>さんを、お願いします。 *<u>Bōi</u> san o, onegai shimasu.*
maid	メイド　*meido*
I need help with the TV.	テレビの使い方を、教えて下さい。 *Terebi no tsukaikata o, oshiete kudasai.*
Please send <u>breakfast</u> to my room.	<u>朝食</u>を、部屋にとどけて下さい。 *<u>Chōshoku</u> o, heya ni todokete kudasi.*
some towels	タオル　*taoru*
some soap	石鹸　*sekken*
some hangers	ハンガー　*hangā*
a pillow	枕　*makura*

a blanket	毛布	*mōfu*
some ice	氷	*kōri*
some ice water	アイス・ウォーター	*aisu wōtā*
an ashtray	灰皿	*haizara*
some toilet paper	トイレット・ペーパー	*toiretto pēpā*
a luggage rack	荷物の置き台	*nimotsu no okidai*

Who is it?   だれですか。   *Dare desu ka.*

Just a minute.   ちょっと、待って下さい。

       Chotto, matte kudasi.

Come in.   どうぞ。   *Dōzo.*

Put it on the <u>table</u> please.   <u>テーブル</u>の上に、置いて下さい。
<u>*Tēburu*</u> *no ue ni oite kudasai.*

   bed   ベッド   *beddo*

I'd like <u>room service</u> please.   <u>ルーム・サービス</u>を、お願いします。
<u>*Rūmu sābisu*</u> *o, onegai shimasu.*

   a masseur/a masseuse   男のあんまさん／女のあんまさん
otoko no anma san/onna no anma san

   a babysitter   子守   *komori*

I'd like a 6 o'clock wake-up call, please.   あす6時に、モーニング・コールを
お願いします。 *Asu roku ji ni, mōningu kōru o onegai shimasu.*

PROBLEMS

There's no electricity.   電気が、つきません。 *Denki ga, tsukimasen.*

The <u>TV</u> doesn't work.   <u>テレビ</u>が、つきません。 <u>*Terebi*</u> *ga, tsukimasen.*

   radio   ラジオ   *rajio*

   electric fan   扇風機   *senpūki*

   lamp   ランプ   *ranpu*

The air conditioning doesn't work.	冷房が、効きません。*Reibō ga, kikimasen.*
There's no heat.	暖房が、効きません。*Danbō ga, kikimasen.*
There's no running <u>water</u>.	水が出ません。<u>*Mizu ga demasen.*</u>
hot water	お湯 *oyu*
The toilet won't flush.	トイレの水が、流れません。*Toire no mizu ga, nagaremasen.*
The toilet is stopped up.	トイレが、つまっています。*Toire ga, tsumatte imasu.*
The sink is stopped up.	洗面台が、つまっています。*Senmen dai ga, tsumatte imasu.*
The bathtub won't drain properly.	(お)風呂の排水が、よくありません。*(O)furo no haisui ga, yoku arimasen.*
I need a new lightbulb.	電球が、切れています。*Denkyū ga, kirete imasu.*
The <u>window</u> won't open.	窓が、開きません。<u>*Mado ga,*</u> *akimasen.*
Venetian blind	ブラインド *buraindo*
The <u>window</u> won't close.	窓が、閉まりません。<u>*Mado ga,*</u> *shimarimasen.*
Venetian blind	ブラインド *buraindo*
Can I get it fixed?	直してもらえますか。*Naoshite moraemasu ka.*
I've locked myself out.	かぎ／キーカードを中においたまま、戸を閉めてしまいました。*Kagi/kī kādo o naka ni oita mama, to o shimete shimaimashita.*
I've lost my <u>key</u>.	鍵を、なくしてしまいました。*Kagi o, nakushite shimaimashita.*
key card	キーカード *kī kādo*

These shoes aren't mine.	私の靴ではありません。
	Watakushi no kutsu dewa arimasen.
This laundry isn't mine.	私の洗濯物ではありません。
	Watakushi no sentakumono dewa arimasen.

ORDERING BREAKFAST

Most large hotels will have dining rooms where breakfast is served, or you may order breakfast sent up to your room. For more phrases dealing with meals, see the food section, starting on page 193.

I'd like _____ .	_____ を下さい。 _____ *o kudasai.*
Do you have _____ ?	_____ はありますか。 _____ *wa arimasu ka.*
May I have some more _____ ?	_____ をもう少し下さい。 _____ *o mō sukoshi kudasai.*
There isn't any _____ .	_____ がありません。 _____ *ga arimasen.*
Could you bring me _____?	_____ を下さい。 _____ *o kudasai.*

FRUIT

Check the price before ordering fruit. It can be expensive.

apple	りんご	*ringo*
orange	オレンジ	*orenji*
melon	メロン	*meron*
Japanese pear	なし	*nashi*
strawberries	いちご	*ichigo*
banana	バナナ	*banana*
pineapple	パイナップル	*painappuru*
grapefruit	グレープフルーツ	*gurēpufurūtsu*

JUICE

As with fruit, check the price before ordering juice.

orange juice	オレンジジュース	*orenji jūsu*
grapefruit juice	グレープフルーツジュース	*gurēpufurūtsu jūsu*
tomato juice	トマトジュース	*tomato jūsu*
pineapple juice	パイナップルジュース	*painappuru jūsu*
apple juice	リンゴジュース	*ringo jūsu*

BEVERAGES

coffee	コーヒー	*kōhī*
tea	紅茶	*kōcha*
tea with lemon	レモンティー	*remon tī*
tea with milk	ミルクティー	*miruku tī*
milk	ミルク／牛乳	*miruku/gyūnyū*
hot milk	温めた牛乳	*atatameta gyūnyū*
hot chocolate	ココア	*kokoa*
iced tea	アイスティー	*aisu tī*
iced coffee	アイスコーヒー	*aisu kōhī*

CEREAL

corn flakes	コーンフレーク	*kōn furēku*
oatmeal	オートミール	*ōtomīru*

EGGS

scrambled eggs	スクランブルエッグ	*sukuranburu eggu*
fried eggs	目玉焼き	*medama yaki*
boiled eggs	ゆで卵	*yudetamago*

soft boiled eggs	半熟のゆで卵	*hanjuku no yudetamago*
hard boiled eggs	堅ゆでのゆで卵	*katayude no yudetamago*
omelet	オムレツ	*omuretsu*

MEAT

bacon	ベーコン	*bēkon*
ham	ハム	*hamu*
sausages	ソーセージ	*sōsēji*

DAIRY

yogurt	ヨーグルト	*yōguruto*
cottage cheese	コテッジチーズ	*kotejji chīzu*
cheese	チーズ	*chīzu*

COMBINATIONS

ham and eggs	ハム・エッグ	*hamu eggu*
bacon and eggs	ベーコン・エッグ	*bēkon eggu*
sausage and eggs	ソーセージと卵	*sōsēji to tamago*
ham omelet	ハム・オムレツ	*hamu omuretsu*
cheese omelet	チーズ・オムレツ	*chīzu omuretsu*

OTHER HOT DISHES

pancakes	ホットケーキ	*hotto kēki*
waffles	ワッフル	*waffuru*
French toast	フレンチ・トースト	*Furenchi tōsuto*

BREAD

toast	トースト	*tōsuto*
rolls	ロールパン	*rōrupan*

croissant	クロワッサン	*kurowassan*
English muffins	マフィン	*mafin*
bagel	ベーゲル	*bēgeru*
Danish pastry	デーニッシュ／菓子パン	*dēnisshu/kashipan*
doughnuts	ドーナツ	*dōnatsu*

ACCOMPANIMENTS

butter	バター	*batā*
jam	ジャム	*jamu*
marmalade	マーマレード	*māmarēdo*
honey	蜂蜜	*hachimitsu*
syrup	シロップ	*shiroppu*

SPECIAL REQUESTS

decaffeinated coffee	カフェインレスコーヒー	*kafein resu kōhī*
skim milk/nonfat milk	スキム・ミルク／無脂肪の牛乳	*sukimu miruku/mu shibō no gyūnyū*
lowfat milk	ローファット・ミルク／低脂肪の牛乳	*rōfatto miruku/tei shibō no gyūnyū*
decaffeinated tea	カフェインレスの紅茶	*kafein resu no kōcha*
sugar substitute	ダイエットの甘味料	*daietto no kanmi ryō*

I'd like it cooked without <u>salt</u>, please.
塩を使わないで、料理して下さい。
Shio o tsukawanai de, ryōri shite kudasai.

| butter or oil | バターやオイル | *batā ya oiru* |

DESK AND PHONE SERVICE

WITH THE DESK CLERK

Could you keep this in your safe?	これを、金庫に預かってもらえますか。 *Kore o, kinko ni azukatte moraemasu ka.*
I'd like to take my things out of your safe.	金庫に預けたものを、出したいのですが。 *Kinko ni azuketa mono o, dashitai no desu ga.*
The key for <u>Room 200</u> please.	<u>200号室</u>の鍵を下さい。 <u>*Ni hyaku gō shitsu*</u> *no kagi o kudasai.*
Room 500	500号室　*go hyaku gō shitsu*
Are there any <u>messages</u> for me?	私あての<u>メッセージ</u>がありますか。 *Watakushi ate no <u>messēji</u> ga arimasu ka.*
letters	手紙　*tegami*
faxes	ファックス　*fakkusu*

WITH THE TELEPHONE OPERATOR

I'd like an outside line.	市内をお願いします。*Shinai o onegai shimasu.*
Hello. I'd like to make <u>a long-distance call</u>.	もしもし、<u>長距離電話</u>をかけたいのですが。 *Moshimoshi, <u>chōkyori denwa</u> o kaketai no desu ga.*
an international call	国際電話　*kokusai denwa*
The number is <u>Osaka 111-2222</u>.	番号は、<u>大阪の111-2222</u>です。 *Bangō wa, <u>Ōsaka no ichi ichi ichi no nī nī nī nī nī</u> desu.*
Nagoya 333-4444	名古屋の333-4444　*Nagoya no san san san no yon yon yon yon*

Hello, operator! I was cut off. / もしもし、電話が切れてしまいました。 *Moshimoshi, denwa ga kirete shimaimashita.*

Could you try it again? / もう一度、かけてもらえますか。 *Mō ichido, kakete moraemasu ka.*

CHECKING OUT

I'm checking out <u>this morning</u>. / 今朝、たちます。 <u>*Kesa*</u>*, tachimasu.*

soon / もうじき　*mō jiki*

around noon / 昼頃　*hiru goro*

early tomorrow / 明日早く　*asu hayaku*

tomorrow morning / 明日の朝　*asu no asa*

Please have my bill ready. / 勘定書を、用意しておいて下さい。 *Kanjō gaki o, yōi shite oite kudasai.*

Would you send someone to carry my luggage down? / 荷物をおろすのに、だれかよこして下さい。 *Nimotsu o orosu no ni, dareka yokoshite kudasai.*

May I have my bill, please. My room is <u>600</u>. / お勘定を、お願いします。部屋は、<u>600</u>号室です。 *Okanjō o, onegai shimasu. Heya wa, <u>roppyaku</u> gō shitsu desu.*

I don't have much time. Could you hurry please? / あまり、時間がありません。急いでもらえますか。 *Amari, jikan ga arimasen. Isoide moraemasu ka.*

Does this include the tax and service charge? / サービス料と税金が、入っていますか。 *Sābisu ryō to zeikin ga, haitte imasu ka.*

There seems to be an error in the bill. / 勘定書に、間違いがあるようですが。 *Kanjō gaki ni, machigai ga aru yō desu ga.*

Could you check it again?	すみませんが、もう一度、確かめて もらえますか。 *Sumimasen ga, mō ichido, tashikamete moraemasu ka.*
Could you get me a taxi?	タクシーを、呼んでもらえますか。 *Takushī o, yonde moraemasu ka.*
Can I check my baggage till <u>noon</u>?	荷物を、<u>お昼</u>まで預かってもらえ ますか。*Nimotsu o, <u>ohiru</u> made azukatte moraemasu ka.*
evening	夕方　*yūgata*

JAPANESE-STYLE LODGING

RYOKAN: JAPANESE INNS

Staying at a *ryokan* is a good way to experience everyday Japanese customs firsthand. These inns offer traditional and authentic Japanese flavor, from the architecture and furnishings to the pace and style of life. You'll have everything you need to be comfortable, but the daily rituals of bathing, dressing, eating, and sleeping will be quite different from what you're used to. *Ryokan* range in quality and price (as with Western-style hotels) from luxurious to simple. Some inns have private bathrooms, and some are used to dealing with Western guests. Dinner and breakfast are included in the room rate. There are thousands of *ryokan* in Japan, and many of them are members of the Japan Ryokan Association (JRA), which ensures high standards of service and facilities. The Japan National Tourist Organization Tourist Information Centers (TICs) or a travel agency can help you choose one that's appropriate for your taste and budget. Website for the Japan Ryokan Association: *www.ryokan.or.jp*

MINSHUKU: FAMILY GUEST HOUSES

Minshuku are guest houses that take in travelers. They are often located in resort and vacation areas, and they charge reasonable rates. Because most are family-run operations, guests are usually treated as members of the family. This means no maid service: you prepare your own bed (Japanese *futon*, or mattress on the floor) at night, and take it up in the morning. You eat with the family—breakfast and dinner are included in the rate—and there's no special service. Your bill will be a good deal lower than at *ryokan* or hotels. There's no service charge, and no 10 percent tax. You can get more information on *minshuku* lodgings from the Japan Minshuku Association at the Japan Minshuku Center in Tokyo. Website for the Japan Minshuku Center: *www.minshuku.jp*

LANGUAGE FOR JAPANESE-STYLE ACCOMMODATIONS

Most of the phrases in this section can be used for both *ryokan* and *minshuku*. In some cases, however, the phrase cannot be used for one or the other. For example, in a *minshuku* you would *not* say, "I'd like a suite." And in a *ryokan* you would *not* say, "Where is the futon (mattress and bedding)?" because the maid will make up the bed for you. When such a phrase occurs, there is an **R** for *ryokan*, or an **M** for *minshuku*, and the letter is crossed out. **M̶** means don't say this at a *minshuku*, and **R̶** means don't say this at a *ryokan*.

CHECKING IN

You remove your shoes when you arrive. Then you step up onto the floor proper, where you'll find slippers. This is the real beginning of your stay. The staff will usually be there to greet you.

Excuse me for bothering you. (The equivalent of "Hello" to announce your arrival.)	ごめんください。 *Gomen kudasai.*
My name is _____, and I have a reservation.	私は、_____と申します。予約がしてあるはずですが。 *Watakushi wa, (last name) to mōshimasu. Yoyaku ga shite aru hazu desu ga.*

I/We don't have a reservation, but could I/we stay?	予約がないのですが、泊めていただけますか。 *Yoyaku ga nai no desu ga, tomete itadakemasu ka.*
I'm alone.	一人です。 *Hitori desu.*
Two of us.	二人です。 *Futari desu.*
Three of us.	三人です。 *San nin desu.*
Four of us.	四人です。 *Yonin desu.*
✂ I'd like <u>a suite</u>.	<u>次の間付きの部屋</u>を、お願いします。 <u>*Tsugi no ma tsuki*</u> *no heya o, onegai shimasu.*
✂ a room with a private bathroom	(お) 風呂とトイレ付きの部屋 *(o)furo to toire tsuki no heya*
✂ a room on the ground floor	一階の部屋 *ikkai no heya*
✂ a room on the second floor	二階の部屋 *nikai no heya*

RATES

How much would it be for a night?	一泊、いかほどですか。 *Ippaku, ikahodo desu ka.*
✂ Does that include tax and service charge?	税金とサービス料が、入っていますか。 *Zeikin to sābisu ryō ga, haitte imasu ka.*
✂ Does that include dinner and breakfast?	朝晩の二食付きですか。 *Asa ban no ni shoku tsuki desu ka.*
Do you have a less expensive room?	もう少し、安い部屋がありますか。 *Mō sukoshi, yasui heya ga arimasu ka.*
I'd like to stay <u>just tonight</u>.	<u>今晩だけ</u>、お世話になりたいのですが。 <u>*Konban dake*</u>*, osewa ni naritai no desu ga.*
two days	二日 *futsuka*
three days	三日 *mikka*

IN THE ROOM

In the *ryokan*, the room maid will show you to your room. Since the floor is covered with *tatami*, or straw mats, be sure to remove your slippers before you enter. Once inside, you'll find a *yukata*, or informal cotton *kimono*, for each guest. You can change into the *yukata* if you like (you can wear this anywhere at the *ryokan*, indoors and out). Then the maid brings you tea. Introduce yourself and others in your party, and mention how long you'll be staying. It is also customary to present the maid with a small tip (about 3,000 yen will cover your entire stay) at this time, although you may do it at your departure if you prefer. Place the money in an envelope or fold a sheet of paper around it before you give it to the maid, and you'll be doing it the Japanese way! At a *minshuku*, say the same thing, but *with no tip*.

How do you do? I'll be staying here (under your care) for two days or so.	二日ほど、お世話になります。どうぞ、よろしく。	*Futsuka hodo, osewa ni narimasu. Dōzo, yoroshiku.*
This is my <u>wife</u>.	これは、<u>家内</u>です。	*Kore wa, <u>kanai</u> desu.*
husband	主人	*shujin*
friend	友達	*tomodachi*

At this time the maid will bring a register for you to sign. It will probably be in Japanese, so you will need help. Here's a list of the items the register might contain. Show it to the maid, and she can point to the equivalent items on the register.

Ryokan or Minshuku Register

passport number	旅券番号	*ryoken bangō*
name	名前	*namae*
family name	姓	*sei*
given name	名	*mei*
male	男	*otoko*
female	女	*onna*

date of birth	生年月日	*seinen gappi*
year	年	*nen*
month	月	*tsuki*
day	日	*hi*
nationality	国籍	*kokuseki*
occupation	職業	*shokugyō*
home address	住所	*jūsho*
length of stay	滞在期間	*taizai kikan*
date	日付	*hizuke*
signature	署名	*shomei*
I can't read Japanese.	日本語が読めません。	*Nihon go ga yomemasen.*
Could you help me fill it out?	書くのを、手伝ってもらえますか。	*Kaku no o, tetsudatte moraemasu ka.*
What does it say?	何と書いてありますか。	*Nan to kaite arimasu ka.*

THE BATH

Ofuro? Literally, it means bath; practically, it can mean, "Do you want your bath now?" or "When would you like your bath?" or "Please take your bath now, because others are waiting." While this interest in your bath may seem unusual to foreigners, it is normal for Japanese, and for good reason. The Japanese bath is a ritual meant for relaxing and unwinding as much as for cleansing. At a *ryokan*, many people like to take a bath before dinner. The bath at the *ryokan* or the *minshuku* may be communal—that is, several people can use it at one time. If so, there will be separate facilities or separate times for men and women.

The law of the Japanese bath: **NO SOAP INSIDE THE TUB.** Rinse, soap, and scrub yourself outside—you'll find spigots, basins, and perhaps a small stool to sit on—then rinse off all the soap and enter the tub. It's deep, and the water is usually very hot. If you're alone, you may adjust the temperature by adding some cold water from the tap. But remember that you do not drain the water after you, that others will use the same water, and that Japanese like their bath water unimaginably hot. Now enjoy a nice, relaxing soak!

Where is the bath?	お風呂は、どこですか。*Ofuru wa, doko desu ka.*
Ⓜ Can I take a bath whenever I want?	お風呂は、いつでも入れますか。*Ofuro wa, itsu demo hairemasu ka.*
Ⓜ Is there a specific time for the bath?	お風呂の時間がありますか。*Ofuro no jikan ga arimasu ka.*

THE TOILET

The toilet is not located in the bath area, but in a room by itself, usually with a small sink. Leave your slippers outside the door, and put on the ones you find just inside the door.

Where is the toilet?	お手洗いは、どこですか。*Otearai wa, doko desu ka.*
Is there a Western-style toilet?	洋式のお手洗いがありますか。*Yōshiki no otearai ga arimasu ka.*
Ⓜ Is there a toilet on this floor?	この階に、お手洗いがありますか。*Kono kai ni, otearai ga arimasu ka.*

MEALS

At most *ryokan*, your maid serves your meals in your room. At the *minshuku*, you often eat with the family. The food is probably Japanese style. If you know ahead of time you won't want breakfast or dinner, you should tell them so.

I won't need <u>dinner</u>.	晩御飯／夕食は、結構です。 *Ban gohan/yūshoku wa, kekkō desu.*	
breakfast	朝御飯／朝食 *asa gohan/chōshoku*	
✗ What time is <u>dinner</u>?	夕食は、何時でしょうか。*Yūshoku wa, nan ji deshō ka.*	
breakfast	朝食 *chōshoku*	
✗ I'd like <u>dinner</u> at 7 o'clock.	晩御飯は、7時にお願いします。 *Ban gohan wa, shichi ji ni onegai shimasu.*	
breakfast	朝御飯 *asa gohan*	
✗ Could I get a Western-style breakfast?	朝食は、洋式をお願いできますか。 *Chōshoku wa, yōshiki o onegai dekimasu ka.*	
✗ Could I have a knife and fork with my meals, too?	食事には、ナイフとフォークもお願いします。*Shokuji niwa, naifu to fōku mo onegai shimasu.*	
Where is the dining room?	食事の部屋は、どこでしょうか。 *Shokuji no heya wa, doko deshō ka.*	

Before and after the meal, whether at a *ryokan* or *minshuku*, there are certain ritual phrases to say aloud; they are expressions of thanks for the meal.

Before beginning to eat	いただきます。*Itadakimasu.*	
After the meal	ごちそうさまでした。*Gochisō sama deshita.*	

COMMUNICATING

The following phrases are used with the front desk staff of the *ryokan*, or with the people who run the *minshuku*. Some fulfill ritual requirements as well as provide information. It's customary, for example, to say, "I'm going out" when leaving, and "I'm back" when returning.

The *minshuku* proprietors:

the husband	ご主人	*goshujin*
the wife	奥さん	*okusan*

Ⓜ Could you send the maid to my room? — 係りの方を、部屋へお願いします。 *Kakari no kata o, heya e onegai shimasu.*

Ⓜ May I have my shoes please? — 靴を、お願いします。 *Kutsu o, onegai shimasu.*

I'm going out. — 行ってまいります。／出かけてきます。 *Itte mairimasu./Dekakete kimasu.*

I'll be back <u>soon</u>. — <u>すぐ</u>、戻ってきます。 <u>*Sugu*</u>, *modotte kimasu.*

  by evening — 夕方までに *yūgata made ni*

I'm back. — ただいま。 *Tadaima.*

CHECKING OUT

I enjoyed my stay very much. — 大変、お世話になりました。 *Taihen, osewa ni narimashita.*

It was wonderful. — とても、素晴らしかったです。 *Totemo, subarashikatta desu.*

Thank you very much. — ありがとうございました。 *Arigatō gozaimashita.*

I'll come back again. — また来ます。 *Mata kimasu.*

YOUTH HOSTELS

There are two kinds of youth hostels in Japan: public or government operated, and privately run. The latter are affiliated with Japan Youth Hostels Inc. (JYH). The Japan National Tourist Organization can provide you with information and listings of facilities. You may want to stay at a youth hostel in Japan although you may not be a member. You can become a member by joining the International Youth Hostel Federation while you are in Japan, or buying a guest card at a hostel where you want to stay. You can stay at a youth hostel even if you're not so young! The web site for the Japan Youth Hostels Inc. is *www.jyh.or.jp/english/*.

Is there a youth hostel nearby?	近くに、ユース・ホステルがありますか。*Chikaku ni, yūsu hosuteru ga arimasu ka.*
Can I stay here? I'm a member.	私は会員ですが泊まれますか。*Watakushi wa kaiin desu ga, tomaremasu ka.*
Here's my membership card.	これが、私の会員証です。*Kore ga, watakushi no kaiin shō desu.*
When is meal time?	食事の時間は、何時ですか。*Shokuji no jikan wa, nan ji desu ka.*
Where's the dining room.	食堂は、どこですか。*Shokudō wa, doko desu ka.*
Can I cook for myself?	自炊できますか。*Jisui dekimasu ka.*
Is there a bath time?	お風呂の時間がありますか。*Ofuruo no jikan ga arimasu ka.*
Can I use my sleeping bag?	スリーピング・バッグが、使えますか。*Surīpingu baggu ga, tsukaemasu ka.*
Can I <u>rent</u> sleeping sheets?	敷布が、借りられますか。*Shikifu ga, <u>kariraremasu ka</u>.*
buy	買えます *kaemasu*
Is there a curfew?	門限は、ありますか。*Mongen wa, arimasu ka.*

When is wake-up time?	起床時間は、何時ですか。 *Kishō jikan wa, nan ji desu ka.*
When is "lights out"?	消灯時間は、何時ですか。 *Shōtō jikan wa, nan ji desu ka.*
What time do I have to vacate the room?	何時までに、部屋を空けなければなりませんか。 *Nan ji made ni, heya o akenakereba narimasen ka.*

ALTERNATIVE LODGING

AIRBNB

AIRbnb has arrived in Japan, but only relatively recently and in a somewhat limited capacity as compared with other countries. If you're interested, you can check the website.

CAPSULE HOTELS

Capsule hotels are just like they sound—overnight lodging consisting of rows of small, confined, capsule-like sleeping spaces, each for one person, and usually accessed by ladders. Showers and toilets are in separate areas. They're clean and cheap.

GETTING AROUND TOWN

TAXIS

Cruising taxis are plentiful in cities and large towns. You'll find taxi stands at train stations, near hotels, and in busy areas. Because most taxis have navigation systems, give the driver the address, telephone number, or name of your destination, and he or she can take you there. Ask someone to write the information in Japanese beforehand, because the driver may not understand English.

Entering and leaving the cab: *Don't* open or close the door yourself. The driver controls the door, which will swing open to let you in or out. Because the driver sits in the front right of the cab, you'll enter and leave the back left side of the cab. This may take some getting used to!

Fares: Meters show the fare in digits. A 20 percent surcharge is added from 10 P.M. until 5 A.M.

Tips: The driver doesn't expect a tip. If he or she does something special for you, like carrying luggage or waiting while you make a stop, you can give a tip. Otherwise, it's not necessary.

NOTE: Uber and other such companies are in Japan, but on a smaller scale as compared to the United States. Most Uber cars belong to cab companies, and Uber car availability and areas of service are quite limited. You can use your app for information.

How long will it take to <u>Ginza</u> by cab?	銀座まで、タクシーでどのくらい時間がかかりますか。*<u>Ginza</u> made, takushī de dono kurai jikan ga kakarimasu ka.*
Tokyo Station	東京駅　*Tōkyō Eki*
the Imperial Hotel	帝国ホテル　*Teikoku Hoteru*

How much will it cost to go to <u>Shinjuku</u> by cab?

新宿まで、タクシーはいくらかかり
ますか。*<u>Shinjuku</u> made, takushī wa ikura kakarimasu ka.*

  Meiji Shrine

明治神宮　*Meiji Jingū*

How far is it?

距離は、どのくらいありますか。
Kyori wa, dono kurai arimasu ka.

Where can I get a taxi?

タクシーは、どこで乗れますか。
Takushī wa, doko de noremasu ka.

Can I get a cab in the street around here?

この辺で、タクシーがひろえますか。
Kono hen de, takushī ga hiroemasu ka.

Would you call me a cab please?

タクシーを呼んでもらえますか。
Takushī o, yonde Moraemasu ka.

Would you write this address in Japanese?

この住所を、日本語で書いてもらえ
ますか。*Kono jūsho o, Nihon go de kaite moraemasu ka.*

Go to the address on this paper please.

この紙に書いてある住所まで、行っ
て下さい。*Kono kami ni kaite aru jūsho made, itte kudasai.*

Take me to <u>the Kabuki Theater</u> please.

歌舞伎座まで、お願いします。
<u>Kabuki-za</u> made, onegai shimasu.

  Haneda Airport

羽田空港　*Haneda Kūkō*

I'd like to go near <u>Roppongi intersection</u>.

<u>六本木の交差点</u>のそばまで、行って
下さい。*<u>Roppongi no kōsaten</u> no soba made, itte kudasai.*

  Zojoji Temple in Shiba

芝の増上寺　*Shiba no Zōjōji*

  Nomura Building in Shinjuku

新宿の野村ビル　*Shinjuku no Nomura Biru*

Can I get there by <u>1</u> o'clock?

<u>一</u>時までに、着けますか。
<u>Ichi</u> ji made ni, tsukemasu ka.

  2

二　*ni*

Could you go faster, please?

急いでもらえますか。*Isoide moraemasu ka.*

There's no need to hurry.	急がなくても、けっこうです。 *Isoganakutemo, kekkō desu.*
I think it's around here.	この辺のはずですが。 *Kono hen no hazu desu ga.*
Could you stop <u>just before</u> the next intersection?	次の交差点の<u>手前</u>で止めて下さい。 *Tsugi no kōsaten no <u>temae</u> de tomete kudasai.*
right after	すぐ後 *sugu ato*
Around here is fine.	この辺で、けっこうです。 *Kono hen de, kekkō desu.*
Stop here please.	ここで、止めて下さい。 *Koko de, tomete kudasai.*
Please wait here for a moment.	ここで、ちょっと待ってもらえますか。 *Koko de, chotto matte moraemasu ka.*
How much do I owe you?	いくらですか。 *Ikura desu ka.*

SUBWAYS AND COMMUTER TRAINS

Most major Japanese cities have fast, clean, and efficient subway and commuter train systems. The latter are not quite the Western equivalent of commuter trains. They're actually a complex system of public and private trains crisscrossing and encircling the urban areas, and linking with the subways. In Tokyo, the *Yamanote sen* is the line that encircles, or loops around, the city's downtown area; in Osaka, the loop line is called the *Kanjo sen*.

Subway entrances are marked by these symbols:

You can use the subways and commuter trains easily if you have a map or guide, and there are many available. The station signs are in Roman letters, or *romaji*, so you'll be able to read them. You can get useful information at the Tokyo Metro website. The Metro network map is available for downloading. The website is *www.tokyometro.jp/en*

STATION NUMBERING AND COLOR CODING

Train lines and stations are identified by different colors, numbers, and letters. You can just follow them to your destination. Announcements on the trains are useful too. You'll understand the destination, the next station, and when to change trains. These sentences will help you on your way.

What color is <u>Ginza</u> Line?	銀座線は何色ですか。*Ginza sen wa nani iro desu ka.*	
Tozai	東西 *Tōzai*	
What are the color and number for Meguro Station on the <u>Yamanote</u> Line?	山手線目黒駅の色とナンバーは何ですか。*Yamanote sen Meguro eki no iro to nanbā wa nan desu ka.*	
Nanboku	南北 *Nanboku*	
subway	地下鉄	*chikatetsu*
commuter train	電車	*densha*
Is there a subway in this city?	この市には、地下鉄がありますか。*Kono shi niwa, chikatetsu ga arimasu ka.*	
Is there a <u>commuter train</u> map in English?	英語の、電車の地図がありますか。*Eigo no, densha no chizu ga arimasu ka.*	
subway	地下鉄 *chikatetsu*	
Where can I get a commuter train map in English?	英語の電車の地図は、どこで買えますか。*Eigo no densha no chizu wa, doko de kaemasu ka.*	
When is the <u>morning</u> rush hour?	朝のラッシュ・アワーは、何時頃ですか。*Asa no rasshu awā wa, nan ji goro desu ka.*	
evening	夕方 *yūgata*	

When is the earliest train of the day?	一番電車は、何時ですか。 *Ichiban densha wa, nan ji desu ka.*
When does the last train depart?	終電は何時に出ますか。 *Shūden wa nan ji ni demasu ka.*
Is there a <u>train</u> station nearby?	近くに、電車の駅がありますか。 *Chikaku ni, <u>densha</u> no eki ga arimasu ka.*
subway	地下鉄 *chikatetsu*
Could you tell me how to get to the nearest train station?	最寄りの電車の駅への行き方を教えて下さい。 *Moyori no densha no eki e no ikikata o oshiete kudasai.*
Where is the <u>Yamanote line</u>?	山手線の駅は、どこですか。 <u>Yamanote Sen</u> wa, doko desu ka.
Marunouchi line	丸の内線 *Marunouchi Sen*
Ginza line	銀座線 *Ginza Sen*
Toyoko line	東横線 *Tōyoko Sen*
Which line should I take to <u>Ginza</u>?	<u>銀座</u>に行くには何線がいいですか。 <u>Ginza</u> ni iku niwa nani sen ga ii desu ka.
Akasaka	赤坂 *Akasaka*
Excuse me, could you help me?	すみませんが、ちょっと教えて下さい。 *Sumimasen ga, chotto oshiete kudasai.*
Which machine should I use?	どの販売機を使ったらいいですか。 *Dono hanbai ki o tsukattara ii desu ka.*
Do I have to change trains?	乗り換えがありますか。 *Norikae ga arimasu ka.*
At which station do I have to change?	乗り換えは、どの駅ですか。 *Norikae wa, dono eki desu ka.*

Which line do I change to?	何線に、乗り換えますか。*Nani sen ni, norikaemasu ka.*
Which track does the train leave from?	何番線から出ますか。*Nan ban sen kara demasu ka.*
Where is the platform for the train to <u>Shibuya</u>?	<u>渋谷</u>行きのホームは、どこですか。*<u>Shibuya</u> yuki no hōmu wa, doko desu ka.*
Yotsuya	四谷　*Yotsuya*
Is this the right platform for the train to <u>Harajuku</u>?	<u>原宿</u>へ行くには、このホームでいいですか。*<u>Harajuku</u> e iku niwa, kono hōmu de ii desu ka.*
Toranomon	虎ノ門　*Toranomon*
Does the express stop at <u>Nakano</u>?	快速は、<u>中野</u>に止まりますか。*Kaisoku wa, <u>Nakano</u> ni tomarimasu ka.*
Ogikubo	荻窪　*Ogikubo*
Is this seat free?	この席は、あいていますか。*Kono seki wa, aite imasu ka.*
Where is the <u>east</u> exit?	<u>東</u>口は、どこですか。*<u>Higashiguchi</u> wa, doko desu ka.*
west	西　*nishi*
north	北　*kita*
south	南　*minami*
Where is the exit to <u>the Wako Building</u>?	<u>和光ビル</u>への出口は、どこですか。*<u>Wakō Biru</u> e no deguchi wa, doko desu ka.*
Hibiya Park	日比谷公園　*Hibiya Kōen*
I've lost my ticket.	切符をなくしてしまいました。*Kippu o nakushite shimaimashita.*

Where is the lost and found office?	遺失物係は、どこですか。 *Ishitsubutsu gakari wa, doko desu ka.*
I've left my <u>camera</u> on the train.	電車の中に、<u>カメラ</u>を置き忘れてしまいました。 *Densha no naka ni, <u>kamera</u> o okiwasurete shimaimashita.*
package	荷物 *nimotsu*

MONORAIL

The monorail operates between Hamamatsucho in Tokyo and Haneda Airport. Some people find it a convenient way to get from town to their flights.

Where do I get the monorail?	モノレールは、どこで乗れますか。 *Monorēru wa, doko de noremasu ka.*
How long does it take to go to Haneda?	羽田まで、どのくらい時間がかかりますか。 *Haneda made, dono kurai jikan ga kakarimasu ka.*
How often does it run?	何分おきに出ますか。 *Nan pun oki ni demasu ka.*
How much is the fare?	料金は、いくらですか。 *Ryōkin wa, ikura desu ka.*

BUSES

If you travel by bus, it's a good idea to have someone write down your destination so you can show it to the driver, who may not understand English.

Where can I get a bus to Ginza?	銀座行きのバス停は、どこですか。 *Ginza yuki no basu tei wa, doko desu ka.*

Where's the nearest bus stop for Shinjuku?
新宿行きの、最寄りのバス停はどこですか。*Shinjuku yuki no, moyori no basu tei wa doko desu ka.*

Can I get a bus to Harajuku around here?
この近くで、原宿行きのバスに乗れますか。*Kono chikaku de, Harajuku yuki no basu ni noremasu ka.*

Which bus do I take to go to Asakusa?
浅草行きのバスは、どれですか。*Asakusa yuki no basu wa, dore desu ka.*

Where does this bus go?
このバスは、どこ行きですか。*Kono basu wa, doko yuki desu ka.*

Does this bus go to Shibuya?
このバスは、渋谷に行きますか。*Kono basu wa, Shibuya ni ikimasu ka.*

Does this bus stop at the Kabuki Theater?
このバスは、歌舞伎座で止まりますか。*Kono basu wa, Kabuki-za de tomarimasu ka.*

Where do I get off to go to the British Consulate?
イギリス領事館に行くには、どこで降りればいいですか。*Igirisu Ryōjikan ni iku niwa, doko de orireba ii desu ka.*

Do I need to change buses to go to the National Theater?
国立劇場に行くには、乗り換えがありますか。*Kokuritsu Gekijō ni iku niwa, norikae ga arimasu ka.*

How often does the bus for Tokyo Station come?
東京駅行きのバスは、何分おきに出ますか。*Tōkyō Eki yuki no basu wa, nan pun oki ni demasu ka.*

When does the next bus to Ikebukuro come?
次の池袋行きのバスは、いつですか。*Tsugi no Ikebukuro yuki no basu wa, itsu desu ka.*

How long does it take from here to Akasaka?
ここから赤坂まで、どのくらい時間がかかりますか。*Koko kara Akasaka made, dono kurai jikan ga kakarimasu ka.*

How many stops are there from here to Tokyo Tower?	東京タワーは、ここからいくつ目ですか。*Tōkyō Tawā wa, koko kara ikutsu me desu ka.*
How much will it be to Aoyama?	青山まで、いくらですか。*Aoyama made, ikura desu ka.*
Do I have to pay the exact change?	料金は、きっかり払わなければなりませんか。*Ryōkin wa, kikkari harawanakereba narimasen ka.*
Can I get change?	おつりをもらえますか。*Otsuri o moraemasu ka.*
Where do I put the fare?	料金は、どこに入れますか。*Ryōkin wa, doko ni iremasu ka.*
Could you tell me when to get off?	いつ降りるか、教えてもらえますか。*Itsu oriru ka, oshiete moraemasu ka.*

SIGHTSEEING

Japan is so rich in things to see and do that your only problem will be limiting yourself to those you have time for. If your tastes run to the traditional, you'll find that the Japan of yesteryear is very much alive today. There are many places where the past is preserved—cities like Kyoto, for example. And in towns like Kanazawa and Kurashiki, you can see what feudal Japan was like. Throughout Japan there are homes, temples, and shrines built according to traditional Japanese styles of architecture. And the centuries-old art forms are still intact: brush painting, flower arranging, ceramics, tea ceremony, and woodblock prints, among others. The stylized entertainment of theatrical arts like Kabuki, Noh, and Bunraku also reflect the preservation of traditional values. The old culture is everywhere.

Do you prefer things contemporary? Then high-tech Japan is for you: the excitement and vitality of the cities, the world of Japanese industry, the taste and purity of modern Japanese design. You'll find sightseeing easy in Japan. The country is well equipped to accommodate tourists, and the Japanese like foreign visitors. They'll do everything they can to help you enjoy their country.

INQUIRIES

Are there English guidebooks for <u>Tokyo</u>?	東京について、英語のガイドブックがありますか。*Tōkyō ni tsuite, eigo no gaidobukku ga arimasu ka.*
Kyoto	京都　*Kyōto*
Which guidebook would you recommend?	どのガイドブックがいいか、教えて下さい。*Dono gaidobukku ga ii ka, oshiete kudasai.*
Where can I buy the guidebook?	そのガイドブックは、どこで買えますか。*Sono gaidobukku wa, doko de kaemasu ka.*
Could you tell me the points of interest <u>here</u>?	<u>ここ</u>での名所を、教えて下さい。<u>*Koko*</u> *de no meisho o, oshiete kudasai.*
there	そこ　*soko*
I'm interested in <u>antiques</u>.	私は、<u>こっとう</u>品に興味があります。*Watakushi wa, <u>kottō hin</u> ni kyōmi ga arimasu.*
architecture	建築　*kenchiku*
art	美術　*bijutsu*
Buddhist temples	お寺　*otera*
ceramics	陶磁器　*tōjiki*
crafts	工芸　*kōgei*
festivals	お祭り　*omatsuri*
flower arrangement	生け花　*ikebana*
folk art	民芸　*mingei*
furniture	家具　*kagu*
high technology	ハイテク　*haiteku*
historical sites	旧跡　*kyūseki*

Japanese cuisine	日本料理	*Nihon ryōri*
Japanese gardens	日本庭園	*Nihon teien*
martial arts	武術	*bujutsu*
Japanese painting	日本画	*Nihon ga*
photography	写真	*shashin*
pottery	陶器	*tōki*
sculpture	彫刻	*chōkoku*
Shinto shrines	神社	*jinja*
tea ceremony	茶道	*sadō*

What would you recommend that I see <u>here</u>?

<u>ここ</u>の 見どころで、おすすめがあります か。<u>*Koko*</u> *no midokoro de, osusume ga arimasu ka.*

there そこ *soko*

in that city その都市 *sono toshi*

Is _____ worth going to see?

_____ は、見に行く価値がありますか。 _____ *wa, mi ni iku kachi ga arimasu ka.*

What are the main attractions there?

そこでのみものには、どんなものが ありますか。*Soko de no mimono niwa, donna mono ga arimasu ka.*

Is it easy to get there?

そこには、簡単に行けますか。*Soko niwa, kantan ni ikemasu ka.*

Where is the tourist information center?

旅行案内所は、どこですか。*Ryokō annai jo wa, doko desu ka.*

We have <u>a half day</u> free here.

ここでは、<u>半日</u>時間があります。*Koko dewa, <u>han nichi</u> jikan ga arimasu.*

a day 一日 *ichi nichi*

a few days 数日 *sūjitsu*

a week 一週間 *isshūkan*

We'd like to see the <u>aquarium</u>.

<u>水族館</u>を、見たいのですが。 <u>*Suizokukan*</u> *o, mitai no desu ga.*

botanical garden	植物園	*shokubutsu en*
business district	ビジネス街	*bijinesu gai*
castle	お城	*oshiro*
downtown area	繁華街	*hanka gai*
gardens	庭園	*teien*
harbor	港	*minato*
lake	湖	*mizuumi*
market	市場	*ichiba*
museum	美術館／博物館	*bijutsukan/ hakubutsukan*
old town	旧市街	*kyū shigai*
palace	宮殿	*kyūden*
park	公園	*kōen*
shrine	神社	*jinja*
stock exchange	証券取引所	*shōken torihiki jo*
temple	お寺	*otera*
zoo	動物園	*dōbutsu en*

SIGHTSEEING TOURS

Considering how difficult driving in Japan can be for foreigners, organized sightseeing tours are a convenient way to get around. The JNTO TICs or any travel agency can help you find a suitable one. You can spend a few hours seeing some major points of interest, or a few days or weeks seeing much more. You can travel by bus, train, or plane, or a combination of all three. And you'll have competent, English-speaking guides.

Are there sightseeing buses in the city?	市内の、観光バスがありますか。 *Shinai no, kankō basu ga arimasu ka.*

Are there sightseeing buses to <u>Hakone</u>?	箱根への、観光バスがありますか。 *<u>Hakone</u> e no, kankō basu ga arimasu ka.*
Nara	奈良　*Nara*
Are there <u>morning</u> bus tours?	午前の観光バスがありますか。 *<u>Gozen</u> no kankō basu ga arimasu ka.*
afternoon	午後　*gogo*
evening	夜　*yoru*
all-day	一日　*ichi nichi*
two-day	二日　*futsuka*
three-day	三日　*mikka*
Are there group tours to <u>Kyoto</u>?	京都への、グループツアーがありますか。*<u>Kyōto</u> e no, gurūpu tsuā ga arimasu ka.*
Hokkaido	北海道　*Hokkaidō*
Shikoku	四国　*Shikoku*
Kyushu	九州　*Kyūshū*
What kind of transportation do you use?	どんな交通機関を使いますか。 *Donna kōtsū kikan o tsukaimasu ka.*
Are the meals and lodging included in the tour fare?	食費と宿泊費は、ツアーの代金に入っていますか。*Shoku hi to shukuhaku hi wa, tsuā no daikin ni haitte imasu ka.*
Are the meals Western or Japanese?	食事は洋食ですか、それとも和食ですか。*Shokuji wa yōshoku desu ka, soretomo washoku desu ka.*
Is the lodging Western style?	泊まる場所は洋式ですか。 *Tomaru basho wa yōshiki desu ka.*
Is there a chance to stay at a Japanese inn?	旅館に泊まる機会がありますか。 *Ryokan ni tomaru kikai ga arimasu ka.*

Where does the tour go?	そのツアーでは、何が見られますか。 *Sono tsuā dewa, nani ga miraremasu ka.*
<u>How many hours</u> does the tour take?	そのツアーは、<u>何時間</u>かかりますか。 *Sono tsuā wa, <u>nan jikan</u> kakarimasu ka.*
how many days	何日 *nan nichi*
When does the tour <u>start</u>?	ツアーは、何時に<u>始まります</u>か。 *Tsuā wa, nan ji ni <u>hajimarimasu</u> ka.*
finish	終わります *owarimasu*
Where does the tour start?	ツアーは、どこから出ますか。*Tsuā wa, doko kara demasu ka.*
At which hotels do you have pickup service?	どのホテルで、ピックアップ・サービスがありますか。*Dono hoteru de, pikku-appu sābisu ga arimasu ka.*
Can I join the tour at the _____ Hotel?	そのツアーには、_____ ホテルから乗れますか。*Sono tsuā niwa, _____ Hoteru kara noremasu ka.*
Is lunch included in the tour fare?	ランチは、ツアーの料金に入っていますか。*Ranchi wa, tsuā no ryōkin ni haitte imasu ka.*
Is there any free time for shopping?	ショッピングのための、自由時間がありますか。*Shoppingu no tame no, jiyū jikan ga arimasu ka.*
How much is the fare for the tour?	そのツアーの料金は、いくらですか。*Sono tsuā no ryōkin wa, ikura desu ka.*
I'd like <u>one ticket</u> for that tour.	そのツアーの<u>券を、一枚</u>ください。*Sono tsuā no <u>ken o, ichi mai</u> kudasai.*
two tickets	券を、二枚 *ken o, ni mai*
three tickets	券を、三枚 *ken o, san mai*
four tickets	券を、四枚 *ken o, yon mai*

CAR WITH DRIVER

This is the Western equivalent of limousine service, but the car is not limousine sized. It's a convenient way to get around, especially in places like Kyoto, where you may want to visit several temples or shrines on the outskirts of town. The "hire" car, as the Japanese call it, has the added advantage of the driver's knowing the sights. And a driver who speaks some English can be a helpful guide. It's not as expensive as you might think, especially if a few of you share the costs. Tip the driver 7 or 8 percent at the end of your excursion.

Is a limousine available for sightseeing?	観光に、ハイヤーが雇えますか。 *Kankō ni, haiyā ga yatoemasu ka.*
Is an English-speaking chauffeur available?	英語が話せる運転手がいますか。 *Eigo ga hanaseru untenshu ga imasu ka.*
Is the rate <u>by meter</u>?	料金は、<u>メーター制</u>ですか。 *Ryōkin wa, <u>mētā sei</u> desu ka.*
by the hour	時間制 *jikan sei*
by the half day	半日制 *han nichi sei*
by the day	一日制 *ichi nichi sei*
How much is the <u>hourly</u> rate?	一時間の料金は、いくらですか。 <u>*Ichi jikan*</u> *no ryōkin wa, ikura desu ka.*
half-day	半日 *han nichi*
daily	一日 *ichi nichi*
Where can I get a limousine?	ハイヤーは、どこで雇えますか。 *Haiyā wa, doko de yatoemasu ka.*
Do I need to call?	電話しなければなりませんか。 *Denwa shinakereba narimasen ka.*

TOUR GUIDES

Is a tour guide available?	観光ガイドが雇えますか。*Kankō gaido ga yatoemasu ka.*

Is there an English-speaking guide?	英語を話すガイドがいますか。 *Eigo o hanasu gaido ga imasu ka.*
How much does a guide charge <u>per hour</u>?	ガイドの料金は、<u>一時間</u>いくらですか。 *Gaido no ryōkin wa, <u>ichi jikan</u> ikura desu ka.*
per day	一日 *ichi nichi*
I'd like an English-speaking guide for a <u>half day</u>.	英語が話せるガイドを、<u>半日</u>頼みたいのですが。 *Eigo ga hanaseru gaido o, <u>han nichi</u> tanomitai no desu ga.*
a day	一日 *ichi nichi*
two days	二日 *futsuka*
How can I arrange for a guide?	ガイドは、どうやって手配できますか。 *Gaido wa, dō yatte tehai dekimasu ka.*
Could you arrange for the guide for me?	ガイドを、手配してもらえますか。 *Gaido o, tehai shite moraemasu ka.*

SIGHTSEEING ON YOUR OWN

If you want to get out and see things on your own, some preliminary inquiries can help. You can use these phrases with hotel staff, tourist information center personnel, or Japanese friends or acquaintances.

I'd like to look around <u>Kyoto</u> on my own.	自分で、<u>京都</u>を見て回りたいのですが。 *Jibun de, <u>Kyōto</u> o mite mawaritai no desu ga.*
here	ここ *koko*
What's the best way to spend <u>a day</u> sightseeing on my own?	自分で<u>一日</u>見物するには、どんな仕方が一番いいですか。*Jibun de <u>ichi nichi</u> kenbutsu suru niwa, donna shikata ga ichiban ii desu ka.*
two days	二日 *futsuka*
What should I see sightseeing on my own?	自分で見物するには、何を見るべきでしょうか。*Jibun de kenbutsu suru niwa, nani o miru beki deshō ka.*

Could you tell me what sightseeing sequence I should follow?	どんな順序で回ればいいか、教えてください。*Donna junjo de mawareba ii ka, oshiete kudasai.*
I'd like to see <u>traditional</u> architecture.	<u>伝統的</u>な建築を見たいのですが。<u>*Dentō teki*</u> *na kenchiku o mitai no desu ga.*
typical	典型的　*tenkei teki*
modern	モダン　*modan*
I'd like to see a festival.	お祭りが、見たいのですが。*Omatsuri ga, mitai no desu ga.*
Is there a festival somewhere <u>today</u>?	<u>今日</u>どこかで、お祭りがありますか。<u>*Kyō*</u> *dokoka de, omatsuri ga arimasu ka.*
tomorrow	あした　*ashita*
this week	今週　*konshū*
Where can I see _____ ?	_____は、どこで見られますか。_____ *wa, doko de miraremasu ka.*
Which museum would be best for seeing _____?	_____を見るには、どの博物館が一番いいですか。_____ *o miru niwa, dono hakubutsukan ga ichiban ii desu ka.*
I'd like to go to _____, _____, and _____.	_____と、_____と、_____に行きたいのですが。_____ *to,* _____ *to,* _____ *ni ikitai no desu ga.*
Could you tell me how to go to _____ ?	_____への行き方を、教えてください。_____ *e no ikikata o, oshiete kudasai.*
Can I get to _____ by train and bus?	_____へは、電車やバスを使って行けますか。_____ *e wa, densha ya basu o tsukatte ikemasu ka.*
Which line do I take to go to _____ ?	_____へ行くには、何線に乗ればいいですか。_____ *e iku niwa, nani sen ni noreba ii desu ka.*

Where can I get the _____ line?	_____線は、どこで乗れますか。 _____ sen wa, doko de noremasu ka.
How far is _____ from the station?	駅から_____まで、どのくらいの距離がありますか。 Eki kara _____ made, dono kurai no kyori ga arimasu ka.
Can I get there from the station on foot?	駅からそこまで、歩いて行けますか。 Eki kara soko made, aruite ikemasu ka.
Can I find it easily?	すぐ、見つかりますか。 Sugu, mitsukarimasu ka.
Can I walk from _____ to _____ ?	_____ から_____ まで、歩いて行けますか。 _____ kara _____ made, aruite ikemasu ka.

WHILE SIGHTSEEING: GETTING IN

What time does it <u>open</u>?	何時に<u>開きます</u>か。 Nan ji ni <u>akimasu</u> ka.
close	閉まります shimarimasu
Is it open <u>on Saturdays</u>?	<u>土曜日</u>に、開いていますか。 <u>Doyōbi ni</u>, aite imasu ka.
on Sundays	日曜日に nichiyōbi ni
now	今 ima
Is it still open?	まだ、開いていますか。 Mada, aite imasu ka.
How long does it stay open?	閉まるまで、どのくらい時間がありますか。 Shimaru made, dono kurai jikan ga arimasu ka.
Is there an admission fee?	入場料が、いりますか。 Nyūjō ryō ga, irimasu ka.
How much is the admission?	入場料は、いくらですか。 Nyūjō ryō wa, ikura desu ka.

Is there a discount for <u>students</u>?	<u>学生</u>の割引が、ありますか。 *<u>Gakusei</u> no waribiki ga, arimasu ka.*
senior citizens	シニア　*shinia*
children	子供　*kodomo*
What's the minimum age for the discount? (senior citizens)	割引は、何才からですか。*Waribiki wa, nan sai kara desu ka.*
What's the age limit for the discount? (children)	割引は、何才までですか。*Waribiki wa, nan sai made desu ka.*
Am I allowed to take pictures inside?	中で、写真を撮ってもかまいませんか。*Naka de, shashin o tottemo kamaimasen ka.*
Where is the <u>entrance</u>?	<u>入り口</u>は、どこですか。 *<u>Iriguchi</u> wa, doko desu ka.*
gift shop	売店　*baiten*
exit	出口　*deguchi*
Do you have an English <u>guidebook</u>?	英語の<u>ガイド・ブック</u>がありますか。 *Eigo no <u>gaido bukku</u> ga arimasu ka.*
catalog	カタログ　*katarogu*
How much is the <u>guidebook</u>?	<u>ガイド・ブック</u>は、いくらですか。 *<u>Gaido bukku</u> wa, ikura desu ka.*
catalog	カタログ　*katarogu*
Do I have to take off my shoes?	くつを、脱がねばなりませんか。 *Kutsu o, nuganeba narimasen ka.*
Can I just look around?	自由に、見て回れますか。*Jiyū ni, mite mawaremasu ka.*
Do I have to wait for a guided tour?	ガイドの案内を、待たなければなりませんか。*Gaido no annai o, matanakereba narimasen ka.*
How long do we have to wait?	どのくらい、待たなければなりませんか。*Dono kurai, matanakereba narimasen ka.*

ASKING ABOUT THE SIGHTS

What is <u>it</u>?	<u>それは、何ですか</u>。<u>Sore wa, nan desu ka</u>.
that building	あの建物　ano tatemono
that monument	あの記念碑　ano kinen hi
How old is it?	それは、どのくらい古いものですか。Sore wa, dono kurai furui mono desu ka.
Is it original?	それは、オリジナルのものですか。Sore wa, orijinaru no mono desu ka.
Who was the <u>architect</u>?	<u>建築家</u>は、誰ですか。<u>Kenchikuka</u> wa, dare desu ka.
artist	芸術家　geijutsuka
craftsman	工芸家　kōgeika
painter	画家　gaka
sculptor	彫刻家　chōkokuka
Who <u>made</u> this?	これは、誰が<u>作りました</u>か。Kore wa, dare ga <u>tsukurimashita</u> ka.
painted	描きました　kakimashita
What's the purpose of ＿＿＿?	＿＿＿の目的は、何ですか。＿＿＿ no mokuteki wa, nan desu ka.
How long did it take to complete?	完成までに、どのくらい時間がかかりましたか。Kansei made ni, dono kurai jikan ga kakarimashita ka.
Is it an <u>everday</u> object?	それは、<u>毎日</u>使うものですか。Sore wa, <u>mainichi</u> tsukau mono desu ka.
a religious	宗教の目的で　shūkyō no mokuteki de
a ceremonial	儀式の目的で　gishiki no mokuteki de
What was it used for?	それは、何のために使われましたか。Sore wa, nan no tame ni tsukawaremashita ka.

| What is it made of? | 材料は、何ですか。 *Zairyō wa, nan desu ka.* |
| How was it made? | それは、どんな方法で作られましたか。 *Sore wa, donna hōhō de tsukuraremashita ka.* |

POINTS OF INTEREST

The high points of sightseeing in Japan include castles, gardens, hot springs, museums, palaces and imperial villas, shrines, and temples. Several in each category are listed so you can pronounce the names of some of the major attractions. The categories are not exclusive; that is, when you visit a temple, you may also find a garden and a museum there. And this list is by no means exhaustive.

Because Japanese festivals are especially colorful and unique, there's also a list, by month, of a few that you might enjoy. There are many more: no matter when you visit Japan, you can find a festival to attend.

CASTLES

Japanese castles are spectacular: Himeji Castle, one of the few remaining original ones, has a five-storied dungeon at the center, and some buildings are preserved as national treasures. Osaka Castle is famous for its stone walls. Dramatic Nijo Castle, built in 1603, was where the Tokugawa shogun stayed when he visited Kyoto.

Name	Location	Name	Pronunciation
Hikone Castle	Hikone	彦根城	*Hikone Jō*
Himeji Castle	Himeji	姫路城	*Himeji Jō*
Hirosaki Castle	Hirosaki	弘前城	*Hirosaki Jō*
Inuyama Castle	Inuyama	犬山城	*Inuyama Jō*
Kumamoto Castle	Kumamoto	熊本城	*Kumamoto Jō*
Matsue Castle	Matsue	松江城	*Matsue Jō*
Matsumoto Castle	Matsumoto	松本城	*Matsumoto Jō*

Matsuyama Castle	Matsuyama	松山城	*Matsuyama Jō*
Nagoya Castle	Nagoya	名古屋城	*Nagoya Jō*
Nijo Castle	Kyoto	二条城	*Nijō Jō*
Odawara Castle	Odawara	小田原城	*Odawara Jō*
Osaka Castle	Osaka	大阪城	*Ōsaka Jō*
Shimabara Castle	Shimabara	島原城	*Shimabara Jō*

GARDENS

Japan is a garden-lover's dream. There are gardens of every size and shape, each one different from the next. Some 132 of them have been designated masterpieces to be preserved and maintained under the Valuable Cultural Properties Act of Japan. Although the first three on this list are widely known as the "big three" of Japanese gardens, most Japanese say that it's difficult to choose a best or favorite one!

Name	Location	Name	Pronunciation
Kairakuen Garden	Mito	偕楽園	*Kairakuen*
Kenrokuen Garden	Kanazawa	兼六園	*Kenrokuen*
Korakuen Garden	Okayama	後楽園	*Kōrakuen*
Korakuen Garden	Tokyo	後楽園	*Kōrakuen*
Moss Garden	Kyoto	苔寺	*Kokedera*
Rikugien Garden	Tokyo	六義園	*Rikugien*
Ritsurin Garden	Takamatsu	栗林公園	*Ritsurin Kōen*
Rock Garden	Kyoto	龍安寺の石庭	*Ryōanji no Sekitei*
Shinjuku Gyoen Garden	Tokyo	新宿御苑	*Shinjuku Gyoen*

HOT SPRINGS

Two of the most famous hot springs are Noboribetsu in Hokkaido and Beppu in Oita Prefecture, Kyushu. The former features a Valley of Hell: columns of steam rising from the ground, which is part of an old crater. The latter also has a "hell": boiling mud ponds.

Name	Location	Name	Pronunciation
Arima Hot Springs	Hyogo Prefecture	有馬温泉	*Arima Onsen*
Atami Hot Springs	Shizuoka Prefecture	熱海	*Atami*
Beppu Hot Springs	Oita Prefecture	別府温泉	*Beppu Onsen*
Dogo Hot Springs	Ehime Prefecture	道後温泉	*Dōgo Onsen*
Hakone Hot Springs	Kanagawa Prefecture	箱根	*Hakone*
Ibusuki Hot Springs	Kagoshima Prefecture	指宿温泉	*Ibusuki Onsen*
Ito Hot Springs	Shizuoka Prefecture	伊東温泉	*Itō Onsen*
Jozankei Hot Springs	Hokkaido	定山渓温泉	*Jōtankei Onsen*
Kinugawa Hot Springs	Tochigi Prefecture	鬼怒川温泉	*Kinugawa Onsen*
Kusatsu Hot Springs	Gunma Prefecture	草津温泉	*Kusatsu Onsen*
Noboribetsu Hot Springs	Hokkaido	登別温泉	*Noboribetsu Onsen*
Yugawara Hot Springs	Kanagawa Prefecture	湯河原温泉	*Yugawara Onsen*
Yuzawa Hot Springs	Niigata Prefecture	湯沢温泉	*Yuzawa Onsen*

MUSEUMS

In Tokyo, be sure to see the Tokyo National Museum. Specializing in Japanese and Far Eastern ancient and medieval art, it houses more than 115,000 objects. It is the largest museum in Japan. In Kyoto, the Kyoto National Museum is a must. It was established in 1868 as a repository for art objects and treasures from temples, shrines, and individual collections. There are now more than 10,000 objects. Also in Kyoto, don't miss the Kyoto Municipal Museum of Traditional Industry. Because most of Kyoto's traditional industry is handicrafts, there are outstanding displays of lacquer, bamboo, silk, paper, and ceramic objects. You can also see demonstrations of centuries-old production methods for these arts and crafts.

If you visit Kurashiki, one of the highlights is the Kurashiki Folkcraft Museum, renowned throughout Japan for its collection of craft objects used in daily life. The building itself is an old rice granary, symbolic of the town's historic role in the rice trade.

Name	Location	Name	Pronunciation
Edo-Tokyo Museum	Tokyo	江戸東京博物館	*Edo-Tōkyō Hakubutsukan*
Fujita Art Museum	Osaka	藤田美術館	*Fujita Bijutsukan*
Kobe City Museum	Kobe	神戸市立博物館	*Kōbe Shiritsu Hakubutsukan*
Kyoto Municipal Museum of Traditional Industry	Kyoto	京都伝統産業ふれあい館	*Kyōto Dentō Sangyō Fureaikan*
Kyoto National Museum	Kyoto	京都国立博物館	*Kyōto Kokuritsu Hakubutsukan*
Kurashiki Folkcraft Museum	Kurashiki	倉敷民芸館	*Kurashiki Mingeikan*
Nara National Museum	Nara	奈良国立博物館	*Nara Kokuritsu Hakubutsukan*
National Museum of Western Art	Tokyo	国立西洋美術館	*Kokuritsu Seiyō Bijutsukan*

Ohara Art Gallery	Kurashiki	大原美術館	*Ōhara Bijutsukan*
Osaka Japan Folk Art Museum	Osaka	大阪日本民芸館	*Ōsaka Nippon Mingeikan*
Tokugawa Art Museum	Nagoya	徳川美術館	*Tokugawa Bijutsukan*
Tokyo National Art Museum	Tokyo	東京国立博物館	*Tōkyō Kokuritsu Hakubutsukan*

PALACES AND IMPERIAL VILLAS

The Imperial Palace, with its gardens covering 250 acres in the heart of Tokyo, is where the imperial family resides. The Kyoto Imperial Palace was the residence from 1331 until 1868, when the family moved to Tokyo. Also in Kyoto, the Katsura Imperial Villa represents a high point of traditional Japanese architecture and landscape gardening. To visit the Kyoto Imperial Palace and the Katsura Imperial Villa (and the Shugakuin Imperial Villa as well), you must apply in advance for permission. Passes are issued by the Kyoto Office of the Imperial Household Agency. You must have your passport with you when you pick up your pass. For the palace pass, you apply in person shortly before your visit; for the villas, you apply in person, by phone, online, or by mail one month to one week in advance. You must be in Japan to apply.

Name	Location	Name	Pronunciation
Hama Imperial Villa	Tokyo	浜離宮	*Hama Rikyū*
Imperial Palace	Tokyo	皇居	*Kōkyo*
Katsura Imperial Villa	Kyoto	桂離宮	*Katsura Rikyū*
Kyoto Imperial Palace	Kyoto	京都御所	*Kyōto Gosho*
Shugakuin Imperial Villa	Kyoto	修学院離宮	*Shūgakuin Rikyū*

SHRINES

Japanese shrines are sacred Shinto places of worship. Shinto, the indigenous religion of Japan, is today as much a value system as a religion. In fact, most Japanese would say that they are Buddhists as well as Shintoists, and see no conflict or contradiction in this dual allegiance. Shinto embodies the deep Japanese respect for nature; the shrines are places of great natural beauty.

The shrines to visit include the Meiji Shrine in Tokyo, the Heian Shrine in Kyoto, the Toshogu Shrine in Nikko, and the Ise Shrine at Ise. The Ise Shrine is the most venerated of all *Shinto shrines*.

Name	Location	Name	Pronunciation
Atsuta Shrine	Nagoya	熱田神宮	*Atsuta Jingū*
Dazaifu Shrine	Fukuoka	太宰府天満宮	*Dazaifu Tenmangū*
Fushimi Inari Shrine	Kyoto	伏見稲荷神社	*Fushimi Inari Jinja*
Heian Shrine	Kyoto	平安神宮	*Heian Jingū*
Ikuta Shrine	Kobe	生田神社	*Ikuta Jinja*
Ise Shrine	Ise	伊勢神宮	*Ise Jingū*
Itsukushima Shrine	Miyajima	厳島神社	*Itsukushima Jinja*
Izumo Grand Shrine	Izumo	出雲大社	*Izumo Taisha*
Kasuga Grand Shrine	Nara	春日大社	*Kasuga Taisha*
Kashima Shrine	Kashima	鹿島神宮	*Kashima Jingū*
Kitano Shrine	Kyoto	北野天神	*Kitano Tenjin*
Kotohira Shrine	Kotohira	琴平神社	*Kotohira Jinja*
Meiji Shrine	Tokyo	明治神宮	*Meiji Jingū*
Sumiyoshi Grand Shrine	Osaka	住吉大社	*Sumiyoshi Taisha*

Toshogu Shrine	Nikko	東照宮	*Tōshōgū*
Tsurugaoka Hachimangu Shrine	Kamakura	鶴岡八幡宮	*Tsurugaoka Hachimangū*
Yasaka Shrine	Kyoto	八坂神社	*Yasaka Jinja*

TEMPLES

Japan's Buddhist temples are so varied that choosing from among them is especially difficult. *Todaiji*, near Nara, is famous as the site of the world's largest bronze statue of Buddha. The building that houses it is the world's largest wooden structure. *Horyuji*, also in Nara, has about 40 buildings, each one of them designated either a National Treasure or an Important Cultural Property. These buildings contain a fabulous collection of Japanese sculpture and art treasures.

Name	Location	Name	Pronunciation
Asakusa Kannon	Tokyo	浅草観音	*Asakusa Kannon*
Byodoin	Uji	平等院	*Byōdōin*
Chuguji	Nara	中宮寺	*Chūgūji*
Chusonji	Hiraizumi	中尊寺	*Chūsonji*
Daitokuji	Kyoto	大徳寺	*Daitokuji*
Enryakuji	Hieisan	延暦寺	*Enryakuji*
Ginkakuji	Kyoto	銀閣寺	*Ginkakuji*
Horyuji	Nara	法隆寺	*Hōryūji*
Kinkakuji	Kyoto	金閣寺	*Kinkakuji*
Kiyomizudera	Kyoto	清水寺	*Kiyomizudera*
Kofukuji	Nara	興福寺	*Kōfukuji*
Koryuji	Kyoto	広隆寺	*Kōryūji*
Kotokuji	Kamakura	高徳寺	*Kōtokuji*

Nanzenji	Kyoto	南禅寺	*Nanzenji*
Nishi Honganji	Kyoto	西本願寺	*Nishi Honganji*
Ryoanji	Kyoto	龍安寺	*Ryōanji*
Saihoji	Kyoto	西芳寺	*Saihōji*
Sanjusangendo	Kyoto	三十三間堂	*Sanjūsangendō*
Tenryuji	Kyoto	天龍寺	*Tenryūji*
Todaiji	Nara	東大寺	*Tōdaiji*
Toji	Kyoto	東寺	*Tōji*
Toshodaiji	Nara	唐招提寺	*Tōshōdaiji*
Yakushiji	Nara	薬師寺	*Yakushiji*

FESTIVALS

Here are just a few of the multitude of festivals held throughout Japan each year. Check with local sources in Japan to find others you can attend during your visit.

festival		お祭り	*omatsuri*
January		一月	*ichigatsu*
6	New Year Firemen's Parade (Tokyo)	消防出初め式	*Shōbō Dezomeshiki*
15	Grass-Burning Festival on Wakakusayama Hill (Nara)	若草山の山焼き	*Wakakusayama no Yamayaki*

February	二月		*nigatsu*
First Fri.–Sun.	Snow Festival (Sapporo)	札幌 雪祭り	*Sapporo Yuki Matsuri*
2, 3, or 4	Bean-Throwing Ceremony (nationwide)	節分	*Setsubun*
2, 3, or 4	Lantern Festival of Kasuga Shrine (Nara)	春日大社 万燈篭	*Kasuga Taisha Mandōrō*
March	三月		*sangatsu*
3	Doll Festival for Girls (nationwide)	雛祭り	*Hina Matsuri*
12	Water-Drawing Ceremony of Todaiji (Nara)	東大寺 二月堂 お水取り	*Tōdaiji Nigatsudō Omizutori*
April	四月		*shigatsu*
8	Buddha's Birthday, at Buddhist temples (nationwide)	花祭り	*Hana Matsuri*
16–17	Yayoi Festival of Futarasan Shrine (Nikko)	二荒山 神社の 弥生祭り	*Futarasan Jinja no Yayoi Matsuri*
May	五月		*gogatsu*
3–5	Hakata Dontaku Parade (Hakata)	博多 どんたく	*Hakata Dontaku*
Second Sat. and Sun., odd-numbered years	Festival of Kanda Myojin Shrine (Tokyo)	神田祭り	*Kanda Matsuri*

Third Sat. and Sun.	Festival of Asakusa Shrine (Tokyo)	三社祭	*Sanja Matsuri*
15	Hollyhock Festival of Shimogamo and Kamigamo Shrines (Kyoto)	葵祭り	*Aoi Matsuri*
17–18	Grand Festival of Toshogu Shrine (Nikko)	東照宮 春祭り	*Tōshōgū Haru Matsuri*

June		六月	**rokugatsu**
14	Rice-Planting Festival at Sumiyoshi Shrine (Osaka)	住吉の 御田植え	*Sumiyoshi no Onta Ue*

July		七月	**shichigatsu**
7	Star Festival (nationwide)	七夕	*Tanabata*
13–16	Bon Festival (nationwide)	お盆	*Obon*
mid-July	Music Festival of Itsukushima Shrine (Miyajima)	管絃祭	*Kangensai*
16–24	Gion Festival of Yasaka Shrine (Kyoto)	祇園祭	*Gion Matsuri*
24–25	Tenjin Festival of Tenmangu Shrine (Osaka)	天神祭り	*Tenjin Matsuri*

August		八月	**hachigatsu**
1–4	Sansa Dance of Morioka (Morioka)	さんさ踊り	*Sansa Odori*

3–7	Float Festival of Aomori (Aomori)	ねぶた	*Nebuta*
5–7	Bamboo Pole and Lantern Balancing Festival (Akita)	かんとう	*Kantō*
6–8	Star Festival (Sendai)	七夕	*Tanabata*
12–15	Awa Odori Folk Dance (Tokushima City)	阿波踊り	*Awa Odori*
16	Daimonji Bonfire on Mount Nyoigatake (Kyoto)	大文字焼き	*Daimonji Yaki*

| **September** | 九月 | | ***kugatsu*** |
| 16 | Horseback Archery of Tsurugaoka Hachimangu Shrine (Kamakura) | 流鏑馬 | *Yabusame* |

October	十月		***jūgatsu***
7–9	Okunchi Festival of Suwa Shrine (Nagasaki)	おくんち	*Okunchi*
11–13	Oeshiki Festival of Honmonji Temple (Tokyo)	お会式	*Oeshiki*
17	Autumn Festival of Toshogu Shrine (Nikko)	東照宮秋祭り	*Tōshōgū Aki Matsuri*

| 22 | Festival of the Ages, Heian Shrine (Kyoto) | 時代祭 | *Jidai Matsuri* |

November 十一月 *jūichigatsu*

| 3 | Feudal Lord's Procession (Hakone) | 大名行列 | *Daimyō Gyōretsu* |
| 15 | Children's Shrine-Visiting Day [for 3-year-old boys and girls, 5-year-old boys, and 7-year-old girls] (nationwide) | 七五三 | *Shichigosan* |

December 十二月 *jūnigatsu*

| 17 | On Matsuri of Kasuga Shrine (Nara) | 御祭り | *On matsuri* |
| mid-December | Year-End Market at Asakusa Kannon Temple (Tokyo) | 年の市 | *Toshi no Ichi* |

RELIGIOUS SERVICES

Although the predominant religions in Japan are Buddhism and Shintoism, there are Christian, Jewish, Muslim, and other places of worship. In the large cities, you may find not only your religious denomination, but also services in your language. If not, these phrases will help.

Where can I find a directory of <u>churches</u>?	どこに、<u>教会</u>のリストがありますか。	*Doko ni, <u>kyōkai</u> no risuto ga arimasu ka.*
religious organizations	宗教団体	*shūkyō dantai*
Is there a <u>Catholic church</u> near here?	近くに、<u>カトリック教の教会</u>があります か。	*Chikaku ni, <u>katorikku kyō no kyōkai</u> ga arimasu ka.*
Protestant church	プロテスタントの教会	*purotesutanto no kyōkai*
synagogue	ユダヤ教の寺院	*yudaya kyō no jiin*
mosque	回教の寺院	*kaikyō no jiin*
Buddhist temple	お寺	*otera*
In what language do they conduct the service?	礼拝式は、何語ですか。	*Reihai shiki wa, nani go desu ka.*
Is there a service in English?	英語での礼拝式がありますか。	*Eigo de no reihai shiki ga arimasu ka.*
What time is the service?	礼拝は、何時に始まりますか。	*Reihai wa, nan ji ni hajimarimasu ka.*

I'd like to speak to a <u>priest</u>.	<u>神父さん</u>と話したいのですが。 *<u>Shinpu san</u> to hanashitai no desu ga.*
minister	牧師さん　*bokushi san*
rabbi	ラビ　*rabi*
I'd like to attend services here today.	今日の礼拝式に出席したいのですが。 *Kyō no reihai shiki ni shusseki shitai no desu ga.*
I enjoyed the services very much.	素晴らしい礼拝式でした。 *Subarashii reihai shiki deshita.*
Are there any other activities here <u>today</u>?	<u>今日</u>は、他に何かありますか。<u>*Kyō*</u> *wa, hoka ni nanika arimasu ka.*
this week	今週　*konshū*
next week	来週　*raishū*
this month	今月　*kongetsu*
I'd like to come back again.	また来たいです。*Mata kitai desu.*
Thank you. Goodbye.	ありがとうございました。さようなら。 *Arigatō gozaimashita. Sayōnara.*
I'll see you again.	また、お目にかかります。*Mata,* *ome ni kakarimasu.*

PLANNING TRIPS

During your stay you may want to plan some longer excursions. Tourists can get around Japan by plane, train, or boat.

TRAINS

Don't expect to find porters in Japanese train stations. And there are many staircases to climb. You'll do well to travel light!

SUPER EXPRESS OR BULLET TRAINS

Shinkansen	新幹線	*shinkansen*

The bullet trains, or Shinkansen as they're known in Japan, are world famous for speed, safety, and comfort. There are nine Shinkansen lines. Some lines have different kinds of trains, faster ones with fewer stops, and slower ones with more stops, as you can see on the chart on the next page. You can specify the one you want when buying your ticket.

OTHER TYPES OF TRAINS

Limited express	特急	*tokkyū*
Ordinary express	急行	*kyukō*
Local trains	普通	*futsū*

Fares and Classes

You need a basic fare ticket for all train travel. And if you travel by Shinkansen, limited express, or ordinary express, you pay a supplementary fare as well. There are three classes of seats on these trains: Green Car (first class), reserved seats, and unreserved seats. Green Car and reserved seats also cost extra. Before you depart for Japan, you might want to inquire at your local Japan Air Lines (JAL) or All Nippon Airways (ANA) ticket office and some travel agencies or online about the money-saving Japan Railpass.

Green Car	グリーン車	*gurīn sha*
reserved seats	指定席	*shitei seki*
unreserved seats	自由席	*jiyū seki*

Line	Route	Train Name (listed from faster ones with fewer stops to slower ones with more stops)
Tokaido Shinkansen	Tokyo – Shin-Osaka	Nozomi Hikari Hikari Rail Star Kodama
Sanyo Shinkansen	Shin-Osaka – Hakata	Mizuho Sakura
Tohoku Shinkansen	Tokyo – Shin-Aomori	Hayate Yamabiko Nasuno
Akita Shinkansen	Morioka – Akita	Komachi
Yamagata Shinkansen	Fukushima – Shinjo	Tsubasa
Joetsu Shinkansen	Tokyo – Niigata	Toki Max Toki Tanigawa Max Tanigawa
Hokuriku Shinkansen	Tokyo – Kanazawa	Kagayaki Hakutaka Tsurugi Asama
Kyushu Shinkansen	Hakata – Kagoshima-Chuo	Mizuho Sakura Tsubame
Hokkaido Shinkansen	Shin-Aomori – Shin-Hakodate-Hokuto	Hayabusa Hayate

INQUIRIES

Is there a timetable in English?	英語の時刻表が、ありますか。 *Eigo no jikoku hyō ga, arimasu ka.*
Where can I get a timetable in English?	英語の時刻表は、どこでもらえますか。 *Eigo no jikoku hyō wa, doko de moraemasu ka.*
Which line do I take to go to <u>Kyoto</u>?	京都行きは、何線ですか。 <u>*Kyōto*</u> *yuki wa, nani sen desu ka.*
Hakone	箱根 *Hakone*
Which station does the train for <u>Kamakura</u> leave from?	鎌倉行きの列車は、どの駅から出ますか。 <u>*Kamakura*</u> *yuki no ressha wa, dono eki kara demasu ka.*
Aomori	青森 *Aomori*
Where can I buy a ticket for the <u>Shinkansen</u>?	新幹線の切符は、どこで買えますか。 <u>*Shinkansen*</u> *no kippu wa, doko de kaemasu ka.*
JR	ジェイアール *Jeiāru*
Can I buy a ticket in advance?	前売り券が、買えますか。 *Maeuri ken ga, kaemasu ka.*
Can I buy a ticket on the day of the trip?	当日券が、買えますか。 *Tōjitsu ken ga, kaemasu ka.*
Where is the <u>ticket window/counter</u>?	切符売り場は、どこですか。 <u>*Kippu uriba*</u> *wa, doko desu ka.*
ticket machine	切符の販売機 *kippu no hanbaiki*
ticket window/ counter for reservations	緑の窓口 *midori no madoguchi*
Shinkansen ticket window/counter for today's trains	新幹線の当日券の窓口 *Shinkansen no tōjitsu ken no madoguchi*
Where is the window/ counter for reserved tickets?	前売り券の窓口は、どこですか。 *Maeuri ken no madoguchi wa, doko desu ka.*

TRAIN INFORMATION

Where is the information center?	案内所は、どこですか。 *Annai jo wa, doko desu ka.*
I'd like to go to <u>Hakata</u>.	博多に行きたいのですが。 <u>*Hakata*</u> *ni ikitai no desu ga.*
Sapporo	札幌 *Sapporo*
Can I stop over?	途中下車が、できますか。 *Tochū gesha ga, dekimasu ka.*
Can I get to Hiroshima by way of <u>Nagano</u>?	長野経由で、広島へ行けますか。 <u>*Nagano*</u> *keiyu de, Hiroshima e ikemasu ka.*
Nara	奈良 *Nara*
Are there <u>limited express</u> trains to Odawara?	小田原へは、特急がありますか。 *Odawara e wa,* <u>*tokkyū*</u> *ga arimasu ka.*
ordinary express	急行 *kyūkō*
Is there a through train to <u>Nara</u>?	奈良への、直通列車がありますか。 <u>*Nara*</u> *e no, chokutsū ressha ga arimasu ka.*
Ise	伊勢 *Ise*
Do I have to change trains?	乗り換えがありますか。 *Norikae ga arimasu ka.*
Where do I have to change trains?	どこで、乗り換えですか。 *Doko de, norikae desu ka.*
Is there a convenient connecting train for <u>Yonago</u>?	米子へは、便利な接続列車があります か。 <u>*Yonago*</u> *e wa, benri na setsuzoku ressha ga arimasu ka.*
Hida Takayama	飛騨高山 *Hida Takayama*
How long do I have to wait?	待ち時間は、どのくらいですか。 *Machi jikan wa, dono kurai desu ka.*
Does the Kodama stop at <u>Atami</u>?	こだまは、熱海に止まりますか。 *Kodama wa,* <u>*Atami*</u> *ni tomarimasu ka.*
Kyoto	京都 *Kyōto*

Does the Hikari stop at <u>Odawara</u>?	ひかりは、<u>小田原</u>に止まりますか。 *Hikari wa, <u>Odawara</u> ni tomarimasu ka.*
Kurashiki	倉敷　*Kurashiki*
When is the <u>earliest</u> train of the day for Nikko?	日光行きの<u>始発</u>は、何時ですか。 *Nikkō yuki no <u>shihatsu</u> wa, nan ji desu ka.*
last	最終　*saishū*
What's the difference in cost between the limited express and ordinary express?	特急と急行の料金の差は、いくらですか。*Tokkyū to kyūkō no ryōkin no sa wa, ikura desu ka.*

BUYING TICKETS

When traveling on intercity trains in Japan, you should buy your tickets in advance. Trains are popular, and choice seats fill up fast. Check with a travel agency, and get the train and class you want. You can, of course, buy tickets at the station or online as well.

I'd like a <u>one-way</u> ticket to Kyoto.	京都への、<u>片道</u>を一枚下さい。 *Kyōto e no, <u>katamichi</u> o ichi mai kudasai.*
a round-trip ticket	往復　*ōfuku*
a ticket for a reserved seat	座席指定券　*zaseki shitei ken*
a first class ticket	グリーン車の券　*gurīn sha no ken*
an unreserved ticket	自由席の券　*jiyū seki no ken*
I'd like two tickets to Kyoto for <u>today</u>.	<u>今日</u>の、京都行きを二枚下さい。 *<u>Kyō</u> no, Kyōto yuki o ni mai kudasai.*
tomorrow	あした　*ashita*
the day after tomorrow	あさって　*asatte*

Is there a discount for <u>a round-trip ticket</u>?	<u>往復券</u>の割引が、ありますか。<u>Ōfuku ken</u> no waribiki ga, arimasu ka.
children	子供　kodomo
senior citizens	シニア　shinia
We'd like <u>unreserved seats</u>.	<u>自由席</u>を、お願いします。<u>Jiyū seki</u> o, onegai shimasu.
reserved seats	指定席　shitei seki
first class seats	グリーン車の席　gurīn sha no seki
the sleeping car	寝台車の席　shindai sha no seki
Is there a <u>nonsmoking</u> section?	<u>禁煙席</u>がありますか。<u>Kin-en</u> seki ga arimasu ka.
smoking	喫煙　kitsuen
Can I get a seat by the <u>window</u>?	<u>窓側</u>の席が、ありますか。<u>Mado gawa</u> no seki ga, arimasu ka.
aisle	通路側　tsūro gawa
How much is the fare?	料金は、いくらですか。Ryōkin wa, ikura desu ka.
Does that include the <u>limited express</u> charge?	それは、<u>特急券</u>も含んでいますか。Sore wa, <u>tokkyū</u> ken mo fukunde imasu ka.
ordinary express	急行　kyūkō

WAITING FOR THE TRAIN

Where's the <u>newsstand</u>?	<u>新聞売り場</u>は、どこですか。<u>Shinbun uriba</u> wa, doko desu ka.
restaurant	食堂／レストラン　shokudō/ resutoran
toilet	トイレ　toire
waiting room	待合い室　machiai shitsu
Where is the <u>track for the Shinkansen</u>?	<u>新幹線乗り場</u>は、どこですか。<u>Shinkansen noriba</u> wa, doko desu ka.
track 10	10番ホーム　jū ban hōmu

the track for Hikari 3	ひかり3号のホーム *Hikari san gō no hōmu*
Which track does the train for Hakata leave from?	博多行きの列車は、何番ホームから出ますか。*Hakata yuki no ressha wa, nan ban hōmu kara demasu ka.*
Which track does the train from Hakata arrive at?	博多からの列車は、何番ホームに着きますか。*Hakata kara no ressha wa, nan ban hōmu ni tsukimasu ka.*
What time does the <u>train</u> for Atami leave?	熱海行きの<u>列車</u>は、何時に出ますか。*Atami yuki no <u>ressha</u> wa, nan ji ni demasu ka.*
next train	次の列車 *tsugi no ressha*
Is this the platform for the train to <u>Ueno</u>?	<u>上野</u>行きの列車のホームは、ここですか。*<u>Ueno</u> yuki no ressha no hōmu wa, koko desu ka.*
Aomori	青森 *Aomori*
Will the train for <u>Nagano</u> leave on time?	<u>長野</u>行きの列車は、定刻に出ますか。*<u>Nagano</u> yuki no ressha wa, teikoku ni demasu ka.*
Kanazawa	金沢 *Kanazawa*

ON THE TRAIN

Is this seat free?	この席は、あいていますか。*Kono seki wa, aite imasu ka.*
I think that's my seat.	それは、私の席だと思いますが。*Sore wa, watakushi no seki da to omoimasu ga.*
Where's the <u>dining car</u>?	<u>食堂車</u>は、何号車ですか。*<u>Shokudō sha</u> wa, nan gō sha desu ka.*
buffet car	ビュッフェ車 *byuffe sha*
sleeping car	寝台車 *shindai sha*
telephone	電話 *denwa*
Can I change to first class?	グリーン車／一等に、かえられますか。*Gurīn sha/ittō ni, kaeraremasu ka.*

Where are we now?	今、どの辺ですか。 *Ima, dono hen desu ka.*
What time do we arrive at Kyoto?	京都には、何時に着きますか。 *Kyōto niwa, nan ji ni tsukimasu ka.*

FOOD: EKIBEN

Ekiben (literally, station box lunch) is one of the best features of riding Japanese trains. Also called *obento*, the Japanese-style meals come in many varieties. There are choices of food, and containers of many shapes and sizes, some reusable—you can keep them if you like! Buy *obento* at the station before the trip, or on the train from vendors. In the past, at some stations along the way, *obento* vendors waited for the trains. Passengers jumped off, bought a box lunch, and boarded again, all within two or three minutes. No more. But you can still buy good local specialties from the onboard vendors when the train is passing through an area known for those items.

What's the next stop?	次の停車駅は、どこですか。 *Tsugi no teisha eki wa, doko desu ka.*
Is there a special obento in this area?	この地域には特別のお弁当があります か。 *Kono chiiki niwa tokubetsu no obentō ga arimasu ka.*
What is in the obento?	そのお弁当には何が入っています か。 *Sono obentō niwa nani ga haitte imasu ka.*

FOOD: VENDORS

Although some trains have dining cars and buffet cars, you can eat at your seat if you prefer. Vendors come through quite often, and they sell a variety of foods, from the delicious Japanese box lunches (*obento*), to sandwiches and other snack foods.

Excuse me. Do you have <u>beer</u>?	ちょっと、すみません。ビールがあ ります か。 *Chotto, sumimasen. Bīru ga arimasu ka.*
candy	キャンディー *kyandī*
chocolate	チョコレート *chokorēto*

coffee	コーヒー	*kōhī*
cola	コーラ	*kōra*
ice cream	アイスクリーム	*aisukurīmu*
Japanese tea	お茶	*ocha*
Japanese box lunches	お弁当	*obentō*
juice	ジュース	*jūsu*
mandarin oranges	みかん	*mikan*
nuts	ナッツ	*nattsu*
peanuts	ピーナッツ	*pīnattsu*
pudding	プリン	*purin*
rice crackers	(お) せんべい	*(o)senbei*
sake	お酒	*osake*
sandwiches	サンドイッチ	*sandoitchi*
tea	紅茶	*kōcha*
whiskey	ウイスキー	*uisukī*

What kind of <u>juice</u> do you have?　どんな<u>ジュース</u>が、ありますか。 *Donna jūsu ga, arimasu ka.*

　box lunches　お弁当　*obentō*

What is that?　それは、何ですか。 *Sore wa, nan desu ka.*

Give me a beer, please.　ビールを下さい。 *Bīru o kudasai.*

Give me Japanese tea and a box lunch, please.　お茶とお弁当を下さい。 *Ocha to obentō o kudasai.*

How much is it?　いくらですか。 *Ikura desu ka.*

LOST AND FOUND

Where is the lost and found office?　遺失物の取扱所は、どこですか。 *Ishitsubutsu no toriatsukaijo wa, doko desu ka.*

I've lost my <u>camera</u>.	カメラを、なくしてしまいました。 *Kamera o, nakushite shimaimashita.*
luggage	荷物　*nimotsu*
traveler's checks	トラベラーズ チェック *toraberāzu chekku*
passport	パスポート　*pasupōto*
I got on the train at <u>Yokohama</u> station.	<u>横浜</u>駅で乗りました。*Yokohama eki de norimashita.*
Shizuoka	静岡　*Shizuoka*
My train arrived here at <u>10:30 A.M.</u>	私の列車は、ここに<u>午前10時半</u>に着きました。*Watakushi no ressha wa, koko ni gozen <u>jū ji han</u> ni tsukimashita.*
4:15 P.M.	午後4時15分　*gogo yo ji jū go fun*
My seat was in the <u>middle</u> of the seventh car.	私の席は、七号車の<u>真ん中辺</u>でした。*Watakushi no seki wa, nana gō sha no <u>mannaka hen</u> deshita.*
front	前の方　*mae no hō*
back	後ろの方　*ushiro no hō*
My seat was by the <u>window</u>.	席は、<u>窓</u>側でした。*Seki wa, <u>mado</u> gawa deshita.*
aisle	通路　*tsūro*

AIR TRAVEL

Besides the two major airlines, All Nippon Airways (ANA) and Japan Airlines (JAL), there are regional, local, and commuter airlines such as Star Flyer (SFJ), JAL Express (JEX), J-Air (JAIR), Air Do (ADO), Skymark Airlines (SKY), Japan Air Commuter (JAC), and Air Japan (AJX). For domestic travel in Japan, air travel is a timesaving option. Although most airline personnel know some English, the Japanese phrases can be helpful, especially at local airports.

When traveling on domestic flights, don't count on food being served. You might get coffee, tea, soft drinks, or a snack, but full meal service is not customary. Check first, so you can eat before your flight if you're hungry.

Smoking is prohibited on airplanes and inside terminals.

INQUIRIES

Is there a flight to <u>Sendai</u>?	<u>仙台</u>への飛行機が、ありますか。 *<u>Sendai</u> e no hikōki ga, arimasu ka.*
Beppu	別府　*Beppu*
Is it a <u>nonstop</u> flight?	それは、<u>ノン・ストップ</u>ですか。 *Sore wa, <u>non·sutoppu</u> desu ka.*
direct	直行便　*chokkō bin*
Where does it stop over?	途中で、どこに止まりますか。 *Tochū de, doko ni tomarimasu ka.*
Is there a daily flight to <u>Toyama</u>?	<u>富山</u>への便は、毎日ありますか。*<u>Toyama</u> e no bin wa, mainichi arimasu ka.*
Takamatsu	高松　*Takamatsu*
Is that a <u>Japan Air Lines</u> flight?	それは、<u>日航</u>の便ですか。*Sore wa, <u>Nikkō</u> no bin desu ka.*
All Nippon Airways	全日空　*Zennikkū*
Which day of the week does the flight to <u>Okayama</u> leave?	岡山行きの便は、何曜日に出ますか。 *<u>Okayama</u> yuki no bin wa, nani yōbi ni demasu ka.*
Kumamoto	熊本　*Kumamoto*
What type of aircraft do they use for that flight?	その便には、どんな飛行機を使いますか。*Sono bin niwa, donna hikōki o tsukaimasu ka.*
Is there a connecting flight to <u>Oita</u>?	<u>大分</u>への乗り継ぎ便が、ありますか。*<u>Ōita</u> e no noritsugi bin ga, arimasu ka.*
Kochi	高知　*Kōchi*

Is there meal service in flight?	機内で、食事のサービスがありますか。 *Kinai de, shokuji no sābisu ga arimasu ka.*
Should I buy my air ticket in advance?	航空券は、前売りを買っておくべきですか。 *Kōkū ken wa, mae uri o katte oku beki desu ka.*
Can I get a ticket at the airport the day of the trip?	当日、空港で券が買えますか。 *Tōjitsu, kūkō de ken ga kaemasu ka.*
Is there a discount for a round-trip ticket?	往復券には、割引がありますか。 *Ōfuku ken niwa, waribiki ga arimasu ka.*
Is there a discount for <u>children</u>?	<u>子供</u>の割引が、ありますか。 *<u>Kodomo</u> no waribiki ga, arimasu ka.*
senior citizens	シニア *shinia*

BUYING TICKETS

Can I get a ticket to Okinawa for <u>today</u>?	<u>今日</u>の沖縄行きの券が、ありますか。 *<u>Kyō</u> no Okinawa yuki no ken ga, arimasu ka.*
tomorrow	あした *ashita*
the day after tomorrow	あさって *asatte*
I'd like a <u>one-way</u> ticket to Osaka.	大阪行きの、<u>片道</u>券を一枚下さい。 *Ōsaka yuki no, <u>katamichi</u> ken o ichi mai kudasai.*
round trip	往復 *ōfuku*
<u>Two tickets</u> to Sapporo, please.	札幌行きの券を、<u>二枚</u>下さい。 *Sapporo yuki no ken o, <u>ni mai</u> kudasai.*
three	三枚 *san mai*
four	四枚 *yo mai*

Is there <u>a morning flight</u> to Kagoshima?

鹿児島行きの、朝の便がありますか。
Kagoshima yuki no, <u>asa no bin</u> ga arimasu ka.

an afternoon flight

昼間の便　*hiruma no bin*

an evening flight

夜の便　*yoru no bin*

I'd like a ticket to Osaka on <u>August 10</u>.

八月十日の大阪行きの券を、一枚下さい。*<u>Hachi gatsu tōka</u> no Ōsaka yuki no ken o ichi mai kudasai.*

September 20

九月二十日　*ku gatsu hatsuka*

October 30

十月三十日　*jū gatsu san jū nichi*

When is the next available flight to Osaka?

次に乗れる大阪行きの便は、何時ですか。*Tsugi ni noreru Ōsaka yuki no bin wa, nan ji desu ka.*

Is there <u>an earlier</u> flight than that?

それより早い便が、ありますか。*Sore yori <u>hayai</u> bin ga, arimasu ka.*

a later

遅い　*osoi*

What's the air fare to <u>Nagasaki</u>.

長崎まで、いくらですか。*<u>Nagasaki</u> made, ikura desu ka.*

Hiroshima

広島　*Hiroshima*

What's the flying time to <u>Okinawa</u>?

沖縄までの飛行時間は、どのくらいですか。*<u>Okinawa</u> made no hikō jikan wa, dono kurai desu ka.*

Hakodate

函館　*Hakodate*

Is there a limit on the number of bags?

荷物の数には、制限がありますか。*Nimotsu no kazu niwa, seigen ga arimasu ka.*

When do I have to check in?

何時にチェック・インしなければなりませんか。*Nan ji ni chekku in shinakereba narimasen ka.*

Do I need to reconfirm the reservation?

予約の再確認は、必要ですか。*Yoyaku no sai kakunin wa, hitsuyō desu ka.*

INFORMATION ABOUT THE AIRPORT

Where is the airport?	空港は、どこにありますか。*Kūkō wa, doko ni arimasu ka.*
Is the airport far?	空港まで、遠いですか。*Kūkō made, tōi desu ka.*
How can I get to the airport?	空港へは、どう行ったらいいですか。*Kūkō e wa, dō ittara ii desu ka.*
Is there a <u>train</u> to the airport?	空港へは、電車がありますか。*Kūkō e wa, <u>densha</u> ga arimasu ka.*
bus	バス　*basu*
hotel bus	ホテルのバス　*hoteru no basu*
subway	地下鉄　*chikatetsu*
What is the best way to get to the airport?	空港への、一番いい行き方は何ですか。*Kūkō e no, ichiban ii ikikata wa nan desu ka.*
How much does the <u>train</u> to the airport cost?	空港まで、電車だといくらかかりますか。*Kūkō made, <u>densha</u> da to ikura kakarimasu ka.*
taxi	タクシー　*takushī*
bus	バス　*basu*
How long does the <u>train</u> take to the airport?	空港まで、電車だとどのくらい時間がかかりますか。*Kūkō made, <u>densha</u> da to dono kurai jikan ga kakarimasu ka.*
taxi	タクシー　*takushī*
bus	バス　*basu*

AT THE AIRPORT

I'd like to check in this suitcase.	このスーツケースを、チェック・インします。*Kono sūtsukēsu o, chekkuin shimasu.*

This is carry-on. これは、機内持ち込み品です。*Kore wa, kinai mochikomi hin desu.*

Can I get a seat by the <u>window</u>? 窓側の席を、もらえますか。<u>*Mado gawa no seki o, moraemasu ka.*</u>

aisle 通路 *tsūro*

When is the departure? 何時発ですか。*Nan ji hatsu desu ka.*

What's the departure gate? 出発ゲートは、何番ですか。*Shuppatsu gēto wa, nan ban desu ka.*

What's the arrival time? 何時着ですか。*Nan ji chaku desu ka.*

INTERNATIONAL AIR TRAVEL

I'd like a ticket to <u>Hong Kong</u>. <u>香港</u>への券を、一枚下さい。<u>*Honkon*</u> *e no ken o, ichi mai kudasai.*

Manila マニラ *Manira*

When is the first available flight to <u>Jakarta</u>? すぐ乗れる<u>ジャカルタ</u>行きの便は、いつ出ますか。*Sugu noreru* <u>*Jakaruta*</u> *yuki no bin wa, itsu demasu ka.*

Bangkok バンコック *Bankokku*

Is there a direct flight to <u>Taipei</u> from this airport? この空港から、<u>台北</u>への直行便がありますか。*Kono kūkō kara,* <u>*Taihoku*</u> *e no chokkō bin ga arimasu ka.*

Guam ガム島 *Gamu tō*

What's the air fare to <u>Singapore</u>? <u>シンガポール</u>まで、いくらですか。<u>*Shingapōru*</u> *made, ikura desu ka.*

Kuala Lumpur クアラランプール *Kuararunpūru*

How long does the flight take? 飛行時間は、何時間ですか。*Hikō jikan wa, nan jikan desu ka.*

Is that a <u>lunch</u> flight? その便では、<u>ランチ</u>が出ますか。*Sono bin dewa,* <u>*ranchi*</u> *ga demasu ka.*

dinner ディナー *dīnā*

When is the <u>departure</u> time?	出発時刻は、何時ですか。 *Shuppatsu jikoku wa, nan ji desu ka.*
arrival	到着　*tōchaku*

BOAT TRAVEL: STEAMSHIP, FERRY, HYDROFOIL, HOVERCRAFT

Is there a cruise ship on the Inland Sea?	瀬戸内海に、クルーズ・シップがありますか。*Setonaikai ni, kurūzu shippu ga arimasu ka.*
Can I go to <u>Hokkaido</u> by ship?	北海道に、船で行けますか。*Hokkaidō ni, fune de ikemasu ka.*
Okinawa	沖縄　*Okinawa*
What type of ship is it?	どんな種類の船ですか。*Donna shurui no fune desu ka.*
Do you need to make a reservation?	予約の必要が、ありますか。*Yoyaku no hitsuyō ga, arimasu ka.*
When does the next <u>ship</u> leave?	次の船は、いつ出ますか。*Tsugi no fune wa, itsu demasu ka.*
ferry	連絡船　*renrakusen*
hydrofoil	水中翼船　*suichū yokusen*
hovercraft	ホーバー・クラフト　*hōbā kurafuto*
Where is the <u>harbor</u>?	港は、どこですか。*Minato wa, doko desu ka.*
ticket office	切符売り場　*kippu uriba*
pier	埠頭　*futō*
How long does the <u>crossing</u> take?	渡るには、どのくらい時間がかかりますか。*Wataru niwa, dono kurai jikan ga kakarimasu ka.*
cruise	航海　*kōkai*

When do we board?	乗船時間は、何時ですか。*Jōsen jikan wa, nan ji desu ka.*
Do we stop at any ports?	途中で、他の港にとまりますか。*Tochū de, hoka no minato ni tomarimasu ka.*
How long do we remain in port?	その港では、どのくらい停泊しますか。*Sono minato dewa, dono kurai teihaku shimasu ka.*
I'd like a <u>first class</u> ticket.	<u>一等</u>の券を下さい。*<u>Ittō</u> no ken o kudasai.*
second class	二等 *nitō*
special class	特等 *tokutō*
Is there a restaurant on board?	船に、レストランがありますか。*Fune ni, resutoran ga arimasu ka.*
Can we buy something to eat on board?	船で、何か食べ物が買えますか。*Fune de, nanika tabemono ga kaemasu ka.*
I don't feel well.	気分が、すぐれません。*Kibun ga, suguremasen.*
Do you have something for seasickness?	何か、船酔いの薬がありますか。*Nanika, funayoi no kusuri ga arimasu ka.*
Do we have time to go ashore at this port?	この港では、上陸する時間があります か。*Kono minato dewa, jōriku suru jikan ga arimasu ka.*
What time do we have to be back on board?	何時までに、船に戻ってこなければ なりませんか。*Nan ji made ni, fune ni modotte konakereba narimasen ka.*
When do we arrive at <u>Sado</u>?	<u>佐渡</u>には、何時に着きますか。*<u>Sado</u> niwa, nan ji ni tsukimasu ka.*
Beppu	別府 *Beppu*

A FEW ITINERARIES

If you want to sightsee, here are a few suggestions: some in-Tokyo tours, some side trips from Tokyo, and one to Kyoto and Nara. For the convenience of a package tour, make arrangements with a travel agency. On your own, you can get to any of these places by public transportation, by car, or a combination of the two.

TOKYO

MEIJI SHRINE

The Meiji Shrine is one of the grandest in Japan. It's easy to reach, located right near Harajuku station. Walk through the entrance, a huge *torii* gate made of 1,700-year-old cedar trees, then along the pebbled path to the Iris Garden; in June, there are 100 varieties in full bloom! There's a teahouse nearby and small pavilions with traditional thatched roofs. Stroll through the thickly wooded gardens, then back along the pebbled path until you come to the main shrine buildings, or *honden*. There you may see couples with newborn babies, brought for naming and blessing by the priests. During the New Year holiday week, festive crowds come to pay their respects.

When you leave, walk down the wide boulevard known as *Omote Sando*. It's a trendy area of small coffee shops, boutiques, restaurants, craft shops, and other amusements. You can easily spend several hours there.

Do I have a chance to see a Shinto ceremony at the shrine?	神社では、神道の儀式を見る機会が ありますか。 *Jinja dewa, shintō no gishiki o miru kikai ga arimasu ka.*
What's the meaning of rinsing the mouth and washing the hands?	口をすすいだり、手を洗ったりする のは、どんな意味ですか。 *Kuchi o susuidari, te o arattari suru no wa, donna imi desu ka.*

Who comes here to pray?	誰が、お祈りに来ますか。*Dare ga, oinori ni kimasu ka.*
What's the proper way to pray?	正しいお祈りの仕方を、教えて下さい。*Tadashii oinori no shikata o, oshiete kudasai.*
Are you supposed to throw money when you pray?	お祈りするとき、おさいせんをあげるべきですか。*Oinori suru toki, osaisen o ageru beki desu ka.*
How much money shall I throw?	おさいせんは、いくらあげればいいですか。*Osaisen wa, ikura agereba ii desu ka.*
May I try a fortune?	おみくじを引いてみてもいいですか。*Omikuji o, hiite mitemo ii desu ka.*

IMPERIAL PALACE, NATIONAL DIET, GINZA

Begin at the Imperial Palace, located in the heart of Tokyo; depending on where you're staying, you might be able to walk from your hotel. The palace itself is open to visitors only at the New Year and on the Emperor's birthday. But you can visit the East Garden, Imperial Palace Plaza, and the *Nijubashi* Bridge, all popular with Tokyoites. From there, walk to the National Diet Building, the home of Japan's legislature, in Kasumigaseki, where you'll find other government buildings, too.

From Kasumigaseki, you can go to Ginza, the most famous shopping area in Japan. At the center of the Ginza district is the *Chuo-dori*, the largest street, which runs northeast to southwest. The intersection of *Chuo-dori* and *Harumi-dori* is a good starting point. Elegant galleries, boutiques, department stores, and restaurants line the streets. Be sure to explore the narrow streets that run parallel to the main roads. These side streets and alleys contain tiny shops, restaurants, coffee houses, bars, and other amusements. You can spend several hours or several days wandering through Ginza, and there will still be more to see next time!

Is this the main residence for the Emperor and his family?	これが、皇居ですか。 *Kore ga, kōkyo desu ka.*
How big is the palace area?	皇居の広さは、どのくらいですか。 *Kōkyo no hirosa wa, dono kurai desu ka.*
Have all the Emperors lived here?	歴代の天皇は、みんなここに住まわれましたか。 *Rekidai no tennō wa, minna koko ni sumawaremashita ka.*
When was it built?	いつ建造されましたか。 *Itsu kenzō saremashita ka.*
Is the Diet in session now?	今、国会は審議中ですか。 *Ima, kokkai wa shingi chū desu ka.*
Can I go inside?	中に入れますか。 *Naka ni hairemasu ka.*
Is there a guided tour of the Diet Building?	議事堂見学の、ガイド付きツアーがありますか。 *Gijidō kengaku no, gaido tsuki tsuā ga arimasu ka.*
Is Ginza more expensive than other shopping areas?	銀座は、他のショッピング街に比べて高いですか。 *Ginza wa, hoka no shoppingu gai ni kurabete takai desu ka.*
Are the stores open at night, too?	(お) 店は、夜も開いていますか。 *(O)mise wa, yoru mo aite imasu ka.*
Is the <u>Kabuki Theater</u> within walking distance of Ginza?	歌舞伎座は、銀座から歩いて行けますか。 *Kabuki za wa, Ginza kara aruite ikemasu ka.*
Tsukiji Fish Market	築地の魚市場　 *Tsukiji no uo ichiba*

ASAKUSA AND UENO

The main attraction in the Asakusa area is the *Asakusa Kannon* Temple. You'll see a huge paper lantern at the *Kaminarimon* (gate). Through the gate, a long arcade leads up to the temple. Known as *Nakamise*, this colorful arcade is lined with small shops open to the walkway. They sell traditional Japanese sweets and rice crackers, clothing, toys, and other souvenirs. The temple itself dates back to 645 A.D. *Kannon* is the goddess of mercy, and many visitors pray for relief from physical ailments at a huge incense brazier close to the entrance. After you leave the temple, you might look at some more shops in the arcade and then have lunch at a nearby restaurant. The *Asakusa Kannon* Temple area is not far from the Tokyo National Museum in Ueno, a must on your tour, and is also accessible to the Ueno Zoo, where you can see the pandas. While in the Asakusa-Ueno area, be sure to visit the spectacular Edo-Tokyo Museum.

Is this area an old part of Tokyo?	この辺は、昔の東京の下町ですか。 *Kono hen wa, mukashi no Tōkyō no shitamachi desu ka.*
Is it always crowded?	いつも、こんでいますか。 *Itsumo, konde imasu ka.*
Do you think I should go to the Tokyo National Museum?	国立博物館へは、行くべきですか。 *Kokuritsu Hakubutsu kan e wa, iku beki desu ka.*
What type of collection are they exhibiting now?	今、どんなものを展示していますか。 *Ima, donna mono o tenji shite imasu ka.*
How early is it open?	何時から、開いていますか。 *Nan ji kara, aite imasu ka.*
How late is it open?	何時まで、開いていますか。 *Nan ji made, aite imasu ka.*
How long does a quick look around the zoo take?	動物園を急いで見て回るのに、どのくらい時間がかかりますか。 *Dōbutsu en o isoide mite mawaru no ni, dono kurai jikan ga kakarimasu ka.*
Can I see pandas at the zoo?	パンダを見ることが、できますか。 *Panda o miru koto ga, dekimasu ka.*

How do I get to the Edo-Tokyo Museum?	江戸東京博物館へは、どう行けばいいですか。 *Edo-Tōkyō Hakubutsukan e wa, dō ikeba ii desu ka.*

NEWER AREAS

For visitors to Tokyo, the possibilities seem endless. As in many major capital cities, there's always something new. For example, Odaiba is a popular leisure destination among young Japanese. So are Roppongi Hills and Omotesando Hills, among others, which are huge and fashionable shopping/restaurant/business/residential complexes.

DAY TRIPS FROM TOKYO

KAMAKURA AND YOKOHAMA

Spend a morning visiting Kamakura, on Japan's Pacific coast. You can get there in about an hour by bus, train, or car. Once the seat of Japan's feudal government, Kamakura offers many attractions in a quiet, peaceful setting. The highlight is the *Daibutsu*, a 700-year-old bronze statue of Buddha, the second largest in Japan. Near the Kamakura station is the *Tsurugaoka Hachimangu* Shrine, which has two museums on its grounds. Also well worth seeing are *Engakuji* and *Kenchoji*, both ranked among the five outstanding Zen temples in Kamakura. You can have lunch at one of Kamakura's fine small restaurants, and then on your way back to Tokyo stop at the port city of Yokohama, about a half hour from Kamakura, and roughly halfway between Kamakura and Tokyo. Visit the *Sankei-en* Garden, which contains many historic buildings, then go to Yamashita Park for a panoramic view of the city and harbor. Walk to nearby Chinatown, where you can wander through the exotic streets at your leisure, visiting the small shops, sampling Chinese delicacies, and perhaps having dinner at one of the superb restaurants before you return to Tokyo.

When was Kamakura the capital?	鎌倉が首都だったのは、いつ頃ですか。 *Kamakura ga shuto datta no wa, itsu goro desu ka.*
How tall is the Great Buddha?	大仏の高さは、どのくらいですか。 *Daibutsu no takasa wa, dono kurai desu ka.*
What are the special handicrafts in Kamakura?	鎌倉には、何か特別の手工芸品があ ります か。 *Kamakura niwa, nanika tokubetsu no shukōgei hin ga arimasu ka.*
Where is the shopping/ restaurant area in Yokohama?	横浜のショッピング／レストラン街は、 どこですか。 *Yokohama no shoppingu/resutoran gai wa, doko desu ka.*
What type of Chinese food do they have?	どんな種類の、中華料理がありますか。 *Donna shurui no, chūka ryōri ga arimasu ka.*
Which one is a <u>Cantonese</u> style restaurant?	どれが、<u>広東</u>料理のレストラン ですか。 *Dore ga, <u>Kanton</u> ryōri no resutoran desu ka.*
Bejing	北京 *Pekin*
Shanghai	上海 *Shanhai*
Szechuan	四川 *Shisen*
Hunan	湖南 *Konan*

If you like things contemporary and urban, you should visit Minato Mirai—the port town of the future. It's an experimental mega-city revitalization and development project inside Yokohama. You can easily spend a whole day there. It features shops, restaurants, cultural events, concerts, exhibitions, museums, parks, and much more!

HAKONE AND MOUNT FUJI

Hakone can be reached by train from Tokyo's Shinjuku station in about an hour and a half, or by bus or car. It's the center of the Fuji-Hakone-Izu National Park, an area of hot springs, pine forests, scenic mountain slopes, and places of historic interest. Nearby Mount Fuji, the venerated 12,388-foot high (3,776 meters) dormant volcano with the perfect cone shape, can be seen from many places in and near Hakone. One of the best viewing spots is beautiful Lake Ashi, which on a clear day shows Mount Fuji's inverted reflection. There are sightseeing boats on the lake. Have lunch at one of the fine hotels in Hakone (perhaps lakeside), and then take a cable-car or funicular railway for spectacular views along the slopes of Mount Sounzan. There's a good open-air museum for sculpture nearby. Among the many other attractions in Hakone are the *Owakudani* and *Kowakidani* valleys, where sulphurous fumes rise from rock crevices. You might also want to take a bus trip partway up Mount Fuji before your return to Tokyo. This one-day excursion can easily extend to several days if you have the time—or you could return to Hakone someday.

Do you think I can see Mount Fuji today?	今日は、富士山が見えるでしょうか。 *Kyō wa, Fujisan ga mieru deshō ka.*
Is it difficult to climb Mount Fuji?	富士山に登るのは、難しいですか。 *Fujisan ni noboru no wa, muzukashii desu ka.*
What are the local handicrafts in Hakone?	箱根には、そこの工芸品があります か。*Hakone niwa, soko no kōgei hin ga arimasu ka.*
Can you swim in the lakes?	湖では、泳げますか。*Mizuumi dewa, oyogemasu ka.*
Is it possible to try a hot spring bath?	温泉に、入ってみることができますか。 *Onsen ni, haitte miru koto ga dekimasu ka.*

NIKKO

Nikko is two hours by train from Tokyo, in a northerly direction. It's known for great scenic beauty, with gentle mountain slopes, cedar trees, lakes, rivers, streams, and waterfalls. When you arrive, go directly to the *Toshogu* Shrine, which was built in 1636 as the mausoleum of *Ieyasu*, founder of the *Tokugawa* shogunate. Many consider it an architectural masterpiece. *Toshogu* is located in a complex of shrines, temples, and museums, and you can get one ticket to admit you to all of them. Begin with *Toshogu*, for it will require some time to see everything. Proceed down the *Omote-Sando*, and pass through the carved and decorated *Yomeimon* gate to the treasures inside. You could spend all day here, seeing the various buildings in the complex. But if you have time, go by bus or taxi along the 48 hairpin curves on the road that climbs to Lake *Chuzenji*, 10 miles (16 biometers) to the west. *Kegon* Falls, 328 feet (100 meters) high, is spectacular. The scenery is worth the side trip.

Is the Toshogu Shrine still owned by the Tokugawa family?	東照宮は、今でも徳川家のものですか。*Tōshōgū wa, ima demo Tokugawa ke no mono desu ka.*
Are the colors original?	色はもともとのものですか。*Iro wa, motomoto no mono desu ka.*

TRIPS OF TWO DAYS OR MORE

KYOTO AND NARA

If you have more than a day to spend outside Tokyo (ideally more than two days), visit Kyoto and Nara. Kyoto is easy to reach by plane, train (there are many Shinkansen daily), bus, or car. The plane trip is about 55 minutes, and the train about 2–3 hours. The capital of Japan from 794 to 1868, Kyoto is still considered by many to be the true repository of traditional Japanese culture. The main attractions are centuries-old temples, shrines, and gardens. There are approximately 400 Shinto shrines and 1,650 Buddhist temples located along thousand-year-old streets and paths. Once you arrive, you can obtain detailed walking tour maps from the Tourist Information Center, or you can arrange with a travel agency for a guided tour.

From Kyoto, Nara is about a 35-minute train ride. Although Nara is much smaller than Kyoto, its history is even older. Many temples contain Buddhist antiquities and other priceless treasures. The famous Deer Park is a 15-minute walk east of the *Kintetsu* Nara station. Over 1,000 tame deer roam the park. Also within walking distance is *Todaiji*, a temple famous for the world's largest bronze statue of Buddha. Walk to *Kofukuji*, a five-story pagoda, and then to the Nara National Museum. If you have time, stop and see the *Kasuga* Grand Shrine and *Shin-Yakushiji*, another temple, before returning to Kyoto.

ENTERTAINMENT AND DIVERSIONS

Japan has a wide variety of amusements that visitors are sure to enjoy. You'll find films, plays, dance, music, sports—all the entertainment and recreation you're used to, plus some that may be new to you, like traditional Japanese theatrical productions, martial arts, and sports.

SCHEDULES

For current schedules of events, you can find weekly English-language publications in most hotels, at JNTO Tourist Information Centers, at travel agencies, and in many restaurants and shops that deal with visitors. You can also get this sort of information in the English-language newspapers such as the *Japan Times*, the *Asahi Weekly*, the *Daily Yomiuri*, the *Tokyo Weekender*, and the *Tokyo Journal*—and, of course, on the Internet.

Where can I find English schedules for current entertainment?	今やっている催し物の英語のスケジュールは、どこを見ればわかりますか。 *Ima yatte iru moyōshimono no eigo no sukejūru wa, doko o mireba wakarimasu ka.*
Where can I buy an English-language newspaper?	英語の新聞は、どこで買えますか。 *Eigo no shinbun wa, doko de kaemasu ka.*

TICKETS

Tickets for most theatrical and many sporting events can be purchased in advance at ticket bureaus known as Play Guides. There are Play Guides at many locations in downtown areas, major train terminals, department stores, and many convenience stores. Be sure to purchase your tickets before the day of the event; Play Guides can't sell you tickets on the same day as the performance (but box offices can).

Is there a Play Guide nearby?	近くに、プレイガイドがありますか。 *Chikaku ni, purei gaido ga arimasu ka.*
Where's the Play Guide?	プレイガイドは、どこにありますか。 *Purei gaido wa, doko ni arimasu ka.*

FILMS AND THEATER

Foreign-made films are shown with their original sound tracks and Japanese titles. Japanese films, of course, have Japanese sound tracks, but you might enjoy them just the same: a good *samurai* adventure film is always exciting! For theater fans, there are good stage productions in Tokyo and other Japanese cities.

Let's go to the <u>movies</u>.	映画に行きましょう。 *<u>Eiga</u> ni ikimashō.*
theater	観劇　*kangeki*
I'd like to go see a <u>film</u>.	映画が見たいのですが。 *<u>Eiga</u> ga mitai no desu ga.*
play	演劇　*engeki*
Are there any good <u>films</u> in town?	どこかで、面白い映画をやっていますか。*Dokoka de, omoshiroi <u>eiga</u> o yatte imasu ka.*
plays	演劇　*engeki*
Could you recommend one?	どれか一つ、推薦してもらえますか。 *Doreka hitotsu, suisen shite moraemasu ka.*
I'm an anime fan.	私はアニメのファンです。*Watakushi wa anime no fan desu.*
Where's the <u>movie theater</u>?	映画館は、どこですか。*<u>Eiga kan</u> wa, doko desu ka.*
theater	劇場　*gekijō*

What's the title of the <u>film</u>?	映画の題名は、何ですか。*Eiga no daimei wa, nan desu ka.*
play	劇　*geki*
Who's the <u>director of the film</u>?	映画監督は、誰ですか。*Eiga kantoku wa, dare desu ka.*
director of the play	演出家　*enshutsu ka*
Who's playing the lead?	誰が、主演していますか。*Dare ga, shuen shite imasu ka.*
Is it a <u>comedy</u>?	それは、喜劇ですか。*Sore wa, kigeki desu ka.*
historical drama	時代物　*jidaimono*
musical	ミュージカル　*myūjikaru*
mystery	ミステリー　*misuterī*
romance	恋愛物　*ren-aimono*
science fiction film	サイエンス・フィクション *saiensu fikushon*
thriller/horror movie	スリラー　*surirā*
tragedy	悲劇　*higeki*
Western	西部劇　*seibu geki*
war film	戦争映画　*sensō eiga*
Is it <u>a Japanese</u> film?	それは、<u>日本の</u>映画ですか。*Sore wa, Nihon no eiga desu ka.*
an American	アメリカの　*Amerika no*
a British	イギリスの　*Igirisu no*
Do they show it in the original language?	原語で、上演しますか。*Gengo de, jōen shimasu ka.*
Is it dubbed in Japanese?	日本語に、吹き替えられていますか。*Nihongo ni, fukikaerarete imasu ka.*
Does it have English subtitles?	英語の字幕が、ありますか。*Eigo no jimaku ga, arimasu ka.*

Is it a first-run film?	それは、封切りの映画ですか。 *Sore wa, fūkiri no eiga desu ka.*
What kind of story is it?	どんな筋ですか。 *Donna suji desu ka.*
Are the performers Americans or Japanese?	出演者はアメリカ人ですか、それとも日本人ですか。 *Shutsuen sha wa Amerika jin desu ka, soretomo Nihon jin desu ka.*
Do they speak English or Japanese?	出演者は英語を話しますか、それとも日本語を話しますか。 *Shutsuen sha wa eigo o hanashimasu ka, soretomo Nihongo o hanashimasu ka.*
Is there a Broadway show being performed now?	今、ブロードウェーのショーをやっていますか。 *Ima, Burōdowē no shō o yatte imasu ka.*
What time does the <u>first</u> show begin?	<u>最初の</u>ショーは、何時に始まりますか。 <u>Saisho no</u> *shō wa, nan ji ni hajimarimasu ka.*
last	最後の *saigo no*
What time does the show end?	ショーは、何時に終わりますか。 *Shō wa, nan ji ni owarimasu ka.*
What time does the performance <u>begin</u>?	<u>開演</u>は、何時ですか。 <u>Kaien</u> *wa, nan ji desu ka.*
end	終演 *shūen*
How long will it run?	いつまで、上演しますか。 *Itsu made, jōen shimasu ka.*
Is there a matinee?	マチネーは、ありますか。 *Machinē wa, arimasu ka.*
Where can I buy a ticket?	券は、どこで買えますか。 *Ken wa, doko de kaemasu ka.*
Where's the box office?	切符売り場は、どこですか。 *Kippu uriba wa, doko desu ka.*

Do you have any tickets left for <u>tonight</u>?	今晩の券が、まだありますか。 <u>Konban</u> no ken ga, mada arimasu ka.
the next show	次のショー　tsugi no shō
I'd like to buy <u>a ticket</u> for tonight.	今晩の<u>券</u>を、<u>一枚</u>下さい。Konban no <u>ken o, ichi mai</u> kudasai.
two tickets	券を、二枚　ken o, ni mai
three tickets	券を、三枚　ken o, san mai
four tickets	券を、四枚　ken o, yo mai
I'd like to buy a ticket for <u>tomorrow</u> night.	<u>あした</u>の晩の券を、一枚下さい。 <u>Ashita no</u> ban no ken o, ichi mai kudasai.
Friday	金曜日の　kinyōbi no
Saturday	土曜日の　doyōbi no
Sunday	日曜日の　nichiyōbi no
Monday	月曜日の　getsuyōbi no
Tuesday	火曜日の　kayōbi no
Wednesday	水曜日の　suiyōbi no
Thursday	木曜日の　mokuyōbi no
Do you have seats in the <u>orchestra</u>?	<u>舞台に近い</u>席が、ありますか。 <u>Butai ni chikai</u> seki ga, arimasu ka.
balcony	二階の正面の　nikai no shōmen no
mezzanine	中二階の　chū nikai no
Do you have better seats than that?	それよりいい席がありますか。Sore yori ii seki ga arimasu ka.
Do you have seats a little more <u>forward</u>?	もう少し<u>前の</u>席が、ありますか。Mō sukoshi <u>mae no</u> seki ga, arimasu ka.
to the rear	後ろの　ushiro no
toward the center	中央寄りの　chūō yori no

Is there a coat check room?	コートを預ける場所が、ありますか。 *Kōto o azukeru basho ga, arimasu ka.*
Is there a program in English?	英語のプログラムが、ありますか。 *Eigo no puroguramu ga, arimasu ka.*
Please show me to my seat.	席まで、案内して下さい。 *Seki made, annai shite kudasai.*

CONCERTS, OPERA, AND BALLET

I'd like to attend <u>a ballet</u>.	<u>バレーを見に</u>行きたいのですが。 <u>*Barē o mini*</u> *ikitai no desu ga.*
a concert	コンサートを聴きに *konsāto o kikini*
an opera	オペラを見に *opera o mini*
Do I need to dress formally?	盛装の必要が、ありますか。 *Seisō no hitsuyō ga, arimasu ka.*
What shall I wear?	何を着たらいいでしょうか。 *Nani o kitara ii deshō ka.*
I prefer <u>chamber music</u>.	<u>室内楽</u>が、好みです。 <u>*Shitsunaigaku*</u> *ga, konomi desu.*
classical music	クラシック・ミュージック *kurashikku myūjikku*
concertos	協奏曲 *kyōsōkyoku*
country music	カントリーミュージック *kantorī myūjikku*
folk songs	フォーク・ソング *fōkusongu*
Japanese traditional music	邦楽 *hōgaku*
jazz	ジャズ *jazu*
J-POP	ジェイポップ *jeipoppu*
modern music	モダン・ミュージック *modan myūjikku*

popular songs	ポピュラー・ソング	*popyurā songu*
rock music	ロック・ミュージック	*rokku myūjikku*
symphonies	シンフォニー	*shinfonī*
classical ballet	古典バレー	*koten barē*
modern ballet	モダンバレー	*modan barē*
modern dance	モダン・ダンス	*modan dansu*

Where's the <u>concert hall</u>?
コンサート・ホールは、どこにあり
ますか。*Konsāto hōru wa, doko ni arimasu ka.*

opera house	オペラ劇場	*opera gekijō*
ballet theater	バレー劇場	*barē gekijō*

Is it nearby?
それは、近くにありますか。*Sore wa, chikaku ni arimasu ka.*

Is <u>a ballet</u> being performed now?
今、<u>バレー</u>をやっていますか。*Ima, <u>barē</u> o yatte imasu ka.*

an opera	オペラ	*opera*
a concert	コンサート	*konsāo*

Which <u>ballet company</u> is performing?
どの<u>バレー団</u>が、上演していますか。
Dono <u>barē dan</u> ga, jōen shite imasu ka.

opera company 歌劇団 *kageki dan*

Which <u>orchestra</u> is playing?
どの<u>管弦楽団</u>が、演奏していますか。
Dono <u>kangengaku dan</u> ga ensō shite imasu ka.

symphony orchestra
交響楽団／オーケストラ
kōkyōgaku dan/ōkesutora

band	楽団	*gakudan*
group	グループ	*gurūpu*

Is that a Japanese <u>ballet company</u>?
それは、日本の<u>バレー団</u>ですか。
Sore wa, Nihon no <u>barē dan</u> desu ka.

opera company	歌劇団	*kageki dan*
orchestra	管弦楽団	*kangengaku dan*

Is that a foreign <u>ballet company</u>?
それは、外国の<u>バレー団</u>ですか。
Sore wa, gaikoku no <u>barē dan</u> desu ka.

opera company	歌劇団	*kageki dan*
orchestra	管弦楽団	*kangengaku dan*

Which country do they come from?
どの国から来ましたか。 *Dono kuni kara kimashita ka.*

What are they <u>performing</u>?
何を<u>上演</u>していますか。 *Nani o <u>jōen</u> shite imasu ka.*

playing	演奏	*ensō*

Who's <u>conducting</u>?
誰が、<u>指揮</u>していますか。 *Dare ga, <u>shiki shite</u> imasu ka.*

dancing	踊って	*odotte*
playing	演奏して	*ensō shite*
singing	歌って	*utatte*

Who is the <u>composer</u>?
<u>作曲家</u>は、誰ですか。 *<u>Sakkyoku ka</u> wa, dare desu ka.*

lead dancer	主演のダンサー	*shuen no dansā*
lead singer	主演の歌手	*shuen no kashu*
pianist	ピアニスト	*pianisuto*
violinist	バイオリニスト	*baiorinisuto*

What time does tonight's performance start?
今晩の公演は、何時に始まりますか。
Konban no kōen wa, nan ji ni hajimarimasu ka.

Are tonight's tickets <u>sold out</u>?
今晩の券は、<u>売り切れ</u>ですか。
Konban no ken wa, <u>urikire desu</u> ka.

still available	まだあります	*mada arimasu*

Should I get tickets in advance?
前売り券を、買うべきですか。
Maeuri ken o, kau beki desu ka.

What are the least expensive seats?	一番安い券は、いくらですか。 *Ichiban yasui ken wa, ikura desu ka.*
I'd like to get good seats.	いい席が、欲しいのですが。*Ii seki ga, hoshii no desu ga.*
How much are the front-row seats?	前列の席は、いくらですか。 *Zenretsu no seki wa, ikura desu ka.*
I'll take any seats available.	あれば、どの席でもいいから下さい。 *Areba, dono seki demo ii kara kudasai.*
Could you show me where our seats are on the chart?	座席表で、席がどこか教えて下さい。 *Zaseki hyō de, seki ga doko ka oshiete kudasai.*
Can I <u>see</u> well from there?	そこから、よく<u>見えます</u>か。*Soko kara, yoku <u>miemasu</u> ka.*
hear	聞こえます *kikoemasu*
Is there an intermission?	途中で、休憩がありますか。*Tochū de, kyūkei ga arimasu ka.*

BUNRAKU, KABUKI, AND NOH

Bunraku, *Kabuki*, and *Noh* are the three major forms of traditional Japanese theater. They originated many centuries ago. Although the performances are in Japanese, English-language programs are usually available, so you can follow the story. The performance lasts longer than you may expect: A five-hour show is not unusual. If the performance lasts through a meal time, you can buy a box lunch from vendors at the theater and eat right at your seat. It's standard practice, not considered rude. You don't have to stay for the entire event— just leave whenever you like.

Bunraku is a kind of Japanese puppet theater dating from the seventeenth century. It features a special type of accompaniment: *shamisen* music, and a reciter who sings or chants both the storyline and the lines for each character in the play. The puppets are unique; each is between three and five feet high, with eyes and mouths that open and close, even eyebrows that move. Each is manipulated by three puppeteers wearing black hoods that cover their heads and faces.

Kabuki is perhaps the most popular of these classical amusements. The only one of the three where the actors speak (or chant) their own parts, *Kabuki* features highly stylized delivery and movement, stunning costumes and makeup, and male actors only. There are three basic types of drama: one deals with warriors and nobles, one with the common people, and another incorporates dance. *Kabuki* is performed on a revolving stage, with a runway extending into the audience. Except for certain plays, music played on classical Japanese instruments is a key element of *Kabuki*.

Noh is highly stylized dance-drama, originally performed at *Shinto* religious festivals. The actors wear elaborate, elegant costumes, but no makeup. Instead they wear masks representing different types of people; the actors have to develop the characters through movements, not facial expressions. The plays are performed on a square stage with no curtain. The orchestra sits at the rear. There are drums of different sizes, and a special *Noh* flute. The main characters express themselves through dance. All speaking is done by a special chorus that sings or chants the narration and the lines. *Noh* often reminds Westerners of classical Greek drama.

In which city can I see <u>Bunraku</u>?	文楽は、どの都市で見られますか。 *<u>Bunraku</u> wa, dono toshi de miraremasu ka.*
Kabuki	歌舞伎　*kabuki*
Noh	能　*nō*
Is <u>Bunraku</u> being performed in Tokyo now?	東京では今、文楽が上演されていますか。*Tōkyō dewa ima, <u>bunraku</u> ga jōen sarete imasu ka.*
Kabuki	歌舞伎　*kabuki*
Noh	能　*nō*

Is Kabuki being performed in <u>Osaka</u> now?	大阪では今、歌舞伎が上演されていますか。*Ōsaka dewa ima, kabuki ga jōen sarete imasu ka.*
Kyoto	京都　*Kyōto*
What kind of play are they performing?	出し物は何ですか。*Dashimono wa nan desu ka.*
When does it <u>start</u>?	何時に<u>始まります</u>か。*Nan ji ni hajimarimasu ka.*
finish	終わります　*owarimasu*
How long does the performance last?	上演の長さは、どのくらいですか。*Jōen no nagasa wa, dono kurai desu ka.*
Is there a place to eat during the intermission?	幕間に、何か食べられる場所がありますか。*Makuai ni, nanika taberareru basho ga arimasu ka.*
Is there a matinee?	昼の興行が、ありますか。*Hiru no kōgyō ga, arimasu ka.*
Are advance tickets necessary?	前売り券が、必要ですか。*Maeuri ken ga, hitsuyō desu ka.*
Where can I buy the tickets?	券は、どこで買えますか。*Ken wa, doko de kaemasu ka.*
How much will it be?	券は、いくらでしょうか。*Ken wa, ikura deshō ka.*
Do they have a program in English?	英語のプログラムが、ありますか。*Eigo no puroguramu ga, arimasu ka.*

BUNRAKU

puppets	人形	*ningyō*
puppeteers	人形つかい	*ningyō tsukai*
ballad-drama	浄瑠璃	*jōruri*
reciter	浄瑠璃語り	*jōruri gatari*

KABUKI

actor playing a female role	女形	*oyama*
actor playing a good male character	立ち役	*tachiyaku*
actor playing a bad male character	敵役	*katakiyaku*
runway	花道	*hanamichi*
revolving stage	回り舞台	*mawari butai*
quick change of costume	早変わり	*hayagawari*

NOH

Noh stage	能舞台	*nō butai*
Noh masks	能面	*nō men*
Noh singing	謡曲	*yōkyoku*
main character	シテ	*shite*
assisting character	ワキ	*waki*

FLOWER ARRANGEMENT
AND TEA CEREMONY

Flower arrangement, or *ikebana*, originally emphasized natural materials—flowers, leaves, grasses, and branches—and the way they were used to express harmony with nature. The fundamental traditions continue: the arrangement of the main branches or sprays signify sky, earth, and mankind. Today some avant-garde schools use artificial materials as well as natural ones.

The formal art of the tea ceremony was perfected in the fifteenth century. A deeply aesthetic experience, the tea ceremony has precise rituals of form and etiquette for host and guests. They include the tea room itself, the selection of the tea bowls, the making and serving of the tea, and the appreciation of the hospitality. Tea is a basic part of Japanese life. The custom of serving tea to family or guests in the home may be considered an informal extension of the ritual tea ceremony.

You can see flower arrangement or tea ceremony demonstrations; you might even want to attend a few classes. The arrangements can be made easily. Check the notices online or in the English-language media, or consult with your travel agent, a JNTO Tourist Information Center, or the hotel staff.

Where can I go to see <u>flower arrangement</u>?	<u>華道</u>を見るには、どこへ行けばいいですか。_Kadō o miru niwa, doko e ikeba ii desu ka._
tea ceremony	茶道　_sadō_
Which school is giving a demonstration?	どの流派が、実演しますか。_Dono ryūha ga, jitsuen shimasu ka._
Can I participate in the <u>tea ceremony</u> demonstration?	<u>お茶</u>の実演に、参加できますか。_Ocha no jitsuen ni, sanka dekimasu ka._
flower arrangement	お花　_ohana_
Do they have demonstrations every day?	実演は、毎日ありますか。_Jitsuen wa, mainichi arimasu ka._
Which day of the week do they have demonstrations?	実演は、何曜日にありますか。_Jitsuen wa, nani yōbi ni arimasu ka._
What time does the demonstration start?	実演は、何時に始まりますか。_Jitsuen wa, nan ji ni hajimarimasu ka._
How long does the demonstration last?	実演の長さは、どのくらいですか。_Jitsuen no nagasa wa, dono kurai desu ka._
Can I also get a brief lesson?	簡単なお稽古を、受けることもできますか。_Kantan na okeiko o, ukeru koto mo dekimasu ka._

Do I need to make a reservation in advance?	前もって、予約の必要がありますか。 *Mae motte, yoyaku no hitsuyō ga arimasu ka.*	
How far in advance do I have to make a reservation?	どのくらい前に、予約しなければなりませんか。 *Dono kurai mae ni, yoyaku shinakereba narimasen ka.*	
Is there an admission fee?	見学料が、ありますか。 *Kengaku ryō ga, arimasu ka.*	
How much will it be?	見学料は、いくらですか。 *Kengaku ryō wa, ikura desu ka.*	

FLOWER ARRANGEMENT

headmaster	家元	*iemoto*
container	容器	*yōki*
bowl	鉢	*hachi*
basin	水盤	*suiban*
cut (v.)	切り取る	*kiritoru*
prune (v.)	せん定する	*sentei suru*
bend (v.)	曲げる	*mageru*
asymmetrical	非対称的な	*hi taishō teki na*

TEA CEREMONY

powdered tea	抹茶	*matcha*
tea bowl	茶碗	*chawan*
tea utensils	茶道具	*cha dōgu*
tea whisk	茶筅	*chasen*
tea cannister (ceramic)	茶入れ	*chaire*
tea cannister (lacquered wood)	なつめ	*natsume*
tea ladle	茶杓	*chashaku*
tea napkin (host's)	茶巾	*chakin*

tea napkin (guests')	ふくさ	*fukusa*
tea kettle	茶釜	*chagama*
tea urn	茶つぼ	*chatsubo*
tea etiquette	点前／お点前	*temae/otemae*

RADIO AND TELEVISION

The American military radio station, the American Forces Network Pacific (AFN), broadcasts in English round the clock, with brief newscasts on the hour. For more extensive news coverage, sports, and commentary, tune in Nippon Hoso Kyokai (NHK), the government broadcasting corporation, which has a brief daily news program in English. Check online for Internet radio and TV schedules and much more.

Many foreigners enjoy Japanese TV, even without understanding the language. You can see traditional Japanese entertainment such as *Kabuki*, Western and Japanese sports events, game shows and musical revues, even soap operas. There are also reruns of popular American series and sitcoms. Many hotels have multiplex systems or cable, which show the programs in the original language. Occasionally you can see an English-language program on Japanese networks. And for news, you can tune in to Cable News Network (CNN). Watching TV online is a good option.

radio	ラジオ	*rajio*
television	テレビ	*terebi*
cable TV	ケーブル・テレビ	*kēburu terebi*
satellite broadcasting	衛星放送	*eisei hōsō*
How can I get the cable channels?	ケーブル・テレビのチャンネルは、どうやってつけますか。*Kēburu terebi no channeru wa, dō yatte tsukemasu ka.*
Which channel is CNN?	シー・エヌ・エヌは、どのチャンネルですか。*Shī Enu Enu wa, dono channeru desu ka.*

Where can I find a TV schedule in English?	英語のテレビ番組表は、どこで見つけられますか。 *Eigo no terebi bangumi hyō wa, doko de mitsukeraremasu ka.*

NIGHTLIFE

Japanese cities offer the usual variety of after-hours diversion, with one important difference: the costs can be astronomical. To avoid unpleasant surprises when your check arrives, you should know beforehand what kind of place it is. While some bars and clubs are reasonable and affordable for most foreign visitors, many are not. A few drinks, a dish of peanuts or rice crackers, and some conversation with a hostess or host could add up to the yen equivalent of hundreds of dollars. Not all Japanese nightspots welcome foreigners; some might not admit you unless you're with a Japanese. Such places are usually frequented exclusively by expense-account customers, and the staff might not speak English.

Before you set out for an evening on the town—or for a drink or two anywhere other than your hotel bar—ask a Japanese friend or acquaintance, or check with your hotel staff or a Tourist Information Center, to get suggestions for the kind of place you want. DO NOT CHOOSE A BAR, NIGHTCLUB, OR CABARET ON YOUR OWN. And remember that appearances can be misleading. A modest-looking place could turn out to be extremely expensive. ASK FIRST!

This section contains phrases useful for various kinds of nightlife. For ordering once inside, refer to the food and drink section on page 193, which gives complete listings for beverages and snacks.

BARS

I'd like to go to a <u>bar</u>.	バーに、行きたいのですが。 *Bā ni, ikitai no desu ga.*
karaoke bar	カラオケバー *karaoke bā*

Is there <u>an inexpensive</u> bar nearby?

近くに、<u>安い</u>バーがありますか。
Chikaku ni, <u>yasui</u> bā ga arimasu ka.

   a quiet

   静かな　*shizuka na*

   a pleasant

   楽しい　*tanoshii*

Do you know of a bar <u>with nice atmosphere</u>?

<u>いい雰囲気の</u>バーを、ご存じですか。
<u>Ii fun-iki no</u> bā o, gozonji desu ka.

   with no hostesses

   ホステスのいない　*hosutesu no inai*

   with a nice reputation

   評判のいい　*hyōban no ii*

   with clearly listed prices

   値段がはっきりした　*nedan ga hakkiri shita*

Where is a bar that's popular among <u>young people</u>?

<u>若い人</u>に人気のあるバーは、どこにありますか。*<u>Wakai hito</u> ni ninki no aru bā wa, doko ni arimasu ka.*

   students

   学生　*gakusei*

   women

   女性　*josei*

   office workers

   サラリーマン　*sararīman*

Where is a gay bar?

ゲイバーはどこにありますか。*Gei bā wa doko ni arimasu ka.*

Is there a bar I can go to without worrying about the bill?

(お) 勘定を心配しないで行けるバーが、ありますか。*(O)kanjō o shinpai shinai de ikeru bā ga, arimasu ka.*

Would you suggest which bar I should go to?

どのバーに行ったらいいか、教えて下さい。*Dono bā ni ittara ii ka, oshiete kudasai.*

Do you have a bar you go to often?

行きつけのバーが、ありますか。*Ikitsuke no bā ga, arimasu ka.*

Do they have a minimum charge?

最低料金が、ありますか。*Saitei ryōkin ga, arimasu ka.*

Do I have to buy drinks for the hostesses?	ホステスの飲み代を、払わなければなりませんか。*Hosutesu no nomidai o, harawanakereba narimasen ka.*
Are strangers welcome there?	ふりの客でも、構いませんか。*Furi no kyaku demo, kamaimasen ka.*
How much will it be for <u>a bottle of beer</u> there?	そこでは、<u>ビール一本</u>いくらぐらいしますか。*Soko dewa, <u>bīru ippon</u> ikura gurai shimasu ka.*
a shot of whiskey	ウイスキー一杯 *uisukī ippai*
Do you think <u>5,000 yen</u> per person is enough?	そこでは、一人<u>五千円</u>あれば足りますか。*Soko dewa, hitori <u>gosen en</u> areba tarimasu ka.*
10,000 yen	一万円 *ichiman en*
15,000 yen	一万五千円 *ichiman gosen en*
20,000 yen	二万円 *ni man en*

NIGHTCLUBS

I'd like to visit a nightclub.	ナイト・クラブへ、行ってみたいのですが。*Naito kurabu e, itte mitai no desu ga.*
Are the nightclubs extremely expensive?	ナイト・クラブは、とても高いですか。*Naito kurabu wa, totemo takai desu ka.*
For example, how much does it cost per person?	例えば、一人当たりいくらかかりますか。*Tatoeba, hitori arari ikura kakarimasu ka.*
Do you know <u>the best</u> nightclub?	<u>最高の</u>ナイト・クラブを、教えてくれませんか。*<u>Saikō no</u> naito kurabu o, oshiete kuremasen ka.*
a cozy	居心地のいい *igokochi no ii*
an inexpensive	安い *yasui*
a nice	いい *ii*

| a posh | 豪華な　*gōka na* |
| a small | 小さい　*chiisai* |

Could you recommend a reasonable nightclub?	手頃な値段のナイト・クラブを、教えてくれませんか。*Tegoro na nedan no naito kurabu o, oshiete kuremasen ka.*
Do I need to make a reservation?	予約の必要が、ありますか。*Yoyaku no hitsuyō ga, arimasu ka.*
Do they have a cover charge?	カバー・チャージがありますか。*Kabā chāji ga arimasu ka.*
How much is the <u>hostess fee</u>?	<u>ホステスの料金</u>は、いくらですか。*Hosutesu no ryōkin wa, ikura desu ka.*
cover charge	カバー・チャージ　*kabā chāji*
Is the hostess fee by the hour?	ホステス料金は、時間制ですか。*Hosutesu ryōkin wa, jikan sei desu ka.*
Are couples welcome?	カップルでも、歓迎されますか。*Kappuru demo, kangei saremasu ka.*
Do they have a floor show?	フロアー・ショーが、ありますか。*Furoā shō ga, arimasu ka.*
What kind of a floor show do they have?	どんな種類のフロアー・ショーですか。*Donna shurui no furoā shō desu ka.*
What time does the floor show start?	フロアー・ショーは、何時に始まりますか。*Furoā shō wa, nan ji ni hajimarimasu ka.*
Do they have a good dance band?	踊るのに、いいバンドが入っていますか。*Odoru no ni, ii bando ga haitte imasu ka.*
What kind of music does the band play?	そのバンドは、どんな曲を演奏しますか。*Sono bando wa, donna kyoku o ensō shimasu ka.*

Can I have dinner there, too?	そこで、食事もできますか。 *Soko de, shokuji mo dekimasu ka.*
What kind of clothes do I need to wear?	どんな服装を、するべきですか。 *Donna fukusō o, suru beki desu ka.*

SNACK BARS

Japanese bars and nightclubs close relatively early—11 P.M. to 11:30 P.M. in most cases. For those who prefer to continue their evening on the town, there are the so-called snack bars. Despite the name, these are also drinking places. The difference is that because they're called snack bars and they serve food, they're allowed to stay open late.

Is there <u>a nice</u> snack bar nearby?	近くに、<u>いい</u>スナック・バーがありますか。 *Chikaku ni, ii sunakku bā ga arimasu ka.*
an interesting	面白い *omoshiroi*
an inexpensive	安い *yasui*
a quiet	静かな *shizuka na*
Where is it?	それは、どこにありますか。 *Sore wa, doko ni arimasu ka.*
What's the name of the snack bar?	そのスナック・バーの名前は何ですか。 *Sono sunakku bā no namae wa nan desu ka.*
What time does it open?	何時に開きますか。 *Nan ji ni akimasu ka.*
Is it open now?	今、開いていますか。 *Ima, aite imasu ka.*
How late is it open?	何時まで開いていますか。 *Nan ji made aite imasu ka.*
What kind of <u>drinks</u> do they serve?	どんな<u>飲み物</u>がありますか。 *Donna nomimono ga arimasu ka.*
food	食べ物 *tabemono*
Do I need to order food?	食べ物を、注文する必要がありますか。 *Tabemono o, chūmon suru hitsuyō ga arimasu ka.*

Is it okay to just have drinks?	飲むだけで、いいですか。 *Nomu dake de, ii desu ka.*
Is the price reasonable?	値段は、手頃ですか。 *Nedan wa, tegoro desu ka.*

BEER HALLS AND BEER GARDENS

Beer halls and beer gardens are good places to go to eat and drink at reasonable prices. They're popular with Japanese who want to relax after work. The beer halls are open all year round, and the beer gardens are open during the summer, many on the roofs of department stores or office buildings.

beer hall	ビアホール *biahōru*
beer garden	ビアガーデン *biagāden*
What time do they <u>open</u>?	何時に<u>開きます</u>か。 *Nan ji ni akimasu ka.*
close	閉まります *shimarimasu*
Are they open at lunchtime?	ランチ・タイムにも、開いていますか。 *Ranchi taimu nimo, aite imasu ka.*
Do they serve only beer?	あるのは、ビールだけですか。 *Aru no wa, bīru dake desu ka.*
Do they serve other drinks besides beer?	ビールのほかにも、何か飲み物がありますか。 *Bīru no hoka nimo, nanika nomimono ga arimasu ka.*
Is there ale?	<u>エール</u>がありますか。 *Ēru ga arimasu ka.*
dark beer	黒ビール *kuro bīru*
draft beer	生ビール *nama bīru*
lager beer	普通のビール *futsū no bīru*
light beer	ライト・ビール *raito bīru*
stout	スタウト *sutauto*

Do they have <u>imported</u> beer?	<u>外国の</u>ビールが、ありますか。 <u>*Gaikoku no*</u> *bīru ga, arimasu ka.*
American	アメリカの　*Amerika no*
German	ドイツの　*Doitsu no*
Do they serve food?	何か、食べ物がありますか。 *Nanika, tabemono ga arimasu ka.*
Can I have a light meal?	軽い食事が、できますか。*Karui shokuji ga, dekimasu ka.*
Do they serve dinner?	ディナーが、ありますか。*Dinā ga, arimasu ka.*
What kind of food do they have?	どんな食べ物が、ありますか。 *Donna tabemono ga, arimasu ka.*

WINE BAR

Japanese wine consumption is increasing, and wine bars are exceedingly popular. Men and women, both young and not so young, go there to enjoy good wine and light meals at reasonable prices.

Is there a wine bar nearby?	近くに、ワインバーがありますか。 *Chikaku ni wain bā ga arimasu ka.*
What kind of wine do they serve?	どんなワインがありますか。*Donna wain ga arimasu ka?*
Do they have <u>Japanese</u> wine?	<u>日本の</u>ワインがありますか。<u>*Nihon no*</u> *wain ga arimasu ka.*
American	アメリカの　*Amerika no*
French	フランスの　*Furansu no*
German	ドイツの　*Doitsu no*
Chilean	チリの　*Chiri no*

TACHINOMIYA

As the name, which means "to stand and drink," indicates, a tachinomiya is a counter-only bar serving beer, sake, and shochu (distilled liquor with about 25 percent alcoholic content). This is a traditional and informal way of inexpensive drinking popular among office workers after the end of the work day. Tachinomiyas usually serve traditional snacks such as yakitori (char-grilled skewered chicken).

Is there a tachinomiya near here?	近くに立ち飲み屋がありますか。 *Chikaku ni tachinomiya ga arimasu ka.*
Give me <u>beer</u>, please.	<u>ビール</u>をください <u>*Bīru*</u> *o kudasai.*
osake	お酒 *osake*
shochu	焼酎 *shōchū*

KARAOKE

Karaoke (kah-rah-oh-keh), now popular worldwide, originated in Japan. Although many bars and snack bars provide karaoke facilities, an establishment unique to Japan is the so-called karaoke box. It isn't a box, but an establishment with karaoke as the main attraction. What you get is a comfortable private room with a karaoke machine. Some fancy ones have special lighting effects and mirrored balls. You can eat and drink while you enjoy singing. The places can be plain and cheap or luxurious and costly. The people who run them usually don't speak English. If you want to go to a karaoke place, it's best to go with Japanese friends.

I would like to go to a karaoke place.	からおけに行きたいのですが。 *Karaoke ni ikitai no desu ga.*
Is there a karaoke place nearby?	近くにからおけがありますか。 *Chikaku ni karaoke ga arimasu ka.*
Where is it?	どこにありますか。 *Doko ni arimasu ka.*
What is the charge?	料金はいくらですか。 *Ryōkin wa ikura desu ka.*
Can you tell me how to use a karaoke machine?	からおけ装置の使い方を教えてください。 *Karaoke sōchi no tsukaikata o oshiete kudasai.*

GAMES

If you want to relax the Japanese way, try their games. Here are phrases for a few.

GAME CENTERS

Although they're considered western, game centers have the latest high-tech arcade game machines Japan has to offer. Some games may be very familiar to you, but others are uniquely Japanese. You can find them in the streets, shopping arcades, and shopping malls in cities throughout Japan. One caution: Many areas have a local law prohibiting players under age 16 after 6 P.M. and under age 18 after 10 P.M.

I would like to go to a game center.	ゲームセンターに行きたいのですが。 *Gēmu sentā ni ikitai no desu ga.*
Is there a game center nearby?	近くにゲームセンターがありますか。 *Chikaku ni gēmu sentā ga arimasu ka.*
Where is it?	どこにありますか。*Doko ni arimasu ka.*
How do I pay?	どのように払いますか。*Donoyō ni haraimasu ka.*
Can you tell me how to use a game machine?	ゲーム機の使い方を教えてください。 *Gēmu ki no tsukaikata o oshiete kudasai.*

PACHINKO

Pachinko is a vertical pinball game played in parlors all over Japan. You can't miss the places: Just follow the blaring music and the sound of thousands of tiny steel balls crashing against each other. Enter and you'll see scores of people, each sitting on a stool in front of a machine, turning the trajectory knob with singular concentration, and staring straight ahead. Addicts tell of the old days before automatic knobs, when you launched each ball with a thumb-operated lever. What do you get for your efforts? Cash in your winning balls for prizes such as chocolate, socks, fruit, razors, dolls, CDs, DVDs, and more.

Do you play pachinko?	パチンコをしますか。*Pachinko o shimasu ka.*
I'd like to try pachinko.	パチンコを、やってみたいです。*Pachinko o, yatte mitai desu.*
Could you take me to a pachinko parlor?	パチンコ屋へ、連れていってもらえますか。*Pachinko ya e, tsurete itte moraemasu ka.*
Where do I buy pachinko balls?	玉は、どこで買いますか。*Tama wa, doko de kaimasu ka.*
How much should I spend for the balls?	玉は、いくら買ったらいいですか。*Tama wa, ikura kattara ii desu ka.*
Which machine should I use?	どの台を使ったらいいですか。*Dono dai o tsukattara ii desu ka.*
Is there a knack to shooting the balls?	球を打つのに、こつがありますか。*Tama o utsu no ni, kotsu ga arimasu ka.*
How many balls do I need to win a prize?	景品をもらうには、玉がいくつ必要ですか。*Keihin o morau niwa, tama ga ikutsu hitsuyō desu ka.*
What kind of prizes do they have?	どんな景品が、ありますか。*Donna keihin ga, arimasu ka.*
Where can I exchange the balls for prizes?	玉は、どこで景品にかえますか。*Tama wa, doko de keihin ni kaemasu ka.*

GO AND SHOGI

These are two of Japan's oldest traditional board games. *Shogi* is similar to chess, but the opponent's captured pieces can be used. *Go* is a territorial game, played with flat, round, black and white stones. It's been in Japan for about 1,300 years and originally came from China. You probably won't master the fine points of *go* and *shogi* in a short time, but you can learn the basics, and then continue to play back home.

Do you <u>play go</u>?	碁を、打ちますか。*Go o, uchimasu ka.*
play shogi	将棋をさします *shōgi o sashimasu*
I <u>don't know</u> how to play go.	碁の打ち方を、<u>知りません</u>。*Go no uchikata o, shirimasen.*
know	知っています *shitte imasu*
I <u>don't know</u> how to play shogi.	将棋のさし方を、<u>知りません</u>。*Shōgi no sashikata o, <u>shirimasen</u>.*
know	知っています *shitte imasu*
Could you play <u>go</u> with me?	碁のお相手を、お願いできますか。*<u>Go</u> no oaite o, onegai dekimasu ka.*
shogi	将棋 *shōgi*
Could you teach me <u>how to play go</u>?	碁の打ち方を、教えてもらえますか。*<u>Go no uchikata</u> o, oshiete moraemasu ka.*
how to play shogi	将棋のさし方 *shōgi no sashikata*
Is it difficult to learn <u>go</u>?	碁を習うのは、難しいですか。*<u>Go</u> o narau no wa, muzukashii desu ka.*
shogi	将棋 *shōgi*
Do you have a <u>go board and stones</u>?	碁盤と碁石を、お持ちですか。*<u>Go ban to go ishi</u> o, omochi desu ka.*
shogi board and pieces	将棋盤と駒 *shōgi ban to koma*
How do you decide the winner and loser?	勝ち負けは、どうやって決めますか。*Kachi make wa, dō yatte kimemasu ka.*

How do you capture your opponent's <u>stones</u>?	相手の<u>石</u>は、どうやって取りますか。 *Aite no <u>ishi</u> wa, dō yatte torimasu ka.*
pieces	駒　*koma*

MAHJONG

A domino-like game of Chinese origin, mahjong has gone through cycles of popularity in the West, but it is still played in Japan.

Do you play mahjong?	マージャンを、しますか。*Mājan o, shimasu ka.*
I <u>don't know</u> how to play mahjong.	マージャンの仕方を、<u>知りません</u>。 *Mājan no shikata o, <u>shirimasen</u>.*
know	知っています　*shitte imasu*
I'd like to play mahjong.	マージャンを、したいのですが。 *Mājan o, shitai no desu ga.*
Do you think you can get two more people?	もう二人、集められますか。*Mō futari, atsumeraremasu ka.*
I'd like to learn how to play mahjong.	マージャンの仕方を、習いたいのですが。*Mājan no shikata o, naraitai no desu ga.*
Is it difficult to learn mahjong?	マージャンを習うのは、難しいですか。*Mājan o narau no wa, muzukashii desu ka.*
Can you teach me how to play mahjong?	マージャンのやり方を、教えてくれますか。*Mājan no yarikata o, oshiete kuremasu ka.*
Do you have a mahjong set?	マージャンのセットを、持っていますか。*Mājan no setto o, motte imasu ka.*
What are the basic rules of mahjong?	マージャンの、基本的なルールは何ですか。*Mājan no, kihon teki na rūru wa nan desu ka.*

SPECTATOR SPORTS

If you enjoy spectator sports, you'll find a lot to watch in Japan. The big two are sumo, the most popular of the traditional Japanese sports, and baseball.

SUMO

Professional sumo, or traditional Japanese wrestling, has a centuries-old history. There are six major tournaments a year, three in January, May, and September at Tokyo's *Kuramae Kokugikan Sumo Hall*, and the others in March at Osaka, in July at Nagoya, and in November at Fukuoka. Each tournament lasts 15 days and is televised every day from 4 P.M. to 6 P.M. The sumo events are colorful: They last from early morning until late afternoon, with spectators usually arriving by early afternoon to catch the main events. The 250- to 400-pound (114- to 182-kilogram) wrestlers provide a lot of drama with their topknots and loincloths, ceremonial aprons, and costumed retainers. Just before the match, the wrestlers throw salt into the ring in an old *Shinto* purification ritual. The match itself is usually over in seconds: It lasts just long enough for one wrestler to throw his opponent out of the ring or make any part of his body except the feet touch the ground.

I'm interested in sumo.	相撲に、興味があります。*Sumō ni, kyōmi ga arimasu.*
Is there a sumo tournament going on now?	今、相撲をやっていますか。*Ima, sumō o yatte imasu ka.*
Where is the sumo tournament now?	今、相撲はどこでやっていますか。*Ima, sumō wa doko de yatte imasu ka.*
<u>When</u> is the next sumo tournament?	次の場所は、<u>いつ</u>ですか。*Tsugi no basho wa, <u>itsu</u> desu ka.*
where	どこ *doko*

Which day of the 15-day sumo tournament is today?	今日は、場所の何日目ですか。*Kyō wa, basho no nan nichi me desu ka.*
Which channel has live sumo broadcasts?	何チャンネルが、相撲の生中継をしていますか。*Nan channeru ga, sumō no nama chūkei o shite imasu ka.*
I'd like to go to see sumo.	相撲を、見に行きたいのですが。*Sumō o, mini ikitai no desu ga.*
Is it difficult to buy sumo tickets?	相撲の券を買うのは、難しいですか。*Sumō no ken o kau no wa, muzukashii desu ka.*
Where can I buy tickets?	相撲の券は、どこで買えますか。*Sumō no ken wa, doko de kaemasu ka.*
Can I buy sumo tickets at the Play Guide?	相撲の券は、プレイガイドで買えますか。*Sumō no ken wa, purei gaido de kaemasu ka.*
I'd like good seats for sumo.	相撲の、いい席が欲しいのですが。*Sumō no, ii seki ga hoshii no desu ga.*
How much does a good seat cost?	いい席は、いくらしますか。*Ii seki wa, ikura shimasu ka.*
When do the sumo matches <u>start</u>?	取り組みは、何時に<u>始まります</u>か。*Torikumi wa, nan ji ni <u>hajimarimasu</u> ka.*
end	終わります　*owarimasu*
When do the matches with the senior wrestlers start?	幕の内の力士の取り組みは、いつ始まりますか。*Maku no uchi no rikishi no torikumi wa, itsu hajimarimasu ka.*
How many matches with the senior wrestlers are there?	幕の内の力士の取り組みは、いくつありますか。*Maku no uchi no rikishi no torikumi wa, ikutsu arimasu ka.*

Where is the sumo hall?	国技館は、どこにありますか。 *Kokugikan wa, doko ni arimasu ka.*	
What's the best time to get there?	そこへは、何時ごろ着けば一番いいですか。*Soko e wa, nan ji goro tsukeba ichiban ii desu ka.*	
Can I get something to eat and drink there?	そこでは、食べ物や飲み物が買えますか。*Soko dewa, tabemono ya nomimono ga kaemasu ka.*	
sumo wrestler	力士	*rikishi*
sumo match	取り組み	*torikumi*
judge	行司	*gyōji*
ring	土俵	*dohyō*
grand champion	横綱	*yokozuna*
What's that wrestler's name?	あの力士の名前は、何ですか。*Ano rikishi no namae wa, nan desu ka.*	
How much does he weigh?	体重は、どのくらいありますか。*Taijū wa, dono kurai arimasu ka.*	
How tall is he?	背の高さは、どのくらいですか。*Se no takasa wa, dono kurai desu ka.*	

BASEBALL

Baseball is so popular in Japan that even high school tournaments attract huge crowds and TV audiences. There are two professional leagues, the Central and the Pacific, each composed of six teams. The playoff at the end of the season is called the Japan Series. Among the 800 or so ballplayers on the major and minor league teams, about 8 percent are foreigners, and many of them are Americans.

I like to watch baseball.	野球を見るのが、好きです。*Yakyū o miru no ga, suki desu.*
Is this the baseball season?	野球は、今シーズン中ですか。*Yakyū wa, ima shīzun chū desu ka.*

Are they <u>professional</u> baseball games?	プロ野球の試合ですか。*Puro yakyū no shiai desu ka.*
college	大学　*daigaku*
high school	高校　*kōkō*
Do you have a professional baseball team in this city?	この都市には、プロ野球のチームがありますか。*Kono toshi niwa, puro yakyū no chīmu ga arimasu ka.*
Is there a professional baseball game <u>today</u>?	<u>今日</u>、プロ野球の試合がありますか。*Kyō, puro yakyū no shiai ga arimasu ka.*
tomorrow	あした　*ashita*
this weekend	この週末　*kono shūmatsu*
Is the game televised?	試合は、テレビ中継されますか。*Shiai wa, terebi chūkei saremasu ka.*
Which channel will broadcast the game?	試合を放送するのは、どのチャンネルですか。*Shiai o hōsō suru no wa, dono channeru desu ka.*
I'd like to go see the game.	野球の試合を、見に行きたいです。*Yakyū no shiai o, mini ikitai desu.*
Where is the ballpark?	球場は、どこにありますか。*Kyūjō wa, doko ni arimasu ka.*
Which teams are playing?	どのチームが、試合しますか。*Dono chīmu ga, shiai shimasu ka.*
Is it a day or a night game?	試合は昼間ですか、それともナイターですか。*Shiai wa hiruma desu ka, soretomo naitā desu ka.*
What time does the game start?	試合は、何時に始まりますか。*Shiai wa, nan ji ni hajimarimasu ka.*
Where can I buy baseball tickets?	野球の券は、どこで買えますか。*Yakyū no ken wa, doko de kaemasu ka.*
Can I buy baseball tickets at a Play Guide?	プレイガイドで、野球の券が買えますか。*Purei gaido de, yakyū no ken ga kaemasu ka.*

Can I buy the tickets at the ballpark on the day of the game?	試合の日に、球場で券が買えますか。	*Shiai no hi ni, kyūjō de ken ga kaemasu ka.*
I'd like seats <u>behind home plate</u>.	<u>ネット裏</u>の席を下さい。	<u>*Netto ura*</u> *no seki o kudasai.*
on the first base side	一塁側の内野	*ichirui gawa no naiya*
on the third base side	三塁側の内野	*sanrui gawa no naiya*
along left field	左翼の外野	*sayoku no gaiya*
along right field	右翼の外野	*uyoku no gaiya*

pitcher	ピッチャー	*pitchā*
catcher	キャッチャー	*kyatchā*
first baseman	一塁手	*ichiruishu*
second baseman	二塁手	*niruishu*
third baseman	三塁手	*sanruishu*
shortstop	ショート	*shōto*
left fielder	レフト	*refuto*
center fielder	センター	*sentā*
right fielder	ライト	*raito*
manager	監督	*kantoku*
umpire	アンパイア	*anpaia*
batter	バッター	*battā*
strike	ストライク	*sutoraiku*
ball	ボール	*bōru*
strikeout	三振	*sanshin*
walk	フォア・ボール	*foa bōru*
hit	ヒット	*hitto*

bunt	バント	*banto*
base hit	一塁打	*ichiruida*
double	二塁打	*niruida*
triple	三塁打	*sanruida*
home run	ホームラン	*hōmuran*
steal	盗塁	*tōrui*
safe	セーフ	*sēfu*
out	アウト	*auto*
score	得点／スコア	*tokuten/sukoa*
inning	回／イニング	*kai/iningu*
top	表	*omote*
bottom	裏	*ura*
Who is <u>pitching</u>?	<u>ピッチャー</u>はだれですか。 *<u>Pitchā</u> wa dare desu ka.*	
catching	キャッチャー	*kyatchā*
at bat	バッター	*battā*

JUDO, KARATE, AND KENDO

Is there a <u>judo</u> demonstration?	<u>柔道</u>の実演がありますか。 *<u>Jūdō</u> no jitsuen ga arimasu ka.*	
karate	空手	*karate*
kendo	剣道	*kendō*
Where is it?	それは、どこでありますか。 *Sore wa, doko de arimasu ka.*	
Where can I see a <u>judo</u> practice?	<u>柔道</u>の稽古は、どこで見られますか。 *<u>Jūdō</u> no keiko wa, doko de miraremasu ka.*	
karate	空手	*karate*
kendo	剣道	*kendō*

What day of the week can I see the <u>demonstration</u>?	実演は、何曜日に見られますか。 *Jitsuen wa, nani yōbi ni miraremasu ka.*
practice	稽古 *keiko*
What time does the <u>demonstration</u> begin?	実演は、何時に始まりますか。 *Jitsuen wa, nan ji ni hajimarimasu ka.*
practice	稽古 *keiko*
What time does it end?	何時に終わりますか。 *Nan ji ni owarimasu ka.*
Is there an admission fee?	入場料が、ありますか。 *Nyūjō ryō ga, arimasu ka.*
Can I participate in the practice?	稽古に、参加できますか。 *Keiko ni, sanka dekimasu ka.*
Is there a <u>judo</u> tournament being held now?	今、<u>柔道</u>のトーナメントが行われています。 *Ima, jūdō no tōnamento ga okonawarete imasu ka.*
karate	空手 *karate*
kendo	剣道 *kendō*
What kind of tournament is it?	どんな種類のトーナメントですか。 *Donna shurui no tōnamento desu ka.*
Where is the tournament held?	トーナメントは、どこでありますか。 *Tōnamento wa, doko de arimasu ka.*
Where can I buy a ticket?	入場券は、どこで買えますか。 *Nyūjō ken wa, doko de kaemasu ka.*
judo/karate/kendo suit	柔道／空手／剣道着 *jūdō/karate/kendō gi*
bamboo sword	竹刀 *shinai*
face guard	面 *men*
arm guard	小手 *kote*
instructor	師範 *shihan*
match	試合 *shiai*

win	勝ち	*kachi*
loss	負け	*make*
draw	引き分け	*hikiwake*
Which grade black belt does the player have?	あの選手は、何段ですか。*Ano senshu wa, nan dan desu ka.*	

SOCCER

Since soccer is very popular in Japan, you can see good games played by professional, university, or company teams.

Is this the soccer season?	サッカーは今、シーズン中ですか。*Sakkā wa ima, shīzun chū desu ka.*
Is there a soccer match <u>today</u>?	<u>今日</u>、サッカーの試合がありますか。*Kyō, sakkā no shiai ga arimasu ka.*
tomorrow	あした *ashita*
this weekend	この週末 *kono shūmatsu*
Is the soccer game televised?	試合は、テレビ中継されますか。*Shiai wa, terebi chūkei saremasu ka.*
Which channel will broadcast the soccer match?	サッカーの試合を放送するのは、どのチャンネルですか。*Sakkā no shiai o hōsō suru no wa, dono channeru desu ka.*
I'd like to go to a soccer game.	サッカーの試合を、見に行きたいです。*Sakkā no shiai o, mini ikitai desu.*
Where is the soccer stadium?	サッカーの競技場は、どこにありますか。*Sakkā no kyōgijō wa, doko ni arimasu ka.*
Which teams are playing?	どのチームが、試合しますか。*Dono chīmu ga, shiai shimasu ka.*
What time does the game start?	試合は、何時に始まりますか。*Shiai wa, nan ji ni hajimarimasu ka.*
Where can I buy soccer tickets?	サッカーの券は、どこで買えますか。*Sakkā no ken wa, doko de kaemasu ka.*

Can I buy soccer tickets at a Play Guide?	プレイガイドで、サッカーの券が買えますか。*Purei gaido de, sakkā no ken ga kaemasu ka.*
Can I buy tickets at the soccer stadium on the day of the game?	試合の日に、競技場で券が買えますか。*Shiai no hi ni, kyōgijō de ken ga kaemasu ka.*

PARTICIPATORY SPORTS

GYM/HEALTH CLUB

Is there a gym/health club <u>in this hotel</u>?	このホテルに、ジム／ヘルス・クラブがありますか。<u>*Kono hoteru ni*</u>, *jimu/herusu kurabu ga arimasu ka.*
nearby	この近くに　*kono chikaku ni*
What hours is the gym/health club open?	ジム／ヘルス・クラブは、何時から何時まで開いていますか。*Jimu/herusu kurabu wa, nan ji kara nan ji made aite imasu ka.*
Can I use the gym/health club facilities on a pay-per-visit basis?	一回ごとの料金払いで、ジム／ヘルス・クラブの施設が利用できますか。*Ikkai goto no ryōkinbaraide, jimu/herusu kurabu no shisetsu o riyō dekimasu ka.*
How much is the fee?	料金は、いくらですか。*Ryōkin wa, ikura desu ka.*
Do I have to become a member to use the gym/health club facilities?	ジム／ヘルス・クラブの施設を利用するには、会員にならねばなりませんか。*Jimu/herusu kurabu no shisetsu o riyō suru niwa, kaiin ni naraneba narimasen ka.*
Is there a <u>temporary</u> membership?	<u>仮の</u>会員制度が、ありますか。<u>*Kari no*</u> *kaiin seido ga, arimasu ka.*
short-term	短期の　*tanki no*

How much is a <u>temporary</u> membership?	<u>仮の</u>会員制度は、いくらですか。 *<u>Kari no</u> kaiin seido wa, ikura desu ka.*
short-term	短期の　*tanki no*
Is there <u>an outdoor swimming pool</u>?	<u>屋外プール</u>が、ありますか。 *<u>Okugai pūru</u> ga, arimasu ka.*
an indoor swimming pool	屋内プール　*okunai pūru*
an indoor jogging track	屋内ジョギング・コース　*okunai jogingu kōsu*
Can I borrow a towel?	タオルが、借りられますか。*Taoru ga, kariraremasu ka.*
Is there an instructor?	インストラクターは、いますか。 *Insutorakutā wa, imasu ka.*
I don't know how to use this machine.	この機械の使い方が、わかりません。 *Kono kikai no tsukaikata ga, wakarimasen.*
Show me how to use this machine, please.	この機械の使い方を、教えて下さい。 *Kono kikai no tsukaikata o, oshiete kudasai.*
Are there <u>aerobics</u> classes?	<u>エアロビックス</u>のクラスがありますか。 *<u>Earobikkusu</u> no kurasu ga arimasu ka.*
spinning	スピニング　*supiningu*
step	ステップ　*suteppu*
Give me a class schedule, please.	クラスのスケジュールを下さい。 *Kurasu no sukejūru o kudasai.*
Which ones are the <u>beginners'</u> classes?	どれが、<u>初心者の</u>クラスですか。 *Dore ga, <u>shoshinsha no</u> kurasu desu ka.*
advanced	上級の　*jōkyū no*
Is there a personal trainer available?	個人レッスンのインストラクターがいますか。*Kojin ressun no insutorakutā ga imasu ka.*

BICYCLING

Where can I rent a bike?
自転車は、どこで借りられますか。
Jitensha wa, doko de kariraremasu ka.

Can I rent a <u>ten-speed bike</u>?
<u>十段変速</u>の自転車が、借りられますか。
Jū dan hensoku no jitensha ga, kariraremasu ka.

  mountain bike
    マウンテン・バイク　*maunten baiku*

How much is the <u>fee</u>?
<u>料金</u>は、いくらですか。*Ryōkin wa, ikura desu ka.*

  deposit
    保証金　*hoshōkin*

Is the fee by the hour?
料金は、時間制ですか。*Ryōkin wa, jikan sei desu ka.*

Does the law require a helmet?
ヘルメットをかぶる法律がありますか。*Herumetto o kaburu hōritsu ga arimasu ka.*

Can I rent a helmet?
ヘルメットが、借りられますか。*Herumetto ga kariraremasu ka.*

Is there a bicycling course nearby?
近くに、サイクリング・コースがありますか。*Chikaku ni, saikuringu kōsu ga arimasu ka.*

GOLF

Although golf is extremely popular in Japan, it's not easy to go out for a casual game. The courses are crowded, and even at a public course, you have to make reservations in advance. Japanese courses are well tended, and many offer spectacular scenery. Play tends to be slow. Allow two to two-and-a-half hours for nine holes.

Do you play golf?
ゴルフをしますか。*Gorufu o shimasu ka.*

Where do you play golf?
ゴルフは、どこでしますか。*Gorufu wa, doko de shimasu ka.*

Could you tell me where I can play golf?	ゴルフがどこでできるか、教えてもらえますか。 *Gorufu ga doko de dekiru ka, oshiete moraemasu ka.*
Is there a public golf course?	公共のゴルフ・コースが、ありますか。 *Kōkyō no gorufu kōsu ga, arimasu ka.*
Is there a hotel with a golf course?	ゴルフ・コースの あるホテルが、ありますか。 *Gorufu kōsu no aru hoteru ga, arimasu ka.*
If I call today for a reservation, when can I play golf?	今日の予約申し込みで、いつゴルフができますか。 *Kyō no yoyaku mōshikomi de, itsu gorufu ga dekimasu ka.*
How much is the greens fee?	グリーン・フィーは、いくらですか。 *Gurīn fī wa, ikura desu ka.*
Do I have to hire a caddy?	キャディーを、雇わなければなりませんか。 *Kyadī o, yatowanakereba narimasen ka.*
Do I have to rent a golf cart?	ゴルフ・カートを、借りなければなりませんか。 *Gorufu kāto o, karinakereba narimasen ka.*
How much does the caddy cost per round?	キャディーは、一ラウンドいくらしますか。 *Kyadī wa, ichi raundo ikura shimasu ka.*
Can I rent <u>golf clubs</u>?	<u>ゴルフ・クラブ</u>が、借りられますか。 *<u>Gorufu kurabu</u> ga, kariraremasu ka.*
a golf cart	ゴルフ・カート　*gorufu kāto*
Is it <u>a difficult</u> course?	このコースは、<u>難しい</u>ですか。 *Kono kōsu wa, <u>muzukashii</u> desu ka.*
an easy	<u>易しい</u>　*yasashii*
What's par?	パーは、いくつですか。 *Pā wa, ikutsu desu ka.*
Can I use the clubhouse facilities?	クラブ・ハウスの施設が、使えますか。 *Kurabu hausu no shisetsu ga, tsukaemasu ka.*

TENNIS

I love to play tennis.	テニスをするのが、大好きです。 *Tenisu o suru no ga, daisuki desu.*
Do you play tennis?	テニスをしますか。 *Tenisu o shimasu ka.*
Where do you play tennis?	テニスは、どこでしますか。 *Tenisu wa, doko de shimasu ka.*
Could you tell me where I can play tennis?	どこでテニスができるか、教えて下さい。 *Doko de tenisu ga dekiru ka, oshiete kudasai.*
Is there a public tennis court?	公共のテニス・コートが、ありますか。 *Kōkyō no tenisu kōto ga, arimasu ka.*
Is there a hotel with a tennis court?	テニス・コートのあるホテルが、ありますか。 *Tenisu kōto no aru hoteru ga, arimasu ka.*
Is the hotel tennis court for guests only?	ホテルのテニス・コートは、泊まり客専用ですか。 *Hoteru no tenisu kōto wa, tomari kyaku sen-yō desu ka.*
Can you play tennis at the hotel tennis court if you're not a guest there?	泊まり客ではなくても、ホテルのテニス・コートでテニスができますか。 *Tomari kyaku dewa nakutemo, hoteru no tenisu kōto de tenisu ga dekimasu ka.*
Can guests use the hotel tennis court free?	泊まり客は、ホテルのテニス・コートが、無料で使えますか。 *Tomari kyaku wa, hoteru no tenisu kōto ga, muryō de tsukaemasu ka.*
Is there a discount for hotel guests?	泊まり客の、料金割引がありますか。 *Tomari kyaku no, ryōkin waribiki ga arimasu ka.*
Which hours are the tennis courts open?	テニス・コートは、何時から何時まで開いていますか。 *Tenisu kōto wa, nan ji kara nan ji made aite imasu ka.*

Is the fee by <u>the hour</u>?	料金は、時間制ですか。 *Ryōkin wa, <u>jikan</u> sei desu ka.*
the half day	半日 *han nichi*
Can I rent a racket?	ラケットが、借りられますか。 *Raketto ga, kariraremasu ka.*

SWIMMING

Japan has good beaches, but they're crowded—don't expect to enjoy the sun and sand in solitude. Pools are crowded, too. Your hotel pool may be your best bet.

I like swimming.	泳ぐのが、好きです。 *Oyogu no ga, suki desu.*
Do you like swimming?	泳ぐのが、好きですか。 *Oyogu no ga, suki desu ka.*
Where do you go swimming?	どこへ、泳ぎに行きますか。 *Doko e, oyogi ni ikimasu ka.*
Could you tell me where I can swim?	どこで泳げるか、教えて下さい。 *Doko de oyogeru ka, oshiete kudasai.*
Is there a swimming pool nearby?	近くに、プールがありますか。 *Chikaku ni, pūru ga arimasu ka.*
Is it a public swimming pool?	それは、公共のプールですか。 *Sore wa, kōkyō no pūru desu ka.*
Is there a hotel with a swimming pool?	プールのあるホテルが、ありますか。 *Pūru no aru hoteru ga, arimasu ka.*
Can hotel guests swim free of charge?	泊まり客は、無料で泳げますか。 *Tomari kyaku wa, muryō de oyogemasu ka.*
Is the hotel swimming pool for guests only?	ホテルのプールは、泊まり客専用ですか。 *Hoteru no pūru wa, tomari kyaku sen-yō desu ka.*
Can you swim at the hotel pool if you're not a guest there?	泊まり客ではなくても、ホテルのプールで泳げますか。 *Tomari kyaku dewa nakutemo, hoteru no pūru de oyogemasu ka.*

How much is the charge?	料金は、いくらですか。*Ryōkin wa, ikura desu ka.*
What hours is the pool open?	プールは、何時から何時まで開いていますか。*Pūru wa, nan ji kara nan ji made aite imasu ka.*
Is there a <u>nice</u> beach around here?	近くに、<u>いい</u>海岸がありますか。*Chikaku ni, <u>ii</u> kaigan ga arimasu ka.*
beautiful	きれいな　*kirei na*
Where is the closest beach where I can swim?	一番近くて泳げる海岸は、どこですか。*Ichiban chikakute oyogeru kaigan wa, doko desu ka.*
How can I get there?	そこへは、どう行けばいいですか。*Soko e wa, dō ikeba ii desu ka.*
Is there a <u>train</u> that goes there?	そこまで、<u>電車</u>がありますか。*Soko made, <u>densha</u> ga arimasu ka.*
bus	バス　*basu*
How long does it take to get there <u>by train</u>?	そこまで、<u>電車</u>でどのくらい時間がかかりますか。*Soko made, <u>densha de</u> dono kurai jikan ga kakarimasu ka.*
by bus	バスで　*basu de*
Is the water <u>cold</u>?	水は、<u>冷たい</u>ですか。*Mizu wa, <u>tsumetai</u> desu ka.*
clean	きれい　*kirei*
calm	穏やか　*odayaka*
Is the beach sandy?	海岸は、砂浜ですか。*Kaigan wa, sunahama desu ka.*
Are there big waves?	大きい波が、ありますか。*Ōkii nami ga, arimasu ka.*
Is it safe for children?	子供にも、安全ですか。*Kodomo ni mo, anzen desu ka.*

Are there lifeguards on duty?	見張りが、出ていますか。 *Mihari ga, dete imasu ka.*
Are there <u>jellyfish</u>?	<u>くらげ</u>がいますか。 <u>*Kurage*</u> *ga imasu ka.*
sharks	さめ *same*
Can I rent <u>an air mattress</u>?	<u>エアー・マットレス</u>が、借りられますか。 <u>*Eā mattoresu*</u> *ga, kariraremasu ka.*
a beach chair	ビーチ・チェアー *bīchi cheā*
a beach towel	ビーチ・タオル *bīchi taoru*
a beach umbrella	ビーチ・パラソル *bīchi parasoru*
a boat	ボート *bōto*
jet ski	ジェットスキー *jetto sukī*
a motor boat	モーター・ボート *mōtā bōto*
a sailboat	ヨット *yotto*
a sailing board	セーリング・ボード *sēringu bōdo*
a surf board	サーフ・ボード *sāfu bōdo*
a swimming tube	浮輪 *ukiwa*
skin-diving equipment	スキン・ダイビング用具 *sukin daibingu yōgu*
snorkeling equipment	スノーケリング用具 *sunōkeringu yōgu*
water skis	水上スキー *suijō sukī*
How much is it <u>per hour</u>?	<u>一時間</u>、いくらですか。 <u>*Ichi jikan*</u>, *ikura desu ka.*
per day	一日 *ichi nichi*
Do you want a deposit?	保証金が、いりますか。 *Hoshō kin ga, irimasu ka.*
How much is the deposit?	保証金は、いくらですか。 *Hoshō kin wa, ikura desu ka.*

SKIING AND SNOWBOARDING

Japan has excellent ski areas, both on Honshu, where the 1998 Winter Olympics were held at Nagano, and Hokkaido, where the 1972 Winter Olympics were held at Sapporo. Transportation to the ski areas is usually by car, bus, or train (or, to Hokkaido, by plane); it's wise to book travel reservations ahead of time.

Do you like <u>skiing</u>?	スキーが、好きですか。 *Sukī ga, suki desu ka.*
snowboarding	スノー・ボード　*sunō bōdo*
Where do you go for <u>skiing</u>?	どこへ、スキーをしに行きますか。 *Doko e, sukī o shini ikimasu ka.*
snowboarding	スノー・ボード　*sunō bōdo*
Is this the <u>ski</u> season?	今は、スキー・シーズンですか。 *Ima wa, sukī shīzun desu ka.*
snowboarding	スノー・ボード　*sunō bōdo*
Where can I <u>ski</u> now?	今、どこでスキーができますか。 *Ima, doko de sukī ga dekimasu ka.*
snowboard	スノー・ボード　*sunō bōdo*
Where is a nearby ski resort?	近くのスキー場は、どこにありますか。 *Chikaku no sukī jō wa, doko ni arimasu ka.*
How can I get there?	そこまで、どう行けばいいですか。 *Soko made, dō ikeba ii desu ka.*
Is there a <u>train</u> that goes there?	そこへ行く汽車が、ありますか。 *Soko e iku kisha ga, arimasu ka.*
bus	バス　*basu*
How long does it take to get there?	そこまで、どのくらい時間がかかりますか。 *Soko made, dono kurai jikan ga kakarimasu ka.*
Tell me how to get there, please.	そこへの行き方を、教えて下さい。 *Soko e no ikikata o, oshiete kudasai.*
Is the ski resort crowded?	スキー場は、こんでいますか。 *Sukī jō wa, konde imasu ka.*

Is the ski slope <u>difficult</u>?	ゲレンデは、難しいですか。 *Gerende wa, <u>muzukashii</u> desu ka.*
steep	急　*kyū*
How is the snow quality?	雪質は、どうですか。*Yuki shitsu wa, dō desu ka.*
Is the snow <u>powdery</u>?	雪は、粉雪ですか。*Yuki wa, <u>kona yuki</u> desu ka.*
wet	べた雪　*beta yuki*
How much is the snow accumulation?	積雪は、どのくらいですか。*Sekisetsu wa, dono kurai desu ka.*
Do they have a ski <u>lift</u>?	<u>リフト</u>が、ありますか。*<u>Rifuto</u> ga, arimasu ka.*
ropeway	ロープ・ウェイ　*rōpu wei*
cable car	ゴンドラ　*gondora*
How long do I have to wait?	どのくらい、待たなければなりませんか。*Dono kurai, matanakereba narimasen ka.*
Should I make a reservation for a <u>hotel</u>?	<u>ホテル</u>の予約は、するべきですか。*<u>Hoteru</u> no yoyaku wa, suru beki desu ka.*
ryokan	旅館　*ryokan*
minshuku	民宿　*minshuku*
Can I rent <u>ski</u> equipment at the ski resort?	スキー場で、<u>スキー</u>用具が借りられますか。*Sukī jō de, <u>sukī</u> yōgu ga kariraremasu ka.*
snowboarding	スノー・ボード　*sunō bōdo*
Can I rent <u>skis</u>?	<u>スキー</u>が、借りられますか。*<u>Sukī</u> ga, kariraremasuka.*
ski shoes	スキー・シューズ　*sukī shūzu*
poles	ストック　*sutokku*
a snowboard	スノー・ボード　*sunō bōdo*

FISHING

Do you like fishing?	釣りが、好きですか。*Tsuri ga, suki desu ka.*
Where do you go fishing?	どこへ、釣りに行きますか。*Doko e, tsuri ni ikimasu ka.*
Where is a nearby fishing spot?	近くの釣り場は、どこにありますか。*Chikaku no tsuri ba wa, doko ni arimasu ka.*
How can I get there?	そこまで、どう行けばいいですか。*Soko made, dō ikeba ii desu ka.*
How long does it take to get there?	そこまで、どのくらい時間がかかりますか。*Soko made, dono kurai jikan ga kakarimasu ka.*
I like <u>river</u> fishing.	<u>川</u>釣りが、好きです。<u>*Kawa*</u> *zuri ga, suki desu.*
ocean	海　*umi*
surf	磯　*iso*
offshore	沖　*oki*
What can you catch now?	今、何が釣れていますか。*Ima, nani ga tsurete imasu ka.*
What kind of fishing equipment do you use?	どんな釣り道具を、使いますか。*Donna tsuri dōgu o, tsukaimasu ka.*
Where can I rent <u>fishing equipment</u>?	<u>釣り道具</u>は、どこで借りられますか。<u>*Tsuri dōgu*</u> *wa, doko de kariraremasu ka.*
a fishing boat	釣り船　*tsuri bune*
Where can I buy fishing gear?	釣り道具は、どこで買えますか。*Tsuri dōgu wa, doko de kaemasu ka.*
Where can I join a chartered fishing boat?	釣り船には、どこで乗れますか。*Tsuri bune niwa, doko de noremasu ka.*
What time does the fishing boat <u>leave</u>?	釣り船は、何時に<u>出ます</u>か。*Tsuri bune wa, nan ji ni <u>demasu</u> ka.*
return	戻ります　*modorimasu*

Do I need to make a reservation?	予約の必要が、ありますか。*Yoyaku no hitsuyō ga, arimasu ka.*
What's the charge?	料金は、いくらですか。*Ryōkin wa, ikura desu ka.*
Do I need to take my own food and drinks?	食べ物と飲み物は、持参する必要がありますか。*Tabemono to nomimono wa, jisan suru hitsuyō ga arimasu ka.*
Can I buy bait?	餌は、買えますか。*Esa wa, kaemasu ka.*
What kind of bait is it?	どんな種類の餌ですか。*Donna shurui no esa desu ka.*
Is there a fishing rights charge?	入漁料が、ありますか。*Nyūgyo ryō ga, arimasu ka.*

CAMPING AND COUNTRYSIDE

Although camping is not as widespread in Japan as in some other countries, you can find some fine campsites. The best source of information is the JNTO Tourist Information Centers.

Where is the Tourist Information Center?	観光案内所は、どこにありますか。*Kankō annai jo wa, doko ni arimasu ka.*
Is there a camping site near here?	近くに、キャンプ場がありますか。*Chikaku ni, kyanpu jō ga arimasu ka.*
I like camping <u>at a lake</u>.	<u>湖のそば</u>のキャンプ場が、好きです。*<u>Mizuumi no soba</u> no kyanpu jō ga, suki desu.*
on a mountain	山　*yama*
at the seashore	海岸　*kaigan*

Could you recommend a site?	どのキャンプ場がいいか、教えて下さい。*Dono kyanpu jō ga ii ka, oshiete kudasai.*
Could you tell me how to get there?	そこまでどう行けばいいか、教えてもらえますか。*Soko made dō ikeba ii ka, oshiete moraemasu ka.*
Where is it on the map?	そこは、地図のどこにありますか。*Soko wa, chizu no doko ni arimasu ka.*
Do I need to make a reservation?	予約の必要がありますか。*Yoyaku no hitsuyō ga arimasu ka.*
Can I camp for the night?	泊まりがけで、キャンプできますか。*Tomarigake de, kyanpu dekimasu ka.*
Where can I spend the night?	どこに泊まれますか。*Doko ni tomaremasu ka.*
Is there <u>drinking water</u>?	<u>飲み水</u>が、ありますか。*<u>Nomimizu</u> ga, arimasu ka.*
running water	水道　*suidō*
gas	ガス　*gasu*
electricity	電気　*denki*
a children's playground	子供の遊び場　*kodomo no asobi ba*
a grocery	食料品店　*shokuryōhin ten*
Are there <u>toilets</u>?	<u>トイレ</u>が、ありますか。*<u>Toire</u> ga, arimasu ka.*
baths	お風呂　*ofuro*
showers	シャワー　*shawā*
tents	テント　*tento*
cooking facilities	料理の設備　*ryōri no setsubi*
Can I rent <u>a sleeping bag</u>?	<u>スリーピング・バッグ</u>が、借りられますか。*<u>Surīpingu baggu</u> ga, kariraremasu ka.*

a blanket	毛布　*mōfu*
cooking utensils	炊事用具　*suiji yōgu*
a lamp	ランプ　*ranpu*
a tent	テント　*tento*
I intend on staying <u>a day</u>.	<u>一日</u>滞在の予定です。<u>*Ichi nichi*</u>, *taizai no yotei desu.*
two days	二日　*futsuka*
three days	三日　*mikka*
How much is the charge per person per day?	料金は、一日一人当たりいくらですか。 *Ryōkin wa, ichi nichi hitori atari ikura desu ka.*
Can I play <u>tennis</u> there?	そこで、<u>テニス</u>ができますか。*Soko de, <u>tenisu</u> ga dekimasu ka.*
basketball	バスケットボール　*basukettobōru*
badminton	バドミントン　*badominton*
ping pong	ピンポン　*pinpon*
volleyball	バレーボール　*barēbōru*
Can I go <u>fishing</u>?	<u>釣り</u>に行けますか。<u>*Tsuri*</u> *ni ikemasu ka.*
swimming	泳ぎ　*oyogi*
bicycling	サイクリング　*saikuringu*
Is there a hiking trail nearby?	近くに、ハイキング・コースがあり ますか。*Chikaku ni, haikingu kōsu ga arimasu ka.*
Is there a map for the hiking trail?	ハイキング・コースの地図が、あり ますか。*Haikingu kōsu no chizu ga, arimasu ka.*
What a beautiful landscape!	素晴らしい景色ですねえ。 *Subarashii keshiki desu nē.*
Look at the <u>barn</u>! (*male speaker*)	あの<u>納屋</u>を、見てごらん。*Ano <u>naya</u> o, mite goran.*

Look at the <u>barn</u>! (*female speaker*)	あの<u>納屋</u>を、見てごらんなさい。 *Ano <u>naya</u> o, mite goran nasai.*	
birds	鳥	*tori*
bridge	橋	*hashi*
cottage	小屋	*koya*
farm	畑	*hatake*
fields	野原	*nohara*
flowers	花	*hana*
forest	森	*mori*
hill	丘	*oka*
lake	湖	*mizuumi*
mountains	山	*yama*
ocean	海	*umi*
plants	草	*kusa*
pond	池	*ike*
rice paddy	水田	*suiden*
river	川	*kawa*
rocks	岩	*iwa*
shrine	神社	*jinja*
stream	小川	*ogawa*
temple	お寺	*otera*
thatch roof	わらぶき屋根	*warabuki yane*
trees	木	*ki*
valley	谷	*tani*
village	村	*mura*
waterfall	滝	*taki*
Where does this path/road lead to?	この道は、どこへ行きますか。 *Kono michi wa, doko e ikimasu ka.*	

How far away is _____?	_____ まで、どのくらい距離がありますか。_____ *made, dono kurai kyori ga arimasu ka.*
How long does it take to get to_____?	_____ まで、どのくらい時間がかかりますか。_____ *made, dono kurai jikan ga kakarimasu ka.*
I'm lost.	道に、迷ってしまいました。*Michi ni, mayotte shimaimashita.*
Can you tell me the way to _____?	_____ への行き方を、教えて下さい。_____ *e no ikikata o, oshiete kudasai.*

OLYMPICS AND PARALYMPICS

OLYMPICS IN JAPAN

1964 Summer Olympics	Tokyo	東京
1972 Winter Olympics	Sapporo	札幌
1998 Winter Olympics	Nagano	長野
2020 Summer Olympics	Tokyo	東京

Tokyo 2020 Olympic and Paralympic Games
東京２０２０オリンピック・パラリンピック大会
Tōkyō Orinpikku Pararinpikku Taikai

July 24–August 9, 2020
２０２０年７月２４日から８月９日まで
*nisen ni jūnen shichigatsu nijūyokka kara
hachigatsu kokonoka made*

host city	主催都市	*shusai toshi*
opening ceremony	開会式	*kaikaishiki*
closing ceremony	閉会式	*heikaishiki*
Olympic record	オリンピック記録	*Orinpikku kiroku*

world record	世界記録	*sekai kiroku*
participating country/countries	参加国	*sankakoku*
team	チーム	*chīmu*
athletes	選手	*senshu*
competition	競技	*kyōgi*
to participate	出場する	*shutsujō suru*
to win	勝つ	*katsu*
to lose	負ける	*makeru*
first (finish)	一位	*ichi i*
second (finish)	二位	*ni i*
third	三位	*san i*
preliminary rounds	予選	*yosen*
semi-final	セミファイナル／準決勝	*semifainaru/jun kesshō*
final	ファイナル／決勝	*fainaru/kesshō*
medal	メダル	*medaru*
gold medal	金メダル	*kin medaru*
silver medal	銀メダル	*gin medaru*
bronze medal	銅メダル	*dō medaru*
sports/athletic events	競技種目	*kyōgi shumoku*
aquatics	水上競技	*suijō kyōgi*
diving	ダイビング	*daibingu*
swimming	競泳	*kyōei*
synchronized swimming	シンクロナイズドスイミング	*shinkuronaizudo suimingu*
water polo	ウォーターポロ／水球	*wōtāporo/suikyū*
archery	アーチェリー	*ācherī*
athletics	陸上競技	*rikujō kyōgi*

badminton	バドミントン	*badominton*
baseball/softball	ベースボール／ソフトボール	*bēsubōru/sofutobōru*
basketball	バスケットボール	*basuketto bōru*
boxing	ボクシング	*bokushingu*
canoe/kayak	カヌー／カヤック	*kanū/kayakku*
cycling	自転車競技	*jitensha kyōgi*
equestrian	馬術	*bajutsu*
fencing	フェンシング	*fenshingu*
field hockey	ホッケー	*hokkē*
football	サッカー	*sakkā*
golf	ゴルフ	*gorufu*
gymnastics	体操	*taisō*
handball	ハンドボール	*handobōru*
judo	柔道	*jūdō*
karate	空手	*karate*
modern pentathlon	近代5種	*kindai go shu*
rowing	ボート／競艇	*bōto/kyōtei*
rugby sevens	7人制ラグビー	*nananinsei ragubī*
sailing	セーリング	*sēringu*
shooting	射撃	*shageki*
skateboarding	スケートボード	*sukētobōdo*
sport climbing	スポーツクライミング	*supōtsu kuraimingu*
surfing	サーフィン	*sāfin*
table tennis	卓球／ピンポン	*takkyū/pinpon*
taekwondo	テコンドー	*tekondō*

tennis	テニス	*tenisu*
triathlon	トライアスロン	*toraiasuron*
volleyball	バレーボール	*barēbōru*
beach volleyball	ビーチバレーボール	*bīchi barēbōru*
weightlifting	ウエイトリフティング	*ueitorifutingu*
wrestling	レスリング	*resuringu*

When does <u>athletics</u> start?	陸上競技はいつ始まりますか。 *Rikujō kyōgi wa itsu hajimarikasu ka.*	
swimming	競泳	*kyōei*
Where is <u>gymnastics</u> held ?	体操はどこで行われますか。*Taisō wa doko de okonawaremasu ka.*	
judo	柔道	*jūdō*
Can I buy a ticket for <u>football</u>?	<u>サッカー</u>のチケットが 買えますか。 *Sakkā no chiketto ga kaemasu ka.*	
table tennis	卓球	*takkyū*
How do I get to the site for <u>golf</u>?	<u>ゴルフ</u>の開催地にはどう 行きますか。 *Gorufu no kaisaichi niwa dō ikimasu ka.*	
sailing	セーリング	*sēringu*
Can I watch <u>boxing</u> on TV?	<u>ボクシング</u>はテレビで見れ ますか。 *Bokushingu wa terebi de miremasu ka.*	
volleyball	バレバレーボール	*barēbōru*
Which channel?	どのチャンネルですか。*Dono channeru desu ka.*	
What time does the coverage start?	放送は何時に始まりますか。*Hōsō wa nanji ni hajimarimasu ka.*	
Who won?	誰が勝ちましたか。*Dare ga kachimashita ka.*	

FOOD AND DRINK

Dining is one of the most pleasurable aspects of visiting Japan. You have a choice of good Western-style restaurants, other Asian restaurants, and an almost endless variety of Japanese food to explore. If you crave American fast food, you can even get that. You won't go hungry in Japan!

Japanese-style eating is unlike Western style. You use chopsticks, the food is different, and table manners are different as well. Therefore, we have separate sections for the two styles.

TIPPING

You don't need to tip anyone in Japanese restaurants. A service charge will be added to your bill, so enjoy your meal and the customary good service. No one expects anything more from you.

TOWELS

Whenever and wherever you drink or dine in Japan, you'll begin with a refreshing hot or cold damp towel for your hands and face.

hot or cold towel	おしぼり	*oshibori*

JAPANESE RESTAURANTS

Japanese cuisine is characterized by freshness, presentation, and variety. Some restaurants offer a selection of different kinds of dishes. Others specialize in one type of food or style of cooking, often prepared in front of you at your table or on a grill. Many (though not all) Japanese eateries display replicas of their offerings outside the front door in glass cases. The dishes look quite real and may tempt you to enter. It makes ordering easy: just point to what you want. You can't do this everywhere, but sometimes it works quite well!

Here are some of the most popular Japanese dishes:

sushi (お) すし *(o)sushi*

Small blocks of vinegared rice, topped with pieces of raw fish or other seafood, and hot Japanese horseradish. Some items, like shrimp, may be cooked; others, like mackerel, may be pickled or smoked. These and other ingredients may also be rolled in seaweed, or combined in a bowl or lacquer box. Sushi is eaten with soy sauce.

tempura 天ぷら *tenpura*

Batter-fried seafood and vegetables, served with a dipping sauce containing grated radish.

yakitori 焼き鳥 *yakitori*

Grilled chicken and vegetables on small skewers.

sukiyaki すき焼き *sukiyaki*

Beef and vegetables cooked in a seasoned sauce, then dipped into a lightly beaten raw egg.

shabu shabu しゃぶしゃぶ *shabu shabu*

Thinly sliced beef and vegetables cooked in a hot broth, eaten with different dipping sauces.

sashimi (お) 刺身 *(o)sashimi*

Fresh, sliced fish or shellfish, eaten raw, dipped in soy sauce and hot Japanese horseradish.

yosenabe 寄せ鍋 *yosenabe*

Seafood, chicken, and vegetables cooked in broth, eaten with several kinds of dipping sauce, and perhaps Japanese noodles.

teppanyaki 鉄板焼 *teppan yaki*

Beef, chicken, seafood, and vegetables cooked on a grill in front of you and served with various sauces.

kushikatsu 串かつ *kushikatsu*

Pork, chicken, seafood, and vegetables, skewered on bamboo sticks, breaded, and deep fried, then eaten with salt, hot mustard, and sauces.

tonkatsu　　　　　トンカツ　　　*tonkatsu*

Pork cutlets, breaded, deep fried, and eaten with a special sauce and thinly shredded cabbage.

soba and udon　　そばとうどん　　*soba to udon*

Japanese noodles, served in hot or cold broth, or with dipping sauce.

ramen　　　　　　ラーメン　　　　*rāmen*

Chinese noodles, served in hot broth or chilled.

okonomiyaki,　　お好み焼き、　　*okonomiyaki,*
monjayaki　　　　もんじゃ焼き　　*monjayaki*

Japanese-style savory pancakes with vegetables and other ingredients. The former is west-Japan style, and the latter is east-Japan style.

SOME SPECIAL CUISINES

Here are some kinds of cooking you may encounter or seek out during your stay in Japan.

kaiseki ryori　　　懐石料理　　　*kaiseki ryōri*

This elaborate and elegant meal consists of a succession of many small dishes served in a formal style. The ingredients change with the seasons and may include fowl and seafood, and nowadays occasionally meat.

shojin ryori　　　　精進料理　　　*shōjin ryōri*

Originally Buddhist temple food, made up of vegetarian ingredients only.

kyodo ryori　　　　郷土料理　　　*kyōdo ryōri*

Local or regional specialties—this may consist of one dish or an entire meal that typifies the cooking of a particular area.

robata yaki　　　　ろばた焼き　　*robata yaki*

Literally "fireside cooking," these meals were originally served to travelers. Now they feature country-style service, food, and atmosphere.

fugu ryori ふぐ料理 *fugu ryōri*

Meals featuring blowfish, from which the poisonous organs have been removed by licensed chefs.

unagi ryori うなぎ料理 *unagi ryōri*

Meals featuring eel.

tofu ryori 豆腐料理 *tōfu ryōri*

Meals featuring beancurd.

GENERAL INQUIRIES

I'd like to have <u>yakitori</u>.	焼き鳥が、食べたいのですが。 *<u>Yakitori</u> ga, tabetai no desu ga.*	
tempura	天ぷら *tenpura*	
Is there a <u>ramen restaurant</u> neaby?	近くに、<u>ラーメン屋</u>がありますか。 *Chikaku ni, <u>rāmen ya</u> ga arimasu ka.*	
soba restaurant	(お) そば屋 *(o)soba ya*	
I'd like to go to a <u>sushi</u> restaurant.	(お) すし屋へ、行きたいのですが。 *(O)sushi ya e, ikitai no desu ga.*	
kaiten sushi (conveyor belt sushi)	回転すし *kaiten sushi*	
Would you recommend <u>a good</u> sushi restaurant?	<u>おいしい</u>(お)すし屋を、教えて下さい。 *<u>Oishii</u> (o)sushi ya o, oshiete kudasai.*	
the best	最高の *saikō no*	
an inexpensive	高くない *takakunai*	
a nearby	近くの *chikaku no*	
How much will it cost per person?	だいたい、一人当たりいくらですか。 *Daitai, hitori atari ikura desu ka.*	

ARRIVING

At many Japanese restaurants you have a choice of where to sit: the counter, a table, a private room, or a Japanese room. Some of the best cooking is done behind a counter. If you're sitting right there, you get each morsel the moment it's prepared or cooked. At a sushi or tempura restaurant, it's the best place to sit.

A Japanese room is private, but you remove your shoes (with no exceptions) before entering, and you sit on cushions on the tatami floor, in front of a low dining table. You may request your desired seating arrangements when you make a reservation or when you arrive at the restaurant.

Good afternoon.	こんにちは。	*Konnichiwa.*
Good evening.	今晩は。	*Konbanwa.*
My name is _____. I have a reservation at 6.	私は、_____ですが。六時に予約がしてあります。*Watakushi wa, _____ desu ga. Roku ji ni yoyaku ga shite arimasu.*	
Is the <u>counter</u> available?	<u>カウンター</u>は、あいていますか。<u>*Kauntā*</u> *wa, aite imasu ka.*	
a table	テーブル	*tēburu*
a private room	個室	*koshitsu*
a Japanese room	お座敷	*ozashiki*
We'll wait till the counter is available.	カウンターがあくまで、待ます。*Kauntā ga akumade, machimasu.*	
How long do we have to wait?	どのくらい、待たねばなりませんか。*Dono kurai, mataneba narimasen ka.*	
Either the counter or a table is fine.	カウンターでも、テーブルでも、かまいません。*Kauntā demo, tēburu demo, kamaimasen.*	
Could you seat us now?	いますぐ、座れますか。*Ima sugu, suwaremasu ka.*	

AT THE TABLE

You'll probably order certain kinds of drinks at a Japanese restaurant: sake (hot, room temperature, chilled, or on the rocks), beer, Japanese whiskey (for starters or during the meal),

Japanese tea toward the end (or at the start if you prefer). You might not be able to get cocktails or mixed drinks.

Is there a menu in English?	英語のメニューが、ありますか。 *Eigo no menyū ga, arimasu ka.*
No drinks, thank you.	飲み物は、けっこうです。 *Nomimono wa, kekkō desu.*
Japanese <u>tea</u>, please.	<u>お茶</u>を下さい。<u>*Ocha*</u> *o kudasai.*
water	水　*mizu*
What kinds of drinks do you serve?	どんな飲み物が、ありますか。 *Donna nomimono ga, arimasu ka.*
Bring us <u>sake</u>, please.	<u>お酒</u>を、下さい。<u>*Osake*</u> *o, kudasai.*
beer	ビール　*bīru*
shochu	焼酎　*shōchū*
Give us <u>hot sake</u>, please.	お酒は、<u>熱燗</u>を下さい。*Osake wa,* <u>*atsukan*</u> *o kudasai.*
chilled sake	冷酒　*reishu*
room temperature sake	冷や　*hiya*
Give us one <u>large bottle</u> of beer, please.	ビールは、<u>大ビン</u>を一本下さい。 *Bīru wa, <u>ō bin</u> o ippon kudasai.*
medium size bottle	中ビン　*chū bin*
small bottle	小ビン　*ko bin*
Give us <u>two</u> large bottles of beer, please.	ビールは、大ビンを<u>二本</u>下さい。 *Bīru wa, ō bin o <u>ni hon</u> kudasai.*
three	三本　*san bon*
four	四本　*yon hon*
five	五本　*go hon*
Give me <u>whiskey and water</u>, please.	<u>水割り</u>を、下さい。<u>*Mizu wari*</u> *o,* *kudasai.*
whiskey and soda	ハイボール　　　　*haibōru*
whiskey on the rocks	オン・ザ・ロック　*on za rokku*

Give us two bottles of <u>hot sake</u>, please.	熱燗を、二本下さい。<u>*Atsukan o*</u>, *ni hon kudasai.*
chilled sake	冷酒　*reishu*
Do you have nonalcoholic drinks?	アルコール分のない飲み物が、ありますか。*Arukōru bun no nai nomimono ga, arimasu ka.*
Could you bring something to eat with drinks?	何か、おつまみを持ってきて下さい。*Nanika, otsumami o motte kite kudasai.*
What kinds of appetizers do you have?	どんなおつまみが、ありますか。*Donna otsumami ga, arimasu ka.*
Could you bring us something good?	何か、適当な物を持ってきて下さい。*Nanika, tekitō na mono o motte kite kudasai.*
Do you have a set meal/prix fixe menu?	セット・コース／定食が、ありますか。*Setto kōsu/teishoku ga, arimasu ka.*
What's good today?	今日は、何がおいしいですか。*Kyō wa, nani ga oishii desu ka.*
Do you serve anything special for this region?	何か、この土地の特産物がありますか。*Nanika, kono tochi no tokusan butsu ga arimasu ka.*
Is it <u>raw</u>?	それは、<u>なまですか</u>。*Sore wa, <u>nama desu</u> ka.*
cooked	料理してあります　*ryōri shite arimasu*
alive	生きています　*ikite imasu*
hot (spicy)	辛いです　*karai desu*
salty	塩辛いです　*shiokarai desu*
How is it cooked?	それは、どんな風に料理しますか。*Sore wa, donna fū ni ryōri shimasu ka.*

I'll have this.	これを、お願いします。	*Kore o, onegai shimasu.*
Can you make an assorted dish?	盛り合わせを、お願いできますか。	*Moriawase o, onegai dekimasu ka.*

SOME BASIC FOODS

bean curd	（お）豆腐	*(o)tōfu*
bean paste soup	味噌汁	*miso shiru*
clear soup	（お）吸物	*(o)suimono*
Japanese horseradish	わさび	*wasabi*
Japanese hot pepper	唐辛子	*tōgarashi*
Japanese pickles	（お）漬け物	*(o)tsukemono*
Japanese rice wine	（お）酒	*(o)sake*
Japanese tea	お茶	*ocha*
green tea	緑茶	*ryokucha*
roasted tea	ほうじ茶	*hōjicha*
pickled plums	梅干し	*umeboshi*
pickled radish	たくあん	*takuan*
cooked rice	ご飯	*gohan*
uncooked rice	（お）米	*(o)kome*
seaweed	海苔	*nori*
bean paste	（お）味噌	*(o)miso*
soy sauce	（お）しょうゆ	*(o)shōyu*
sweet rice wine	みりん	*mirin*
Japanese soup stock	だし	*dashi*
dried fish	干物	*himono*

EATING THE JAPANESE WAY: A FEW POINTERS

Menus are not always provided. Some restaurants just serve what they have that day. Others might bring a succession of items served in a set order. Just tell them when you've had enough.

Prices are not always listed. This may mean it's a very expensive place, or that prices vary from day to day, as in a sushi shop. To avoid any surprises with your check, inquire about the price range beforehand.

Desserts are not traditional with Japanese meals, but you can usually get fresh fruit (probably expensive) or sweet bean paste. Some places serve ice cream or sherbet as well.

Japanese noodles may be slurped noisily—it's quite proper, and may even indicate you're enjoying the flavor.

Soy sauce is not poured on white rice. The rice is served in individual rice bowls, which may be held in the left hand. Dip food morsels, one at a time, in soy sauce, and then eat together with the rice.

Soup is served in individual lacquer bowls, without spoons. Sip directly from the bowl, with an assist from chopsticks if there are vegetables or other bits of food in it.

Chopsticks are easy! Rest one at the base of the thumb and index finger and between the ends of the ring and middle finger. That chopstick remains stationary. Grasp the other between the ends of the thumb and the first two fingers, and enjoy your food.

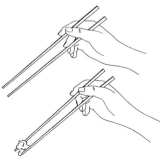

KINDS OF RESTAURANTS

AT A SUSHI RESTAURANT

If you sit at the counter, you usually order sushi one kind at a time (two bite-size pieces). At a table, you might order an assorted sushi tray, or other sushi specialties.

raw fish	刺身　*sashimi*
I'd like to start with assorted sashimi.	始めに、刺身の盛り合わせをお願いします。*Hajime ni, sashimi no moriawase o onegai shimasu.*
I'd like <u>assorted sashimi over rice in a box</u>.	<u>ちらし</u>を下さい。*Chirashi o kudasai.*
assorted sushi rolled in seaweed	のり巻きの盛り合わせ　*norimaki no moriawase*
tuna on rice in a large bowl	鉄火丼　*tekka donburi*
assorted sushi	すしの盛り合わせ　*sushi no moriawase*
I'd like the <u>regular</u> kind.	<u>並み</u>のを下さい。*Nami no o kudasai.*
deluxe	上　*jō*
super deluxe	特上　*tokujō*
I'll start with sushi.	最初から、すしにします。*Saisho kara, sushi ni shimasu.*
What's good today?	今日は、何がおいしいですか。*Kyō wa, nani ga oishii desu ka.*
What is it?	これは何ですか。*Kore wa nan desu ka.*
This one, please.	これを下さい。*Kore o kudasi.*

Some of the names of the seafood used in sushi sound exotic to foreign visitors. Try them; you may like them.

I'll have <u>abalone</u>, please.	<u>あわび</u>を下さい。	<u>Awabi</u> o kudasai.
ark shell	赤貝	akagai
ark shell lip	赤貝のひも	akagai no himo
clam	はまぐり	hamaguri
cockle	とり貝	torigai
conger eel	あなご	anago
crab	かに	kani
cuttlefish	もんごういか	mongō ika
eel	うなぎ	unagi
flounder	平目	hirame
herring roe	数の子	kazunoko
horse clam	みる貝	mirugai
horse mackerel	あじ	aji
mackerel	さば	saba
vinegared mackerel	しめさば	shimesaba
mantis shrimp	しゃこ	shako
marlin	かじき	kajiki
octopus	たこ	tako
omelet	たまご	tamago
porgy	鯛	tai
salmon roe	いくら	ikura
sea bass	すずき	suzuki
sea urchin	うに	uni
shrimp	えび	ebi
live shrimp	おどり	odori
raw shrimp	甘えび	ama ebi

skipjack tuna	かつお	*katsuo*
squid	いか	*ika*
tuna	まぐろ	*maguro*
very fatty tuna	大とろ	*ōtoro*
medium fatty tuna	中とろ	*chū toro*
fatty tuna	とろ	*toro*
yellowtail	はまち	*hamachi*
young gizzard shad	こはだ	*kohada*

Do you have <u>eel</u>? うなぎは、ありますか。*Unagi wa, arimasu ka.*

| swordfish | まかじき | *makajiki* |
| trout | ます | *masu* |

Could you roll <u>flounder</u>, please? 平目を巻いて下さい。*Hirame o maite kudasai.*

| omelet | たまご | *tamago* |
| yellowtail | はまち | *hamachi* |

<u>Tuna</u> roll, please. 鉄火巻を下さい。*Tekka maki o kudasai.*

| cucumber | かっぱ | *kappa* |
| California | カリフォルニア | *Kariforunia* |

Could you make me a hand roll of <u>tuna</u>, please? 鉄火の手巻きを、お願いします。*Tekka no temaki o, onegai shimasu.*

| pickled plum | 梅干し | *umeboshi* |
| eel and cucumber | うなきゅう | *unakyū* |

Would you use a little <u>less</u> Japanese horseradish, please? わさびを、少なめにしてもらえますか。*Wasabi o, <u>sukuname</u> ni shite moraemasu ka.*

| more | 多め | *ōme* |

Another <u>sake</u>, please.	お酒を、もう一本お願いします。 *Osake o, mō ippon onegai shimasu.*
beer	ビール　*bīru*
May I have some more <u>ginger</u>?	<u>しょうが</u>を、もう少しお願いします。 *Shōga o, mō sukoshi onegai shimasu.*
tea	お茶　*ocha*
I'm close to the end.	そろそろ、終わりにします。 *Sorosoro, owari ni shimasu.*
This is my last order.	最後に、これを下さい。*Saigo ni, kore o kudasai.*
I've had plenty.	十分、頂きました。*Jūbun, itadakimashita.*
It was really delicious.	とっても、おいしかったです。 *Tottemo, oishikatta desu.*
Thank you very much for a wonderful meal.	どうも、ごちそうさまでした。 *Dōmo, gochisō sama deshita.*
May I have the check, please?	(お)会計を、お願いします。 *(O)kaikei o, onegai shimasu.*

AT A TEMPURA RESTAURANT

If you sit at a counter, you'll receive your tempura from the chef piece by piece as it is cooked. There's often a set order for the items, but you may request more of those you like. If you sit at a table, you'll choose from a menu of tempura specialties.

Do you have <u>a set menu</u>?	セット・コースは、ありますか。 *Setto kōsu wa, arimasu ka.*
assorted tempura	天ぷらの盛り合わせ　*tenpura no moriawase*
a bowl of tempura on rice	天丼　*tendon*
vegetable tempura	精進揚げ　*shōjin age*

I'll have <u>asparagus</u>, please.	<u>アスパラ</u>を下さい。	<u>Asupara</u> o kudasai.
burdock	ごぼう	gobō
carrot	にんじん	ninjin
chicken	とり	tori
broccoli	ブロッコリ	burokkori
cauliflower	カリフラワー	karifurawā
eggplant	なす	nasu
ginko nuts	銀杏	ginnan
green pepper	ピーマン	pīman
Japanese green pepper	ししとう	shishitō
Japanese mint leaves	しそ	shiso
lotus root	はす	hasu
mushroom	マッシュルーム	masshurūmu
okra	オクラ	okura
onion	玉ねぎ	tamanegi
pumpkin	かぼちゃ	kabocha
scallops	帆立て	hotate
shiitake mushroom	しいたけ	shiitake
shrimp	えび	ebi
smelts	きす	kisu
squid	いか	ika
string beans	さやいんげん	sayaingen
sweet potato	さつまいも	satsumaimo
trefoil	三つ葉	mitsuba
zucchini	ズッキーニ	zukkīni

I'll have <u>crab</u> next, please.	次に、<u>かに</u>を下さい。*Tsugi ni, <u>kani</u> o kudasai.*
eggplant	なす *nasu*
I'll have <u>green pepper</u> again, please.	また、<u>ピーマン</u>を下さい。*Mata, <u>pīman</u> o kudasai.*
scallops	帆立て *hotate*
Could you give me some more <u>tempura dipping sauce</u>?	<u>天つゆ</u>を、もう少しお願いします。*<u>Tentsuyu</u> o, mō sukoshi onegai shimasu.*
grated radish	大根おろし *daikon oroshi*
lemon	レモン *remon*
salt	塩 *shio*
I'm ready for rice and miso soup.	そろそろ、ご飯とおみおつけをお願いします。*Sorosoro, gohan to omiotsuke o onegai shimasu.*
I've had enough, thank you.	もう、けっこうです。*Mō, kekkō desu.*
Thank you for a wonderful meal.	どうも、ごちそうさまでした。*Dōmo, gochisō sama deshita.*
May I have the check, please?	お会計を、お願いします。*Okaikei o, onegai shimasu.*

AT A SUKIYAKI OR SHABU SHABU RESTAURANT

In these restaurants, you sit at a table, and the food is cooked right there, in a flat pan for sukiyaki, and a deeper one for shabu shabu. The server may ask if you want to cook for yourself, or he or she may cook and serve you.

| We don't know how to cook it. | 料理の仕方が、わかりません。*Ryōri no shikata ga, wakarimasen.* |
| Would you cook it for us? | 料理してもらえますか。*Ryōri shite moraemasu ka.* |

We'd like one more order of <u>meat</u>.	肉を、もう一人前お願いします。 *Niku o, mō ichi nin mae onegai shimasu.*
vegetables	野菜　*yasai*
Can you give me some more <u>shabu shabu dipping sauce</u>?	しゃぶしゃぶのたれを、もう少しお願いします。*Shabu shabu no tare o, mō sukoshi onegai shimasu.*
noodles	うどん　*udon*
rice	ご飯　*gohan*
I've had plenty.	たくさん、頂きました。*Takusan, itadakimashita.*
Thank you very much for cooking for us.	お世話様でした。*Osewa sama deshita.*
It was delicious.	とても、おいしかったです。 *Totemo, oishikatta desu.*

AT A YAKITORI RESTAURANT

Yakitori can be expensive or inexpensive, depending on where you go. You can even get yakitori at an open-front street stall, buying a few skewers on the run!

Do you have <u>lunch courses</u>?	ランチのコースが、ありますか。 *Ranchi no kōsu ga, arimasu ka.*
dinner courses	ディナーのコース　*dinā no kōsu*
assorted yakitori	焼き鳥の盛り合わせ　*yakitori no moriawase*
I'll have <u>chicken liver</u>, please.	レバを下さい。*Reba o kudasai.*
chicken wings	とりの手羽　*tori no teba*
chicken meat balls	つくね　*tsukune*
dark meat	しょにく　*shoniku*
duck liver	鴨レバ　*kamo reba*
ginko nuts	ぎんなん　*ginnan*

green pepper	ピーマン	*pīman*
hearts	ハツ	*hatsu*
Japanese green pepper	ししとう	*shishi tō*
leeks	長ねぎ	*naga negi*
loin of duck	鴨ロースト	*kamo rōsuto*
chicken and scallions	ねぎま	*negima*
tree mushrooms	しめじ	*shimeji*
white meat	ささ身	*sasami*

AT A JAPANESE COFFEE SHOP

kissaten/café	喫茶店／カフェ	*kissaten/kafe*

The kissaten is a coffee shop (sometimes referred to as a tea room) where you can get Western-style snacks and light food, Japanese-style light food, or both, depending on the place. A unique feature of most kissaten is the breakfast special, literally "morning service" in Japanese. This is popular with people rushing to work without breakfast. The kissaten are places where you can sit and drink your coffee or tea undisturbed as long as you like.

I'd like to sit at <u>a table</u>.	<u>テーブル</u>を、お願いします。*Tēburu o, onegai shimasu.*
the counter	カウンター　*kauntā*
Do you have a menu?	メニューがありますか。*Menyū ga arimasu ka.*
Do you have a breakfast special?	モーニング・サービスがありますか。*Mōningu sābisu ga arimasu ka.*
What do I get for the breakfast special?	モーニング・サービスには、何がついてきますか。*Mōningu sābisu niwa, nani ga tsuite kimasu ka.*

I'd like to order <u>a breakfast special</u>.	<u>モーニング・サービス</u>を、お願いします。	<u>Mōningu sābisu</u> o, onegai shimasu.
coffee	コーヒー	kōhī
hot coffee	ホット	hotto
iced coffee	アイスコーヒー	aisu kōhī
tea	紅茶	kōcha
tea with lemon	レモン・ティー	remon tī
tea with milk	ミルク・ティー	miruku tī
iced tea	アイス・ティー	aisu tī
cola	コーラ	kōra
Coca Cola	コカ・コーラ	Koka Kōra
Pepsi Cola	ペプシ・コーラ	Pepushi Kōra
ice cream	アイスクリーム	aisukurīmu
chocolate ice cream	チョコレート・アイスクリーム	chokorēto aisukurīmu
coffee ice cream	コーヒー・アイスクリーム	kōhī aisukurīmu
gelato	ジェラート	jerāto
green tea ice cream	抹茶アイスクリーム	matcha aisukurīmu
peach ice cream	ピーチ・アイスクリーム	pīchi aisukurīmu
strawberry ice cream	ストロベリー・アイスクリーム	sutoroberī aisukurīmu
vanilla ice cream	バニラ・アイスクリーム	banira aisukurīmu
sherbet	シャーベット	shābetto
lemon sherbet	レモン・シャーベット	remon shābetto
orange sherbet	オレンジ・シャーベット	orenji shābetto

raspberry sherbet	ラズベリー・シャーベット	*razuberī shābetto*
juice	ジュース	*jūsu*
orange juice	オレンジ・ジュース	*orenji jūsu*
grapefruit juice	グレープフルーツ・ジュース	*gurēpufurūtsu jūsu*
grape juice	グレープ・ジュース	*gurēpu jūsu*
tomato juice	トマト・ジュース	*tomato jūsu*
sandwich	サンドイッチ	*sandoitchi*
assorted sandwiches	ミックス・サンド	*mikkusu sando*
club sandwich	クラブ・サンド	*kurabu sando*
egg sandwich	エッグ・サンド	*eggu sando*
ham sandwich	ハム・サンド	*hamu sando*
ham and cheese sandwich	ハムとチーズのサンドイッチ	*hamu to chīzu no sandoitchi*
tuna sandwich	ツナ・サンド	*tsuna sando*

SOMETHING DIFFERENT

ryotei　　　料亭　　　*ryōtei*

The *ryotei* is a traditional Japanese restaurant in a building all its own, usually with a garden. You dine in private Japanese-style rooms, with servers at your table throughout the meal to assist you. Food is served in many small courses, on exquisite ceramics and lacquer. If requested, *geisha* may entertain. It's an elegant, extremely expensive way to dine. Many *ryotei* require an introduction from another customer before giving you a reservation. A good way to experience the *ryotei* is with a Japanese friend—or host!

WESTERN AND
INTERNATIONAL RESTAURANTS

There is good Western and other ethnic food in Japan with a full range of possibilities from elegant and expensive restaurants to simple and inexpensive ones. When an eating place is called a "restaurant" (reh-soo-toh-rahn), it means they serve food of foreign origin.

GENERAL INQUIRIES

Is there a restaurant nearby?	近くに、レストランがありますか。 *Chikaku ni, resutoran ga arimasu ka.*
Is there a restaurant that is <u>still</u> open?	まだ開いているレストランが、ありますか。 <u>*Mada*</u> *aiteiru resutoran ga, arimasu ka.*
already	もう *mō*
Is there a <u>McDonald's</u> around here?	この辺に、<u>マクドナルド</u>がありますか。 *Kono hen ni, <u>Makudonarudo</u> ga arimasu ka.*
Kentucky Fried Chicken	ケンタッキー　フライドチキン *Kentakkī Furaido Chikin*
Mr. Donut	ミスター・ドーナッツ　*Misutā Dōnattsu*
Baskin-Robbins	サーティーワン・アイスクリーム *Sātīwan Aisukurīmu*
Do you know <u>a good</u> restaurant?	<u>いい</u>レストランを、知っていますか。 <u>*Ii*</u> *resutoran o, shitte imasu ka.*
an inexpensive	安い *yasui*
a quiet	静かな *shizuka na*
the nearest	一番近くにある *ichi ban chikaku ni aru*
the best	一番いい *ichi ban ii*

Can you recommend <u>a nice</u> restaurant?	いいレストランを、教えて下さい。 *Ii resutoran o, oshiete kudasai.*	
small	小さい	*chiisai*
fancy	しゃれた	*shareta*
first class	トップクラスの	*toppu kurasu no*
I'd like to have <u>American</u> food.	<u>アメリカ</u>料理が、食べたいのですが。 *Amerika ryōri ga, tabetai no desu ga.*	
Chinese	中華	*Chūka*
French	フランス	*Furansu*
German	ドイツ	*Doitsu*
Indian	インド	*Indo*
Italian	イタリア	*Itaria*
Korean	韓国	*Kankoku*
Mexican	メキシコ	*Mekishiko*
Russian	ロシア	*Roshia*
Scandinavian	スカンジナビア	*Sukanjinabia*
Spanish	スペイン	*Supein*
Thai	タイ	*Tai*
How much would it be per person?	大体、一人当たりいくらかかりますか。 *Daitai, hitori atari ikura kakarimasu ka.*	
Do they take credit cards?	クレジット・カードが、使えますか。 *Kurejitto kādo ga, tsukaemasu ka.*	
Are they open for <u>lunch</u>?	<u>昼食</u>に、開いていますか。*Chūshoku ni, aite imasu ka.*	
dinner	夕食	*yūshoku*
breakfast	朝食	*chōshoku*
What are their hours?	営業時間は。*Eigyō jikan wa.*	
Do you have the telephone number?	そこの電話番号を、ご存じですか。 *Soko no denwa bangō o, gozonji desu ka.*	

MAKING RESERVATIONS

Do I need to make a reservation?	予約が、必要ですか。 *Yoyaku ga, hitsuyō desu ka.*
Do you take reservations?	予約を、受け付けますか。 *Yoyaku o, uketsukemasu ka.*
I'd like to make a reservation for <u>dinner tonight</u>.	<u>今晩のディナー</u>の予約をしたいのですが。 <u>*Konban no dīnā*</u> *no yoyaku o shitai no desu ga.*
lunch today	今日のランチ　*kyō no ranchi*
lunch tomorrow	あしたのランチ　*ashita no ranchi*
dinner tomorrow	あしたのディナー　*ashita no dīnā*
<u>Two people</u> at 12, please.	十二時に、<u>二人</u>お願いします。 *Jū ni ji ni, <u>futari</u> onegai shimasu.*
Three people	三人　*san nin*
Four people	四人　*yo nin*
Five people	五人　*go nin*
Six people	六人　*roku nin*
Seven people	七人　*nana nin*
Eight people	八人　*hachi nin*
Two people at <u>12:30</u>, please.	十二時半に、二人お願いします。 *<u>Jū ni ji han</u> ni, futari onegai shimasu.*
1:00	一時　*ichi ji*
1:30	一時半　*ichi ji han*
2:00	二時　*ni ji*
6:00	六時　*roku ji*
6:30	六時半　*roku ji han*
7:00	七時　*shichi ji*
7:30	七時半　*shichi ji han*
8:00	八時　*hachi ji*

| My name is _____. | 私の名前は、_____です。*Watakushi no namae wa, _____ desu.* |

ARRIVING

Good afternoon.	こんにちは。*Konnichiwa.*
Good evening.	今晩は。*Konbanwa.*
I have a reservation for 8 o'clock. My name is _____.	八時に、予約してあります。名前は、___です。*Hachi ji ni, yoyaku shite arimasu. Namae wa, _____ desu.*
I'd like a table for four.	四人ですが、テーブルがありますか。*Yonin desu ga, tēburu ga arimasu ka.*
We'd like to sit at the counter.	カウンターを、お願いします。*Kauntā o, onegai shimasu.*
Can we get a table now?	今すぐ、テーブルをもらえますか。*Ima sugu, tēburu o moraemasu ka.*
Do we have to wait?	待たなければなりませんか。*Matanakereba narimasen ka.*
How long do we have to wait?	どのくらい、待たなければなりませんか。*Dono kurai, matanakereba narimasen ka.*

AT THE TABLE

No drinks, thank you.	飲み物は、けっこうです。*Nomimono wa, kekkō desu.*
Give us a menu, please.	メニューを下さい。*Menyū o kudasai.*
We'd like to order drinks first.	始めに、飲み物をお願いします。*Hajime ni, nomimono o onegai shimasu.*

QUESTIONS

| What's the specialty of the house? | ここの自慢料理は、何ですか。*Koko no jiman ryōri wa, nan desu ka.* |

Is there a special today?	今日のスペシャルが、ありますか。 *Kyō no supesharu ga, arimasu ka.*
Do you have a fixed-price <u>lunch</u>?	<u>ランチ</u>の定食が、ありますか。 <u>*Ranchi*</u> *no teishoku ga, arimasu ka.*
dinner	ディナー *dinā*
What's good today?	今日は、何がおいしいですか。*Kyō wa, nani ga oishii desu ka.*
What would you recommend?	おすすめ品は、何ですか。*Osusume hin wa, nan desu ka.*
Can we order now?	今、注文できますか。*Ima, chūmon dekimasu ka.*
We'll take some more time before ordering.	注文には、もう少し時間がいります。 *Chūmon niwa, mō sukoshi jikan ga irimasu.*
Could you bring some bread and butter?	パンとバターを、お願いします。 *Pan to batā o, onegai shimasu.*
Water, please.	水を、下さい。*Mizu o, kudasai.*

ORDERING

I'd like _____.	_____を下さい。_____ *o kudasai.*
I'll have _____.	_____にします。_____ *ni shimasu.*
I don't think I want _____.	_____は、けっこうです。_____ *wa, kekkō desu.*
Do you have _____?	_____がありますか。_____ *ga arimasu ka.*
I'd like to have some _____ first.	始めに、_____をお願いします。 *Hajime ni, _____ o onegai shimasu.*
I'd like to have _____, _____, and _____.	_____と、_____と、_____を下さい。 _____ *to,* _____ *to,* _____ *o kudasai.*
I'd like to have <u>two orders</u> of _____.	_____を、<u>二人前</u>下さい。_____ *o,* <u>*ni nin mae*</u> *kudasai.*

three orders	三人前	*san nin mae*
four orders	四人前	*yo nin mae*

Bring me _____ later.　_____は、後でお願いします。_____ *wa, ato de onegai shimasu.*

May I change A to B?　AをBに、替えられますか。*A o B ni, kaeraremasu ka.*

I like my steak <u>rare</u>.　ステーキは、<u>レア</u>をお願いします。 *Sutēki wa, <u>rea</u> o onegai shimasu.*

medium rare	ミディアム・レア	*midiamu rea*
medium	ミディアム	*midiamu*
well done	ウェル・ダーン	*weru dān*

I'd like it cooked without <u>salt</u>.　<u>塩</u>を使わないで、料理して下さい。 *<u>Shio</u> o tsukawanai de, ryōri shite kudasai.*

butter or oil	バターや油	*batā ya abura*
MSG	化学調味料	*kagaku chōmi ryō*

Does it take long?　時間が、かかりますか。*Jikan ga, kakarimasu ka.*

DRINKS

ALCOHOLIC

Do you have Japanese <u>beer</u>?　日本の<u>ビール</u>がありますか。 *Nihon no <u>bīru</u> ga arimasu ka.*

wine	ワイン	*wain*
whiskey	ウイスキー	*uisukī*

I want it straight, please.　ストレートで下さい。*Sutorēto de kudasai.*

Make it double, please.　ダブルで下さい。*Daburu de kudasai.*

With <u>lemon</u>, please.	<u>レモン</u>を入れて下さい。	<u>Remon</u> o irete kudasai.
lemon peel	レモンの皮	remon no kawa
an olive	オリーブ	orību
onion	オニオン	onion
aperitif	アペリチフ	aperichifu
bourbon	バーボン	bābon
bourbon and soda	バーボンの ハイボール	bābon no haibōru
bourbon and water	バーボンの 水割り	bābon no mizuwari
bourbon on the rocks	バーボンの オン・ザ・ロック	bābon no on za rokku
straight bourbon	バーボンの ストレート	bābon no sutorēto
beer	ビール	bīru
dark beer	黒ビール	kuro bīru
draft beer	生ビール	nama bīru
light beer	ライト・ビール	raito bīru
Bloody Mary	ブラディー・ マリー	Buradī Marī
brandy	ブランディー	burandī
Campari	カンパリ	Kanpari
Campari and soda	カンパリ・ソーダ	Kanpari sōda
champagne	シャンペン	shanpen
cognac	コニャック	konyakku
Dubonnet	デュボネ	Dubone
gin	ジン	jin
gin and tonic	ジン・トニック	jin tonikku
gin fizz	ジン・フィーズ	jin fīzu

gin on the rocks	ジンの オン・ザ・ロック	*jin no on za rokku*
mai tai	マイタイ	*maitai*
manhattan	マンハッタン	*manhattan*
margarita	マーガリータ	*māgarīta*
martini	マティーニ	*matīni*
mimosa	ミモザ	*mimoza*
port	ポート・ワイン	*pōto wain*
prosecco	プロセッコ	*purosekko*
rum	ラム酒	*ramu shu*
rum and coke	ラム・コーク	*ramu kōku*
sangria	サングリア	*sanguria*
screwdriver	スクリュー・ ドライバー	*sukuryū doraibā*
scotch	スコッチ	*sukotchi*
scotch and soda	スコッチの ハイボール	*sukotchi no haibōru*
scotch and water	スコッチの 水割り	*sukotchi no mizuwari*
scotch on the rocks	スコッチの オン・ザ・ロック	*sukotchi no on za rokku*
straight scotch	スコッチの ストレート	*sukotchi no sutorēto*
sherry	シェリー	*sherī*
vermouth	ベルモット	*berumotto*
vodka	ウォッカ	*wokka*
vodka and tonic	ウォッカ・ トニック	*wokka tonikku*
vodka on the rocks	ウォッカの オン・ザ・ロック	*wokka no on za rokku*

NONALCOHOLIC

Is the juice fresh?	ジュースは、新鮮なジュースですか。	*Jūsu wa, shinsen na jūsu desu ka.*
Do you have <u>diet soda</u>?	<u>ダイエットの飲み物</u>が、ありますか。	<u>*Daietto no nomimono*</u> *ga, arimasu ka.*
club soda	炭酸／プレイン・ソーダ	*tansan/purein sōda*
Coca-Cola	コカコーラ	*Koka kōra*
coffee	コーヒー	*kōhī*
American coffee (less strong)	アメリカン・コーヒー	*Amerikan kōhī*
espresso	エスプレッソ	*esupuresso*
iced coffee	アイス・コーヒー	*aisu kōhī*
Diet Coke	ダイエット・コカコーラ	*Daietto Koka Kōra*
Diet Pepsi	ダイエット・ペプシ	*Daietto Pepushi*
Diet 7-up	ダイエット・セブンアップ	*Daietto Sebun-appu*
fruit juice	フルーツ・ジュース	*furūtsu jūsu*
apple juice	リンゴジュース／アップル・ジュース	*ringo jūsu/ appuru jūsu*
grape juice	グレープ・ジュース	*gurēpu jūsu*
grapefruit juice	グレープフルーツ・ジュース	*gurēpufurūtsu jūsu*
orange juice	オレンジ・ジュース	*orenji jūsu*
pineapple juice	パイナップル・ジュース	*painappuru jūsu*

tomato juice	トマト・ジュース	*tomato jūsu*
ginger ale	ジンジャエール	*jinjaēru*
lemonade	レモネード	*remonēdo*
milk	ミルク	*miruku*
mineral water	ミネラル・ウォーター	*mineraru wōtā*
sparkling mineral water	炭酸入りのミネラルウォーター	*tansan iri no mineraru wōtā*
Pepsi Cola	ペプシコーラ	*Pepushi kōra*
7-up	セブンアップ	*Sebun-appu*
Sprite	スプライト	*Supuraito*
tea	紅茶	*kōcha*
tea with lemon	レモン・ティー	*remon tī*
tea with milk	ミルク・ティー	*miruku tī*
iced tea	アイス・ティー	*aisu tī*
tonic water	トニック・ウォーター	*tonikku wōtā*
No ice, please.	氷無しでお願いします。	*Kōri nashi de onegai shimasu.*

ORDERING WINE

I'd like to see your wine list, please.
ワイン・リストを、見せて下さい。
Wain risuto o, misete kudasai.

Do you have <u>French</u> wine?
<u>フランス</u>のワインが、ありますか。
<u>Furansu</u> no wain ga, arimasu ka.

American　アメリカ　*Amerika*

German　ドイツ　*Doitsu*

Italian　イタリア　*Itaria*

Japanese　日本　*Nihon*

We'll have <u>white wine</u>.	<u>ホワイト・ワイン</u>にします。 *<u>Howaito wain</u> ni shimasu.*
red wine	レッド・ワイン　*reddo wain*
rosé	ロゼー　*rozē*
Do you have anything dry?	ドライなワインは、ありますか。 *Dorai na wain wa, arimasu ka.*
Is it dry?	それは、ドライですか。*Sore wa, dorai desu ka.*
Do you have a house wine?	ハウス・ワインが、ありますか。 *Hausu wain ga, arimasu ka.*
Do you recommend anything in particular?	何か、特別のおすすめ品がありますか。 *Nanika, tokubetsu no osusume hin ga arimasu ka.*
Where is it from?	それは、どこのですか。*Sore wa, doko no desu ka.*
What's the name of it?	名前は、何ですか。*Namae wa, nan desu ka.*
What's the vintage?	何年物ですか。*Nan nen mono desu ka.*
How much is a bottle of ＿＿＿?	＿＿＿は、一本いくらですか。＿＿＿ *wa, ippon ikura desu ka.*
I'll try this.	これを、試してみます。*Kore o, tameshite mimasu.*
Can we order by the glass?	グラスで、注文できますか。*Gurasu de, chūmon dekimasu ka.*
I'd like <u>a glass of white wine</u>.	<u>ホワイト・ワイン</u>を一杯下さい。 *<u>Howaito wain</u> o ippai kudasai.*
a glass of red wine	レッド・ワインを一杯　*reddo wain o ippai*
Bring me <u>a bottle</u>, please.	<u>一本</u>、お願いします。*<u>Ippon</u>, onegai shimasu.*
a half bottle	ハーフ・ボトル　*hāfu botoru*

FOOD

APPETIZERS

anchovies	アンチョビ	*anchobi*
antipasto	アンティパスト	*antipasuto*
asparagus	アスパラガス	*asuparagas*
caviar	キャビア	*kyabia*
celery and olives	セロリとオリーブ	*serori to orību*
cheese	チーズ	*chīzu*
clams on the half-shell	生はまぐり	*nama hamaguri*
crabmeat	かに	*kani*
fresh fruit cup	新鮮な果物の フルーツ・カップ	*shinsen na kudamono no furūtsu kappu*
ham	ハム	*hamu*
herring (pickled)	酢づけのにしん	*suzuke no nishin*
lobster	ロブスター	*robusutā*
mushrooms	マッシュルーム／ シャンピニオン	*masshurūmu/ shanpinion*
melon	メロン	*meron*
oysters on the half-shell	生がき	*nama gaki*
pate	パテ	*pate*
prosciutto	生ハム	*nama hamu*
prosciutto and melon	生ハムとメロン	*nama hamu to meron*
salami	サラミ・ ソーセージ	*sarami sōsēji*
sardines	サーディン	*sādin*

sausage	ソーセージ	*sōsēji*
shrimp cocktail	海老のカクテル	*ebi no kakuteru*
smoked salmon	スモークド・サーモン	*sumōkudo sāmon*
snails	エスカルゴ	*esukarugo*

SOUP

borscht	ボルシチ	*borushichi*
chicken soup	チキン・スープ	*chikin sūpu*
clam chowder	クラム・チャウダー	*kuramu chaudā*
consomme	コンソメ	*konsome*
corn soup	コーン・スープ	*kōn sūpu*
cream soup	クリーム・スープ	*kurīmu sūpu*
fish soup	フィッシュ・スープ	*fisshu sūpu*
garlic soup	ガーリック・スープ	*gārikku sūpu*
noodle soup	ヌードル・スープ	*nūdoru sūpu*
onion soup	オニオン・スープ	*onion sūpu*
tomato soup	トマト・スープ	*tomato sūpu*
vegetable soup	ベジタブル・スープ	*bejitaburu sūpu*
vichyssoise	ビシソア	*bishisoa*

SALAD AND DRESSING

Caesar salad	シーザー・サラダ	*Shīzā sarada*
green salad	グリーン・サラダ	*gurīn sarada*
tomato salad	トマト・サラダ	*tomato sarada*

tossed salad	ミックス・サラダ	*mikkusu sarada*
blue cheese dressing	ブルー・チーズの ドレッシング	*burū chīzu no doresshingu*
French dressing	フレンチ・ ドレッシング	*Furenchi doresshingu*
house dressing	ハウス・ ドレッシング	*hausu doresshingu*
Italian dressing	イタリアン・ ドレッシング	*Itarian doresshingu*
Japanese-style dressing	和風 ドレッシング	*wafū doresshingu*
oil and vinegar	オイルと ビネガー	*oiru to binegā*

MAIN COURSE DISHES

For the main course, you can choose some of the best
seafood, fowl, and meat you've ever tasted. Japan has fish and
shellfish in abundance. You've probably heard of the famous
beer-fed Kobe beef cattle. The Japanese prize their beef highly;
some restaurants offer a choice of beef from different parts
of the country. Here are some cooking instructions for your
entrees.

I'd like it <u>baked</u>.	それは、<u>天火で焼いて</u>下さい。*Sore wa, <u>tenpi de yaite</u> kudasai.*
boiled	ゆでて　*yudete*
broiled	直火で焼いて　*jikabi de yaite*
fried	油で揚げて　*abura de agete*
grilled	焼き網で焼いて　*yakiami de yaite*
roasted	ローストにして　*rōsuto ni shite*
sauteed	ソテーにして　*sotē ni shite*
rare	レアにして　*rea ni shite*

medium rare	ミディアム・レアにして *midiamu rea ni shite*	
medium	ミディアムにして	*midiamu ni shite*
well done	ウェル・ダーンにして	*weru dān ni shite*
Do you have any vegetarian dishes?	ベジタリアンのための料理がありますか。*Bejitarian no tame no ryōri ga arimasu ka.*	

FISH AND SHELLFISH

abalone	あわび	*awabi*
clams	はまぐり	*hamaguri*
cod	たら	*tara*
crab	かに	*kani*
eel	うなぎ	*unagi*
flounder	平目	*hirame*
halibut	おひょう	*ohyō*
herring	にしん	*nishin*
lobster	ロブスター／ 伊勢えび	*robusutā/Ise ebi*
mackerel	さば	*saba*
mussels	ムール貝	*mūru gai*
octopus	たこ	*tako*
oysters	かき	*kaki*
porgy	鯛	*tai*
prawns	車えび	*kuruma ebi*
rainbow trout	虹ます	*niji masu*
salmon	さけ	*sake*
sardines	いわし	*iwashi*
scallops	帆立て	*hotate*

sea bass	すずき	*suzuki*
shrimp	えび	*ebi*
smelts	きす	*kisu*
sole	したびらめ	*shitabirame*
Spanish mackerel	さわら	*sawara*
squid	いか	*ika*
swordfish	まかじき	*makajiki*
trout	ます	*masu*
tuna	まぐろ	*maguro*
yellowtail	はまち／ぶり	*hamachi/buri*

FOWL

chicken	とり／にわとり	*tori/niwatori*
capon	おんどり	*ondori*
chicken breast (boneless)	とりのささ身	*tori no sasami*
chicken thigh	とりのもも肉	*tori no momo niku*
chicken wing	とりの手羽	*tori no teba*
ground chicken	とりの挽き肉	*tori no hikiniku*
duck	あひる	*ahiru*
mallard	まがも	*magamo*
partridge	山うずら	*yama uzura*
pheasant	きじ	*kiji*
squab	ひなばと	*hinabato*
quail	うずら	*uzura*
rabbit	うさぎ	*usagi*
turkey	七面鳥	*shichimenchō*

MEAT

bacon	ベーコン	*bēkon*
beef	ビーフ／牛肉	*bīfu/gyū niku*
beefsteak	ビフテキ	*bifuteki*
chateaubriand	シャトー・ブリアン	*shatō burian*
cold cuts	冷肉とチーズの盛り合わせ	*reiniku to chīzu no moriawase*
corned beef	コーン・ビーフ	*kōn bīfu*
filet	ヒレ肉	*hire niku*
filet mignon	ヒレミニオン	*hireminion*
ground beef	牛の挽き肉	*gyū no hikiniku*
ground pork	豚の挽き肉	*buta no hikiniku*
ham	ハム	*hamu*
hamburger steak	ハンバーガー・ステーキ	*hanbāgā sutēki*
kidneys	腎臓	*jinzō*
lamb	ラム／子羊	*ramu/ko hitsuji*
lamb chop	ラム・チョップ	*ramu choppu*
leg of lamb	子羊の足	*kohitsuji no ashi*
liver	レバー／肝臓	*rebā/kanzō*
meatballs	ミート・ボール	*mīto bōru*
minute steak	ミニッツ・ステーキ	*minittsu sutēki*
mutton	羊肉	*yō niku*
ox tail	オックス・テール	*okkusu tēru*
pepper steak	ペパー・ステーキ	*pepā sutēki*
pork	ポーク／豚肉	*pōku/buta niku*

pork chop	ポーク・チョップ	*pōku choppu*
roast beef	ロースト・ビーフ	*rōsuto bīfu*
roast pork	ロースト・ポーク	*rōsuto pōku*
sausage	ソーセージ	*sōsēji*
sirloin	サーロイン／ロース	*sāroin/rōsu*
steak	ステーキ	*sutēki*
stew meat	シチュー肉	*shichū niku*
T-bone steak	ティーボン・ステーキ	*tībon sutēki*
tenderloin	テンダロイン	*tendaroin*
tongue	タン	*tan*
tournedos	トルヌードー	*torunūdō*
veal	子牛	*ko ushi*

VEGETABLES

asparagus	アスパラガス	*asuparagasu*
avocado	アボカド	*abokado*
basil	バジリコ	*bajiriko*
broccoli	ブロッコリ	*burokkori*
brussels sprouts	芽キャベツ	*me kyabetsu*
cabbage	キャベツ	*kyabetsu*
carrot	人参	*ninjin*
cauliflower	カリフラワー	*karifurawā*
celery	セロリ	*serori*
corn	コーン／とうもろこし	*kōn/tōmorokoshi*
cucumber	きゅうり	*kyūri*
eggplant	なす	*nasu*

endive	エンダイブ	*endaibu*
garlic	ガーリック／ にんにく	*gārikku/ninniku*
green pepper	ピーマン	*pīman*
leek	長ねぎ	*naganegi*
lettuce	レタス	*retasu*
olive	オリーブ	*orību*
onion	玉ねぎ／オニオン	*tamanegi/onion*
parsley	パセリ	*paseri*
potato	ポテト／ じゃがいも	*poteto/jagaimo*
radish	ラディッシュ／ 二十日大根	*radisshu/ hatsuka daikon*
red pepper	赤いピーマン	*akai pīman*
spring onion	細ねぎ	*hosonegi*
spinach	ほうれん草	*hōrensō*
string beans	さやいんげん	*sayaingen*
sweet potato	さつまいも	*satsumaimo*
tomato	トマト	*tomato*
turnip	かぶ	*kabu*
watercress	クレソン	*kureson*
zucchini	ズッキーニ	*zukkīni*

BREAD

Not all restaurants provide bread as a matter of course. You may have to ask for it. You may be asked if you want bread or rice. It's an either-or question, as if the two are so similar you wouldn't want both. And if you're asked, you <u>will</u> get one or the other, not both!

We'd like some <u>bread</u>, please.	<u>パン</u>を、お願いします。	<u>Pan</u> o, onegai shimasu.
bagels	ベーゲル	bēgeru
croissant	クロワッサン	kurowassan
French bread	フランス・パン	Furansu pan
garlic toast	ガーリック・トースト	gārikku tōsuto
Italian bread	イタリア・パン	Itaria pan
rolls	ロール・パン	rōru pan
rye	ライ・ブレッド／黒パン	rai bureddo/ kuro pan
toast	トースト	tōsuto
white bread	白パン	shiro pan

PASTA, RICE, AND POTATOES

You're going to see and hear different words for rice in Japan. In restaurants where Western food is served, rice is *raisu*, served on a plate. In Japanese-style meals, rice is *gohan*, served in a bowl. It is the same rice!

baked potato	ベークド・ポテト	bēkudo poteto
boiled potato	ゆでたじゃがいも	yudeta jagaimo
French fries	フレンチ・フライ	Furenchi furai
macaroni	マカロニ	makaroni
mashed potatoes	マッシュ・ポテト	masshu poteto
rice	ライス	raisu
pasta	パスタ	pasuta
spaghetti	スパゲッティー	supagettī

ACCOMPANIMENTS

butter	バター	*batā*
cream	クリーム	*kurīmu*
honey	はちみつ	*hachimitsu*
horseradish	ホースラデッシュ／西洋わさび	*hōsu raddishu/ seiyō wasabi*
jam	ジャム	*jamu*
ketchup	ケチャップ	*kechappu*
lemon	レモン	*remon*
lime	ライム／ゆず	*raimu/yuzu*
margarine	マーガリン	*māgarin*
marmalade	マーマレード	*māmarēdo*
mayonnaise	マヨネーズ	*mayonēzu*
milk	ミルク／牛乳	*miruku/gyūnyū*
mustard	マスタード／からし	*masutādo/karashi*
oil	オイル	*oiru*
olive oil	オリーブ・オイル	*orību oiru*
paprika	パプリカ	*papurika*
pepper	こしょう	*koshō*
salt	(お) 塩	*(o)shio*
soy sauce	(お) しょうゆ	*(o)shōyu*
sugar	(お) 砂糖	*(o)satō*
syrup	シロップ	*shiroppu*
Tabasco	タバスコ	*Tabasuko*
vinegar	(お) 酢	*(o)su*
Worcestershire sauce	ウースター・ソース	*ūsutā sōsu*

CHEESE

Although cheese is relatively new to the Japanese diet, excellent cheeses, both domestic and imported, are readily available. Not all Japanese are familiar with the names of different kinds of cheese. Ask for what you want—it may be there even if it isn't known by name. Asking to see a cheese tray usually gets you the whole assortment.

What kind of cheese do you have?	チーズは、どんな種類がありますか。	*Chīzu wa, donna shurui ga arimasu ka.*
Do you have a cheese tray?	チーズを盛った、お盆がありますか。	*Chīzu o motta, obon ga arimasu ka.*
Can I see them (the cheeses)?	チーズを、見せてもらえますか。	*Chīzu o, misete moraemasu ka.*
Give me some <u>blue cheese</u>, please.	<u>ブルー・チーズ</u>を下さい。	<u>*Burū chīzu*</u> *o kudasai.*
Brie	ブリー	*Burī*
Camembert	カマンベール	*Kamanbēru*
Cheddar cheese	チェダー	*Chedā*
Edam cheese	エダム	*Edamu*
Swiss cheese	スイス・チーズ	*Suisu chīzu*
Please bring some crackers, too.	クラッカーも、お願いします。	*Kurakkā mo, onegai shimasu.*

FRUIT

Excellent fresh fruit is available throughout Japan, though often expensive. Check the price before ordering.

apple	りんご	*ringo*
banana	バナナ	*banana*
blueberries	ブルーベリー	*burūberī*
cherries	さくらんぼ／チェリー	*sakuranbo/cherī*
fig	いちじく	*ichijiku*

grapes	ぶどう	*budō*
grapefruit	グレープフルーツ	*gurēpufurūtsu*
kiwi	キーウィー	*kīwī*
loquat	びわ	*biwa*
mango	マンゴー	*mangō*
melon	メロン	*meron*
nectarine	ネクタリン	*nekutarin*
orange	オレンジ	*orenji*
papaya	パパイヤ	*papaiya*
peach	桃	*momo*
pear	洋なし	*yō nashi*
Japanese pear	なし	*nashi*
persimmon	柿	*kaki*
pineapple	パイナップル	*painappuru*
plum	プラム／すもも	*puramu/sumomo*
strawberries	いちご	*ichigo*
tangerine	みかん	*mikan*
watermelon	西瓜	*suika*

NUTS

almonds	アーモンド	*āmondo*
Brazil nuts	ブラジル・ナッツ	*Burajiru nattsu*
cashews	カシュー・ナッツ	*kashū nattsu*
chestnuts	栗	*kuri*
hazelnuts	ヘーゼル・ナッツ	*hēzeru nattsu*
Macadamia nuts	マカデミア・ナッツ	*Makademia nattsu*
peanuts	ピーナッツ	*pīnattsu*

| pecans | ペカン | *pekan* |
| walnuts | くるみ | *kurumi* |

DESSERTS

cake	ケーキ	*kēki*
cheesecake	チーズ・ケーキ	*chīzu kēki*
chocolate cake	チョコレート・ケーキ	*chokorēto kēki*
layer cake	レヤ・ケーキ	*reya kēki*
strawberry shortcake	いちごの ショート・ケーキ	*ichigo no shōto kēki*
cookies	クッキー	*kukkī*
custard	カスタード	*kasutādo*
fruit compote/cup	フルーツ・カップ	*furūtsu kappu*
ice cream	アイスクリーム	*aisukurīmu*
coffee ice cream	コーヒー・アイスクリーム	*kōhī aisukurīmu*
chocolate ice cream	チョコレート・アイスクリーム	*chokorēto aisukurīmu*
chocolate sundae	チョコレート・サンデー	*chokorēto sandē*
ginger ice cream	ジンジャー・アイスクリーム	*jinjā aisukurīmu*
green tea ice cream	抹茶 アイスクリーム	*matcha aisukurīmu*
hot fudge sundae	ホットファッジ・サンデー	*hotto fajji sandē*
peach melba	ピーチ・メルバ	*pīchi meruba*
strawberry sundae	ストロベリー・サンデー	*sutoroberī sandē*
vanilla ice cream	バニラ・アイスクリーム	*banira aisukurīmu*

mousse	ムース	*mūsu*
chocolate mousse	チョコレート・ムース	*chokorēto mūsu*
pastry	ペストリー	*pesutorī*
chestnut tart	チェスナッツ・タート	*chesunattsu tāto*
cream puff	シュークリーム	*shūkurīmu*
eclair	エクレア	*ekurea*
fruit tart	フルーツ・タート	*furūtsu tāto*
petit four	ペティ・フォー／小型ケーキ	*peti fō/kogata kēki*
pie	パイ	*pai*
apple pie	アップル・パイ	*appuru pai*
blueberry pie	ブルーベリー・パイ	*burūberī pai*
lemon meringue pie	レモンメレンゲ・パイ	*remon merenge pai*
pudding	プリン	*purin*
sherbet	シャーベット	*shābetto*
lemon sherbet	レモン・シャーベット	*remon shābetto*
orange sherbet	オレンジ・シャーベット	*orenji shābetto*
soufflé	スフレ	*sufure*
chocolate soufflé	チョコレート・スフレ	*chokorēto sufure*
grapefruit soufflé	グレープフルーツ・スフレ	*gurēpufurūtsu sufure*

ADDITIONAL REQUESTS

Waiter/waitress!	ちょっと、すみませんが。 *Chotto, sumimasen ga.*
Could you bring me <u>a knife</u>, please?	<u>ナイフ</u>を、お願いします。 <u>*Naifu*</u> *o, onegai shimasu.*
a fork	フォーク *fōku*
a spoon	スプーン *supūn*
a teaspoon	小さじ *kosaji*
a tablespoon	大さじ *ōsaji*
a glass	コップ *koppu*
a cup	コーヒー茶碗 *kōhī jawan*
a saucer	受け皿 *ukezara*
a plate	お皿 *osara*
a bowl	ボール *bōru*
a napkin	ナプキン *napukin*
some toothpicks	楊枝 *yōji*
Please bring me some more <u>water</u>.	<u>水</u>を、もう少し下さい。 <u>*Mizu*</u> *o, mō sukoshi kudasai.*
bread	パン *pan*
butter	バター *batā*
rice	ライス *raisu*
wine	ワイン *wain*
Please bring me <u>another bottle of wine</u>.	<u>ワインをもう一本</u>、お願いします。 <u>*Wain o mō ippon*</u>, *onegai shimasu.*
another glass of wine	ワインをもう一杯 *wain o mō ippai*
another order of this	これをもう一人前 *kore o mō ichinin mae*
Show me the menu again, please.	メニューを、もう一度見せて下さい。 *Menyū o, mō ichido misete kudasai.*

COMPLAINTS

It's not what I ordered.	これは、注文したのと違います。 *Kore wa, chūmon shita no to chigaimasu.*
The meat is too rare.	肉が、まだ生です。 *Niku ga, mada nama desu.*
The meat is too well done.	肉が、焼け過ぎです。 *Niku ga, yakesugi desu.*
This is undercooked.	これはまだ、料理が足りません。 *Kore wa mada, ryōri ga tarimasen.*
This is overcooked.	これは、料理のし過ぎです。 *Kore wa, ryōri no shisugi desu.*
This isn't <u>hot</u>.	これは、<u>熱く</u>ありません。 *Kore wa, atsuku arimasen.*
cold	冷たく *tsumetaku*
fresh	新鮮では *shinsen dewa*
Would you get the manager, please?	マネージャーを、呼んで下さい。 *Manējā o, yonde kudasai.*

THE CHECK

Check, please.	お会計／お勘定を、お願いします。 *Okaikei/okanjō o, onegai shimasu.*
Separate checks, please.	会計は、別々にお願いします。 *Kaikei wa, betsubetsu ni onegai shimasu.*
Do you take <u>credit cards</u>?	<u>クレジット・カード</u>が、使えますか。 *Kurejitto kādo ga, tsukaemasu ka.*
traveler's checks	トラベラーズ・チェック *toraberāzu chekku*
Which credit cards do you take?	どのクレジット・カードが、使えますか。 *Dono kurejitto kādo ga, tsukaemasu ka.*

Are the tax and service charge included?	税金とサービス料が、入っていますか。	*Zeikin to sābisu ryō ga, haitte imasu ka.*
Is this correct?	これは、あっていますか。	*Kore wa, atte imasu ka.*
I don't think the bill is right.	会計に、間違いがあるみたいですが。	*Kaikei ni, machigai ga aru mitai desu ga.*
What are these charges for?	この代金は、何のためですか。	*Kono daikin wa, nan no tame desu ka.*
I didn't order this.	これは、注文しませんでした。	*Kore wa, chūmon shimasen deshita.*
May I have a receipt, please?	レシートを、お願いします。	*Reshīto o, onegai shimasu.*

LIGHT FOOD AND SNACKS

biscuits	ビスケット	*bisuketto*
cake	ケーキ	*kēki*
candy	キャンディー	*kyandī*
cheese	チーズ	*chīzu*
cocoa	ココア	*kokoa*
coffee	コーヒー	*kōhī*
Coke	コーク	*kōku*
cookies	クッキー	*kukkī*
crackers	クラッカー	*kurakkā*
French toast	フレンチ・トースト	*Furenchi tōsuto*
French fries	フレンチ・フライ	*Furenchi furai*
fried eggs	目玉焼き	*medama yaki*
fruit	果物	*kudamono*

ham	ハム	*hamu*
hamburger	ハンバーガー	*hanbāgā*
hard boiled eggs	ゆで卵	*yude tamago*
hot dog	ホットドッグ	*hotto doggu*
ice cream	アイスクリーム	*aisukurīmu*
omelet	オムレツ	*omuretsu*
potato chips	ポテトチップ	*poteto chippu*
sandwich	サンドイッチ	*sandoitchi*
toast	トースト	*tōsuto*
waffles	ワッフル	*waffuru*

DIETARY CONCERNS

diet	ダイエット	*daietto*
no sugar	無糖	*mutō*
low sugar	低糖	*teitō*
reduced sugar	減糖	*gentō*
no sodium	無塩	*muen*
low sodium	低塩	*teien*
reduced sodium	減塩	*gen-en*
no fat	無脂肪	*mushibō*
low fat	低脂肪	*teishibō*
skim	スキム	*sukimu*
zero calorie	ゼロカロリー	*zero karorī*
low calorie	ローカロリー	*rō karorī*
no artificial coloring	無着色	*muchakushoku*
organic (food)	有機（食品）	*yūki (shokuhin)*
natural (food)	自然（食品）	*shizen (shokuhin)*

no chemicals	無農薬	*munōyaku*
high fiber	高繊維質	*kō sen-ishitsu*
decaffeinated	デカフェ	*dekafe*
artificial sweetener	人工甘味料	*jinkō kanmiryō*

I'd like one with <u>low sugar</u>. <u>低糖</u>のが欲しいです。*<u>Teitō</u> no ga hoshii desu.*

zero calories	ゼロカロリー	*zero karorī*

I'm looking for one with <u>no sodium</u>. <u>無塩</u>の を探しています。*<u>Muen</u> no o sagashite imasu.*

no chemicals	無農薬	*munōyaku*

Do you have one with <u>low fat</u>? <u>無脂肪</u>のはありますか。*Mushibō no ga arimasu ka.*

reduced sodium	減塩	*gen-en*

Do you have a sugar substitute? 人工甘味料がありますか。*Jinkō kanmiryō ga arimasu ka.*

I'm a <u>vegetarian</u>. 私は<u>ベジタリアン</u>です。*Watakushi wa <u>bejitarian</u> desu.*

vegan ビーガン（純菜食主義者） *bīgan (jun saishoku shugi sha)*

I'm allergic to <u>nuts</u>. <u>ナッツ</u>にアレルギーです。*<u>Nattsu</u> ni arerugī desu.*

eggs	卵	*tamago*
wheat	小麦	*komugi*

I can't eat <u>shellfish</u>. <u>エビ</u>や<u>カニ</u>や<u>貝類</u>が食べられません。*Ebi ya kani ya kairui ga taberaremasen.*

chocolate	チョコレート	*chokorēto*
grapefruit	グレープフルーツ	*gurēpufurūtsu*

MEETING PEOPLE

As you travel around seeing the sights, you'll have many opportunities to meet Japanese people. Although Japanese generally prefer formal introductions, sightseeing does provide various situations where you can strike up a casual conversation. You may have questions about the places you're visiting, and Japanese are by nature hospitable; most would try to assist you. This section will help you get the conversation started—and to continue it if it seems appropriate! You can use these phrases with local Japanese people, and with those from out of town, too. Japanese enjoy sightseeing; you'll probably meet a lot of Japanese tourists. For more information on Japanese customs in social situations, see page 22, The Land and the People.

CONVERSATION STARTERS:
WITH LOCAL PEOPLE

Do you live <u>here</u>?	<u>ここに</u>、お住まいですか。	<u>Koko ni</u>, osumai desu ka.
in Tokyo	東京に	Tōkyō ni
in Osaka	大阪に	Ōsaka ni
in Kyoto	京都に	Kyōto ni
I've always wanted to come here.	ここに来たいと、いつも思っていました。	Koko ni kitai to, itsumo omotte imashita.
It's a wonderful place.	素晴らしい所ですねえ。	Subarashii tokoro desu nē.
I've really been enjoying it here.	ここで、何もかも楽しんでいます。	Koko de, nanimo ka mo tanoshinde imasu.
I've been to _____, _____, and _____.	今まで、_____と、_____と、_____へ行きました。	Ima made, _____ to, _____ to, _____ e ikimashita.

I'm planning to go to _____, _____, and _____.	これから、_____と、_____と、_____ へ行く予定です。*Kore kara, _____ to, _____ to, _____ e iku yotei desu.*
Is there anything not on my itinerary that you would recommend?	私の旅程以外に、どこか行くべき所 がありますか。*Watakushi no ryotei igai ni, dokoka iku beki tokoro ga arimasu ka.*
Could you explain a little about _____?	_____ について、少し説明してもら えますか。*_____ ni tsuite, sukoshi setsumei shite moraemasu ka.*
Would you recommend a nice place to eat?	素晴らしい食事どころを、教えても らえますか。*Subarashii shokuji dokoro o, oshiete moraemasu ka.*
Where's a good place for souvenir shopping?	おみやげを買うには、どこがいいで しょうか。*Omiyage o kau niwa, doko ga ii deshō ka.*

CONVERSATION STARTERS: WITH OTHER TRAVELERS

Do you live here? (casual)	ここに、住んでいますか。*Koko ni, sunde imasu ka.*
Do you live here? (polite)	ここに、お住まいですか。*Koko ni, osumai desu ka.*
Are you here for sightseeing, or on business?	ここは観光ですか、それともお仕事 ですか。*Koko wa kankō desu ka, soretomo oshigoto desu ka.*
When did you come here? (casual)	ここへは、いつ来ましたか。*Koko e wa, itsu kimashita ka.*
When did you come here? (polite)	ここへは、いついらっしゃいましたか。 *Koko e wa, itsu irasshaimashita ka.*
How do you like it here?	ここは、気に入っていますか。*Koko wa, ki ni itte imasu ka.*

What have you seen here?	今までに、何を見ましたか。*Ima made ni, nani o mimashita ka.*
I've been to _____, _____, and _____.	私は、_____と、_____と、_____を見ました。*Watakushi wa, _____ to, _____ to, _____ o mimashita.*
Have you been to _____?	_____へは、行ったことがありますか。*_____ e wa, itta koto ga arimasu ka.*
I recommend that you go to _____.	_____へは、是非行った方がいいですよ。*_____ e wa, zehi itta hō ga ii desu yo.*
I ate at _____, and it was wonderful.	_____で食べましたが、とてもおいしかったです。*_____ de tabemashita ga, totemo oishikatta desu.*
Are you with <u>a tour group</u>?	<u>観光旅行のグループ</u>と一緒ですか。*<u>Kankō ryokō no gurūpu</u> to issho desu ka.*
your family	ご家族　*gokazoku*
a friend	お友達　*otomodachi*
Are you on your own?	お一人で旅行ですか。*Ohitori de ryokō desu ka.*
How long will you be staying here?	ここにはもう何日、滞在の予定ですか。*Koko niwa mō nan nichi, taizai no yotei desu ka.*
Where are you staying?	どちらに、お泊まりですか。*Dochira ni, otomari desu ka.*
Where are you from?	お住まいは、どちらですか。*Osumai wa, dochira desu ka.*
I hear it's nice there.	そこは、いい所だそうですね。*Soko wa, ii tokoro da sō desu ne.*
What's (<u>Morioka</u>) famous for?	(<u>盛岡</u>)では、何が有名ですか。*(<u>Morioka</u>) dewa, nani ga yūmei desu ka.*

What's the special local food in (Morioka)?

(盛岡)で、特別の食べ物は何ですか。*(Morioka) de, tobubetsu no tabemono wa nan desu ka.*

What's a good <u>hotel</u> to stay at in (Morioka)?

(盛岡)で泊まるには、どの<u>ホテル</u>がいいですか。*(Morioka) de tomaru niwa, dono <u>hoteru</u> ga ii desu ka.*

Japanese inn

旅館　*ryokan*

Could you tell me a good place to eat?

食事するのに、いい場所を教えて下さい。*Shokuji suru no ni, ii basho o oshiete kudasai.*

FOLLOW-UP

What do you think of _____?

_____については、どう思いますか。*_____ ni tsuite wa, dō omoimasu ka.*

Do you like _____?

_____は、好きですか。*_____ wa, suki desu ka.*

I think _____ is very <u>beautiful</u>.

_____は、とても<u>きれいだ</u>と思います。*_____ wa, totemo <u>kirei da</u> to omoimasu.*

interesting

面白い　*omoshiroi*

magnificent

立派だ　*rippa da*

wonderful

素晴らしい　*subarashii*

By the way, let me introduce myself.

ところで、自己紹介させて下さい。*Tokorode, jiko shōkai sasete kudasai.*

My name is _____.

私の名前は、_____です。*Watakushi no namae wa, _____ desu.*

I'm here <u>alone</u>.

<u>一人で</u>、来ています。*<u>Hitori de</u>, kite imasu.*

with my family

家族と　*kazoku to*

with my wife

家内と　*kanai to*

with my husband

主人と　*shujin to*

with my daughter

娘と　*musume to*

with my son

息子と　*musuko to*

with my friend	友達と	*tomodachi to*
with my colleague	同僚と	*dōryō to*
I'm a <u>student</u>.	<u>学生</u>です。	<u>*Gakusei*</u> *desu.*
government official	公務員	*kōmuin*
businessman	ビジネスマン	*bijinesuman*
doctor	医者	*isha*
lawyer	弁護士	*bengoshi*
I'm from <u>the United States</u>.	<u>アメリカ</u>から、来ました。	<u>*Amerika*</u> *kara, kimashita.*
Canada	カナダ	*Kanada*
Italy	イタリア	*Itaria*
I live in <u>New York</u>.	<u>ニューヨーク</u>に、住んでいます。	<u>*Nyūyōku*</u> *ni, sunde imasu.*
Hong Kong	香港	*Honkon*
Cairo	カイロ	*Kairo*
I'm here for <u>sightseeing</u>.	<u>観光</u>で、来ています。	<u>*Kankō*</u> *de, kite imasu.*
business	仕事	*shigoto*
a conference	会議	*kaigi*
I've been in Japan for <u>two days</u>.	日本に来てから、<u>二日</u>になります。	*Nihon ni kite kara,* <u>*futsuka*</u> *ni narimasu.*
three days	三日	*mikka*
four days	四日	*yokka*
one week	一週間	*isshūkan*
I came here <u>today</u>.	ここへは、<u>今日</u>着きました。	*Koko e wa,* <u>*kyō*</u> *tsukimashita.*
yesterday	昨日	*kinō*
two days ago	おととい	*ototoi*
three days ago	さきおととい	*sakiototoi*

It's my first time in <u>Japan</u>.　<u>日本</u>は、初めてです。*Nihon wa, hajimete desu.*

  Sapporo　札幌　*Sapporo*

  Beppu　別府　*Beppu*

I'll stay here <u>overnight</u>.　ここには、<u>一晩</u>泊まります。*Koko niwa, <u>hitoban</u> tomarimasu.*

  for a few days　数日　*sūjitsu*

  for a week　一週間　*isshūkan*

I'm staying at the _____ hotel.　_____ホテルに、泊まっています。*_____ hoteru ni, tomatte imasu.*

I'm <u>single</u>.　私は、<u>独身</u>です。*Watakushi wa, <u>dokushin desu</u>.*

  married　結婚しています　*kekkon shite imasu*

I have a family.　私には、家族があります。*Watakushi niwa, kazoku ga arimasu.*

I have no children.　子供は、いません。*Kodomo wa, imasen.*

I have <u>one</u> child(ren).　子供が、<u>一人</u>います。*Kodomo ga, <u>hitori</u> imasu.*

  two　二人　*futari*

  three　三人　*san nin*

These are pictures of my family.　これが、私の家族の写真です。*Kore ga, watakushi no kazoku no shashin desu.*

Would you like to see them?　ご覧になりますか。*Goran ni narimasu ka.*

Are you a student?　学生さんですか。*Gakusei san desu ka.*

What are you studying?　何を勉強していますか。*Nani o benkyō shite imasu ka.*

What do you do?	お仕事は、何ですか。*Oshigoto wa, nan desu ka.*
Are you <u>single</u>?	<u>独身</u>ですか。<u>*Dokushin desu*</u> *ka.*
married	結婚しています *kekkon shite imasu*
Do you have any children?	お子さんが、いますか。*Okosan ga, imasu ka.*
How many children do you have?	お子さんは、何人ですか。*Okosan wa, nan nin desu ka.*
How old are they?	お子さんは、おいくつですか。*Okosan wa, oikutsu desu ka.*
Is your <u>family</u> here?	<u>ご家族</u>は、ここにおいでですか。<u>*Go kazoku*</u> *wa, koko ni oide desu ka.*
wife	奥さん *okusan*
husband	ご主人 *go shujin*
Do you have any pictures of your <u>family</u>?	<u>ご家族</u>の写真を、お持ちですか。<u>*Go kazoku*</u> *no shashin o, omochi desu ka.*
children	お子さん *okosan*

TAKING PICTURES

Would you like me to take a picture for you?	写真を、お撮りしましょうか。*Shashin o, otori shimashō ka.*
May I take your picture?	あなたの写真を撮っても、よろしいですか。*Anata no shashin o tottemo, yoroshii desu ka.*
Stand here.	そこに立って下さい。*Soko ni tatte kudasai.*
Don't move.	動かないで。*Ugokanai de.*
Smile.	笑って。*Waratte.*
That's it.	はい、終わりました。*Hai, owarimashita.*

Would you take a picture of me, please?	写真を、撮ってもらえますか。 *Shashin o, totte moraemasu ka.*
Thank you.	ありがとうございました。 *Arigatō gozaimashita.*

SAYING GOODBYE

Nice talking to you.	お話しできて、楽しかったです。 *Ohanashi dekite, tanoshikatta desu.*
I hope I'll see you again.	また、お目にかかれるといいですね。 *Mata, ome ni kakareru to ii desu ne.*

GETTING TOGETHER

Could I see you again?	また、お目にかかれますか。 *Mata, ome ni kakaremasu ka.*
Here's my name, hotel, telephone number, and extension.	これが、私の名前、ホテル、電話番号、内線です。 *Kore ga, watakushi no namae, hoteru, denwa bangō, naisen desu.*
Here's my email address.	これが私のメールアドレスです。 *Kore ga watakushi no mēru adoresu desu.*
May I have your email address?	あなたのメールアドレスをもらえますか。 *Anata no mēru adoresu o moraemasu ka.*
Could you give me your telephone number?	あなたの電話番号を、いただけますか。 *Anata no denwa bangō o, itadakemasu ka.*
May I call you?	電話しても、かまいませんか。 *Denwa shitemo, kamaimasen ka.*
Are you doing anything <u>this afternoon</u>?	<u>今日の午後</u>は、何か予定がありますか。 *<u>Kyō no gogo</u> wa, nanika yotei ga arimasu ka.*
this evening	今晩　*konban*
tomorrow	あした　*ashita*
Are you free this evening?	今晩、おひまですか。 *Konban, ohima desu ka.*

What about <u>dinner</u> together?	夕食を、一緒にいかがですか。 *Yūshoku o, issho ni ikaga desu ka.*
drinks	お酒　*osake*
sightseeing	見物　*kenbutsu*
I'd like to invite you for <u>cocktails</u>.	<u>カクテル</u>に、お招きしたいのですが。 *Kakuteru ni, omaneki shitai no desu ga.*
dinner	夕食　*yūshoku*
a show	ショー　*shō*
I hope you can come.	来ていただければ、うれしいのですが。 *Kite itadakereba, ureshii no desu ga.*
Where shall I meet you?	どこで、お会いしましょうか。*Doko de, oai shimashō ka.*
Shall I meet you at <u>my hotel lobby</u>?	<u>私のホテルのロビー</u>で、お会いしましょうか。*Watakushi no hoteru no robī de, oai shimashō ka.*
your hotel lobby	あなたのホテルのロビー　*anata no hoteru no robī*
the restaurant	レストラン　*resutoran*
the cocktail lounge	カクテル・ラウンジ　*kakuteru raunji*
the theater	劇場　*gekijō*
Shall I come to pick you up?	お迎えに、行きましょうか。 *Omukae ni, ikimashō ka.*
What time shall we meet?	何時に、お会いしましょうか。*Nan ji ni, oai shimashō ka.*
Is <u>6:00</u> convenient for you?	<u>六時</u>で、ご都合はいかがですか。 *Roku ji de, go tsugō wa ikaga desu ka.*
6:30	六時半　*rokuji han*
7:00	七時　*shichi ji*
See you then.	では、のちほど。*Dewa, nochi hodo.*
I'm looking forward to seeing you.	会えるのを楽しみにしています。 *Aeru no o tanoshimi ni shite imasu.*

SOCIAL MEDIA

Social media is widely used, especially by young and middle-aged Japanese. As elsewhere, it takes many forms: those that originated overseas and are internationally well known, and those that originated in Japan. But all have enthusiastic users.

Popular social media in Japan are as follows:

LINE	ライン	*Rain*
Twitter	ツイッター	*Tsuittā*
Instagram	インスタグラム	*Insutaguramu*
Facebook	フェイスブック	*Feisubukku*
Snapchat	スナップチャット	*Sunappuchatto*
LinkedIn	リンクトイン	*Rinkutoin*
Google+	グーグルプラス	*Gūgurupurasu*
Skype	スカイプ	*Sukaipu*
FaceTime	フェイスタイム	*Feisutaimu*
WhatsApp	ワッツアップ	*Wattsuappu*
Do you use social media?	何かソーシャルメディアを使っていますか。*Nanika sōsharu media o tsukatte imasu ka.*	
Which social media are you using?	どのソーシャルメディアを使っていますか。*Dono sōsharu media o tsukatte imasu ka.*	
Are you using <u>Line</u>?	<u>ライン</u>を使っていますか。*<u>Rain</u> o tsukatte imasu ka.*	
Twitter	ツイッター	*Tsuittā*
Can I access <u>Skype</u>?	<u>スカイプ</u>ができますか。*<u>Sukaipu</u> ga dekimasu ka.*	
FaceTime	フェイスタイム	*feisutaimu*

How can I find you on <u>Instagram</u>?	<u>インスタグラム</u>でどうやってあなたを見つけられますか？ *Insutaguramu de dō yatte anata o mitsukeraremasu ka.*	
Facebook	フェイスブック	*Feisubukku*
Can I follow you?	あなたをフォローできますか。*Anata o forō dekimasu ka.*	
May I have your username?	ユーザーネームがもらえますか。*Yūzā nēmu ga moraemasu ka.*	
Can I add you as a friend?	フェイスブックで友達に入れますね。*Feisubukku de tomodachi ni iremasu ne.*	
Can I tag you as a friend?	友達のタグつけていいですか？ *Tomodachi no tagu tsukete ii desu ka.*	
Like!	イイネ。*Ii ne.*	
Dislike!	ヤダネ。*Ya da ne.*	
Where is the nearest <u>Internet café</u>?	直ぐそばの<u>インターネットカフェ</u>はどこですか。*Sugu soba no intānetto kafe wa doko desu ka.*	
hotspot	ホットスポット	*hottosupotto*

SHOPPING

How often have you read or heard that Japan is a shoppers' paradise? It's true. Not only can you buy familiar items you need, you can explore the Japanese decorative arts firsthand. During your shopping expeditions, remember that bargaining is not generally practiced in Japan.

I'd like to go shopping today.	今日、買い物に行きたいのですが。 *Kyō, kaimono ni ikitai no desu ga.*
Where can I find a good ____?	いい____は、どこにありますか。 *Ii ____ wa, doko ni arimasu ka.*
antique shop	骨董屋　*kottō ya*
art gallery	画廊　*garō*
bakery	パン屋　*pan ya*
bookstore	本屋　*hon ya*
camera shop	カメラ店　*kamera ten*
ceramics store	瀬戸物屋　*setomono ya*
clothing store	洋服店　*yōfuku ten*
men's clothing store	紳士服の店　*shinshi fuku no mise*
women's clothing store	婦人服の店　*fujin fuku no mise*
confectionery	お菓子屋　*okashi ya*
cosmetics shop	化粧品店　*keshōhin ten*
department store	デパート　*depāto*
drugstore	ドラッグ・ストアー　*doraggu sutoā*
electrical appliance store	電気器具店　*denki kigu ten*
fish market	魚屋　*sakana ya*
florist	花屋　*hana ya*

folkware shop	民芸品店	*mingei hin ten*
grocery store	食料品店	*shokuryō hin ten*
handicrafts shop	手工芸品店	*shu kōgei hin ten*
jewelry store	宝石店／宝飾店	*hōseki ten/ hōshoku ten*
kimono store	呉服屋	*gofuku ya*
liquor store	酒屋	*sakaya*
newsstand	新聞売り場	*shinbun uriba*
optician	眼鏡屋	*megane ya*
pharmacy	薬局	*yakkyoku*
photographer	写真屋	*shashin ya*
photography shop	カメラ屋	*kamera ya*
record store	レコード屋	*rekōdo ya*
shoe store	靴屋	*kutsu ya*
souvenir shop	おみやげ屋	*omiyage ya*
sporting goods store	運道具店	*undō gu ten*
stationery store	文房具屋	*bunbōgu ya*
supermarket	スーパー	*sūpā*
tailor	仕立屋	*shitate ya*
tobacco shop	たばこ屋	*tabako ya*
toiletries shop	化粧品店	*keshō hin ten*
toy store	おもちゃ屋	*omocha ya*
travel agency	旅行代理店	*ryokō dairi ten*
watch and clock store	時計屋	*tokei ya*
woodblock print shop	版画店	*hanga ten*

INQUIRIES ABOUT SHOPPING

Where's the nearest _____?	一番近い_____は、どこにありますか。 *Ichiban chikai _____ wa, doko ni arimasu ka.*
Which _____ do you recommend?	どの_____が、いいでしょうか。 *Dono _____ ga, ii deshō ka.*
Where do they sell _____?	_____は、どこで売っていますか。 *_____ wa, doko de utte imasu ka.*
Where's the main shopping area?	主なショッピング街は、どこにありますか。 *Omo na shoppingu gai wa, doko ni arimasu ka.*
I'd like to go to a shopping arcade.	ショッピング・アーケードに、行きたいのですが。 *Shoppingu ākēdo ni, ikitai no desu ga.*
Is it far?	そこは、遠いですか。 *Soko wa, tōi desu ka.*
Can you tell me how to get there?	そこまで、どうやって行けばいいですか。 *Soko made, dō yatte ikeba ii desu ka.*
Where's a good place to window shop?	ウィンドウショッピングは、どこがいいですか。 *Windō shoppingu wa, doko ga ii desu ka.*

THE CLERK

Here are some things you'll hear while you're shopping. If you're not quite sure what's being said, you can ask the clerk to point to the phrase in the book.

Welcome.	いらっしゃいませ。 *Irasshaimase.*
What are you looking for?	何か、おさがしですか。 *Nanika, osagashi desu ka.*

What <u>color</u> do you want?	どんな色を、お好みですか。*Donna iro o, okonomi desu ka.*
size	サイズ　*saizu*
I'm sorry. We don't have it/any.	すみませんが、あいにくございません。*Sumimasen ga, ainiku gozaimasen.*
Would you like us to order it for you?	ご注文いたしましょうか。*Go chūmon itashimashō ka.*
Please write your name, address and phone number.	お名前とご住所と電話番号を、お願いします。*Onamae to gojūsho to odenwa bangō o, onegai shimasu.*
It should be here <u>in a few days</u>.	<u>数日中に</u>、来ると思います。*Sūjitsu chū ni, kuru to omoimasu.*
next week	来週　*raishū*
We'll call you when it's here.	まいりましたら、お電話いたします。*Mairimashita ra, odenwa itashimasu.*
That will be _____ yen, please.	_____円、ちょうだいいたします。*_____ en, chōdai itashimasu.*
I'm sorry; we don't accept credit cards.	申し訳ございませんが、クレジット・カードは受け付けておりません。*Mōshiwake gozaimasen ga, kurejitto kādo wa uketsukete orimasen.*
We accept <u>Diners Club</u>.	<u>ダイナーズ・クラブ</u>を、受け付けております。*Daināzu Kurabu o, uketsukete orimasu.*
American Express	アメックス　*Amekkusu*
Visa	ビザ　*Biza*
MasterCard	マスターカード　*Masutākādo*
Here's your receipt.	レシートをどうぞ。*Reshīto o dōzo.*
Thank you.	ありがとうございました。*Arigatō gozaimashita.*
Come again.	また、おこし下さい。*Mata, okoshi kudasai.*

IN THE STORE

Excuse me.	すみませんが。*Sumimasen ga.*
Can you help me?	ちょっと、お願いします。*Chotto, onegai shimasu.*
I'd like to see some _____.	_____を、見せてもらえますか。_____ *o, misete moraemasu ka.*
Do you have any _____?	_____は、ありますか。_____ *wa, arimasu ka.*
I'm just looking, thank you.	ちょっと、見ているだけです。*Chotto, mite iru dake desu.*
I'd like something for <u>a child</u>.	何か、<u>子供</u>のものが欲しいのですが。*Nanika, <u>kodomo</u> no mono ga hoshii no desu ga.*
a 5-year-old boy	五才の男の子　*go sai no otoko no ko*
a 10-year-old girl	十才の女の子　*jussai no onna no ko*
I'd like to see <u>that one</u>.	<u>あれ</u>を見たいのですが。*<u>Are</u> o mitai no desu ga.*
this one	これ　*kore*
the one in the window	あのショー・ウィンドーにあるの　*ano shō windō ni aru no*
I'd like to replace this _____.	この_____を、買いかえたいのですが。*Kono _____ o, kaikaetai no desu ga.*
I'm interested in something <u>inexpensive</u>.	<u>高くない</u>ものが欲しいのですが。*<u>Takaku nai</u> mono ga hoshii no desu ga.*
handmade	手作りの　*tezukuri no*
Japanese	日本の　*Nihon no*
Do you have any others?	ほかに、何かありますか。*Hoka ni, nanika arimasu ka.*

I'd like a <u>big</u> one.	大きいのが、欲しいのですが。 *Ōkii no ga, hoshii no desu ga.*
small	小さい *chiisai*
cheap	安い *yasui*
better	もっといい *motto ii*
good	いい *ii*
How much is <u>it</u>?	これは、いくらですか。 *Kore wa, ikura desu ka.*
that one	それ *sore*
Could you write the price down?	値段を、紙に書いてくれませんか。 *Nedan o, kami ni kaite kuremasen ka.*
I want to spend about _____ yen.	予算は、約_____円です。 *Yosan wa, yaku _____ en desu.*
Do you have something <u>less expensive</u>?	もう少し安いのが、ありますか。 *Mō sukoshi yasui no ga, arimasu ka.*
more expensive	もう少し高い *mō sukoshi takai*
I'll take it/this.	これを、下さい。 *Kore o, kudasai.*
May I use <u>a credit card</u>?	クレジット・カードが、使えますか。 *Kurejitto kādo ga, tsukaemasu ka.*
traveler's check	トラベラーズ・チェック *toraberāzu chekku*
Which cards do you take?	どのカードが、使えますか。 *Dono kādo ga, tsukaemasu ka.*
May I have a receipt, please.	レシートを、お願いします。 *Reshīto o, onegai shimasu.*
Could you send it to my hotel?	ホテルに、届けてもらえますか。 *Hoteru ni, todokete moraemasu ka.*
Could you send it to this address?	この住所に、送ってもらえますか。 *Kono jūsho ni, okutte moraemasu ka.*

Could you ship it overseas for me?	海外に、郵送してもらえますか。 *Kaigai ni, yūsō shite moraemasu ka.*
How much would it cost?	郵送料は、いくらですか。 *Yūsō ryō wa, ikura desu ka.*
I'd also like to see _____.	_____ も、見たいのですが。 *_____ mo, mitai no desu ga.*
That's all, thank you.	これで、けっこうです。 *Kore de, kekkō desu.*
I'd like to <u>exchange</u> this.	この品を、<u>交換</u>したいのですが。 *Kono shina o, <u>kōkan</u> shitai no desu ga.*
return	返品 *henpin*
May I have a refund, please?	払い戻ししてもらえますか。 *Haraimodoshi shite moraemasu ka.*
Here's my receipt.	これが、レシートです。 *Kore ga, reshīto desu.*
Thank you for your help.	助けてもらって、助かりました。 *Tasukete moratte, tasukarimashita.*

DEPARTMENT STORES

Japanese department stores carry all the things you would expect, and a lot more as well. The folkware or *mingei* sections have crafts from all over Japan: handmade dolls, toys, pottery, paper crafts, bamboo baskets, lacquer trays, bowls, chopsticks, handmade and dyed fabrics, and more. You'll also find typical Japanese craft items in the housewares section—in a range from everyday pottery to expensive lacquerware. Such items usually come in sets of five, not six or eight as in Western countries.

Don't miss the food section; the entire basement floor is devoted to fresh and packaged foods, both Japanese and Western style.

Where's the <u>men's clothing</u> department? | <u>紳士服</u>売り場は、どこにありますか。 *<u>Shinshi fuku</u> uriba wa, doko ni arimasu ka.*

women's clothing	婦人服	*fujin fuku*
children's clothing	子供服	*kodomo fuku*
shoe	くつ	*kutsu*
housewares	家庭用品の	*kateiyōhin no*
china	瀬戸物	*setomono*
jewelry	宝石	*hōseki*
notions	小間物	*komamono*
furniture	家具	*kagu*
luggage	旅行かばん／スーツ・ケース	*ryokō kaban/sūtsu kēsu*
handicrafts	手工芸品	*shu kōgei hin*
Japanese food	日本食品の	*Nihon shokuhin no*
Western food	西洋食品の	*seiyō shokuhin no*
kimono	呉服	*gofuku*
toy	おもちゃ	*omocha*

Where's the <u>ladies' room</u>? | <u>女性用のトイレ</u>は、どこにありますか。 *<u>Josei yō no toire</u> wa, doko ni arimasu ka.*

men's room	男性用のトイレ	*dansei yō no toire*
elevator	エレベーター	*erebētā*
escalator	エスカレーター	*esukarētā*
snack bar	スナック	*sunakku*
coffee shop	喫茶室	*kissashitsu*
restaurant	レストラン	*resutoran*
telephone	電話	*denwa*
water fountain	水飲み場	*mizunomiba*
information desk	案内所	*annaijo*

BOOKS

Bookstores, newsstands, and stationery stores are usually separate in Japan—although some bookstores do sell newspapers. At bookstores and newsstands in large tourist hotels you can find some American and European newspapers, and also weekly news magazines, usually international or Far East editions. You can also buy English language newspapers written and published in Japan; these are available at most newsstands throughout the country. If you don't see them, ask the vendor. Some big bookstores in large cities have good selections of books in English.

Do you have books in <u>English</u>?	英語の本が、ありますか。 <u>*Eigo no hon ga, arimasu ka.*</u>
French	フランス語 *Furansu go*
Italian	イタリア語 *Itaria go*
German	ドイツ語 *Doitsu go*
Where are the books in English?	英語の本は、どこにありますか。 *Eigo no hon wa, doko ni arimasu ka.*
I want <u>a guidebook</u>.	<u>ガイド・ブック</u>が欲しいのですが。 <u>*Gaido bukku*</u> *ga hoshii no desu ga.*
a map of this city	この都市の地図 *kono toshi no chizu*
a map of Japan	日本の地図 *Nihon no chizu*
a pocket dictionary	ポケット版の辞書 *poketto ban no jisho*
a magazine in English	英語の雑誌 *eigo no zasshi*
a book for learning Japanese	日本語を習うための本 *Nihon go o narau tame no hon*
Where can I find <u>detective stories</u>?	<u>探偵小説</u>は、どこにありますか。 <u>*Tantei shōsetsu*</u> *wa, doko ni arimasu ka.*

history books	歴史の本	*rekishi no hon*
novels	小説	*shōsetsu*
short story books	短編小説	*tanpen shōsetsu*

Do you have English translations of <u>Japanese classics</u>?　<u>日本の古典</u>の、英訳がありますか。 <u>Nihon no koten</u> no, eiyaku ga arimasu ka.

modern Japanese novels	近代日本小説	*kindai Nihon shōsetsu*
current Japanese novels	現代日本小説	*gendai Nihon shōsetsu*

Do you have English translations of <u>Yukio Mishima's</u> books?　<u>三島由紀夫</u>の本の、英訳があります か。<u>Mishima Yukio no</u> hon no, eiyaku ga arimasu ka.

Yasunari Kawabata's	川端康成の	*Kawabata Yasunari no*
Kenzaburo Oe's	大江健三郎の	*Ōe Kenzaburō no*
Junichiro Tanizaki's	谷崎潤一郎の	*Tanizaki Junichirō no*

I'm looking for a copy of _____.	_____を、さがしているのですが。 _____ o, sagashite iru no desu ga.
The title of the book is _____.	本の題名は、_____です。 Hon no daimei wa, _____ desu.
The author of the book is _____.	著者は、_____です。 Chosha wa, _____ desu.
The publisher of the book is _____.	出版社は、_____です。 Shuppansha wa, _____ desu.
I don't know the title/author.	本の題名／著者は、知りません。 Hon no daimei/chosha wa, shirimasen.
I'll take these books.	この本を、お願いします。 Kono hon o, onegai shimasu.

CLOTHING

Shopping for clothing in Japan yields basic styles as well as designs, patterns, and fabrics unavailable anywhere else. Most Japanese designers have boutiques in the department stores and elsewhere; some feature lines of clothing more affordable than you may expect, both high fashion items and simple, well-made sportswear. And don't overlook traditional Japanese clothing. A silk or cotton kimono, either antique or modern, makes a stylish gift—perhaps for yourself!

ITEMS

Could you please show me some <u>belts</u>?	<u>ベルト</u>を、見せて下さい。	<u>Beruto</u> o, misete kudasai.
blouses	ブラウス	burausu
dresses	ドレス	doresu
gloves	手袋	tebukuro
handkerchiefs	ハンカチ	hankachi
handbags	ハンドバッグ	handobaggu
hats	帽子	bōshi
jackets	上着／ジャケット	uwagi/jaketto
jeans	ブルー・ジーン／ジーンズ	burū jīn/jīnzu
overcoats	オーバー	ōbā
pants	スラックス	surakkusu
pocketbooks	ハンドバッグ	handobaggu
raincoats	レイン・コート	rein kōto
robes	化粧着／バス・ローブ	keshōgi/basu rōbu
scarves	スカーフ	sukāfu
shirts	ワイシャツ	waishatsu

casual shirts	スポーツ・シャツ *supōtsu shatsu*
shorts (briefs)	ブリーフ *burīfu*
skirts	スカート *sukāto*
slippers	スリッパ *surippa*
socks	ソックス *sokkusu*
sportswear	スポーツウェア *supōtsu wea*
stockings	ストッキング *sutokkingu*
suits	スーツ *sūtsu*
sweaters	セーター *sētā*
cardigans	カーディガン *kādigan*
swim suits	水着 *mizugi*
tee shirts	ティー・シャツ *tī shatsu*
ties	ネクタイ *nekutai*
trousers	ズボン *zubon*
undershirts	アンダー・シャツ／肌着 *andā shatsu/hadagi*
underwear	下着 *shitagi*
wallets	財布 *saifu*

Is there a special sale today?	今日は、特売がありますか。*Kyō wa, tokubai ga arimasu ka.*
I'd like the _____ with long/short sleeves.	長／半そでの_____が、欲しいのですが。*Naga/han sode no _____ ga, hoshii no desu ga.*
Do you have anything <u>else</u>?	何か、<u>ほか</u>のがありますか。*Nanika, <u>hoka</u> no ga arimasu ka.*

larger	もっと大きい *motto ōkii*
smaller	もっと小さい *motto chiisai*
cheaper	もっと安い *motto yasui*
of better quality	もっと上等な *motto jōtō na*

longer	もっと長い	*motto nagai*
shorter	もっと短い	*motto mijikai*
I'd prefer a different <u>color</u>.	ほかの<u>色</u>のが、いいのですが。	*Hoka no <u>iro</u> no ga, ii no desu ga.*
style	スタイル	*sutairu*
I want something in <u>black</u>.	何か、<u>黒い</u>のがありますか。	*Nanika, <u>kuroi</u> no ga arimasu ka.*
blue	青い	*aoi*
brown	茶色い	*chairoi*
gray	グレー	*gurē*
green	グリーン	*gurīn*
pink	ピンク	*pinku*
purple	紫	*murasaki*
red	赤い	*akai*
white	白い	*shiroi*
yellow	黄色い	*kiiroi*
I'd like <u>a solid color</u>.	<u>無地</u>の を、下さい。	*<u>Muji</u> no o, kudasai.*
a print/floral print	プリント／花模様	*purinto/hana moyō*
stripes	縞模様	*shima moyō*
a plaid	格子縞	*kōshi jima*
checks	チェック	*chekku*
I'd like a <u>darker</u> color.	もう少し、<u>地味</u>なのがありますか。	*Mō sukoshi, <u>jimi</u> na no ga arimasu ka.*
brighter	派手	*hade*
Do you have anything to match this?	これに、合うものがありますか。	*Kore ni, au mono ga arimasu ka.*

Do you have something in <u>cotton</u>?	何か、<u>木綿</u>のものがありますか。 *Nanika, <u>momen</u> no mono ga arimasu ka.*	
wool	ウール	*ūru*
silk	絹／シルク	*kinu/shiruku*
linen	麻／リンネル	*asa/rinneru*
polyester	ポリエステル	*poriesuteru*
leather	皮	*kawa*
patent leather	エナメル	*enameru*
suede	スエード	*suēdo*
vinyl	ビニール	*binīru*
nylon	ナイロン	*nairon*

SIZES

You should try on Japanese clothing before you buy it. Although you can find a good fit in most items, some may be short-waisted for Westerners, and some sleeves may also be short. For women, dress sizes run in odd numbers 7, 9, 11, 13, and so forth, and are not too different from American sizes. Men's suit sizes are roughly the centimeter equivalent of American suit sizes (multiplying the inches by 2.5 instead of the usual 2.54 centimeters).

MEN						
Suits, Coats						
American	36	38	40	42	44	46
British	36	38	40	42	44	46
Continental	46	48	50	52	54	56
Japanese	90	95	100	105	110	115
Shirts						
American	14	14½	15	15½	16	16½	17
British	14	14½	15	15½	16	16½	17
Continental	36	37	38	39	40	41	42
Japanese	36	37	38	39	40	41	42

WOMEN						
Dresses, Blouses, Sportswear, Lingerie						
American	6	8	10	12	14	16
British	8	10	12	14	16	18
Continental	34	36	38	40	42	44
Japanese	5/7	7/9	9/11	11/13	13/15	15/17
	S	S	M	ML	L	LL
Pantyhose, Tights						
American	A	B	C/D	plus E	plus F	
British	small	medium	large	extra large	extra large	
Continental	1	2	3	4	5	
Japanese	S	M	L	BL	BLL	

Please take my measurements.	私のサイズを、計って下さい。 *Watakushi no saizu o, hakatte kudasai.*
I don't know the Japanese sizes.	日本のサイズは、知りません。 *Nihon no saizu wa, shirimasen.*
My <u>American</u> size is _____.	私の<u>アメリカの</u>サイズは、_____です。 *Watakushi no <u>Amerika no</u> saizu wa, desu.*
European	ヨーロッパの　*Yōroppa no*
My size is <u>small</u>.	私のサイズは、<u>スモール</u>です。 *Watakushi no saizu wa, <u>sumōru</u> desu.*
medium	エム・サイズ　*emu saizu*
large	エル・サイズ　*eru saizu*
May I try it on?	試着しても、いいですか。*Shichaku shitemo, ii desu ka.*
Where's the dressing room?	試着室は、どこですか。*Shichaku shitsu wa, doko desu ka.*
Do you have a mirror?	鏡が、ありますか。*Kagami ga, arimasu ka.*
It's too <u>long</u>.	<u>長</u>すぎます。*<u>Naga</u>sugimasu.*
short	短か　*mijika*
tight	きつ　*kitsu*
loose	ゆる　*yuru*
Can you alter it?	直してもらえますか。*Naoshite moraemasu ka.*
The zipper doesn't work.	チャックが、こわれています。 *Chakku ga, kowarete imasu.*
There's a button missing.	ボタンが、なくなっています。 *Botan ga, nakunatte imasu.*
It doesn't fit me.	これは、合いません。*Kore wa, aimasen.*

| It fits very well. | これは、ぴったりです。 *Kore wa, pittari desu.* |
| I'll take it. | これを、下さい。 *Kore o, kudasai.* |

SHOES

It is not easy to find Japanese shoes that fit Western feet.

There is one standard width, EE, and large sizes are hard to find; this is true for both men's and women's shoes. Size charts tend to be inconsistent; it's best to let the salesperson measure your feet.

I'd like to see a pair of <u>shoes</u>.	<u>くつ</u>を、見たいのですが。 <u>*Kutsu*</u> *o, mitai no desu ga.*
boots	ブーツ *būtsu*
casual shoes	普段ばきのくつ *fudanbaki no kutsu*
dressy shoes	改まったときのくつ *aratamatta toki no kutsu*
high-heeled shoes	ハイヒール *haihīru*
low-heeled shoes	ローヒール *rō hīru*
running shoes	ランニング・シューズ *ranningu shūzu*
sandals	サンダル *sandaru*
sneakers	スニーカー／運動靴 *sunīkā/undō gutsu*
tennis shoes	テニス・シューズ *tenisu shūzu*
There's a pair in the window that I like.	ショー・ウィンドーに、好きなのがあります。 *Shō windō ni, suki na no ga arimasu.*
Do they come in <u>another color</u>?	これには、<u>ほかの色</u>のもありますか。 *Kore niwa, <u>hoka no iro</u> no mo arimasu ka.*
calf	子牛の皮 *koushi no kawa*

suede	スエード	*suēdo*
patent leather	エナメル	*enameru*
Can you measure my size?	私のサイズを、計ってもらえますか。 *Watakushi no saizu o, hakatte moraemasu ka.*	
These are too <u>narrow</u>.	これは、<u>せま</u>すぎます。*Kore wa, <u>sema</u>sugimasu.*	
wide	広	*hiro*
loose	ゆる	*yuru*
tight	きつ	*kitsu*
They fit fine.	これは、ぴったりです。*Kore wa, pittari desu.*	
I'll take them.	これを、下さい。*Kore o, kudasai.*	
Do you have shoelaces here?	くつひもは、売っていますか。 *Kutsu himo wa, utte imasu ka.*	

ELECTRICAL APPLIANCES

For a look at the latest in electrical appliances and electronic equipment, visit Tokyo's Akihabara wholesale-retail district. It's the biggest discount center in Japan. While fixed prices are standard almost everywhere else, shops in Akihabara offer large discounts, and bargaining is commonplace, even expected. Save the bargaining phrases listed here for Akihabara or shops clearly marked discount—no others!

Where can I buy electrical applicances?	電気製品は、どこで買えますか。 *Denki seihin wa, doko de kaemasu ka.*
How can I get to Akihabara?	秋葉原には、どう行けばいいですか。 *Akihabara niwa, dō ikeba ii desu ka.*

I want to buy <u>a battery</u>.	<u>電池</u>を買いたいのですが。 <u>Denchi</u> o kaitai no desu ga.	
an answering machine	留守番電話	rusuban denwa
a camcorder	カムコーダー	kamukōdā
a CD player	シーディープレーヤー	shīdī purēyā
a cellular phone	携帯電話	keitai denwa
a computer	コンピュータ	konpyūta
a notebook computer	ノートブック・コンピュータ	nōtobukku conpyūta
a copier	コピー・マシーン／複写機	kopī mashīn/fukusha ki
a cordless telephone	コードレスフォン	kōdoresu fon
a digital camera	デジタルカメラ	dejitaru kamera
a digital music player	デジタルミュージックプレーヤー	dejitaru mūjikku purēyā
a digital tape recorder	デジタル・テープレコーダー	dejitaru tēpu rekōdā
a DVD player	ディービーディープレーヤー	dībīdī purēyā
earphones	イヤフォン	iafon
an electric razor	電気かみそり	denki kamisori
a hair dryer	ヘアー・ドライヤー	heā doraiyā
headphones	ヘッドフォン	heddofon
a keyboard	キーボード	kībōdo
a microphone	マイクロフォン	maikurofon
a microcassette recorder	マイクロ・カセットレコーダー	maikuro kasetto rekōdā

a minicalculator	ポケット型計算器／ポケット電卓 *pokettogata keisan ki/poketto dentaku*
a modem	モデム *modemu*
a mouse	マウス *mausu*
a portable component stereo system	携帯コンポステレオ装置 *keitai konpo sutereo sōchi*
a portable printer	ポータブル プリンター *pōtaburu purintā*
a portable radio	ポータブルラジオ *pōtaburu rajio*
a portable scanner	ポータブル スキャナー *pōtaburu sukyanā*
a record player	レコードプレーヤー *rekōdo purēyā*
a speaker	スピーカー *supīkā*
a video camera	ビデオカメラ *bideo kamera*
Is there a special department for products for use overseas?	海外で使用する製品のための、特別の売り場がありますか。*Kaigai de shiyō suru tame no, tokubetsu no uriba ga arimasu ka.*
What voltage does this take?	これには、何ボルトが必要ですか。*Kore niwa, nan boruto ga hitsuyō desu ka.*
Do you have one suitable for <u>American</u> voltage?	<u>アメリカ</u>のボルトに合うのが、ありますか。<u>*Amerika*</u> *no boruto ni au no ga, arimasu ka.*
South American	南米 *Nanbei*
European	ヨーロッパ *Yōroppa*
Is there a <u>110</u>-volt one?	<u>110</u>ボルトのが、ありますか。<u>*Hyaku jū*</u> *boruto no ga, arimasu ka.*
220	220 *ni hyaku ni jū*

| Do you sell transformers? | 変圧器は、ありますか。*Hen-atsu ki wa, arimasu ka.* |

100 volts	*hyaku boruto*
110 volts	*hyaku jū boruto*
220 volts	*ni hyaku ni jū boruto*

This is out of order/ broken.	これは、こわれています。*Kore wa, kowarete imasu.*
How much is this?	これは、いくらですか。*Kore wa, ikura desu ka.*
It's rather expensive.	ちょっと、高いですねえ。*Chotto, takai desu nē.*
It's more than I expected.	思ったより、高いですねえ。*Omotta yori, takai desu nē.*
That's not the final price, is it?	それが、終わりの値段ではないでしょ。*Sore ga, owari no nedan dewa nai desho.*
Can't you come down a little?	もうちょっと、安くなりませんか。*Mō chotto, yasuku narimasen ka.*
How about _____ yen?	_____円では、どうですか。*_____ en dewa, dō desu ka.*

FOOD AND HOUSEHOLD ITEMS

See the chapter on food (page 193) and the dictionaries (pages 387–421) for more food words.

I'd like _____ .	_____、下さい。 *_____ , kudasai.*
a bag of sugar	砂糖を一袋 *satō o hito fukuro*
a bar of chocolate	チョコレートを一枚 *chokorēto o ichi mai*

a bottle of ketchup	ケチャップを一本	*kechappu o ippon*
a bottle of juice	ジュースを一本	*jūsu o ippon*
a box of candy	キャンディーを一箱	*kyandī o hito hako*
a box of cereal	シリアルを一箱	*shiriaru o hito hako*
a box of chocolate	チョコレートを一箱	*chokorēto o hito hako*
a box of crackers	クラッカーを一箱	*kurakkā o hito hako*
a box of eggs	卵を一箱	*tamago o hito hako*
a box of raisins	干しぶどうを一箱	*hoshi budō o hito hako*
a can of nuts	ナッツを一缶	*nattsu o hito kan*
a can of tuna	マグロの缶詰を一缶	*maguro no kanzume o hito kan*
a half kilo* of grapes	ぶどうを五百グラム	*budō o go hyaku guramu*

Note: Common measurements for purchasing food are a kilo or fractions thereof and 100, 200, and 500 grams. See also the section on numbers (pages 18–21).

a half kilo of tangerines	みかんを五百グラム	*mikan o go hyaku guramu*
a jar of instant coffee	インスタント・コーヒーを一びん	*insutanto kōhī o hito bin*
a jar of jam	ジャムを一びん	*jamu o hito bin*
a jar of mayonnaise	マヨネーズを一びん	*mayonēzu o hito bin*
a jar of mustard	からしを一びん	*karashi o hito bin*
a jar of pepper	こしょうを一びん	*koshō o hito bin*

METRIC WEIGHTS AND MEASURES

Solid Measures
(approximate measurements only)

OUNCES	GRAMS	GRAMS	OUNCES
1/4	7	10	1/3
1/2	14	100	3-1/2
3/4	21	300	10-1/2
1	28	500	18

POUNDS	KILOGRAMS	KILOGRAMS	POUNDS
1	1/2	1	2-1/4
5	2-1/4	3	6-1/2
10	4-1/2	5	11
20	9	10	22
50	23	50	110
100	45	100	220

Liquid Measures
(approximate measurements only)

OUNCES	MILLILITERS	MILLILITERS	OUNCES
1	30	10	1/3
6	175	50	1-1/2
12	350	100	3-1/2
16	475	150	5

GALLONS	LITERS	LITERS	GALLONS
1	3-3/4	1	1/4 (1 quart)
5	19	5	1-1/3
10	38	10	2-1/2

a jar of salt	塩を一びん	*shio o hito bin*
a kilo of apples	リンゴを一キロ	*ringo o ikkiro*
a kilo of bananas	バナナを一キロ	*banana o ikkiro*
a kilo of ham	ハムを一キロ	*hamu o ikkiro*
a liter of milk	ミルクを一リットル	*miruku o ichi rittoru*
a loaf of bread	パンを一本	*pan o ippon*
a package of candy	キャンディーを一袋	*kyandī o hito fukuro*
a slice of cake	ケーキを一切れ	*kēki o hito kire*
a stick of butter	バター一本	*batā ippon*

JEWELRY

I'd like to see <u>a bracelet</u>.	<u>ブレスレット</u>を、見せて下さい。	<u>*Buresuretto*</u> *o, misete kudasai.*
a brooch	ブローチ	*burōchi*
a chain	チェーン／鎖	*chēn/kusari*
some cufflinks	カフス・ボタン	*kafusu botan*
some earrings	イヤリング	*iyaringu*
some earrings for pierced ears	ピアスのイヤリング	*piasu no iyaringu*
a necklace	ネックレス	*nekkuresu*
a pendant	ペンダント	*pendanto*
a pin	飾りピン	*kazari pin*
a ring	指輪	*yubiwa*
a wristwatch	腕時計	*ude dokei*
Is this <u>gold</u>?	それは<u>金</u>ですか。	*Sore wa <u>kin</u> desu ka.*

platinum	プラチナ	*purachina*
silver	銀	*gin*
stainless steel	ステンレス	*sutenresu*

How many karats is it? それは、何金ですか。*Sore wa, nan kin desu ka.*

Is it solid gold? それは、純金ですか。*Sore wa, jun kin desu ka.*

Is it gold plated? それは、金めっきですか。*Sore wa, kin mekki desu ka.*

What kind of stone is that? その石は、何ですか。*Sono ishi wa, nan desu ka.*

I want <u>an amethyst</u>. <u>アメジスト</u>が、欲しいのですが。*<u>Amejisuto</u> ga, hoshii no desu ga.*

an aquamarine	アクアマリン	*akuamarin*
a diamond	ダイアモンド	*daiamondo*
an emerald	エメラルド	*emerarudo*
jade	ひすい	*hisui*
onyx	しまめのう／オニキス	*shimamenō/onikisu*
opal	オパール	*opāru*
pearls	真珠／パール	*shinju/pāru*
cultured pearls	養殖真珠	*yōshoku shinju*
a ruby	ルビー	*rubī*
a sapphire	サファイア	*safaia*
a topaz	トパーズ	*topāzu*
turquoise	トルコ石	*toruko ishi*

How much is it? それは、いくらですか。*Sore wa, ikura desu ka.*

Are these Japanese pearls? これは、日本の真珠ですか。*Kore wa, Nihon no shinju desu ka.*

Are they freshwater or seawater pearls?	これは淡水産の真珠ですか、海の真珠ですか。 *Kore wa tansui san no shinju desu ka, umi no shinju desu ka.*
The luster is wonderful.	素晴らしい光沢です。 *Subarashii kōtaku desu.*
I prefer a baroque/ round shape.	変わった／丸い形の方が、好きなんですが。 *Kawatta/marui katachi no hō ga, suki nandesu ga.*
Can you tell me how to care for them?	手入れの仕方を、教えて下さい。 *Teire no shikata o, oshiete kudasai.*

CLOCKS AND WATCHES

I'd like a wristwatch.	腕時計が、欲しいのですが。 *Ude dokei ga, hoshii no desu ga.*
I want a <u>digital</u> watch.	<u>デジタル</u>の時計が、欲しいです。 *<u>Dejitaru</u> no tokei ga, hoshii desu.*
quartz	クオーツ *kuōtsu*
I want a watch with a <u>calendar</u> function.	<u>カレンダー</u>付きの時計が、欲しいです。 *<u>Karendā</u> tsuki no tokei ga, hoshii desu.*
an alarm	アラーム／ベル *arāmu/beru*
a calculator function	計算機能 *keisan kinō*
I'd like a clock.	時計が、欲しいのですが。 *Tokei ga, hoshii no desu ga.*
I want <u>an alarm clock</u>.	<u>目覚まし時計</u>が、欲しいです。 *<u>Mezamashi dokei</u> ga, hoshii desu.*
a travel alarm	旅行用の目覚まし *ryokō yō no mezamashi*

MUSIC, RECORDS, AND TAPES

Is there a record shop around here?	近くに、レコード店がありますか。 *Chikaku ni, rekōdo ten ga arimasu ka.*
Tell me how to get there, please.	そこへの、道順を教えて下さい。 *Soko e no, michijun o oshiete kudasai.*
Do you sell <u>anime videos</u>?	<u>アニメのビデオ</u>を、売っていますか。 *<u>Anime no bideo</u> o, utte imasu ka.*
CDs	シーディー　*shīdī*
DVDs	ディービーディー　*dībīdī*
music videos	ミュージック・ビデオ　*myūjikku bideo*
records	レコード　*rekōdo*
video tapes	ビデオテープ　*bideo tēpu*
Do you have <u>video games</u>?	<u>ビデオゲーム</u>が、ありますか。 *<u>Bideo gēmu</u> ga, arimasu ka.*
CDs for karaoke	カラオケ用のシーディー *karaoke yō no shīdī*
DVDs for karaoke	カラオケ用のディー ビーディー *karaoke yō no dībīdī*
Where is the <u>American music</u> section?	<u>アメリカの音楽</u>は、どこにありますか。 *<u>Amerika no ongaku</u> wa, doko ni arimasu ka.*
classical music	クラシック　*kurashikku*
country music	カントリーミュージック　*kantorī myūjikku*
hard rock	ハードロック　*hādorokku*
heavy metal	ヘビーメタル　*hebī metaru*
Japanese children's music	日本の童謡　*Nihon no dōyō*
Japanese folk songs	日本の民謡　*Nihon no min-yō*
Japanese popular songs	歌謡曲　*kayōkyoku*

Japanese traditional music	日本の伝統音楽 *Nihon no dentō ongaku*
jazz	ジャズ *jazu*
J-POP	ジェイポップ *jeipoppu*
latest hits	最近のヒット曲 *saikin no hitto kyoku*
opera	オペラ *opera*
pop music	ポピュラーソング *popyurā songu*
rap music	ラップ・ミュージック *rappu myūjikku*
rock music	ロック *rokku*
Can I listen to this CD/DVD/record?	このシーディー／ディービーディー／レコードを聞かせて もらえますか。 *Kono shīdī/dībīdī/rekōdo o, kikasete moraemasu ka.*
Do you have any CD/DVD/record by _____?	＿＿のシーディー／ディービーディー／レコードがありますか。 *_____ no shīdī/dībīdī/rekōdo ga, arimasu ka.*

NEWSPAPERS AND MAGAZINES

Do you carry newspapers/ magazines in English?	英語の新聞／雑誌が、ありますか。 *Eigo no shinbun/zasshi ga, arimasu ka.*
I'd like an English-language newspaper.	英語の新聞が、欲しいのですが。 *Eigo no shinbun ga, hoshii no desu ga.*
May I see what you have, please?	何があるか、見せて下さい。*Nani ga aru ka, misete kudasai.*
Do you have <u>news magazines</u>?	<u>ニュース関係の雑誌</u>が、ありますか。 *<u>Nyūsu kankei no zasshi</u> ga, arimasu ka.*
picture postcards	絵はがき　*ehagaki*
stamps	切手　*kitte*
I'd like these.	これを、下さい。*Kore o, kudasai.*
How much are they?	いくらですか。*Ikura desu ka.*

PHOTOGRAPHIC SUPPLIES

Where is there a <u>camera</u> shop?	<u>カメラ</u>屋は、どこにありますか。 *<u>Kamera</u> ya wa, doko ni arimasu ka.*
photo	写真　*shashin*
Do you develop film here?	フィルムの現像をしますか。 *Firumu no genzō o shimasu ka.*
Can I get photos printed from my <u>memory card</u>?	メモリーカードから写真にしてもらえますか。*<u>Memorī kādo</u> kara shashin ni shite moraemasu ka.*
CD	シーディー　*shīdī*
DVD	ディービーディー　*dībīdī*

I want one print of each.	写真は、一枚ずつ一組お願いします。 *Shashin wa, ichi mai zutsu hitokumi onegai shimasu.*
I want a print with a <u>glossy</u> finish.	<u>光沢</u>仕上げにして下さい。*<u>Kōtaku</u> shiage ni shite kudasai.*
matte	つや消しの *tsuya keshi no*
When will the photos be ready?	仕上がりは、いつですか。*Shiagari wa, itsu desu ka.*
I want an <u>enlargement</u>.	<u>引き伸ばし</u>して下さい。 *<u>Hikinobashi</u> shite kudasai.*
some reprints	焼き増し *yakimashi*
I want size _____.	サイズは、_____にして下さい。 *Saizu wa, _____ ni shite kudasai.*
I want a roll of <u>color</u> film.	<u>カラー</u>フィルムを、一本下さい。 *<u>Karā</u> firumu o, ippon kudasai.*
black-and-white	白黒の *shiro kuro no*
I want a roll of film for slides.	スライド用のフィルムを、一本下さい。 *Suraido yō no firumu o, ippon kudasai.*
I'd like some film for this camera.	このカメラ用のフィルムを下さい。*Kono kamera yō no firumu o kudasai.*
I'd like <u>36 exposures</u>.	<u>三十六枚どり</u>のフィルムを下さい。 *<u>San jū roku mai dori</u> no firumu o kudasai.*
24 exposures	二十四枚どりのフィルム *ni jū yon mai dori no firumu*
indoor type	室内用のフィルム *shitsunai yō no firumu*
outdoor type	屋外用のフィルム *okugai yō no firumu*
Do you have film with ISO _____?	感度が_____のフィルムが、ありますか。*Kando ga _____ no firumu ga, arimasu ka.*

I'd like to buy a <u>camera</u>.	<u>カメラ</u>が買いたいのですが。 *Kamera ga kaitai no desu ga.*
camera with panoramic mode	パノラマ機能付きカメラ *panorama kinō tsuki kamera*
compact camera	コンパクト・カメラ　*konpakuto kamera*
digital camera	デジタルカメラ　*dejitaru kamera*
disposable camera	使い捨てカメラ　*tsukaisute kamera*
zoom camera	ズーム・カメラ　*zūmu kamera*
I'd like to buy an expensive/inexpensive camera.	高級／高くないカメラが買いたいのですが。*Kōkyū/takakunai kamera ga kaitai no desu ga.*
I want <u>an exposure meter</u>.	<u>露出計</u>が欲しいのですが。*Roshutsu kei ga, hoshii no desu ga.*
a battery for a camera	カメラ用の電池　*kamera yō no denchi*
a close-up lens	接写レンズ　*sessha renzu*
a filter	フィルター　*firutā*
a lens	レンズ　*renzu*
a lens cap	レンズ・キャップ　*renzu kyappu*
a lens cleaner	レンズ・クリーナー　*renzu kurīnā*
a memory card	メモリーカード　*memorī kādo*
a selfie stick	自分撮りスティック　*jibundori sutikku*
a telescopic lens	望遠レンズ　*bōen renzu*
a tripod	三脚　*sankyaku*
a wide-angle lens	広角レンズ　*kōkaku renzu*
a zoom lens	ズーム・レンズ　*zūmu renzu*

GIFT SHOPS: JAPANESE

Allow yourself time to browse in Japanese-style gift shops. You're sure to see something you like. Japanese shopkeepers will wrap purchases beautifully, whether they're intended as gifts or not!

I'd like <u>a nice gift</u>.	何かいいおみやげが、買いたいのですが。*Nanika ii <u>omiyage</u> ga, kaitai no desu ga.*
a small gift	小さいおみやげ *chiisai omiyage*
a souvenir	おみやげ／記念品 *omiyage/ kinen hin*
It's for _____.	_____に、あげます。 _____ *ni, agemasu.*
I don't want to spend more than _____ yen.	_____円以下のものが、欲しいのですが。_____ *en ika no mono ga, hoshii no desu ga.*
Could you suggest something?	何がいいでしょうか。*Nani ga ii deshō ka.*
Could you show me your <u>bamboo baskets</u>?	<u>竹かご</u>を、見せてもらえますか。<u>*Take kago*</u> *o, misete moraemasu ka.*
blown glass	口吹きガラス *kuchibuki garasu*
carved objects	彫刻品 *chōkoku hin*
ceramics	陶磁器 *tōjiki*
chopsticks	はし *hashi*
cloisonné	七宝焼 *shippō yaki*
fabric	布／生地 *nuno/kiji*
fans	扇／扇子 *ōgi/sensu*
Japanese chests of drawers	たんす *tansu*
Japanese dolls	日本人形 *Nihon ningyō*

Japanese folk toys	民芸玩具	*mingei gangu*
Japanese games	日本伝統のゲーム	*Nihon dentō no gēmu*
Japanese swords	日本刀	*Nihontō*
kimonos	着物	*kimono*
kites	凧	*tako*
lacquerware	塗り物／漆器	*nurimono/shikki*
masks	お面	*omen*
origami paper	折り紙	*origami*
paper crafts	紙細工	*kami zaiku*
paper lanterns	ちょうちん	*chōchin*
papier-mâché	張り子細工	*hariko zaiku*
porcelain	磁器	*jiki*
rice paper	和紙	*washi*
sake bottles	とっくり	*tokkuri*
sake cups	盃	*sakazuki*
scrolls	掛け軸	*kakejiku*
tea bowls	茶道のお茶碗	*sadō no ochawan*
tea cups	湯飲み茶碗	*yunomi jawan*
tea pots	急須／土瓶	*kyūsu/dobin*
trays	お盆	*obon*
woodblock prints	木版画	*mokuhanga*

Is this handmade?	それは、手作りの品ですか。*Sore wa, tezukuri no shina desu ka.*
Where in Japan is it from?	どの地方の産ですか。*Dono chihō no san desu ka.*

STATIONERY ITEMS

I want to buy a ballpoint pen.	ボールペンを、下さい。	*Bōrupen o, kudasai.*
a deck of cards	トランプ	*toranpu*
some correction fluid	修正液	*shūsei eki*
some correction tape	修正テープ	*shūsei tēpu*
some envelopes	封筒	*fūtō*
an eraser	消しゴム	*keshigomu*
a fountain pen	万年筆	*mannenhitsu*
some glue	接着剤／のり	*setchaku zai/nori*
a bottle of ink	インク	*inku*
ink cartridges	インクのカートリッジ	*inku no kātorijji*
a knife	ナイフ	*naifu*
a magnifier	虫めがね	*mushimegane*
a marker	マジックペン	*majikku pen*
some masking tape	マスキン・テープ	*masukin tēpu*
a mechanical pencil	シャープペンシル	*shāpupenshiru*
a notebook	ノート	*nōto*
some paper clips	クリップ	*kurippu*
some pencils	鉛筆	*enpitsu*
a pencil sharpener	鉛筆削り	*enpitsu kezuri*
some Post-its	ポスト・イット／ふせん	*posuto itto/fusen*
some rubber bands	輪ゴム	*wa gomu*
a ruler	定規	*jōgi*
some safety pins	安全ピン	*anzen pin*

a pair of scissors	はさみ	*hasami*
some Scotch tape	セロテープ	*serotēpu*
a stapler	ホッチキス	*hotchikisu*
some string	ひも	*nimo*
a tape measure	巻尺	*makijaku*
some printing paper	プリント用紙	*purinto yōshi*
some wrapping paper	包装用紙	*hōsō yōshi*
a writing pad	筆記用紙	*hikki yōshi*
some writing paper	便せん	*binsen*

TOBACCO

There are many no-smoking areas in Japan, and smoking is prohibited in many public places. In some *ku* (administrative districts) in Tokyo, smoking in the streets is forbidden except in designated areas. If you're caught, you must pay a penalty. Akihabara, for example, is in one of these districts. So smokers should be aware of these restrictions. At the same time, some restaurants, coffee shops, and bars do allow smoking. You may ask to be seated in a no-smoking area, but don't be surprised if they don't have one.

A pack of cigarettes, please.	たばこを、一箱下さい。*Tabako o, hito hako kudasai.*
I'd like <u>filtered</u> cigarettes.	<u>フィルター付きの</u>たばこを下さい。 <u>*Firutā tsuki no* tabako o, kudasai.</u>
unfiltered	フィルターの付いていない *firutā no tsuite inai*
menthol	はっか入りの　*hakka iri no*
king size	キングサイズの　*kingu saizu no*
mild	マイルドな　*mairudo na*
low nicotine, low tar	ニコチンが少ない　*nikochin ga sukunai*

Are these cigarettes strong/mild?	このたばこは、強い／軽いですか。 *Kono tabako wa, tsuyoi/karui desu ka.*
Do you have American cigarettes?	アメリカのたばこが、ありますか。 *Amerika no tabako ga, arimasu ka.*
What brands?	どんな種類がありますか。 *Donna shurui ga, arimasu ka.*
Please give me some matches, too.	マッチも下さい。 *Matchi mo kudasai.*
Do you sell <u>chewing tobacco</u>?	<u>かみたばこ</u>は、売っていますか。 <u>*Kami tabako*</u> *wa, utte imasu ka.*
cigarette holders	シガレット・ホールダー *shigaretto hōrudā*
cigars	葉巻　*hamaki*
electronic cigarettes/ e-cigarettes	電子たばこ　*denshi tabako*
lighters	ライター　*raitā*
pipes	パイプ　*paipu*
pipe tobacco	きざみたばこ　*kizami tabako*
snuff	かぎたばこ　*kagi tabako*

SMOKING

Is this a <u>smoking</u> area?	ここは、喫煙地域ですか。 *Koko wa, kitsuen chiiki desu ka.*
nonsmoking	禁煙　*kin-en*
Where is a smoking area?	喫煙地域は、どこですか。 *Kitsuen chiiki wa, doko desu ka.*
Would you like a cigarette?	たばこは、いかがですか。 *Tabako wa, ikaga desu ka.*
May I trouble you for <u>a cigarette</u>?	<u>たばこを一本</u>、お願いできますか。 <u>*Tabako o ippon*</u>, *onegai dekimasu ka.*
light	たばこの火を　*tabako no hi o*

No thanks, I don't smoke.	けっこうです。たばこは、吸いません。 *Kekkō desu. Tabako wa, suimasen.*
I've given it up.	たばこは、止めました。*Tabako wa, yamemashita.*
Do you mind if I smoke?	たばこを吸っても、かまいませんか。 *Tabako o suttemo, kamaimasen ka.*
I don't mind if you smoke.	どうぞ、お吸いください。*Dōzo, osui kudasai.*
Would you mind putting out the cigarette?	たばこを、消していただけますか。 *Tabako o, keshite itadakemasu ka.*

TOILETRIES

Is there a store that carries <u>American</u> toiletries?	<u>アメリカの</u>化粧品類を売っている店が、ありますか。<u>*Amerika no*</u> *keshōhin rui o utte iru mise ga, arimasu ka.*
European	ヨーロッパの　*yōroppa no*
Do you have <u>after-shave lotion</u>?	<u>アフターシェーブ・ローション</u>が、ありますか。<u>*Afutāshēbu rōshon*</u> *ga, arimasu ka.*
bobby pins	ヘアー・ピン　*heā pin*
body lotion	ボディー・ローション　*bodī rōshon*
brushes	ブラシ　*burashi*
cleansing cream	クレンジング・クリーム *kurenjingu kurīmu*
cologne	オーデコロン　*ōdekoron*
combs	くし　*kushi*
conditioner	コンディショナー　*kondishonā*
cream rinse	クリーム・リンス　*kurīmu rinsu*
curlers	カーラー　*kārā*

deodorant	デオドラント	*deodoranto*
emery boards	爪やすり	*tsume yasuri*
eye liner	アイライナー	*airainā*
eye pencils	アイペンシル	*ai penshiru*
eye shadow	アイシャドー	*aishadō*
eyebrow pencils	まゆずみ	*mayuzumi*
face powder	おしろい	*oshiroi*
hair color	毛染め	*kezome*
hair spray	ヘアー・スプレー	*heā supurē*
hand lotion	ハンド・ローション	*hando rōshon*
lipstick	口紅	*kuchibeni*
mascara	マスカラ	*masukara*
mirrors	鏡	*kagami*
nail clippers	爪切り	*tsume kiri*
nail files	爪やすり	*tsume yasuri*
nail polish	マニキュア液／エナメル	*manikyua eki/enameru*
nail polish remover	マニキュア落とし／除光液	*manikyua otoshi/jokō eki*
perfume	香水	*kōsui*
razors	かみそり	*kamisori*
razor blades	かみそりの刃	*kamisori no ha*
rouge, blusher	ほお紅	*hōbeni*
safety pins	安全ピン	*anzen pin*
(cuticle) scissors	(あま皮用の)はさみ	*amakawa yō no hasami*
shampoo	シャンプー	*shanpū*

shaving lotion	シェービング・ローション *shēbingu rōshon*
soap	石鹸　*sekken*
sponges	スポンジ　*suponji*
styling gel/mousse	スタイリング・ジェル／ムース *sutairingu jeru/mūsu*
sunscreen	日焼け止め　*hiyake dome*
suntan lotion	サンタン・ローション　*santan rōshon*
tissues	ちり紙／ティッシュー*chirigami/* *tisshū*
toothbrushes	歯ブラシ　*haburashi*
toothpaste	練り歯みがき　*neri hamigaki*
towels	タオル　*taoru*
tweezers	毛抜き　*kenuki*

PERSONAL CARE AND SERVICES

If your hotel doesn't offer these services, ask the desk clerk to recommend someone nearby.

AT THE BARBER

Although tipping for services is not common practice, it is expected at some hair salons in large tourist hotels. If so, you'll see a sign; 10 percent would be appropriate.

Does this hotel have a barbershop?	このホテルには、床屋がありますか。 *Kono hoteru niwa, tokoya ga arimasu ka.*
Do you know where a good barbershop is?	上手な床屋がどこにあるか、知っていますか。*Jōzu na tokoya ga doko ni aru ka, shitte imasu ka.*
Would I have to wait long?	長いこと、待たねばなりませんか。 *Nagai koto, mataneba narimasen ka.*
How much does a haircut cost there?	そこでの散髪は、いくらしますか。 *Soko de no sanpatsu wa, ikura shimasu ka.*
Whose turn is it?	だれの番ですか。 *Dare no ban desu ka.*
I don't have much time.	あまり、時間がありません。 *Amari, jikan ga arimasen.*
I want a haircut.	散髪して下さい。 *Sanpatsu shite kudasai.*
I want a shave.	ひげを、そって下さい。 *Hige o, sotte kudasai.*
Don't cut it too short, please.	あまり、短く刈らないで下さい。 *Amari, mijikaku karanai de kudasai.*

Just a trim, please.	形を、整えるだけでいいです。 *Katachi o, totonoeru dake de ii desu.*
Short in back, long in front.	前は長め、後ろは短めにして下さい。 *Mae wa nagame, ushiro wa mijikame ni shite kudasai.*
Leave it long.	全体、長めのままでいいです。 *Zentai, nagame no mama de ii desu.*
I want it (very) short.	(かなり)短めにして下さい。 *(Kanari) mijikame ni shite kudasai.*
You can cut a little <u>in back</u>.	<u>後ろ</u>を、ちょっと刈って下さい。 *<u>Ushiro</u> o, chotto katte kudasai.*
in front	前 *mae*
off the top	てっぺん *teppen*
on the sides	両側 *ryōgawa*
I part my hair <u>on the left</u>.	分け目は、<u>左側</u>です。*Wakeme wa, <u>hidari gawa</u> desu.*
on the right	右側 *migi gawa*
in the middle	真ん中 *mannaka*
I comb my hair straight back.	髪は、いつもまっすぐ後ろへとかしています。*Kami wa, itsumo massugu ushiro e tokashite imasu.*
Cut a little bit more here.	ここを、もうちょっと刈って下さい。 *Koko o, mō chotto katte kudasai.*
That's enough.	それで、十分です。*Sore de, jūbun desu.*
It's fine that way.	それで、結構です。*Sore de, kekkō desu.*
I don't want tonic.	ヘアー・トニックは、つけないで下さい。*Heā tonikku wa, tsukenai de kudasai.*

I don't want hair oil.   ヘアー・オイルは、使わないで下さい。 *Heā oiru wa, tsukawanai de kudasai.*

I don't want hair spray.   ヘアー・スプレーは、使わないで下さい。 *Heā supurē wa, tsukawanaide kudasai.*

Please use the scissors only.   はさみだけで、刈って下さい。 *Hasami dake de, katte kudasai.*

Please trim my <u>beard</u>.   <u>あごひげ</u>を、刈りそろえて下さい。 *<u>Agohige</u> o, karisoroete kudasai.*

   mustache   口ひげ   *kuchihige*

   sideburns   もみあげ   *momiage*

Thank you very much.   どうも、ありがとうございました。 *Dōmo, arigatō gozaimashita.*

How much do I owe you?   いかほどですか。 *Ikahodo desu ka.*

AT THE HAIR SALON

Check under "At the Barber," page 292, for tipping hints.

Is there a hair salon <u>in</u> the hotel?   ホテルの<u>中に</u>、美容院がありますか。 *Hoteru no <u>naka ni</u>, biyōin ga arimasu ka.*

   near   近くに   *chikaku ni*

Do you know where a good hair salon is?   上手な美容院がどこにあるか、ごぞんじですか。 *Jōzu na biyōin ga doko ni aru ka, gozonji desu ka.*

What are the business hours?   何時から何時まで、やっていますか。 *Nan ji kara nan ji made, yatte imasu ka.*

Are they used to foreigners' hair?   そこの美容師は、外人の髪の毛に慣れていますか。 *Soko no biyōshi wa, gaijin no kami no ke ni narete imasu ka.*

Is it an expensive place?	そこは、高い美容院ですか。*Soko wa, takai biyōin desu ka.*
Can you give me a <u>color rinse</u>?	<u>カラー・リンスをして</u>もらえますか。*<u>Karā rinsu o shite</u> moraemasu ka.*
facial	フェイシャルをして *feisharu o shite*
haircut	カットをして *katto o shite*
manicure	ネイルをして *neiru o shite*
pedicure	ペディキュア *pedikyua*
shampoo	シャンプーをして *shanpū o shite*
shampoo and blow dry	シャンプーの後ブロー・ドライして *shanpū no ato burō dorai shite*
How long does it take?	どのくらい時間がかかりますか。*Donokurai jikan ga kakarimasu ka.*
I'd like to see a color chart.	色の表を、見せて下さい。*Iro no hyō o, misete kudasai.*
I want <u>auburn</u>.	<u>赤茶色を</u>、お願いします。*<u>Akachairo o</u>, onegaishimasu.*
blond	ブロンド *burondo*
brunette	ブルネット *burunetto*
a darker color	もっと濃い色 *motto koi iro*
a lighter color	もっと薄い色 *motto usui iro*
the same color	同じ色 *onaji iro*
Don't apply any hair spray.	ヘアー・スプレーは、使わないで下さい。*Heā supurē wa, tsukawanai de kudasai.*
Not too much hair spray.	ヘアー・スプレーは、あまりかけないで下さい。*Heā supurē wa, amari kakenai de kudasai.*

I want <u>bangs</u>.	<u>前髪を下げて</u>下さい。 *<u>Maegami o</u> <u>sagete</u> kudasai.*
a bun	シニヨン・スタイルにして *shiniyon sutairu ni shite*
it curly	巻き毛／カーリーにして *makige/kārī ni shite*
it straight	まっすぐにして　*massugu ni shite*
it wavy	ウェーブをかけて　*wēbu o kakete*
Is it done?	終わりましたか。*Owarimashita ka.*
Thank you very much.	どうも、ありがとうございました。 *Dōmo, arigatō gozaimashita.*
How much do I owe you?	おいくらですか。*Oikura desu ka.*

AT THE NAIL SALON

You should keep in mind that "manicure" in Japan refers to a type of hair color procedure. If you want your nails done, the word is *neiru*. First, find out if the salon takes walk-ins or if you need an appointment.

Can you recommend a nail salon?	いいネイルサロンを教えてもらえますか。 *Ii neiru saron o oshiete moraemasu ka.*
nail salon	ネイルサロン　*neiru saron*
nail	ネイル／マニキュア　*neiru/manikyua*
pedicure	ペディキュア　*pedikyua*
manicure designs	ネイルアート (nail art) *neiru āto*
<u>Manicure</u>, please.	<u>ネイル</u>をお願いします。　*Neiru o onegaishimasu.*
pedicure	ペディキュア　*pedikyua*
manicure design	ネイルアート　*neiru āto*

Same color please.	同じ色でお願いします。*Onaji iro de onegaishimasu.*
What colors do you have?	どんな色がありますか。*Donna iro ga arimasu ka.*
I'll take this color.	この色にします。*Kono iro ni shimasu.*
Gel, please.	ジェルをお願いします。*Jeru o onegai shimasu.*
I'd like acrylics.	アクリルネイルをお願いします。*Akuriru neiru o onegaishimasu.*
I'd like a French manicure.	フレンチネイルをお願いします。*Furenchi neiru o onegaishimasu.*
Leave them long, please.	長いままでお願いします。 *Nagai mama de onegaishimasu.*
A little shorter, please.	もうちょっと短くしてください。 *Mō chotto mijikaku shite kudasai.*
File them <u>square</u>, please.	<u>スクエアネイル</u>にしてください。<u>*Sukuea neiru*</u> *ni shite kudasai.*
oval	オーバルネイル *ōbaru neiru*
Are they dry yet?	乾きましたか。 *Kawaimashita ka.*

LAUNDRY AND DRY CLEANING

Do you have laundry service in this hotel?	このホテルには、洗濯のサービスがありますか。*Kono hoteru niwa, sentaku no sābisu ga arimasu ka.*
Do you have dry cleaning service in this hotel?	このホテルには、ドライ・クリーニングのサービスがありますか。*Kono hoteru niwa, dorai kurīningu no sābisu ga arimasu ka.*
Where is the nearest <u>laundry</u>?	一番近い<u>洗濯屋</u>は、どこですか。*Ichiban chikai <u>sentaku ya</u> wa, doko desu ka.*

dry cleaner	クリーニング屋	*kurīningu ya*
laundromat	コイン・ランドリー	*koin randorī*

I want this dry cleaned.
これを、ドライ・クリーニングして下さい。*Kore o, dorai kurīningu shite kudasai.*

I want this ironed/pressed.
これに、アイロンをかけて下さい。*Kore ni, airon o kakete kudasai.*

I want this mended.
これを、繕って下さい。*Kore o, tsukurotte kudasai.*

I want this washed.
これを、洗濯して下さい。*Kore o, sentaku shite kudasai.*

When will it be ready?
いつ、できあがりますか。*Itsu, dekiagarimasu ka.*

I need it for <u>tonight</u>.
<u>今晩</u>、必要なんですが。*<u>Konban</u>, hitsuyō nan desu ga.*

    tomorrow
あした　*ashita*

    the day after tomorrow
あさって　*asatte*

Could you do it as soon as possible?
できるだけ早く、仕上げてもらえますか。*Dekiru dake hayaku, shiagete moraemasu ka.*

Can you get the stain out?
このしみを、抜いてもらえますか。*Kono shimi o, nuite moraemasu ka.*

Can you sew this button on?
このボタンを、つけてもらえますか。*Kono botan o, tsukete moraemasu ka.*

I want my shirts <u>well starched</u>.
ワイシャツは、<u>のりをよくきかせて</u>下さい。*Waishatsu wa, <u>nori o yoku kikasete</u> kudasai.*

    lightly starched
薄のりにして　*usu nori ni shite*

I don't want my shirts starched.
ワイシャツに、のりはいりません。*waishatsu ni, nori wa irimasen.*

I want my shirts <u>boxed</u>.	ワイシャツは、<u>箱に入れて</u>下さい。 *Waishatsu wa, <u>hako ni irete</u> kudasai.*
folded	たたんで *tatande*
on hangers	ハンガーにつるして *hangā ni tsurushite*
What time shall I come for them?	何時に、取りに来ればいいですか。 *Nan ji ni, tori ni kureba ii desu ka.*

SHOE REPAIRS

The heel of my high-heeled shoes <u>came off</u>.	ハイヒールのかかとが、<u>とれて</u>しまいました。 *Haihīru no kakato ga, <u>torete</u> shimaimashita.*
broke	折れて *orete*
Can you fix it while I wait?	待っている間に、直してもらえますか。 *Matte iru aida ni, naoshite moraemasu ka.*
I want these shoes repaired.	このくつを、直して下さい。*Kono kutsu o, naoshite kudasai.*
I need new <u>heels</u>.	新しい<u>かかと</u>に、替えて下さい。 *Atarashii <u>kakato</u> ni, kaete kudasai.*
soles	くつ底 *kutsu zoko*
heels and soles	かかととくつ底 *kakato to kutsu zoko*
Would you polish them, too?	靴も、磨いておいてもらえますか。 *Kutsu mo, migaite oite moraemasu ka.*
When will they be ready?	いつ、できあがりますか。*Itsu, dekiagarimasu ka.*

WATCH REPAIRS

I need a battery for this watch.	この時計用の電池が、欲しいのですが。 *Kono tokei yō no denchi ga, hoshii no desu ga.*
Can you fix this watch/clock?	この時計を、直してもらえますか。 *Kono tokei o, naoshite moraemasu ka.*
I dropped it.	おっことしてしまいました。 *Okkotoshite shimaimashita.*
It's stopped.	動きません。*Ugokimasen.*
When will it be ready?	いつ、できあがりますか。*Itsu, dekiagarimasu ka.*

CAMERA REPAIRS

There's something wrong with this camera.	カメラの調子が、悪いのですが。 *Kamera no chōshi ga, warui no desu ga.*
Can you fix it?	直してもらえますか。*Naoshite moraemasu ka.*
The focus is off.	焦点が合いません。*Shōten ga aimasen.*
The screen is blank.	スクリーンが真っ暗です。*Sukurīn ga makkura desu.*
I can't get the memory card out.	メモリーカードが取り出せません。 *Memorī kādo ga toridasemasen.*
How much will it cost to fix it?	修理には、いくらかかりますか。 *Shūri niwa, ikura kakarimasu ka.*
When will it be ready?	いつ、できるでしょうか。*Itsu, dekiru deshō ka.*

HEALTH AND MEDICAL CARE

THE PHARMACY

Where is the nearest pharmacy?	最寄りの薬屋は、どこにありますか。 *Moyori no kusuri ya wa, doko ni arimasu ka.*
Is there an all-night pharmacy?	終夜営業の薬屋が、ありますか。 *Shūya eigyō no kusuri ya ga, arimasu ka.*
Where is the all-night pharmacy?	終夜営業の薬屋は、どこにありますか。 *Shūya eigyō no kusuri ya wa, doko ni arimasu ka.*
What time does the pharmacy <u>open</u>?	その薬屋は、何時に<u>開きます</u>か。 *Sono kusuri ya wa, nan ji ni <u>akimasu</u> ka.*
close	閉まります　*shimarimasu*
Is there a pharmacy that carries American/ European products?	アメリカ／ヨーロッパ製品を売っている薬屋が、ありますか。*Amerika/ Yōroppa seihin o utte iru kusuri ya ga, arimasu ka.*
Something for <u>asthma</u>, please.	ぜんそくの薬を下さい。<u>Zensoku</u> no kusuri o kudasai.
a burn	やけど　*yakedo*
a cold	風邪　*kaze*
a cut	切り傷　*kiri kizu*
constipation	便秘　*benpi*
a cough	せき　*seki*
diarrhea	下痢　*geri*
a fever	熱　*netsu*

hay fever	花粉症	*kafun shō*
a headache	頭痛	*zutsū*
an insect bite	虫刺され	*mushi sasare*
insomnia	不眠症	*fumin shō*
nausea	吐き気	*hakike*
a sunburn	日焼け	*hiyake*
a toothache	歯痛／歯いた	*shitsū/haita*
an upset stomach	胃がおかしいとき	*I ga okashii toki*

Is a prescription needed for the medicine?	その薬には、処方箋が必要ですか。 *Sono kusuri niwa, shohōsen ga hitsuyō desu ka.*
Can you fill this prescription for me now?	この処方箋の薬を、今もらえますか。 *Kono shohōsen no kusuri o, ima moraemasu ka.*
It's an emergency.	急病です。 *Kyūbyō desu.*
Can I wait for it?	薬は、待っていたらもらえますか。 *Kusuri wa, matte itara moraemasu ka.*
How long will it take?	薬をもらうのに、どのくらい時間がかかりますか。 *Kusuri o morau no ni, dono kurai jikan ga kakarimasu ka.*
When can I come for it?	いつ、取りに来ましょうか。 *Itsu, tori ni kimashō ka.*
Do you have contact lens care products for <u>soft lenses</u>?	<u>ソフト・コンタクト・レンズ</u>の、手入れ用の品がありますか。 <u>*Sofuto kontakuto renzu*</u> *no, teire yō no shina ga arimasu ka.*
hard lenses	ハード・コンタクト・レンズ *hādo kontakuto renzu*
May I see what you have?	何があるか、見せてもらえますか。 *Nani ga aru ka, misete moraemasu ka.*

I need a carrying case for <u>hard lenses</u>.	ハード・コンタクト・レンズの、携帯用ケースがありますか。<u>*Hādo kontakuto renzu* no</u>, *keitai yō kēsu ga arimasu ka.*
soft lenses	ソフト・コンタクト・レンズ *sofuto kontakuto renzu*
I would like <u>some adhesive tape</u>.	ばんそうこうを、下さい。<u>*Bansōkō* o</u>, *kudasai.*
some alcohol	アルコール　*arukōru*
an antacid	胃散　*isan*
an antiseptic	消毒薬　*shōdokuyaku*
some aspirin	アスピリン　*asupirin*
an aspirin-free painkiller	アスピリンを含まない鎮痛剤 *asupirin o fukumanai chintsū zai*
some bandages	包帯　*hōtai*
some Band-Aids	バンドエイド　*bando eido*
some condoms	コンドーム　*kondōmu*
some corn plasters	魚の目膏薬　*uonome kōyaku*
some cotton	脱脂綿　*dasshimen*
some cough drops	咳止めドロップ　*sekidome doroppu*
some cough syrup	咳止めシロップ　*sekidome shiroppu*
some (disposable) diapers	(使い捨ての)おしめ *(tsukaisute no) oshime*
some ear drops	耳薬　*mimigusuri*
some eye drops	目薬　*megusuri*
a first-aid kit	救急箱　*kyūkyū bako*
some gauze	ガーゼ　*gāze*
some insect repellent	虫よけの薬　*mushi yoke no kusuri*

some iodine	ヨードチンキ	*yōdochinki*
a laxative	下剤／通じ薬	*gezai/tsūjiyaku*
a razor	かみそり	*kamisori*
some razor blades	かみそりの刃	*kamisori no ha*
some sanitary napkins	生理ナプキン	*seiri napukin*
some sleeping pills	睡眠薬	*suiminyaku*
some suppositories	座薬	*zayaku*
some talcum powder	シッカロール	*shikkarōru*
some tampons	タンポン	*tanpon*
a thermometer	体温計	*taion kei*
some tissues	ちり紙／ティッシュー	*chirigami/tisshū*
some toilet paper	トイレット・ペーパー	*toiretto pēpā*
a toothbrush	歯ブラシ	*ha burashi*
some toothpaste	練り歯みがき	*neri hamigaki*
some tranquilizers	トランキライザー	*torankiraizā*
some vitamins	ビタミン剤	*bitamin zai*

ACCIDENTS AND EMERGENCIES

The telephone number for an ambulance in emergencies is 119 nationwide. A call to this number will secure an ambulance in 5 or 10 minutes, but the operator speaks Japanese only, and gets off the line quickly. For similar service with more time to make yourself understood, some additional numbers are: Tokyo: 03-3212-2323; Kobe: 78-333-0119. They are part of Japan Helpline, a 24/7 nationwide emergency assistance service. The toll-free number is 0570-000-911. The first four phrases listed here will work on the telephone. For more information on securing medical help, see page 306.

Hello. It's an emergency!	もしもし。緊急事態です。*Moshi moshi. Kinkyū jitai desu.*
<u>I'm</u> hurt.	<u>私は</u>、怪我してしまいました。 <u>*Watakushi wa*</u>, *kega shite shimaimashita.*
my husband's	主人が *shujin ga*
my wife's	家内が *kanai ga*
my child's	子供が *kodomo ga*
somebody's	誰か *dareka*
Can you send an ambulance immediately?	大至急、救急車をお願いします。 *Dai shikyū, kyūkyū sha o onegai shimasu.*
We're located at _____.	場所は、_____です。*Basho wa, _____ desu.*
Help!	助けて。*Tasukete.*
Help me, somebody!	誰か、助けて下さい。*Dareka, tasukete kudasai.*
Get a <u>doctor</u>, quick!	すぐ、<u>医者</u>を呼んで下さい。*Sugu, <u>isha</u> o yonde kudasai.*
nurse	看護師 *kango <u>shi</u>*
Call an ambulance!	救急車を、呼んで下さい。*Kyūkyū sha o, yonde kudasai.*
I need first aid.	応急処置が、必要です。*Ōkyū shochi ga, hitsuyō desu.*
I've fallen.	ころんでしまいました。*Konronde shimaimashita.*
I was knocked down.	突き倒されてしまいました。 *Tsukitaosarete shimaimashita.*
I'm having a heart attack.	心臓麻痺です。*Shinzō mahi desu.*
I burned myself.	やけどしてしまいました。*Yakedo shite shimaimashita.*

I cut myself.	切り傷です。*Kiri kizu desu.*
I'm bleeding.	出血しています。*Shukketsu shite imasu.*
I've lost a lot of blood.	ずいぶん、出血しました。*Zuibun, shukketsu shimashita.*
My <u>wrist</u> is sprained.	<u>手首</u>を、ねんざしてしまいました。<u>*Tekubi* o, nenza shite shimaimashita.</u>
ankle	足首　*ashikubi*
I can't bend my <u>elbow</u>.	<u>ひじ</u>が、曲がりません。<u>*Hiji ga,* magarimasen.</u>
knee	ひざ　*hiza*
neck	首　*kubi*
I can't move my <u>arm</u>.	<u>腕</u>が、動かせません。<u>*Ude ga,* ugokasemasen.</u>
leg	足　*ashi*
neck	首　*kubi*
I think the bone is <u>broken</u>.	<u>骨折</u>してしまったみたいです。<u>*Kossetsu* shite shimatta mitai desu.</u>
dislocated	脱臼　*dakkyū*
The leg is swollen.	足が、はれています。*Ashi ga, harete imasu.*

FINDING A DOCTOR

At a large tourist hotel, the staff can usually help you find a doctor. You can also get a list of English-speaking doctors at the U.S. Embassy's American Citizens Services Website at *http://japan.usembassy.gov/e/tacs-main.html*. If you're on your own, here are a few hospitals with English-speaking doctors and staff members:

TOKYO

St. Luke's International Hospital
(03) 3541-5151, *www.luke.or.jp*

Seibo International Catholic Hospital
(03) 3951-1111, *www.seibokai.or.jp*

	Tokyo Adventist Hospital (03) 3392-6151, *www.tokyoeiei.com*
YOKOHAMA	Bluff Clinic (045) 641-6961, *www.bluffclinic.com*
KYOTO	Japan Baptist Hospital (075) 781-5191, *www.jbh.or.jp*
OSAKA	Yodogawa Christian Hospital (06) 6322-2250, *www.ych.or.jp*

Although many Japanese physicians and dentists speak good English, you can't count on finding them everywhere; it's best to be prepared with some Japanese phrases.

Do you know a doctor who speaks English?	英語を話す医者を、知っていますか。 *Eigo o hanasu isha o, shitte imasu ka.*
Do you know an American doctor?	アメリカ人の医者を、知っていますか。 *Amerika jin no isha o, shitte imasu ka.*
Do you know a doctor who studied medicine in America?	アメリカで医学を勉強した医者を、知っていますか。 *Amerika de igaku o benkyō shita isha o, shitte imasu ka.*
Where is that doctor's <u>office</u>?	その医者の診療所／オフィスは、どこですか。 *Sono isha no <u>shinryō jo/ofisu</u> wa, doko desu ka.*
hospital	病院 *byōin*
What are the office hours?	診療時間は、何時から何時までですか。 *Shinryō jikan wa, nan ji kara nan ji made desu ka.*
Can I just walk in?	予約なしに、行けますか。 *Yoyaku nashi ni, ikemasu ka.*
Do I need to make an appointment?	予約の必要が、ありますか。 *Yoyaku no hitsuyō ga, arimasu ka.*

What's the telephone number of the <u>office</u>?	診療所／オフィスの電話番号は、何番ですか。 <u>*Shinryō jo/ofisu* no denwa bangō wa, nan ban desu ka.</u>
hospital	病院　*byōin*
I want to see <u>an internist</u>.	<u>内科の医者</u>に、行きたいのですが。 <u>*Naika no isha* ni, ikitai no desu ga.</u>
an ear, nose, and throat specialist	耳鼻咽喉科の医者　*jibiinkōka no isha*
a dermatologist	皮膚科の医者　*hifuka no isha*
a gastroenterologist	消化器科の医者　*shōkakika no isha*
a gynecologist	婦人科医　*fujinka i*
an obstetrician	産科医　*sanka i*
an ophthalmologist	眼科医　*ganka i*
an orthopedist	整形外科の医者　*seikeigeka no isha*
a pediatrician	小児科医　*shōnika i*
a surgeon	外科医　*geka i*
a urologist	泌尿器科医　*hitsunyōkika i*

WITH THE DOCTOR

This section is divided into two parts: **Telling the Doctor** and **What the Doctor Says**. You use the phrases under **Telling the Doctor** and hand the book to the doctor so he or she can point to the appropriate phrases under **What the Doctor Says**.

Please point to the phrase in the book.	この本の、適当な文を指さして下さい。 *Kono hon no, tekitō na bun o yubisashite kudasai.*

TELLING THE DOCTOR

I don't feel well.	気分が、すぐれません。*Kibun ga, suguremasen.*
I feel sick.	気分が、悪いです。*Kibun ga, warui desu.*
I'm dizzy.	めまいがします。*Memai ga shimasu.*
I feel weak.	体に、力が入りません。*Karada ni, chikara ga hairimasen.*
It hurts me here.	ここが、痛みます。*Koko ga, itamimasu.*
My whole body hurts.	体全体が、痛みます。*Karada zentai ga, itamimasu.*
I feel faint.	気が、遠くなりそうです。*Ki ga, tōku narisō desu.*
I feel nauseated.	吐き気がします。*Hakike ga shimasu.*
I feel a chill.	悪寒がします。*Okan ga shimasu.*
I've been vomiting.	吐いています。*Haite imasu.*
I'm pregnant.	妊娠中です。*Ninshin chū desu.*
I want to sit down for a while.	ちょっと、座りたいのですが。*Chotto, suwaritai no desu ga.*
My temperature is normal (98.6°F, 37°C).	熱は、平熱です。*Netsu wa, heinetsu desu.*
I feel all right now.	今は、大丈夫です。*Ima wa, daijōbu desu.*
I feel better.	今は、よくなりました。*Ima wa, yoku narimashita.*
I feel worse.	気分が、前より悪くなっています。*Kibun ga, mae yori waruku natte imasu.*

My <u>abdomen</u> hurts.	おなかが、痛いんですが。 _Onaka ga, itain desu ga._
ankle	足首　_ashikubi_
arm	腕　_ude_
back	背中　_senaka_
breast	乳房　_chibusa_
cheek	ほお　_hoo_
chest	胸　_mune_
chin	あご　_ago_
ear	耳　_mimi_
elbow	ひじ　_hiji_
eye	目　_me_
face	顔　_kao_
finger	指　_yubi_
foot	足　_ashi_
groin	股の付け根　_mata no tsukene_
hand	手　_te_
head	頭　_atama_
heart	心臓　_shinzō_
heel	かかと　_kakato_
joint	関節　_kansetsu_
knee	ひざ　_hiza_
leg	足　_ashi_
muscle	筋肉　_kin-niku_
neck	首　_kubi_
nose	鼻　_hana_
rib	肋骨　_rokkotsu_
shoulder	肩　_kata_
skin	皮膚／肌　_hifu/hada_

spine	背骨	*sebone*
stomach	胃	*i*
thigh	太もも	*futomomo*
throat	のど	*nodo*
thumb	親指	*oya yubi*
toe	足の指	*ashi no yubi*
tongue	舌	*shita*
wrist	手首	*tekubi*

My <u>lower lip is</u> numb.　<u>下唇</u>が、痺れています。<u>*Shita kuchibiru ga*</u>, *shibirete imasu.*

left arm is	左腕が	*hidari ude ga*
right-hand fingers are	右手の指が	*migi te no yubi ga*
left leg is	左足が	*hidari ashi ga*

My <u>left-hand fingers are</u> tingling.　<u>左手の指</u>が、ちくちくします。<u>*Hidari te no yubi ga*</u>, *chikuchiku shimasu.*

right leg is	右足が	*migi ashi ga*

I have an abcess.　腫れ物があります。*Haremono ga arimasu.*

I have a bee sting.　蜂に刺されてしまいました。*Hachi ni sasarete shimaimashita.*

I have a bruise.　打撲傷です。*Dabokushō desu.*

I have a burn.　やけどしてしまいました。*Yakedo shite shimaimashita.*

I have a burning sensation.　燃えるような感じがします。*Moeru yō na kanji ga shimasu.*

I have the chills.　悪寒がします。*Okan ga shimasu.*

I have <u>a cold</u>.　<u>風邪</u>をひいています。<u>*Kaze o hiite imasu.*</u>

a chest cold	せきのでる風邪	*seki no deru kaze*
a head cold	鼻風邪	*hana kaze*

I'm constipated.	便秘しています。	*Benpi shite imasu.*
I have cramps.	おなかが、痛んでいます。	*Onaka ga, itande imasu.*
I have a cut.	切り傷です。	*Kiri kizu desu.*
I have diarrhea.	下痢をしています。	*Geri o shite imasu.*
I have a fever.	熱があります。	*Netsu ga arimasu.*
I have a headache.	頭痛がします。	*Zutsū ga shimasu.*
I have indigestion.	消化不良です。	*Shōka furyō desu.*
I have an infection.	化膿しているところがあります。	*Kanō shite iru tokoro ga arimasu.*
I have an insect bite.	虫に、刺されてしまいました。	*Mushi ni, sasarete shimaimashita.*
I have an itch.	かゆみがあります。	*Kayumi ga arimasu.*
I have a lump.	しこりがあります。	*Shikori ga arimasu.*
I have a sore throat.	のどが痛いです。	*Nodo ga itai desu.*
I have a stomach ache.	おなかが痛いです。	*Onaka ga itai desu.*
I have a swelling.	腫れているところがあります。	*Harete iru tokoro ga arimasu.*
I have a wound.	怪我をしてしまいました。	*Kega o shite shimaimashita.*
I think I have <u>a broken bone/ fracture</u>.	<u>骨が折れた</u>みたいです。	<u>*Hone ga oreta*</u> *mitai desu.*
dysentery	赤痢	*sekiri*
the flu	流感	*ryūkan*
a stomach ulcer	胃潰瘍	*ikaiyō*
I've had this pain since <u>this morning</u>.	<u>今朝</u>から、痛みがあります。	<u>*Kesa*</u> *kara, itami ga arimasu.*
last night	昨日の晩	*kinō no ban*

yesterday	昨日 *kinō*
the day before yesterday	おととい *ototoi*
last week	先週 *senshū*
It's a <u>dull</u> pain.	鈍い痛みです。<u>*Nibui* itami desu.</u>
sharp	鋭い *surudoi*
throbbing	ズキズキする *zukizuki suru*
I've had this numbness for <u>three days</u>.	この<u>三日間</u>、痺れがあります。*Kono <u>mikka kan</u>, shibire ga arimasu.*
four days	四日間 *yokka kan*
I'm having chest pain.	胸に、痛みがあります。*Mune ni, itami ga arimasu.*
I had a heart attack _____ years ago.	_____年前、心臓麻痺の発作がありました。 *_____ nen mae, shinzō mahi no hossa ga arimashita.*
I'm a diabetic.	私には、糖尿病があります。*Watakushi niwa, tōnyō byō ga arimasu.*
I'm taking <u>this medicine</u>.	今、<u>この薬</u>を使っています。*Ima, <u>kono kusuri</u> o tsukatte imasu.*
insulin	インシュリン *inshurin*
I'm allergic to <u>antibiotics</u>.	<u>抗生物質</u>に過敏です。<u>*Kōsei busshitsu*</u> *ni kabin desu.*
codeine	コデイン *kodein*
penicillin	ペニシリン *penishirin*
There's a history of <u>cancer</u> in my family.	家族には、<u>がん</u>の歴史があります。*Kazoku niwa, <u>gan</u> no rekishi ga arimasu.*
diabetes	糖尿病 *tōnyō byō*
heart disease	心臓病 *shinzō byō*
high blood pressure	高血圧 *kō ketsuatsu*

There's no history of _____ in my family.	家族には、_____の歴史はありません。 *Kazoku niwa, _____ no rekishi wa arimasen.*
Do you know what's wrong with me?	どこが、悪いですか。*Doko ga, warui desu ka.*
Do I have _____?	_____でしょうか。 *_____ deshō ka.*
Is it _____?	_____でしょうか。 *_____ deshō ka.*

(<u>See below, under "What the Doctor Says,"</u> for a list of medical ailments.)

Is it serious?	重いですか。*Omoi desu ka.*
Is it contagious?	うつる恐れがありますか。*Utsuru osore ga arimasu ka.*
Do I have to stay in bed?	寝ていなければなりませんか。*Nete inakereba narimasen ka.*
How long do I have to stay in bed?	どのくらい、寝ていなければなりませんか。*Dono kurai, nete inakereba narimasen ka.*
Do I have to be hospitalized?	入院しなければなりませんか。*Nyūin shinakereba narimasen ka.*
Are you going to give me a prescription?	処方箋がいりますか。*Shohōsen ga irimasu ka.*
What kind of medicine is it?	どんな種類の薬ですか。*Donna shurui no kusuri desu ka.*
Will it make me sleepy?	それを飲むと、眠くなりますか。*Sore o nomu to, nemuku narimasu ka.*
How often must I take this medicine?	この薬は、一日何回飲むのですか。*Kono kusuri wa, ichi nichi nan kai nomu no desu ka.*
When can I continue my trip?	いつから、旅行が続けられますか。*Itsu kara, ryokō ga tsuzukeraremasu ka.*
Thank you very much.	どうも、ありがとうございました。*Dōmo, arigatō gozaimashita.*

Where do I pay?	どこで払えば、よろしいですか。 *Doko de haraeba, yoroshii desu ka.*

WHAT THE DOCTOR SAYS

Where does it hurt?	どこが痛いですか。*Doko ga itai* *desu ka.*
Where were you before you came to Japan?	日本に来る前は、どこにいましたか。 *Nihon ni kuru mae wa, doko ni* *imashita ka.*
I'm going to take your temperature.	熱を計ります。*Netsu o hakarimasu.*
I'll take your pulse.	脈を測ります。*Myaku o hakarimasu.*
I'm going to take your blood pressure.	血圧を測ります。*Ketsuatsu o* *hakarimasu.*
Open your mouth, please.	口を開けて下さい。*Kuchi o akete* *kudasai.*
Stick out your tongue, please.	舌を出して下さい。*Shita o dashite* *kudasai.*
Cough, please.	せきをして下さい。*Seki o shite* *kudasai.*
Breathe deeply, please.	深呼吸をして／深く息を吸って下さい。*Shinkokyū o shite/fukaku iki o* *sutte kudasai.*
Hold your breath, please.	息を止めて下さい。*Iki o tomete* *kudasai.*
Exhale slowly, please.	ゆっくり、息を吐いて下さい。 *Yukkuri, iki o haite kudasai.*
Roll up your sleeve, please.	袖をまくって下さい。*Sode o* *makutte kudasai.*
Take off your clothing to the waist, please.	上半身を脱いで下さい。*Jō hanshin* *o nuide kudasai.*
Remove your trousers/skirt and underwear, please.	ズボン／スカートと、下着を脱いで下さい。*Zubon/sukāto to, shitagi o* *nuide kudasai.*

Put this gown on, please.	このガウンを着てください。*Kono gaun o kite kudasai.*
Lie down, please.	横になって下さい。*Yoko ni natte kudasai.*
Does it hurt when I press here?	ここを押すと、痛みますか。*Koko o osu to, itamimasu ka.*
Stand up, please.	立って下さい。*Tatte kudasai.*
Get dressed, please.	服を着て下さい。*Fuku o kite kudasai.*
Have you ever had this before?	前、こんなになったことがありますか。*Mae, konna ni natta koto ga arimasu ka.*
Are you having shortness of breath?	息切れがしますか。*Iki gire ga shimasu ka.*
Do you have palpitations?	動悸がしますか。*Dōki ga shimasu ka.*
Do you have any numbness here?	ここは、感覚が鈍いですか。*Koko wa, kankaku ga nibui desu ka.*
What medicine have you been taking?	どんな薬を、使っていますか。*Donna kusuri o, tsukatte imasu ka.*
What dosage of insulin do you take?	インシュリンの使用量は、一回どのくらいですか。*Inshurin no shiyō ryō wa, ikkai dono kurai desu ka.*
Is it by injection or oral?	注射ですか、飲み薬ですか。*Chūsha desu ka, nomi gusuri desu ka.*
What treatment have you been having?	どんな治療を、受けていますか。*Donna chiryō o, ukete imasu ka.*
Is there a history of _____ in your family?	家族に、_____の歴史がありますか。*Kazoku ni, _____ no rekishi ga arimasu ka.*
When is your baby due?	出産予定日は、いつですか。*Shussan yotei bi wa, itsu desu ka.*

I want a <u>urine</u> sample.	<u>尿</u>の検査をします。*Nyō no kensa o shimasu.*
stool	便　*ben*
blood	血液　*ketsueki*
I want you to have an X-ray.	レントゲンの写真を撮ります。*Rentogen no shashin o torimasu.*
When was your last tetanus shot?	破傷風の予防注射は、いつしましたか。*Hashōfū no yobō chūsha wa, itsu shimashita ka.*
I'm going to send you to <u>a specialist</u>.	<u>専門医</u>のところへ、行ってもらいます。*Senmon i no tokoro e, itte moraimasu.*
a dermatologist	皮膚科の医者　*hifuka no isha*
an ear, nose, and throat specialist	耳鼻咽喉科医　*jibiinkōka i*
a gastroenterologist	消化器科の医者　*shōkakika no isha*
a gynecologist	婦人科医　*fujinka i*
an obstetrician	産科医　*sanka i*
an ophthalmologist	眼科医　*ganka i*
an orthopedist	整形外科医　*seikeigeka i*
a surgeon	外科医　*geka i*
It's minor.	大したこと、ありません。*Taishita koto, arimasen.*
It's acute.	急性の病気です。*Kyūsei no byōki desu.*
It's infected.	化膿しています。*Kanō shite imasu.*
It's broken.	骨折しています。*Kossetsu shite imasu.*
It's sprained.	捻挫しています。*Nenza shite imasu.*
It's dislocated.	脱臼しています。*Dakkyū shite imasu.*

It's inflamed.	炎症を、起こしています。 *Enshō o, okoshite imasu.*
I'll have to take stitches.	縫わなければなりません。 *Nuwanakereba narimasen.*
I'll have to lance it.	切開しなければなりません。 *Sekkai shinakereba narimasen.*
I'll have to tape it.	テープで、固定しなければなりません。 *Tēpu de, kotei shinakereba narimasen.*
You can't travel until _____ .	旅行は、_____ まで控えて下さい。 *Ryokō wa, _____ made hikaete kudasai.*
I want you to go to the hospital for some tests.	検査のために、病院へ行って下さい。 *Kensa no tame ni, byōin e itte kudasai.*
I want you to go to the hospital for treatment.	治療のために、病院へ行って下さい。 *Chiryō no tame ni, byōin e itte kudasai.*
I want you to go to the hospital for surgery.	手術のために、病院へ行って下さい。 *Shujutsu no tame ni, byōin e itte kudasai.*
Shall I make the arrangements for you to go to the hospital?	病院へ行く手はずを整えましょうか。 *Byōin e iku tehazu o totonoemashō ka.*
You've had a mild heart attack.	軽い心臓発作です。 *Karui shinzō hossa desu.*
Are you allergic to _____ ?	_____ に、アレルギー体質ですか。 *_____ ni, arerugī taishitsu desu ka.*
Are you allergic to any medicines?	アレルギー反応のある薬があります か。 *Arerugī hannō no aru kusuri ga arimasu ka.*
I'm giving you an injection of penicillin.	ペニシリンの注射をします。 *Penishirin no chūsha o shimasu.*
I'm prescribing an antibiotic.	抗生物質を処方します。 *Kōsei busshitsu o shohō shimasu.*

I'm giving you some medicine to take.	薬をあげます。 *Kusuri o agemasu.*
I'm writing a prescription for you.	処方箋を書きましょう。 *Shohōsen o kakimashō.*
We don't use _____ in Japan.	_____は、日本では使っていません。 _____ *wa, Nihon dewa tsukatte imasen.*
This is quite similar to _____.	これは、_____に非常に似ています。 *Kore wa, _____ ni hijō ni nite imasu.*
Take _____ teaspoons of this medicine at a time.	この薬を、一度に小さじ_____杯飲んで下さい。 *Kono kusuri o, ichi do ni kosaji _____ pai/hai/bai nonde kudasai.*
Take it every _____ hours.	_____時間ごとに、飲んで下さい。 _____ *jikan goto ni, nonde kudasai.*
Take _____ tablets with a glass of water.	これを_____錠、水で飲んで下さい。 *Kore o _____ jō, mizu de nonde kudasai.*
Take it _____ times a day.	一日に_____回、飲んで下さい。 *Ichi nichi ni _____ kai, nonde kudasai.*
Take it after meals.	食後に飲んで下さい。 *Shoku go ni nonde kudasai.*
Take it before meals.	食前に飲んで下さい。 *Shoku zen ni nonde kudasai.*
Take it in the morning.	朝飲んで下さい。 *Asa nonde kudasai.*
Take it at night.	夜飲んで下さい。 *Yoru nonde kudasai.*
Use an ice pack on it.	氷のうをあてて下さい。 *Hyōnō o atete kudasai.*
Use wet heat on it.	温湿布をあてて下さい。 *On shippu o atete kudasai.*
I want you to come back after _____ day(s).	_____たったら、また来て下さい。 _____ *tattara, mata kite kudasai.*

I think it's _____ .	_____だと思います。_____ da to omoimasu.
an allergy	アレルギー　arerugī
appendicitis	盲腸炎　mōchō en
arthritis	関節炎　kansetsu en
asthma	ぜんそく　zensoku
a bacterial infection	細菌性炎症　saikin sei enshō
a bladder infection	ぼうこう炎　bōkō en
bronchitis	気管支炎　kikanshi en
a common cold	普通の風邪　futsū no kaze
conjunctivitis	結膜炎　ketsumaku en
dysentery	赤痢　sekiri
hay fever	花粉症　kafunshō
hemorrhoids	痔　ji
gastroenteritis	胃腸炎　ichō en
the heart	心臓　shinzō
hepatitis	肝炎　kan en
influenza	インフルエンザ／流感　infuruenza/ryūkan
a muscle spasm	筋肉のけいれん　kinniku no keiren
muscular	筋肉　kinniku
pneumonia	肺炎　hai en
shingles	帯状疱疹　taijō hōshin
tonsilitis	扁桃腺炎　hentōsen en
an ulcer	潰瘍　kaiyō
a urinary infection	尿道炎　nyōdō en
a viral infection	ウイルス性の化膿　uirusu sei no kanō

AT THE DENTIST

This section is divided into two parts: **Patient** and **Dentist**. You use the phrases under **Patient**, and hand the book to the dentist so he or she can point to the appropriate phrases under **Dentist**.

Please point to the phrase in the book.	この本の、適当な文を指して下さい。 *Kono hon no, tekitō na bun o yubisashite kudasai.*

PATIENT

I have to go to a dentist.	歯医者に、行かなければなりません。 *Ha isha ni, ikanakereba narimasen.*
Can you recommend a dentist?	歯医者を、紹介してもらえますか。 *Ha isha o, shōkai shite moraemasu ka.*
I'd like an appointment with the dentist.	歯医者の予約がしたいのですが。 *Ha isha no yoyaku ga shitai no desu ga.*
I need to see the dentist immediately.	すぐ、歯医者に行かなければなりません。 *Sugu, ha isha ni ikanakereba narimasen.*
I have a really bad toothache.	歯が、ひどく痛みます。 *Ha ga, hidoku itamimasu.*
I think I have <u>a cavity</u>.	<u>虫歯</u>のようですが。 *Mushiba no yō desu ga.*
an abscess	膿んでいる *unde iru*
I've lost a filling.	歯の詰め物を、なくしてしまいました。 *Ha no tsumemono o, nakushite shimaimashita.*
I've broken a tooth.	歯を、折ってしまいました。 *Ha o, otte shimaimashita.*
I can't chew on this side.	こちら側で、噛むことができません。 *Kochira gawa de, kamu koto ga dekimasen.*

My gums hurt.	歯ぐきが、痛んでいます。 *Haguki ga, itande imasu.*
Can you give me a <u>temporary</u> filling?	<u>仮の</u>詰め物を、してもらえますか。 <u>*Kari no*</u> *tsumemono o, shite moraemasu ka.*
porcelain	磁器製の *jiki sei no*
composite	合成剤の *gōsei zai no*
Can you fix this <u>bridge</u>?	この<u>ブリッジ</u>を、直してもらえますか。 *Kono <u>burijji</u> o, naoshite moraemasu ka.*
crown	歯冠 *shikan*
denture	入れ歯 *ireba*

DENTIST

Where does it hurt?	どこが痛みますか。 *Doko ga itamimasu ka.*
Does this hurt?	こうすると、痛みますか。 *Kō suru to, itamimasu ka.*
Is it sensitive to cold/ heat?	冷たいもの／熱いものに、敏感ですか。 *Tsumetai mono /atsui mono ni, binkan desu ka.*
Is it tender?	ここは、敏感ですか。 *Koko wa, binkan desu ka.*
Can you feel this?	こうすると、感じますか。 *Kō suru to, kanjimasu ka.*
I want to take an X-ray.	レントゲンの写真を、取ります。 *Rentogen no shashin o, torimasu.*
I see the problem.	どこが悪いか、わかりました。 *Doko ga warui ka, wakarimashita.*
We should do it now.	今、しなければなりません。 *Ima, shinakereba narimasen.*
It can wait until you get home.	帰国するまで、大丈夫です。 *Kikoku suru made, daijōbu desu.*

I'm going to give you a <u>temporary</u> filling.	<u>仮の</u>詰め物をしましょう。<u>Kari no</u> tsumemono o shimashō.
porcelain	磁器製の jiki sei no
composite	合成剤の gōsei zai no
You need a root canal.	歯根を抜く必要があります。Shikon o nuku hitsuyō ga arimasu.
Would you like some <u>novocaine</u>?	<u>ノボカイン</u>をしましょうか。<u>Nobokain</u> o shimashō ka.
gas	麻酔ガス masui gasu
Open wider, please.	口を、もっと大きく開けてください。Kuchi o, motto ōkiku akete kudasai.
Rinse, please.	口を、すすいでください。Kuchi o, susuide kudasai.
Bite down, please.	かみ合わせてください。Kami awasete kudasai.
I'm giving you a prescription.	処方箋を、あげましょう。Shohōsen o, agemashō.
Rinse with this _____ times daily.	一日_____回、これですすいでください。Ichi nichi _____ kai, kore de susuide kudasai.
This is <u>an antibiotic</u>.	これは、<u>抗生物質</u>です。Kore wa, <u>kōsei busshitsu</u> desu.
a painkiller	痛み止め itami dome
Take _____ tablets/capsules at a time.	錠剤／カプセルを、一度に_____錠飲んで下さい。Jōzai/kapuseru o, ichi do ni _____ jō nonde kudasai.
Take it/them every _____ hours.	_____時間ごとに、飲んで下さい。_____jikan goto ni, nonde kudasai.

TRADITIONAL TREATMENTS

ACUPRESSURE (SHIATSU) AND ACUPUNCTURE (HARI)

Acupuncture is widely practiced in Japan. You can have acupuncture or acupressure treatment at the therapist's office, or where you're staying. Payment is usually by the hour.

Where can I get <u>acupressure</u>?	<u>指圧</u>は、どこで受けられますか。 *<u>Shiatsu</u> wa, doko de ukeraremasu ka.*
acupuncture	針療治 *hari ryōji*
Do you know a good <u>acupressurist</u>?	上手な<u>指圧師</u>を、知っていますか。 *Jōzu na <u>shiatsu shi</u> o, shitte imasu ka.*
acupuncturist	針の療治師 *hari no ryōji shi*
Does he/she come to my place?	私のところへ、来てくれますか。 *Watakushi no tokoro e, kite kuremasu ka.*
How much is it for an hour?	一時間いくらですか。*Ichi jikan ikura desu ka.*
Do I need to make an appointment?	予約するべきですか。*Yoyaku suru beki desu ka.*
Could you get me an acupressurist/ acupuncturist?	指圧師／針の療治師を呼んでもらえますか。*Shiatsu shi/hari no ryōji shi o yonde moraemasu ka.*

WITH THE ACUPRESSURIST OR ACUPUNCTURIST

My problem is here.	ここの具合が、よくありません。 *Koko no guai ga, yoku arimasen.*
My <u>neck</u> is (are) stiff.	<u>首</u>が、こっています。<u>*Kubi*</u> *ga, kotte imasu.*
shoulders	肩 *kata*
back	背中 *senaka*

My <u>head</u> ache(s).	頭が、痛いんです。*Atama ga, itain desu.*
arms	腕 *ude*
back	背中 *senaka*
legs	足 *ashi*
neck	首 *kubi*
shoulders	肩 *kata*
stomach	胃 *i*
waist/hip	腰 *koshi*

WITH THE ACUPRESSURIST

It's too hard.	強すぎます。*Tsuyosugimasu.*
Can you do it more gently?	もうちょっと、弱くして下さい。*Mō chotto, yowaku shite kudasai.*
I can take it harder.	もうちょっと、強くてもいいです。*Mō chotto, tsuyokutemo ii desu.*

WITH THE OPTICIAN

Can you repair these glasses for me?	眼鏡を、直してもらえますか。*Megane o, naoshite moraemasu ka.*
I've broken a lens.	レンズを、割ってしまいました。*Renzu o, watte shimaimashita.*
I've broken the frame.	わくを、こわしてしまいました。*Waku o, kowashite shimaimashita.*
Can you put in a new lens?	新しいレンズを、入れてもらえますか。*Atarashii renzu o, irete moraemasu ka.*
Can you get the prescription from the old lens?	古いレンズから、度をとってもらえますか。*Furui renzu kara, do o totte moraemasu ka.*

Can you tighten the screw?　ねじを、締めてもらえますか。*Neji o, shimete moraemasu ka.*

I need the glasses as soon as possible.　眼鏡は、できるだけ早く欲しいのですが。*Megane wa, dekiru dake hayaku hoshii no desu ga.*

I don't have any others.　代わりの眼鏡は、ありません。*Kawari no megane wa, arimasen.*

I'd like a new pair of eyeglasses.　新しい眼鏡が、欲しいのですが。*Atarashii megane ga, hoshii no desu ga.*

Can you give me a new prescription?　度を、測ってもらえますか。*Do o, hakatte moraemasu ka.*

I'd like the lenses tinted.　レンズに、軽く色をつけて下さい。*Renzu ni, karuku iro o tsukete kudasai.*

Can you show me color samples?　色の見本を、見せてもらえますか。*Iro no mihon o, misete moraemasu ka.*

Are there cheaper frames?　もっと、安いわくがありますか。*Motto, yasui waku ga arimasu ka.*

When will it be ready?　仕上がりは、いつですか。*Shiagari wa, itsu desu ka.*

Do you sell <u>contact lenses</u>?　<u>コンタクト・レンズ</u>は、売っていますか。*<u>Kontakuto renzu</u> wa, utte imasu ka.*

　soft contact lenses　ソフト・コンタクト・レンズ *sofuto kontakuto renzu*

Do you sell sunglasses?　サングラスは、売っていますか。*Sangurasu wa, utte imasu ka.*

COMMUNICATIONS

POST OFFICE

Post offices are identified by this symbol: 〒. It looks like a capital T with a bar above it. Mailboxes on the street have this sign, too; the mailboxes are red. Post offices are open from 9 A.M. to 5 P.M. weekdays. Main post offices are also open Saturdays. Central post offices of major cities are open 24 hours a day, 7 days a week. You can buy stamps at shops and kiosks that display the red symbol.

I want to mail a letter.	手紙を出したいのですが。*Tegami o dashitai no desu ga.*
Where is <u>a mailbox</u>?	<u>ポスト</u>は、どこにありますか。 *<u>Posuto</u> wa, doko ni arimasu ka.*
post office	郵便局　*yūbin kyoku*
Which window sells stamps?	切手の窓口は、どこですか。*Kitte no madoguchi wa, doko desu ka.*
What's the postage for <u>a letter</u> to the United States?	アメリカへの<u>手紙</u>は、いくらですか。*Amerika e no <u>tegami</u> wa, ikura desu ka.*
Express Mail	国際ビジネス便　*kokusai bijinesu bin*
a registered letter	書留　*kakitome*
a special delivery letter	速達　*sokutatsu*
a postcard	葉書　*hagaki*
I'd like <u>6 stamps for Europe</u>.	<u>ヨーロッパへの切手を6枚</u>ください。 *<u>Yōroppa e no kitte o roku mai</u> kudasai.*
7 postcard stamps for South America	南米への、葉書用の切手を七枚 *Nanbei e no, hagaki yō no kitte o nana mai*

How long will it take to <u>the United States</u> by air?	航空便だと、<u>アメリカ</u>まで何日かかりますか。*Kōkū bin da to, <u>Amerika</u> made nan nichi kakarimasu ka.*
Europe	ヨーロッパ *Yōroppa*
South America	南米 *Nanbei*
I want some pretty stamps.	きれいな切手を下さい。*Kirei na kitte o kudasai.*
I'd like to send this parcel.	この小包を、送りたいのですが。*Kono kozutsumi o, okuritai no desu ga.*
Do I need to fill out a customs declaration form?	税関の申告書に、記入しなければなりませんか。*Zeikan no shinkoku sho ni, kinyū shinakereba narimasen ka.*

TELEPHONE

Although almost everyone has a cell phone, public phones are still widely available in Japan.

On a public telephone, a three-minute local call costs 10 yen. Lift the receiver, wait for a dial tone, and deposit coins. If you're going to speak more than three minutes, insert the coins at the beginning or you risk being cut off.

Your best bet is to buy a telephone card. Many phone booths have telephone-card dispensing machines that accept 1,000 yen bills. The cards are also available at kiosks, convenience stores, supermarkets, train stations, and many other places. It's like a disposable fare card. When it's used up, you throw it away.

Most public phones are green or grey. Both take telephone cards; most take coins as well, although some green ones don't. The grey ones have monitor screens with simple instructions for use in English, as well as information about your call.

CELL PHONES AND SIM CARDS

You'll probably be able to use your cell phone in Japan, but check with your phone company about costs beforehand. A convenient, low-cost option is to get a prepaid SIM card, either before departure or in Japan. You can get a prepaid SIM card at airports, electronics stores, convenience stores, and elsewhere, and you will be able to use it immediately. Before buying the card, check the size to make sure it's what you need—is it just for data, or is it for both voice and data?

telephone	電話	*denwa*
landline (telephone)	固定電話	*kotei denwa*
cell phone	携帯／携帯電話	*keitai/keitai denwa*
smart phone	スマートフォン／スマホ	*sumātofon/sumaho*
public phone	公衆電話	*kōshū denwa*
telephone number	電話番号	*denwa bangō*

JAPAN TRAVEL-PHONE

Visitors to Japan will find Japan Travel-Phone helpful. If you're having difficulty communicating, or if you want more detailed information for sightseeing or travel plans, use Travel-Phone—you'll find an English-speaking travel expert on the line to help solve your problems!

You can call from anywhere in Japan except the Tokyo and Kyoto areas. The toll-free numbers are 0088-22-4800 and 0120-44-4800. For calls in the Tokyo and Kyoto areas, use the following numbers, which are not toll-free.

Tokyo Area: 3201-3331 (Tokyo Tourist Information Center)

Kyoto Area: 371-5649 (Kyoto Tourist Information Center)

Elsewhere in Japan: Dial the above-mentioned numbers. Or insert a 10-yen coin, dial 106, and tell the operator (in English): "Collect call, TIC." Your money will be returned after the call.

Where is a <u>public telephone</u>?	公衆電話は、どこにありますか。*Kōshū denwa wa, doko ni arimasu ka.*
telephone booth	電話ボックス　*denwa bokkusu*
I'd like to make a phone call. Could you give me some change?	電話をかけるのに、こまかくしてもらえますか。*Denwa o kakeru no ni, komakaku shite moraemasu ka.*
Where can I buy a prepaid telephone card?	テレフォンカードは、どこで買えますか。*Terefon kādo wa, doko de kaemasu ka.*
I'd like to buy a telephone card, please.	テレフォンカードをください。*Terefon kādo o kudasai.*
1,000-yen	千円　*sen en*
Can I make an international call from this public telephone?	この公衆電話から、国際電話がかけられますか。*Kono kōshū denwa kara, kokusai denwa ga kakeraremasu ka.*
Which public telephone should I use to make an international call?	国際電話をかけるには、どの公衆電話を使うべきですか。*Kokusai denwa o kakeru niwa, dono kōshū denwa o tsukau beki desu ka.*
Can you tell me how to make an international call from a public telephone?	どうやって公衆電話から国際電話をかけるか、教えて下さい。*Dō yatte kōshū denwa kara kokusai denwa o kakeru ka, oshiete kudasai.*
May I use your phone?	電話を、拝借できますか。*Denwa o, haishaku dekimasu ka.*
I want to make a <u>local call</u>.	<u>市内電話</u>を、かけたいのですが。*Shinai denwa o, kaketai no desu ga.*
long-distance call	長距離電話　*chōkyori denwa*
Please show me how to call this number.	この番号のかけ方を、教えて下さい。*Kono bangō no kakekata o, oshiete kudasai.*

Can I dial direct?	ダイヤル直通ですか。 *Daiyaru chokutsū desu ka.*

WITH THE OTHER PARTY

Hello!	もしもし。 *Moshi moshi.*
Is this Mr./Mrs./Miss/Ms. _____'s residence?	(姓)さんの、お宅ですか。 <u>*(last name) san*</u> *no, otaku desu ka.*
May I speak to _____? (Mr.)	(姓)さんを、お願いします。 <u>*(last name) san*</u> *o, onegai shimasu.*
(Mrs.)	(姓)さんの奥さん *(last name) san no okusan*
(son or daughter)	(名)さん *(first name) san*
Is this (company name)?	(会社の名前)ですか。 *(company name) desu ka.*
I want extension _____ .	内線の_____番を、お願いします。 *Naisen no _____ ban o, onegai shimasu.*
<u>General Affairs Department</u>, please.	<u>総務部</u>をお願いします。 <u>*Sōmu bu*</u> *o onegai shimasu.*
Personnel Department	人事部 *jinji bu*
Finance Department	経理部 *keiri bu*
Business Operations Department	営業部 *eigyō bu*
Public Relations Department	渉外部 *shōgai bu*
Sales Department	販売部 *hanbai bu*
Is Mr./Mrs./Miss/Ms. _____ in?	(姓)さんは、いらっしゃいますか。 <u>*(last name) san*</u> *wa, irasshaimasu ka.*
Hello! Is this _____ ?	もしもし、(姓)さんですか。 *Moshi moshi, <u>(last name) san</u> desu ka.*
_____ speaking.	私は、(名前)ですが。 *Watakushi wa, <u>(full name)</u> desu ga.*

IF THE PERSON ISN'T THERE

When will he/she be back?	いつ、お戻りになりますか。 *Itsu, omodori ni narimasu ka.*
Will you tell him/her that (full name) called?	(名前)が電話したと、お伝えいただけますか。 *(full name) ga denwa shita to, otsutae itadakemasu ka.*
Would you tell him/her to call me?	私に電話するように、伝えていただけますか。 *Watakushi ni denwa suru yō ni, tsutaete itadakemasu ka.*
My phone number is _____ .	私の電話番号は、_____ です。 *Watakushi no denwa bangō wa, _____ desu.*
My extension is _____ .	私の内線は、_____ 番です。 *Watakushi no naisen wa, _____ ban desu.*
Please tell him/her to leave a message if I'm not here.	私が出なかったら、伝言を残すようにお伝え下さい。 *Watakushi ga denakattara, dengon o nokosu yō ni otsutae kudasai.*
I'll call him/her again.	また、電話します。 *Mata, denwa shimasu.*
Thank you very much. Goodbye.	どうも、ありがとうございました。では、ごめんください。 *Dōmo, arigatō gozaimashita. Dewa, gomen kudasai.*

FAX

I'd like to <u>send</u> a fax.	ファックスが、<u>送りたい</u>のですが。 *Fakkusu ga, <u>okuritai</u> no desu ga.*
receive	受け取りたい *uketoritai*

Where can I <u>send</u> a fax?	ファックスは、どこで<u>送れます</u>か。 *Fakkusu wa, doko de <u>okuremasu</u> ka.*
receive	受け取れます　*uketoremasu*
Can I use a fax machine in this hotel?	このホテルで、ファックスが使えますか。*Kono hoteru de, fakkusu ga tsukaemasu ka.*
What's a fax number <u>here</u>?	<u>ここ</u>のファックス番号は、何番ですか。 <u>*Koko*</u> *no fakkusu bangō wa, nan ban desu ka.*
there	そちら　*sochira*
I'll fax it to you.	それは、ファックスで送ります。 *Sore wa, fakkusu de okurimasu.*
Fax it to me, please.	それは、ファックスで送ってください。 *Sore wa, fakkusu de okutte kudasai.*

WI-FI AND HOTSPOTS

For your cell phone, computer, or tablet, free Wi-Fi, paid Wi-Fi, and hotspots are widely available.

Is <u>Wi-Fi</u> available nearby?	近くに <u>ワイファイ</u>がありますか。 *Chikaku ni <u>waifai</u> ga arimasu ka.*
Wireless LAN	無線LAN　*musenran*
a hotspot	ホットスポット　*hotto supotto*
Is there <u>Wi-Fi</u> here?	ここに<u>ワイファイ</u>がありますか。*Koko ni <u>waifai</u> ga arimasu ka.*
wireless LAN	無線LAN　*musenran*
Is there a charge?	有料ですか。*Yūryō desu ka.*
The pass code/ password, please.	暗証をください。*Anshō o kudasai.*

Is there an Internet café nearby?	この近くにインターネット・カフェがありますか。 *Kono chikaku ni intānetto·kafe ga arimasu ka.*
Is there a <u>coffee shop</u> with Wi-Fi nearby?	近くに無線LANがある<u>喫茶店</u>がありますか。 *Chikaku ni musenran ga aru <u>kissaten</u> ga arimasu ka.*
fast-food restaurant	ファーストフードの店 *fāsuto·fūdo no mise*
hotel lobby	ホテルのロビー *hoteru no robī*

DRIVING A CAR

Foreigners driving in Japan must contend with certain realities: The steering wheel is on the right side of the car, and you drive on the left side of the road; most expressway signs are in Japanese; nonexpress roads may be narrow and usually have no sidewalks. Speedometers are only in kilometers; streets are crowded with pedestrians, bicycles, vendors, and cars; and penalties for accidents are high. In short, for the visitor to Japan, driving is not recommended.

Do you still want to drive? If so, you'll need an International Driving Permit. You'll also need to be familiar with Japanese road signs and traffic signs, some of which are shown at the end of this section. Many are International Traffic Signs, which are clear and easy to read. The Japan Automobile Federation in Tokyo has a useful booklet called "Rules of the Road," which you should read if you're planning on driving. One final note: There are road checkpoints for intoxicated drivers, and penalties can be severe.

RENTING A CAR

Where can I rent a car?	どこで、車が借りられますか。	*Doko de, kuruma ga kariraremasu ka.*
I'd like to rent a car.	車が、借りたいのですが。	*Kuruma ga, karitai no desu ga.*
Do you have a <u>small car</u>?	<u>小さい車</u>が、ありますか。	<u>*Chiisai kuruma*</u> *ga, arimasu ka.*
mid-size car	中型車	*chūgata sha*
large car	大型車	*ōgata sha*
sport utility vehicle	スポーツ多目的車	*supōtsu tamokuteki sha*
sports car	スポーツ・カー	*supōtsukā*

van	バン　*ban*
minivan	ミニバン　*miniban*
May I see your list of rates?	料金表を、見せてもらえますか。 *Ryōkin hyō o, misete moraemasu ka.*
I prefer automatic transmission.	自動変速の車が、欲しいのですが。 *Jidō hensoku no kuruma ga, hoshii no desu ga.*
I'd like it for <u>a day</u>.	それを、<u>一日</u>貸してください。 *Sore o, <u>ichi nichi</u> kashite kudasai.*
two days	二日　*futsuka*
three days	三日　*mikka*
a week	一週間　*isshūkan*
What's the rate for <u>a day</u>?	<u>一日</u>の料金は、いくらですか。 *<u>Ichi nichi</u> no ryōkin wa, ikura desu ka.*
a week	一週間　*isshūkan*
Does the rate include <u>mileage</u>?	料金には、<u>キロ数</u>も入っていますか。 *Ryōkin niwa, <u>kiro sū</u> mo haitte imasu ka.*
gas	ガソリン代　*gasorin dai*
insurance	保険　*hoken*
How much is the insurance?	保険は、いくらですか。*Hoken wa, ikura desu ka.*
What's the deposit?	保証金は、いくらですか。*Hoshō kin wa, ikura desu ka.*
Do you take credit cards?	クレジット・カードで、払えますか。 *Kurejitto kādo de, haraemasu ka.*
Here's my International Driving Permit.	これが、私の国際免許書です。*Kore ga, watakushi no kokusai menkyo sho desu.*
Please give me some emergency telephone numbers.	緊急の場合に呼べる電話番号を、下さい。 *Kinkyū no baai ni yoberu denwa bangō o, kudasai.*

INFORMATION AND DIRECTIONS

Excuse me, but _____ .	ちょっとすみませんが。 *Chotto sumimasen ga.*
How do I get to _____ ?	_____へは、どう行けばいいですか。 *_____ e wa, dō ikeba ii desu ka.*
I think we're lost.	道に、迷ってしまったみたいです。 *Michi ni, mayotte shimatta mitai desu.*
Where am I?	ここは、どこですか。 *Koko wa, doko desu ka.*
Which is the road to _____ ?	_____へ行く道は、どれですか。 *_____ e iku michi wa, dore desu ka.*
Is this the road to _____ ?	_____へ行くには、この道でいいですか。 *_____ e iku niwa, kono michi de ii desu ka.*
What's the name of this town?	この町の名前は、何ですか。 *Kono machi no namae wa, nan desu ka.*
Is the next <u>town</u> far?	次の町は、遠いですか。 *Tsugi no <u>machi</u> wa, tōi desu ka.*
gas station	ガソリン・スタンド *gasorin sutando*
How far away is _____ ? (distance)	_____へは、どのくらい距離がありますか。 *_____ e wa, dono kurai kyori ga arimasu ka.*
How far away is _____ ? (time)	_____まで、どのくらい時間がかかりますか。 *_____ made, dono kurai jikan ga kakarimasu ka.*
Do you have a road map?	道路地図が、ありますか。 *Dōro chizu ga, arimasu ka.*
Could you show me where _____ is on the map?	_____がどこか、地図で教えて下さい。 *_____ ga doko ka, chizu de oshiete kudasai.*

Could you show me where I am on the map?	私がどこにいるのか、地図で教えて下さい。*Watakushi ga doko ni iru no ka, chizu de oshiete kudasai.*
Is this the <u>fastest</u> way?	これが、<u>一番速い</u>行き方ですか。*Kore ga, <u>ichiban hayai</u> ikikata desu ka.*
easiest	一番分かりやすい *ichiban wakariyasui*
Do I go straight?	まっすぐ行くのですか。*Massugu iku no desu ka.*
Do I turn to the <u>right</u>?	<u>右</u>に曲がるのですか。<u>*Migi*</u> *ni magaru no desu ka.*
left	左 *hidari*
Where is the <u>entrance to the highway</u>?	<u>高速道路への入り口</u>は、どこですか。<u>*Kōsoku dōro e no iriguchi*</u> *wa, doko desu ka.*
tourist information center	旅行案内所 *ryokō annai jo*
gas station	ガソリン・スタンド *gasorin sutando*

THE SERVICE STATION

Is there a gas station nearby?	近くに、ガソリン・スタンドがありますか。*Chikaku ni, gasorin sutando ga arimasu ka.*
I need some gas.	ガソリンを下さい。*Gasorin o kudasai.*
How much is a liter of <u>regular</u>?	<u>レギュラー</u>は、一リットルいくらですか。<u>*Regyurā*</u> *wa, ichi rittoru ikura desu ka.*
super	スーパー／ハイオク *sūpā/haioku*
unleaded	無鉛ガソリン *muen gasorin*
diesel	ディーゼル *dīzeru*

LIQUID MEASURES (APPROXIMATE)

LITERS	U.S. GALLONS	IMPERIAL GALLONS
30	8	6
40	10	8
50	13	11
60	15	13
70	18	15
80	21	17

Give me <u>10</u> liters of regular, please.	レギュラーを、<u>十</u>リットル下さい。 *Regyurā o, <u>jū</u> rittoru kudasai.*	
20	二十 *ni jū*	
30	三十 *san jū*	
Give me <u>3,000</u> yen worth of super, please.	スーパーを、<u>三千</u>円分下さい。 *Sūpā o, <u>san zen</u> en bun kudasai.*	
4,000	四千 *yon sen*	
5,000	五千 *go sen*	
Fill it up, please.	満タンにして下さい。 *Man tan ni shite kudasai.*	
Please check the <u>tires</u>.	<u>タイヤ</u>を調べてくだ さい。 *<u>Taiya</u> o, shirabete kudasai.*	
tire pressure	タイヤの空気圧 *taiya no kūki atsu*	
Can you fix a flat tire?	パンクを、修理してもらえますか。 *Panku o, shūri shite moraemasu ka.*	

TIRE PRESSURE

LBS. PER SQ. IN.	KG. PER SQ.CM.	LBS. PER SQ. IN.	KG. PER SQ.CM.
17	1.2	30	2.1
18	1.3	31	2.2
20	1.4	33	2.3
21	1.5	34	2.4
23	1.6	36	2.5
24	1.7	37	2.6
26	1.8	38	2.7
27	1.9	40	2.8
28	2.0		

Change this tire, please. — このタイヤを、かえて下さい。*Kono taiya o, kaete kudasai.*

Would you clean the windshield? — フロント・ガラスを、ふいてもらえますか。*Furonto garasu o, fuite moraemasu ka.*

DISTANCE MEASURES (APPROXIMATE)

KILOMETERS	MILES
1	0.6
5	3
10	6
20	12
25	15
50	30
75	45
100	60

Do you have a road map of this area?	この地域の、道路地図がありますか。 *Kono chiiki no, dōro chizu ga arimasu ka.*
Where are the rest rooms?	トイレは、どこですか。*Toire wa, doko desu ka.*

PARKING

Parking can be a problem in the cities. There's little street parking available in Tokyo and not much in other cities either. All-night street parking is not allowed. In fact, Japanese must prove they have an off-street parking space when they obtain an automobile registration. A parking garage or parking lot may be your best bet. Some hotels offer parking facilities for their guests.

Excuse me, but _____ .	ちょっと、すみませんが。*Chotto, sumimasen ga.*
Can I park here?	ここに、駐車できますか。*Koko ni, chūsha dekimasu ka.*
Is it illegal to park here?	ここは、駐車禁止ですか。*Koko wa, chūsha kinshi desu ka.*
Is there any street parking nearby?	近くに、路上駐車できる場所がありますか。*Chikaku ni, rojō chūsha dekiru basho ga arimasu ka.*
How much does a parking meter cost per hour?	パーキング・メーターは、一時間いくらしますか。*Pākingu mētā wa, ichi jikan ikura shimasu ka.*
<u>From</u> what time can I park at a parking meter?	何時<u>から</u>、パーキング・メーターで駐車できますか。*Nan ji kara, pākingu mētā de chūsha dekimasu ka.*
Until	まで *made*
Is there a parking garage nearby?	近くに、駐車場がありますか。*Chikaku ni, chūsha jō ga arimasu ka.*

When does the parking garage <u>open</u>?	駐車場は、何時に開きますか。 *Chūsha jō wa, nan ji ni <u>akimasu</u> ka.*
close	閉まります *shimarimasu*
What's the parking fee?	駐車料金は、いくらですか。 *Chūsha ryōkin wa, ikura desu ka.*
I'd like to park <u>for one hour</u>.	<u>一時間</u>駐車したいのですが。 *<u>Ichi jikan</u> chūsha shitai no desu ga.*
for two hours	二時間 *ni jikan*
till noon	昼まで *hiru made*
till 5 o'clock	五時まで *go ji made*
overnight	一晩 *hito ban*
for a day	一日 *ichi nichi*
for two days	二日 *futsuka*
Do I leave the key in the car?	鍵は、車に残しますか。 *Kagi wa, kuruma ni nokoshimasu ka.*

ACCIDENTS AND REPAIRS

Could you help me?	助けてもらえますか。 *Tasukete moraemasu ka.*
I have a flat tire.	パンクです。 *Panku desu.*
Could you help me change the tire?	タイヤを替えるのを、手伝ってもらえますか。 *Taiya o kaeru no o, tetsudatte moraemasu ka.*
I've run out of gas.	ガス欠です。 *Gasu ketsu desu.*
Could you give me some gas?	ガソリンを、少し分けてもらえますか。 *Gasorin o, sukoshi wakete moraemasu ka.*
The car is overheated.	オーバー・ヒートです。 *Ōbā hīto desu.*
Can I get some water?	水を少し、もらえますか。 *Mizu o sukoshi, moraemasu ka.*

The car is stuck in the <u>mud</u>.	車がぬかるみにはまって、出られません。 *Kuruma ga <u>nukarumi</u> ni hamatte, deraremasen.*
ditch	みぞ　*mizo*
Could you <u>give me a hand</u>?	<u>手助けして</u>もらえますか。 *<u>Tedasuke shite</u> moraemasu ka.*
push it	押して　*oshite*
pull it	引っ張って　*hippatte*
The battery is dead.	バッテリーが、あがってしまいました。 *Batterī ga, agatte shimaimashita.*
Do you have a jumper cable?	ジャンパーを、お持ちですか。 *Janpā o, omochi desu ka.*
The radiator is leaking.	ラジエーターが、漏っています。 *Rajiētā ga, motte imasu.*
The keys are locked inside the car.	鍵を車の中に残したまま、ドアをロックしてしまいました。 *Kagi o kuruma no naka ni nokoshita mama, doa o rokku shite shimaimashita.*
I don't have any tools.	修理道具は、持っていません。 *Shūri dōgu wa, motte imasen.*
Could you lend me a <u>flashlight</u>?	<u>懐中電灯</u>を、貸してもらえますか。 *<u>Kaichū dentō</u> o, kashite moraemasu ka.*
hammer	ハンマー　*hanmā*
jack	ジャッキ　*jakki*
monkey wrench	自在スパナ　*jizai supana*
pliers	ペンチ　*penchi*
screwdriver	ドライバー／ねじ回し　*doraibā/ neji mawashi*
My car has broken down.	車が、故障してしまいました。 *Kuruma ga, koshō shite shimaimashita.*

The engine won't start.	エンジンが、かかりません。 *Enjin ga, kakarimasen.*
The car doesn't go.	車が、動きません。 *Kuruma ga, ugokimasen.*
I need <u>an auto mechanic</u>.	<u>車の整備士</u>が、必要です。 <u>*Kuruma no seibishi*</u> *ga, hitsuyō desu.*
a tow truck	レッカー車 *rekkā sha*
Is there a repair shop/ garage near here?	この近くに、修理工場がありますか。 *Kono chikaku ni, shūri kōjō ga arimasu ka.*
Do you know the phone number of a nearby garage?	近くの修理工場の、電話番号を御存知ですか。 *Chikaku no shūri kōjō no, denwa bangō o gozonji desu ka.*
Could you send a <u>mechanic</u>?	<u>修理ができる人</u>を、よこしてもらえますか。 <u>*Shūri ga dekiru hito*</u> *o, yokoshite moraemasu ka.*
tow truck	レッカー車 *rekkā sha*

AT THE GARAGE

There's something wrong with my car.	どこか、車の調子がよくないんですが。 *Dokoka, kuruma no chōshi ga yokunain desu ga.*
I don't know what's wrong with the car.	どこが悪いのか、わかりません。 *Doko ga warui no ka, wakarimasen.*
I think there's something wrong with the <u>battery</u>.	<u>バッテリー</u>が、よくないみたいです。 <u>*Batterī*</u> *ga, yokunai mitai desu.*
brakes	ブレーキ *burēki*
clutch	クラッチ *kuratchi*
electrical system	電気装置 *denki sōchi*
engine	エンジン *enjin*
fan belt	ファン・ベルト *fan beruto*
fuel pump	ガソリン・ポンプ *gasorin ponpu*

gears	ギヤ *giya*
ignition	点火装置 *tenka sōchi*
starter	スターター *sutātā*
steering wheel	ハンドル *handoru*
suspension	サスペンション *sasupenshon*
transmission	トランスミッション *toransumisshon*
water pump	ウォーター・ポンプ *wōtā ponpu*

Can you take a look at the <u>carburetor</u>? — <u>キャブレター</u>を、チェック／点検してもらえますか。 *<u>Kyaburetā</u> o, chekku/tenken shite moraemasu ka.*

distributor	ディストリビューター *disutoribyūtā*
gear box	ギヤ・ボックス *giya bokkusu*
ignition coil	イグニッション・コイル *igunisshon koiru*
thermostat	サーモスタット *sāmosutatto*

What's the problem? — どこが、よくないですか。 *Doko ga, yokunai desu ka.*

Is it fixable? — 直りますか。 *Naorimasu ka.*

Do you have the necessary parts? — 必要な部品が、ありますか。 *Hitsuyō na buhin ga, arimasu ka.*

Is it possible to get it fixed <u>now</u>? — <u>今</u>、直してもらえるでしょうか。 *<u>Ima</u>, naoshite moraeru deshō ka.*

today — 今日中に *kyō jū ni*

How long will it take? — 修理には、どのくらい時間がかかりますか。 *Shūri niwa, dono kurai jikan ga kakarimasu ka.*

Can you repair it temporarily? — 仮の修理をしてもらえますか。 *Kari no shūri o shite moraemasu ka.*

Can you give me an estimate for the repair?	修理の見積もりを、教えて下さい。 *Shūri no mitsumori o, oshiete kudasai.*
Is everything okay now?	直りましたか。*Naorimashita ka.*
May I have an itemized bill and a receipt?	明細書と領収書を、お願いします。 *Meisaisho to ryōshūsho o, onegai shimasu.*
Thank you very much for your help.	おかげで、本当に助かりました。 *Okage de, hontō ni tasukarimashita.*

ROAD SIGNS IN JAPANESE

Most road signs will be the visual kind. But you may see some with just Japanese writing. This list may help you recognize them and understand what they mean.

入り口	entrance
出口	exit
次の出口	next exit
料金所	toll gate
国道	national highway
県道	state (prefectural) highway
非常電話	emergency telephone
通行止め	road closed
車両通行止め	no vehicles
車両進入禁止	no entry
転回禁止	no U-turn
行き止まり	dead end
駐車禁止	no parking
駐停車禁止	no stopping
徐行	slow down

止まれ	stop
一方通行	one way
追い越し禁止	no passing
路肩弱し	soft shoulder
道路工事中	road under construction
まわり道(回り道)	detour
歩行者専用道路	road strictly for pedestrians

GUIDE SIGNS

Emergency Telephone

Parking

National Highway

Prefectural Highway

Entrance to Expressway

Service Area

Toll Gate

Next Exit

Exit

Detour

CAUTION SIGNS

Caution

Slippery

REGULATION SIGNS

Road Closed

No Entry for Vehicles or
Motorcycles

No Vehicles

No Right Turn

No Entry

No U-Turn

No Entry for Vehicles

No Passing

No Parking, No Standing

Minimum Speed

No Parking

Cars Only

No Parking Over 60 Minutes

Bicycles Only

Maximum Speed

Pedestrians and Bicycles Only

Pedestrians Only

One Way

This Lane for Motorcycles
and Lightweight Cars

Stop

Slow Down

Sound Horn

End of Speed Limit Restriction

INDICATION SIGNS

Parking Permitted

Two Way Traffic Dividing Line

Standing Permitted

Traffic Island

AUXILIARY SIGNS

日曜・祝日を除く

8－20

Except Sundays and Holidays

追越し禁止	路肩弱し	注　意
No Passing	Soft Shoulder	Caution

End of Restriction

INDICATION BOARD

Left Turn Permitted

GENERAL INFORMATION

TELLING TIME

A.M.	午前	*gozen*
P.M.	午後	*gogo*
noon	正午	*shōgo*
midnight	真夜中／ 午前零時	*mayonaka/gozen* *rei ji*
o'clock	時	*ji*

First, a list of hours, then a list of minutes, then we'll put them together!

HOURS

1 o'clock	一時	*ichi ji*
2 o'clock	二時	*ni ji*
3 o'clock	三時	*san ji*
4 o'clock	四時	*yo ji*
5 o'clock	五時	*go ji*
6 o'clock	六時	*roku ji*
7 o'clock	七時	*shichi ji*
8 o'clock	八時	*hachi ji*
9 o'clock	九時	*ku ji*
10 o'clock	十時	*jū ji*
11 o'clock	十一時	*jū ichi ji*
12 o'clock	十二時	*jū ni ji*

MINUTES

1 minute	一分	*ippun*
2 minutes	二分	*ni fun*
3 minutes	三分	*san pun*
4 minutes	四分	*yon pun*
5 minutes	五分	*go fun*
6 minutes	六分	*roppun*
7 minutes	七分	*nana fun*
8 minutes	八分	*happun*
9 minutes	九分	*kyū fun*
10 minutes	十分	*juppun*
11 minutes	十一分	*jū ippun*
12 minutes	十二分	*jū ni fun*
13 minutes	十三分	*jū san pun*
14 minutes	十四分	*jū yon pun*
15 minutes	十五分	*jū go fun*
16 minutes	十六分	*jū roppun*
17 minutes	十七分	*jū nana fun*
18 minutes	十八分	*jū happun*
19 minutes	十九分	*jū kyū fun*
20 minutes	二十分	*ni juppun*
21 minutes	二十一分	*ni jū ippun*
22 minutes	二十二分	*ni jū ni fun*
23 minutes	二十三分	*ni jū san pun*
24 minutes	二十四分	*ni jū yon pun*
25 minutes	二十五分	*ni jū go fun*
26 minutes	二十六分	*ni jū roppun*
27 minutes	二十七分	*ni jū nana fun*
28 minutes	二十八分	*ni jū happun*

29 minutes	二十九分	*ni jū kyū fun*
30 minutes	三十分	*san juppun*
31 minutes	三十一分	*san jū ippun*
32 minutes	三十二分	*san jū ni fun*
33 minutes	三十三分	*san jū san pun*
34 minutes	三十四分	*san jū yon pun*
35 minutes	三十五分	*san jū go fun*
36 minutes	三十六分	*san jū roppun*
37 minutes	三十七分	*san jū nana fun*
38 minutes	三十八分	*san jū happun*
39 minutes	三十九分	*san jū kyū fun*
40 minutes	四十分	*yon juppun*
41 minutes	四十一分	*yon jū ippun*
42 minutes	四十二分	*yon jū ni fun*
43 minutes	四十三分	*yon jū san pun*
44 minutes	四十四分	*yon jū yon pun*
45 minutes	四十五分	*yon jū go fun*
46 minutes	四十六分	*yon jū roppun*
47 minutes	四十七分	*yon jū nana fun*
48 minutes	四十八分	*yon jū happun*
49 minutes	四十九分	*yon jū kyū fun*
50 minutes	五十分	*go juppun*
51 minutes	五十一分	*go jū ippun*
52 minutes	五十二分	*go jū ni fun*
53 minutes	五十三分	*go jū san pun*
54 minutes	五十四分	*go jū yon pun*
55 minutes	五十五分	*go jū go fun*
56 minutes	五十六分	*go jū roppun*

57 minutes	五十七分	*go jū nana fun*
58 minutes	五十八分	*go jū happun*
59 minutes	五十九分	*go jū kyū fun*
a quarter after ten	十時十五分	*jū ji jū go fun*
	or	
	十時十五分過ぎ	*jū ji jū go fun sugi*

Using "sugi," which means "past" or "after," is optional.

a quarter to ten	十時十五分前	*jū ji jū go fun mae*

Start using "mae," which means "to" or "before," at 15 minutes
before the hour.

half past ten	十時半	*jū ji han*

"Han" means "half."

What time is it?	何時ですか。	*Nan ji desu ka.*
It's <u>5:00 o'clock</u>.	<u>五時です。</u>	<u>*Go ji desu.*</u>
5:05	五時五分	*go ji go fun*
5:10	五時十分	*go ji juppun*
5:15	五時十五分	*go ji jū go fun*
5:20	五時二十分	*go ji ni juppun*
5:25	五時二十五分	*go ji ni jū go fun*
5:30	五時半	*go ji han*
5:35	五時三十五分	*go ji san jū go fun*
5:40	五時四十分	*go ji yon juppun*
5:45/a quarter to six	五時四十五分／六時十五分前	*go ji yon jū go fun/roku ji jū go fun mae*
5:50 (ten to six)	六時十分前	*roku ji juppun mae*
5:55 (five to six)	六時五分前	*roku ji go fun mae*

To indicate A.M. or P.M., put *gozen* for A.M. and *gogo* for
P.M. before the time.

6:10 A.M.	午前１０時１０分	*gozen jū ji juppun*
9:35 P.M.	午後9時35分	*gogo ku ji san jū go fun*

For time schedules, as in railway and airline timetables, numbers 1 to 59 are used for minutes, not "a quarter to" or "ten to" the hour.

My train leaves at 13:42.	私の汽車は、十三時四十二分に出ます。 *Watakushi no kisha wa, jū san ji yon jū ni fun ni demasu.*	
His plane arrives at 20:50.	彼の飛行機は、二十時五十分に着きます。*Kare no hikōki wa, ni jū ji go juppun ni tsukimasu.*	

Note that transportation timetables are based on the 24-hour clock.

DAYS OF THE WEEK

Sunday	日曜日	*nichiyōbi*
Monday	月曜日	*getsuyōbi*
Tuesday	火曜日	*kayōbi*
Wednesday	水曜日	*suiyōbi*
Thursday	木曜日	*mokuyōbi*
Friday	金曜日	*kinyōbi*
Saturday	土曜日	*doyōbi*

MONTHS OF THE YEAR

January	一月	*ichigatsu*
February	二月	*nigatsu*
March	三月	*sangatsu*
April	四月	*shigatsu*
May	五月	*gogatsu*
June	六月	*rokugatsu*

July	七月	*shichigatsu*
August	八月	*hachigatsu*
September	九月	*kugatsu*
October	十月	*jūgatsu*
November	十一月	*jūichigatsu*
December	十二月	*jūnigatsu*

THE FOUR SEASONS

spring	春	*haru*
summer	夏	*natsu*
fall	秋	*aki*
winter	冬	*fuyu*

TIME PHRASES

today	今日	*kyō*
yesterday	きのう	*kinō*
the day before yesterday	おととい	*ototoi*
tomorrow	あした	*ashita*
the day after tomorrow	あさって	*asatte*
this week	今週	*konshū*
last week	先週	*senshū*
next week	来週	*raishū*
for one week	一週間	*isshūkan*
for two weeks	二週間	*ni shūkan*
in one week	一週間で	*isshūkan de*

in two weeks	二週間で	*ni shūkan de*
for one day	一日	*ichi nichi*
for two days	二日間	*futsuka kan*
for three days	三日間	*mikka kan*
in one day	一日で	*ichi nichi de*
in two days	二日で	*futsuka de*
three days ago	三日前	*mikka mae*
two months ago	二ヶ月前	*ni ka getsu mae*
three months ago	三ヶ月前	*san ka getsu mae*
five years ago	五年前	*go nen mae*
this year	今年	*kotoshi*
last year	去年	*kyonen*
next year	来年	*rainen*
this morning	けさ	*kesa*
this afternoon	今日の午後	*kyō no gogo*
tonight	今晩	*konban*
tomorrow night	あしたの晩	*ashita no ban*
for six years	六年間	*roku nen kan*
for seven months	七ヶ月間	*nana ka getsu kan*
in the morning	午前中	*gozen chū*
in the afternoon	午後	*gogo*
in the early evening	夕方	*yūgata*
in the evening	夜	*yoru*
in summer	夏に	*natsu ni*
in winter	冬に	*fuyu ni*
by Tuesday	火曜日までに	*kayōbi made ni*
by June	六月までに	*roku gatsu made ni*
by morning	朝までに	*asa made ni*

What's today's date?	今日は、何日ですか。*Kyō wa, nan nichi desu ka.*	
It's the (<u>fifteenth</u>).	(<u>十五日</u>)です。(*<u>Jū go nichi</u>) desu.*	
What day is today?	今日は、何曜日ですか。*Kyō wa, nani yōbi desu ka.*	
It's (<u>Thursday</u>).	(<u>木曜日</u>)です。(*<u>Mokuyōbi</u>) desu.*	

DAYS OF THE MONTH

1st	一日	*tsuitachi*
2nd	二日	*futsuka*
3rd	三日	*mikka*
4th	四日	*yokka*
5th	五日	*itsuka*
6th	六日	*muika*
7th	七日	*nanoka*
8th	八日	*yōka*
9th	九日	*kokonoka*
10th	十日	*tōka*
11th	十一日	*jū ichi nichi*
12th	十二日	*jū ni nichi*
13th	十三日	*jū san nichi*
14th	十四日	*jū yokka*
15th	十五日	*jū go nichi*
16th	十六日	*jū roku nichi*
17th	十七日	*jū shichi nichi*
18th	十八日	*jū hachi nichi*
19th	十九日	*jū ku nichi*
20th	二十日	*hatsuka*

21st	二十一日	*ni jū ichi nichi*
22nd	二十二日	*ni jū ni nichi*
23rd	二十三日	*ni jū san nichi*
24th	二十四日	*ni jū yokka*
25th	二十五日	*ni jū go nichi*
26th	二十六日	*ni jū roku nichi*
27th	二十七日	*ni jū shichi nichi*
28th	二十八日	*ni jū hachi nichi*
29th	二十九日	*ni jū ku nichi*
30th	三十日	*san jū nichi*
31st	三十一日	*san jū ichi nichi*

COUNTING YEARS

one year	一年	*ichi nen*
two years	二年	*ni nen*
three years	三年	*san nen*
four years	四年	*yo nen*
five years	五年	*go nen*
six years	六年	*roku nen*
seven years	七年	*nana nen/shichi nen*
eight years	八年	*hachi nen*
nine years	九年	*ku nen/kyū nen*
ten years	十年	*jū nen*

COUNTING DAYS

one day	一日	*ichi nichi*
two days	二日	*futsuka*
three days	三日	*mikka*
four days	四日	*yokka*
five days	五日	*itsuka*
six days	六日	*muika*
seven days	七日	*nanoka*
eight days	八日	*yōka*
nine days	九日	*kokonoka*
ten days	十日	*tōka*
eleven days	十一日	*jū ichi nichi*
twelve days	十二日	*jū ni nichi*
thirteen days	十三日	*jū san nichi*

COUNTING WEEKS

one week	一週間	*isshūkan*
two weeks	二週間	*ni shūkan*
three weeks	三週間	*san shūkan*
four weeks	四週間	*yon shūkan*
five weeks	五週間	*go shūkan*
six weeks	六週間	*roku shūkan*
seven weeks	七週間	*nana shūkan*
eight weeks	八週間	*hasshūkan*
nine weeks	九週間	*kyū shūkan*
ten weeks	十週間	*jusshūkan*

COUNTING DIFFERENT KINDS OF THINGS

	1 (one) ichi	2 (two) ni	3 (three) san	4 (four) shi/yon	5 (five) go
long, skinny objects (pencils, sticks, bottles, and so forth)					
	一本 ippon	二本 ni hon	三本 san bon	四本 yon hon	五本 go hon
thin, flat objects (paper, bills, cloth, plates, tickets, and so forth)					
	一枚 ichi mai	二枚 ni mai	三枚 san mai	四枚 yo mai	五枚 go mai
bound objects (books, magazines, notebooks, and so forth)					
	一冊 issatsu	二冊 ni satsu	三冊 san satsu	四冊 yon satsu	五冊 go satsu
liquid or dry measures (glasses or cups of water, coffee, tea, sugar, and so forth)					
	一杯 ippai	二杯 ni hai	三杯 san bai	四杯 yon hai	五杯 go hai
vehicles, machines					
	一台 ichi dai	二台 ni dai	三台 san dai	四台 yon dai	五台 go dai
things to wear (jackets, sweaters, shirts, coats, and so forth)					
	一着 itchaku	二着 ni chaku	三着 san chaku	四着 yon chaku	五着 go chaku

pairs of things to wear on feet or legs (socks, shoes, slippers, and so forth)

一足	二足	三足	四足	五足
issoku	ni soku	san zoku	yon soku	go soku

sets of dishes, pairs of people, and so forth

一組	二組	三組	四組	五組
hito kumi	futa kumi	mi kumi	yo kumi	itsu kumi/ go kumi

boxes, cases, and so forth

一箱	二箱	三箱	四箱	五箱
hito hako	futa hako	mi hako	yo hako	itsu hako/ go hako

floors of buildings

一階	二階	三階	四階	五階
ikkai	ni kai	san gai	yon kai	go kai

houses, buildings

一軒	二軒	三軒	四軒	五軒
ikken	ni ken	san gen	yon ken	go ken

small and medium-size animals, insects, fish

一匹	二匹	三匹	四匹	五匹
ippiki	ni hiki	san biki	yon hiki	go hiki

large animals (horses, cows, elephants, and so forth)

一頭	二頭	三頭	四頭	五頭
ittō	*ni tō*	*san tō*	*yon tō*	*go tō*

birds

一羽	二羽	三羽	四羽	五羽
ichi wa	*ni wa*	*san ba*	*yo wa*	*go wa*

bunches (grapes, bananas, and so forth)

一房	二房	三房	四房	五房
hito fusa	*futa fusa*	*mi fusa*	*yo fusa*	*itsu fusa*

copies (newspapers, documents, brochures, and so forth)

一部	二部	三部	四部	五部
ichi bu	*ni bu*	*san bu*	*yon bu*	*go bu*

portions, servings

一人前	二人前	三人前	四人前	五人前
ichi nin mae	*ni nin mae*	*san nin mae*	*yo nin mae*	*go nin mae*

slices

一切れ	二切れ	三切れ	四切れ	五切れ
hito kire	*futa kire*	*mi kire*	*yo kire*	*itsu kire*

small objects not in the categories listed above

一個／一つ	二個／二つ	三個／三つ	四個／四つ	五個／五つ
ikko/hitotsu	*ni ko/futatsu*	*sanko/mittsu*	*yonko/yottsu*	*goko/itsutsu*

NATIONAL HOLIDAYS

January 1
   New Year's Day   元日   *ganjitsu*

January, the second Monday
   Adulthood Day   成人の日   *seijin no hi*

February 11
   National Foundation   建国記念日   *kenkoku kinen bi*
   Day

March 20 or 21
   Vernal Equinox Day   春分の日   *shunbun no hi*

April 29
   Showa Day   昭和の日   *shōwa no hi*

May 3
   Constitution Day   憲法記念日   *kenpō kinen bi*

May 4
   Greenery Day   緑の日   *midori no hi*

May 5
   Children's Day   子供の日   *kodomo no hi*

July, the third Monday
   Marine Day   海の日   *umi no hi*

August 11
   Mountain Day   山の日   *yama no hi*

September, the third Monday
   Respect for the   敬老の日   *keirō no hi*
   Aged Day

September 23 or 24
   Autumnal Equinox   秋分の日   *shūbun no hi*
   Day

October, the second Monday

    Health-Sports Day   体育の日   *taiiku no hi*

November 3

    Culture Day   文化の日   *bunka no hi*

November 23

    Labor Thanksgiving   勤労感謝の日   *kinrō kansha no hi*
    Day

December 23

    Emperor's Birthday   天皇誕生日   *tennō tanjō bi*

COUNTRIES

Afghanistan	アフガニスタン	*Afuganisutan*
Algeria	アルジェリア	*Arujeria*
Argentina	アルゼンチン	*Aruzenchin*
Australia	オーストラリア	*Ōsutoraria*
Austria	オーストリア	*Ōsutoria*
Bangladesh	バングラデシュ	*Banguradeshu*
Belarus	ベラルーシ	*Berarūshi*
Belgium	ベルギー	*Berugī*
Bolivia	ボリビア	*Boribia*
Bosnia and Herzegovina	ボスニア・ヘルツェゴビナ	*Bosunia-Herutsegobina*
Brazil	ブラジル	*Burajiru*
Brunei	ブルネイ	*Burunei*
Bulgaria	ブルガリア	*Burugaria*
Burkina Faso	ブルキナファソ	*Burukinafaso*
Burundi	ブルンジ	*Burunji*
Cambodia	カンボジア	*Kanbojia*

Cameroon	カメルーン	*Kamerūn*
Canada	カナダ	*Kanada*
Chile	チリ	*Chiri*
China	中国	*Chūgoku*
Colombia	コロンビア	*Koronbia*
Congo	コンゴ	*Kongo*
Costa Rica	コスタリカ	*Kosutarika*
Côte d' lvoire	コートジボワール	*Kōtojibowāru*
Croatia	クロアチア	*Kuroachia*
Cuba	キューバ	*Kyūba*
Czech Republic	チェコ	*Cheko*
Denmark	デンマーク	*Denmāku*
Djibouti	ジブチ	*Jibuchi*
Dominican Republic	ドミニカ	*Dominika*
Ecuador	エクアドル	*Ekuadoru*
Egypt	エジプト	*Ejiputo*
El Salvador	エルサルバドル	*Erusarubadoru*
Ethiopia	エチオピア	*Echiopia*
England/ United Kingdom (See also United Kingdom.)	英国	*Eikoku*
Fiji	フィジー	*Fijī*
Finland	フィンランド	*Finrando*
France	フランス	*Furansu*
Gabon	ガボン	*Gabon*
Georgia	ジョージア	*Jōjia*
Germany	ドイツ	*Doitsu*
Ghana	ガーナ	*Gāna*
Greece	ギリシャ	*Girisha*
Guatemala	ガテマラ	*Gatemara*

Guinea	ギニア	*Ginia*
Haiti	ハイチ	*Haichi*
Holland (See also Netherlands.)	オランダ	*Oranda*
Honduras	ホンジュラス	*Honjurasu*
Hungary	ハンガリー	*Hangarī*
India	インド	*Indo*
Indonesia	インドネシア	*Indoneshia*
Iran	イラン	*Iran*
Iraq	イラク	*Iraku*
Ireland	アイルランド	*Airurando*
Israel	イスラエル	*Isuraeru*
Italy	イタリア	*Itaria*
Jamaica	ジャマイカ	*Jamaika*
Jordan	ヨルダン	*Yorudan*
Kazakhstan	カザフスタン	*Kazafusutan*
Kenya	ケニア	*Kenia*
Korea (South)	韓国	*Kankoku*
Kuwait	クウェート	*Kuwēto*
Kyrgyzstan	キルギスタン	*Kirugisutan*
Laos	ラオス	*Raosu*
Lebanon	レバノン	*Rebanon*
Liberia	リベリア	*Riberia*
Libya	リビア	*Ribia*
Luxembourg	ルクセンブルグ	*Rukusenburugu*
Macedonia	マセドニア	*Masedonia*
Madagascar	マダガスカル	*Madagasukaru*
Malawi	マラウイ	*Maraui*
Malaysia	マレーシア	*Marēshia*
Marshall Islands	マーシャル諸島	*Māsharu Shotō*

Mauritania	モーリタニア	*Mōritania*
Mexico	メキシコ	*Mekishiko*
Micronesia	ミクロネシア	*Mikuroneshia*
Mongolia	モンゴリア	*Mongoria*
Montenegro	モンテネグロ	*Monteneguro*
Morocco	モロッコ	*Morokko*
Mozambique	モザンビーク	*Mozanbīku*
Myanmar	ミャンマー	*Myanmā*
Nepal	ネパール	*Nepāru*
Netherlands	オランダ	*Oranda*
New Zealand	ニュージーランド	*Nyūjīrando*
Nicaragua	ニカラグア	*Nikaragua*
Nigeria	ナイジェリア	*Naijeria*
Norway	ノルウェー	*Noruwē*
Oman	オマーン	*Omān*
Pakistan	パキスタン	*Pakisutan*
Panama	パナマ	*Panama*
Papua New Guinea	パプア ニューギニア	*Papua Nyūginia*
Paraguay	パラグアイ	*Paraguai*
Peru	ペルー	*Perū*
Philippines	フィリピン	*Firipin*
Poland	ポーランド	*Pōrando*
Portugal	ポルトガル	*Porutogaru*
Qatar	カタール	*Katāru*
Romania	ルーマニア	*Rūmania*
Russian Federation	ロシア	*Roshia*
Rwanda	ルワンダ	*Ruwanda*
Saudi Arabia	サウジアラビア	*Saujiarabia*
Senegal	セネガル	*Senegaru*
Serbia	セルビア	*Serubia*

Singapore	シンガポール	*Shingapōru*
Slovakia	スロバキア	*Surobakia*
Slovenia	スロベニア	*Surobenia*
South Africa	南アフリカ	*Minami Afurika*
Spain	スペイン	*Supein*
Sri Lanka	スリランカ	*Suriranka*
Sudan	スーダン	*Sūdan*
Sweden	スウェーデン	*Suwēden*
Switzerland	スイス	*Suisu*
Syria	シリア	*Shiria*
Taiwan	台湾	*Taiwan*
Tanzania	タンザニア	*Tanzania*
Thailand	タイ	*Tai*
Tunisia	チュニジア	*Chunijia*
Turkey	トルコ	*Toruko*
Uganda	ウガンダ	*Uganda*
Ukraine	ウクライナ	*Ukuraina*
United Arab Emirates	アラブ首長国連邦	*Arabu Shuchō Koku Renpō*
United Kingdom of Great Britain and Northern Ireland	英国／イギリス	*Eikoku/Igirisu*
United States of America	アメリカ	*Amerika*
Uruguay	ウルグアイ	*Uruguai*
Uzbekistan	ウズベキスタン	*Uzubekisutan*
Venezuela	ベネズエラ	*Benezuera*
Vietnam	ベトナム	*Betonamu*
Yemen	イエメン	*Iemen*
Zambia	ザンビア	*Zanbia*
Zimbabwe	ジンバブエ	*Jinbabue*

NATIONALITIES

To express nationality, add *jin* to the Japanese expressions for the countries listed above. For example, to say "American," look up the country United States, which is *Amerika*, and add *jin*. Thus American is *Amerika jin*. *Jin* literally means "person."

person	人	*jin*

COUNTING TIMES

once	一度	*ichi do*
twice	二度	*ni do*
three times	三度	*san do*
four times	四度	*yon do*
five times	五度	*go do*

the first time	初めて	*hajimete*
the second time	二度目	*ni do me*
the third time	三度目	*san do me*
the fourth time	四度目	*yon do me*
the fifth time	五度目	*go do me*

SIGNS

Most signs are in Japanese characters. With this list, you can recognize the characters and understand the meaning.

入口	Entrance
出口	Exit
東口	East Exit

西口	West Exit
南口	South Exit
北口	North Exit
お手洗い	Lavatory
便所	Lavatory
男	Men
女	Women
大人	Adult
小人	Child
危険	Danger
立入禁止	Keep Out
消火器	Fire Extinguisher
火気厳禁	No Matches
有料	Fee Required
無料	Free Admission
本日休業	Closed Today
準備中	Temporarily Closed
禁煙	No Smoking
土足厳禁	No Shoes (no street shoes allowed on the floor)
コインロッカー	Pay Locker
指定席	Reserved Seat
自由席	Nonreserved Seat
満席	Full
駐車場	Parking Place
病院	Hospital
空き	Vacant
使用中	Occupied
ベルを押してください	Please Ring
引く	Pull
押す	Push

注意	Caution
非常口	Emergency Exit
触れるな	Don't Touch
案内所	Information
猛犬に注意	Beware of Dog
会計	Cashier
貸し出し／貸します	For Rent, For Hire
ノックせずにお入り ください	Enter Without Knocking
入場禁止	No Entry
入場お断り	No Admittance
私有地	Private Property
警告	Warning
止まれ	Stop
売り切れ	Sold Out
魚釣禁止	No Fishing
水泳禁止	No Swimming
階段	Stairs
エスカレーター	Escalator
エレベーター	Elevator
セール	On Sale
特売	Bargain Sale
大安売り	Special Bargain Sale
割引き	Discount

METRIC CONVERSIONS

If you're not used to the metric system, you'll need the tables and conversion charts for your visit to Japan.

SOME CONVENIENT ROUGH EQUIVALENTS

These are rough approximations, but they'll help you to "think metric" when you don't have your pocket calculator handy.

3 kilometers	about 2 miles
30 grams	about 1 ounce
100 grams	about 3.5 ounces
1 kilogram	about 2 pounds
1 liter	about 1 quart
1 hectare	about 1 acre

CENTIMETERS/INCHES

It is usually unnecessary to make exact conversions from inches to the metric system, but for an approximate idea of how they compare, use the following guide.

To convert **centimeters into inches**, multiply by .39.

To convert **inches into centimeters**, multiply by 2.54.

Centimeters

Inches

METERS/FEET

1 meter	=	39.37 inches	1 foot	=	0.3 meters
	=	3.28 feet	1 yard	=	0.9 meters
	=	1.09 yards			

How tall are you in meters? See for yourself.

FEET/INCHES	METERS/CENTIMETERS
5'	1m 52cm
5' 1"	1m 55cm
5' 2"	1m 57cm
5' 3"	1m 60cm
5' 4"	1m 62cm
5' 5"	1m 65cm
5' 6"	1m 68cm
5' 7"	1m 71cm
5' 8"	1m 73cm
5' 9"	1m 76cm
5' 10"	1m 78cm
5' 11"	1m 81cm
6'	1m 83cm
6' 1"	1m 86cm

LIQUID MEASUREMENTS

1 liter = 1.06 quarts

4 liters = 1.06 gallons

For quick approximate conversion, multiply the number of gallons by 4 to get liters. Divide the number of liters by 4 to get gallons.

WHEN YOU WEIGH YOURSELF

1 kilogram = 2.2 pounds

1 pound = 0.45 kilogram

KILOGRAMS	POUNDS
40	88
45	99
50	110
55	121
60	132
65	143
70	154
75	165
80	176
85	187
90	198
95	209
100	220

USEFUL WEBSITES

The Japan National Tourist Organization is run by the Japanese government. It has a comprehensive, informative, easy-to-use website. It can also lead you to many other relevant websites. The home address is *http://www.jnto.go.jp/eng/*. Another all-purpose convenient website is *http://japan-guide.com*.

QUICK GRAMMAR GUIDE

Japanese is a complex language, and a detailed grammatical presentation is far beyond the scope of this book. However, this list of some major characteristics of the language may give you an idea of how Japanese works and can help you use the phrases with confidence.

WORD ORDER

The word order of a Japanese sentence is subject-object-verb. The verb always comes at the end. Subordinate clauses must come before the main clause. For example, the sentence *I'm studying Japanese* becomes *Japanese-am-studying. I won't go if it rains* becomes *It-rains-if I-won't-go.* Notice how the subordinate clause, *if it rains*, changes position so that the main clause can be at the end of the sentence.

ARTICLES

There are no articles in Japanese. That is, there is nothing that corresponds to the English words *a*, *an*, or *the*.

NOUNS

Japanese nouns do not have plural forms. **Hon** means a book, the book, books, or the books.

PARTICLES

Japanese contains many particles. A particle is a word that shows the relationship of a word, a phrase, or a clause to the rest of the sentence. Some particles show grammatical function, such as subject, object, or indirect object. Some have meaning themselves, like English prepositions. But since they always follow the word or words they mark, they are postpositions. Here are some of the more common particles and some of their uses.

ga	Subject marker
wa	Topic marker
o	Direct object marker
ka	Question marker
no	Possessive marker
ni	Indirect object marker; also translates English *to* (or *at* when it indicates where something is located)
e	Translates English *to*
de	Translates English *at* when it indicates where an action takes place

PRONOUNS

The subject and object pronouns are usually omitted if the meaning is clear without them. They can be included when necessary. For example:

I'm an American.   <u>Amerikajin</u> <u>desu</u>.

American   am

ADJECTIVES

In English, adjectives (such as *big, small,* and *attractive*) are words that modify or describe nouns. In Japanese, one group of adjectives has verb-like characteristics. Often called verbal adjectives, the endings change according to tense. (*Suzushii* means "It's cool." *Suzushikatta* means "It was cool.") The other group of adjectives has noun-like characteristics. Often called adjectival nouns, they are invariable in form and are usually followed by the word *na,* as in *kirei na hito,* which means "a pretty person" (the adjective is *kirei,* "pretty"). Both groups can function like English adjectives, that is, to modify nouns that follow.

VERBS

There are two tenses in Japanese: nonpast and past. We can think of the nonpast as including the present and future tense meanings:

| I study at the library. | <u>Toshokan</u> <u>de</u> <u>benkyō shimasu.</u> |
| | library   at   study |

| I'm studying at the library. | <u>Toshokan</u> <u>de</u> <u>benkyō shite imasu.</u> |
| | library   at   studying am |

| I'll study at the library soon. | <u>Sugu toshokan</u> <u>de</u> <u>benkyō shimasu.</u> |
| | soon   library   at   study will |

The past tense looks like this:

| I studied at the library. | <u>Toshokan</u> <u>de</u> <u>benkyō shimashita.</u> |
| | library   at   studied |

Negatives of nonpast verbs are made by changing -masu to -masen:

| I understand. | Wakarimasu. |

| I don't understand. | Wakarimasen. |

In the case of the past, -mashita becomes -masen deshita:

I understood.	Wakarimashita.
I didn't understand.	Wakarimasen deshita.

LEVELS OF LANGUAGE

The Japanese language reflects the importance of interpersonal relationships in Japanese society. Of course, other languages have ways of expressing varying degrees of formality in a relationship or a situation. But Japanese has more ways than most. To fulfill the linguistic requirements of dealing with respect, courtesy, and relative social status in Japanese takes a knowledge of the culture and the language that ordinarily results from considerable time and study.

Many of the social and other distinctions are conveyed in the verbs. There are entire sets of endings for different levels of language. This book uses a level of politeness that will be appropriate for your trip. We may characterize it as "polite" (formal), as opposed to "plain" (informal).

	polite	plain
I understand.	Wakarimasu.	Wakaru.
I'm eating.	Tabete imasu.	Tabete iru.

You should be aware that there is much more to this dimension of the Japanese language, and that while you will be correct in using the verb forms presented in this book, you will hear a great many others.

MALE AND FEMALE LANGUAGE

Another aspect of the interpersonal distinctions in Japanese is the difference between male and female language. Japanese men and women are bound by certain rules of language usage, and some of these carry over to foreigners as well. The only difference that we treat here is the use of the polite or honorific particle before certain words. We indicate this for you with an *o* in parenthesis.

Japanese rice wine   (o)sake

This means that a woman should pronounce the *o*. For a man, it's optional.

NUMBERS

A word about numbers may be helpful here. Japanese uses classifiers for counting different categories of things. For speakers of English or other European languages, this can be confusing at first. It means that when you've learned to count from 1 to 10 or to 100 or 1,000, you can't necessarily use those numbers for counting books or days or people. For example, some cardinal numbers:

one	ichi
two	ni
three	san

But:

one *book*	hon o issatsu
one *dog*	inu o ippiki

Not an *ichi* in sight! So, before you count anything, check for the classifier, or counter, you need. You'll find many listed throughout the book, under the appropriate headings. Others appear on pages 361–365, General Information section.

WRITING SYSTEM

You probably won't be reading or writing Japanese on your trip, but you will see those fascinating characters everywhere, and you might want to know something about them. You might even get to recognize a few!

Traditionally, Japanese is written vertically, from top to bottom and from right to left. But it is also written horizontally and from left to right as in English. There are three kinds of characters used in the writing:

kanji   hiragana   katakana

All three are used together in Japanese words and sentences.

KANJI

Although Japanese and Chinese are completely separate languages, Japanese adopted written symbols and much vocabulary from Chinese, beginning in the fourth or fifth century. In Japan these symbols or Chinese characters are called kanji. They represent both meaning and sound, and it is often the case that one kanji has more than one reading (or pronunciation) and meaning. Japanese people learn about 2,000 kanji by the end of high school. Those are the basic characters used in newspapers, magazines, and school textbooks. Most Japanese know several thousand additional kanji as well.

Kanji can be very simple, with one or two strokes, or quite complicated, with many strokes needed to make one character. Some kanji look like pictures, or line drawings, of the words they represent:

| mountain | yama | 山 |
| river | kawa | 川 |

Put these two together, and you have the Japanese family name Yamakawa: 山川

HIRAGANA AND KATAKANA

Hiragana and katakana are used to represent the sounds of syllables. Each is a kind of alphabet of 46 characters or sounds. Hiragana is used for native Japanese words, and katakana is used for words of foreign origin.

| Welcome to Japan, Mr. Smith. | Sumisu スミス katakana | san さん、 hiragana | Nihon 日本 kanji | e yōkoso. へようこそ。 hiragana |

HIRAGANA

a	あ	i	い	u	う	e	え	o	お
ka	か	ki	き	ku	く	ke	け	ko	こ
sa	さ	shi	し	su	す	se	せ	so	そ
ta	た	chi	ち	tsu	つ	te	て	to	と
na	な	ni	に	nu	ぬ	ne	ね	no	の
ha	は	hi	ひ	fu	ふ	he	へ	ho	ほ
ma	ま	mi	み	mu	む	me	め	mo	も
ya	や			yu	ゆ			yo	よ
ra	ら	ri	り	ru	る	re	れ	ro	ろ
wa	わ							o	を
n	ん								
ga	が	gi	ぎ	gu	ぐ	ge	げ	go	ご
za	ざ	ji	じ	zu	ず	ze	ぜ	zo	ぞ
da	だ	ji	ぢ	zu	づ	de	で	do	ど
ba	ば	bi	び	bu	ぶ	be	べ	bo	ぼ
pa	ぱ	pi	ぴ	pu	ぷ	pe	ぺ	po	ぽ
kya	きゃ			kyu	きゅ			kyo	きょ
sha	しゃ			shu	しゅ			sho	しょ
cha	ちゃ			chu	ちゅ			cho	ちょ
nya	にゃ			nyu	にゅ			nyo	にょ
hya	ひゃ			hyu	ひゅ			hyo	ひょ
mya	みゃ			myu	みゅ			myo	みょ
rya	りゃ			ryu	りゅ			ryo	りょ
gya	ぎゃ			gyu	ぎゅ			gyo	ぎょ
ja	じゃ			ju	じゅ			jo	じょ
bya	びゃ			byu	びゅ			byo	びょ
pya	ぴゃ			pyu	ぴゅ			pyo	ぴょ

KATAKANA

a	ア	i	イ	u	ウ	e	エ	o	オ
ka	カ	ki	キ	ku	ク	ke	ケ	ko	コ
sa	サ	shi	シ	su	ス	se	セ	so	ソ
ta	タ	chi	チ	tsu	ツ	te	テ	to	ト
na	ナ	ni	ニ	nu	ヌ	ne	ネ	no	ノ
ha	ハ	hi	ヒ	fu	フ	he	ヘ	ho	ホ
ma	マ	mi	ミ	mu	ム	me	メ	mo	モ
ya	ヤ			yu	ユ			yo	ヨ
ra	ラ	ri	リ	ru	ル	re	レ	ro	ロ
wa	ワ							o	ヲ
n	ン								
ga	ガ	gi	ギ	gu	グ	ge	ゲ	go	ゴ
za	ザ	ji	ジ	zu	ズ	ze	ゼ	zo	ゾ
da	ダ	ji	ヂ	zu	ヅ	de	デ	do	ド
ba	バ	bi	ビ	bu	ブ	be	ベ	bo	ボ
pa	パ	pi	ピ	pu	プ	pe	ペ	po	ポ
fa	ファ	fi	フィ	fu	フ	fe	フェ	fo	フォ
kya	キャ			kyu	キュ			kyo	キョ
sha	シャ			shu	シュ			sho	ショ
cha	チャ			chu	チュ			cho	チョ
nya	ニャ			nyu	ニュ			nyo	ニョ
hya	ヒャ			hyu	ヒュ			hyo	ヒョ
mya	ミャ			myu	ミュ			myo	ミョ
rya	リャ			ryu	リュ			ryo	リョ
gya	ギャ			gyu	ギュ			gyo	ギョ
ja	ジャ			ju	ジュ			jo	ジョ
bya	ビャ			byu	ビュ			byo	ビョ
pya	ピャ			pyu	ピュ			pyo	ピョ

Notes on Hiragana

In Japanese, わ and は are pronounced *wa* and *ha*, respectively. But when は is used as a topic marker, it is pronounced *wa*.

In the expressions *Konnichiwa*, "Good afternoon," and *Konbanwa*, "Good evening," は, not わ, is used.

When へ (*he*) is used as a locational particle, the pronunciation changes to *e*, as in え.

ENGLISH-JAPANESE DICTIONARY

A

abalone あわび　*awabi*

abdomen おなか　*onaka*

accident 事故　*jiko*

acrylics アクリルネイル　*akuriru neiru*

acupressure 指圧　*shiatsu*

acupressurist 指圧師　*shiatsu shi*

acupuncture 針療治　*hari ryōji*

acupuncturist 針の療治師　*hari no ryōjishi*

ad 広告　*kōkoku*

adapter plug プラグのアダプター　*puragu no adaputā*

address 住所　*jūsho*

adhesive tape ばんそうこう　*bansōkō*

admission fee 入場料　*nyūjō ryō*

aerobics エアロビックス　*earobikkusu*

aerogram 航空書簡　*kōkū shokan*

Africa アフリカ　*Afurika*

after のあとで　*no ato de*

afternoon 午後　*gogo*

again もう一度　*mō ichido*

age limit 年齢制限　*nenrei seigen*

air conditioner 冷房　*reibō*

airplane 飛行機　*hikōki*

airport 飛行場／空港　*hikōjō/kūkō*

aisle 通路　*tsūro*

alcohol アルコール　*arukōru*

ale エール　*ēru*

allergy アレルギー　*arerugī*

almonds アーモンド　*āmondo*

alone ひとり　*hitori*

also も／また　*mo/mata*

to alter (clothing) 直す　*naosu*

altogether 全部で　*zenbu de*

always いつも　*itsumo*

ambulance 救急車　*kyūkyūsha*

America アメリカ　*Amerika*

American (adj.) アメリカの　*Amerika no*

American (person) アメリカ人　*Amerika jin*

American music アメリカの音楽　*Amerika no ongaku*

American products アメリカ製品　*Amerika seihin*

and (between nouns) と　*to*

and (between sentences) そして　*soshite*

anime アニメ　*anime*

ankle 足首　*ashikubi*

another 外の　*hoka no*

antacid 胃散　*isan*

antibiotics 抗生物質　*kōsei busshitsu*

antiques 骨董　*kottō hin*

antiseptic 消毒薬　*shōdokuyaku*

aperitif アペリチフ　*aperichifu*

appendicitis 盲腸炎　*mōchō en*

appetizers 前菜／つまみ　*zensai/tsumami*

apple りんご　*ringo*

appointment 予約　*yoyaku*

April 四月　*shigatsu*

aquamarine アクアマリン　*akuamarin*

aquarium 水族館　*suizokukan*

Arabic (lang.) アラビア語 *Arabia go*

architect 建築家 *kenchikuka*

architecture 建築 *kenchiku*

area 地域 *chiiki*

arm 腕 *ude*

around (approximate time) _____頃 _____ *goro*

arrival 到着 *tōchaku*

arrival time 到着の時間 *tōchaku no jikan*

to arrive 着く *tsuku*

art 美術 *bijutsu*

art gallery 画廊 *garō*

artificial sweetener 人工甘味料 *jinkō kanmiryō*

artist 芸術家 *geijutsuka*

to go ashore 上陸する *jōriku suru*

arthritis 関節炎 *kansetsu en*

aspirin アスピリン *asupirin*

aspirin-free painkiller アスピリンを含まない鎮痛剤 *asupirin o fukumanai chintsūzai*

assorted food 盛り合わせ *moriawase*

assorted sandwiches ミックスサンド *mikkusu sando*

asthma ぜんそく *zensoku*

at _____で _____ *de*

ATM エーティーエム *ē·tī·emu*

atmosphere 雰囲気 *fun-iki*

attache case アタッシェ・ケース *atasshe kēsu*

attractions みもの *mimono*

  main attractions 主なみもの *omo na mimono*

auburn 赤茶色 *akachairo*

August 八月 *hachigatsu*

aunt (someone else's) おばさん *obasan*

aunt (your own) おば *oba*

Australia オーストラリア *Ōsutoraria*

author 著者 *chosha*

auto mechanic 車の整備士 *kuruma no seibishi*

auto repair shop 修理工場 *shūri kōjō*

automatic transmission 自動変速／オートマチック *jidō hensoku/ōtomachikku*

autumn leaves 紅葉 *kōyō*

awful-tasting まずい *mazui*

B

baby 赤ん坊 *akanbō*

baby bottle 哺乳ビン *honyū bin*

baby-sitter 子守 *komori*

baby wipes おしりふき *oshiri fuki*

back (location) うしろ *ushiro*

back (body) 背中 *senaka*

bacon ベーコン *bēkon*

bad 悪い *warui*

badminton バドミントン *badominton*

bagel ベーゲル *bēgeru*

baggage 荷物 *nimotsu*

baked 天火で焼いた *tenpi de yaita*

bakery パン屋 *pan ya*

balcony (theater) 二階の正面（の席） *nikai no shōmen (no seki)*

ballet バレー *barē*

  classical ballet 古典バレー *koten barē*

  modern ballet モダン・バレー *modan barē*

  ballet theater バレー劇場 *barē gekijō*

ballpoint pen ボールペン *bōrupen*

bamboo 竹 *take*

bamboo basket 竹のかご *take no kago*

bamboo craft shop 竹細工の店 *takezaiku no mise*

banana バナナ *banana*

band 楽団 *gakudan*

bandages 包帯 *hōtai*

Band-Aids バンドエイド *bandoeido*

bangs 前髪 *maegami*

bank 銀行 *ginkō*

bar バー *bā*

barbershop 床屋 *tokoya*

bargain sale 特売 *tokubai*

barn 納屋 *naya*

baseball 野球 *yakyū*

   ball game 試合 *shiai*

   professional baseball プロ野球 *puro yakyū*

   ballpark 野球場 *yakyujō*

basket かご *kago*

basketball バスケットボール *basuketto bōru*

bath 風呂／お風呂／浴室 *furo/ofuro/yokushitsu*

bathing suit 水着 *mizugi*

bathtub 風呂／お風呂／浴そう *furo/ofuro/yokusō*

bathroom お手洗い／トイレ／お便所 *otearai/toire/obenjo*

batter-fried food 天ぷら *tenpura*

battery 電池 *denchi*

battery (car) バッテリー *batterī*

bay 湾 *wan*

beach 海岸 *kaigan*

   beach umbrella ビーチ・パラソル *bīchi parasoru*

bean curd 豆腐 *tōfu*

beard あごひげ *ago hige*

beautiful, pretty きれい *kirei*

bed ベッド *beddo*

beef 牛肉／ビーフ *gyūniku/bīfu*

   roast beef ロースト・ビーフ *rōsuto bīfu*

beef cooked in broth しゃぶしゃぶ *shabu shabu*

beef cooked in seasoned sauce すき焼き *sukiyaki*

beefsteak ビフテキ *bifuteki*

beer ビール *bīru*

before ＿＿＿ ＿＿＿ の前に *no mae ni*

beginner 初心者 *shoshinsha*

bellhop ボーイ *bōi*

belt ベルト *beruto*

better もっといい *motto ii*

bicycle, bike 自転車 *jitensha*

bicycling サイクリング *saikuringu*

bicycling course サイクリング・コース *saikuringu kōsu*

big 大きい *ōkii*

bills (currency) お札 *osatsu*

bird 鳥 *tori*

birthdate 生年月日 *seinen gappi*

biscuits ビスケット *bisuketto*

black 黒い *kuroi*

black-and-white 白黒(の) *shiro kuro (no)*

blanket 毛布 *mōfu*

blender ミキサー *mikisā*

blond ブロンド *burondo*

blood 血 *chi*

blood pressure 血圧 *ketsuatsu*

blouse ブラウス *burausu*

blow dry ブロー・ドライ *burō dorai*

blown glass 口吹きガラス *kuchibuki garasu*

blue 青い *aoi*

boat ボート／船 *bōto/fune*

bobby pins ヘアー・ピン *heā pin*

body 体 *karada*

body lotion ボディー・ローション *bodī rōshon*

boiled ゆでた／煮た *yudeta/nita*

bone 骨 *hone*

book 本 *hon*

bookstore 本屋 *hon-ya*

boots ブーツ *būtsu*

bottle びん *bin*

large bottle 大びん *ō bin*
medium-size bottle 中びん *chū bin*
small bottle 小びん *ko bin*
bourbon バーボン *bābon*
bow (n.) おじぎ *ojigi*
to bow おじぎする *ojigi suru*
bowl ボール *bōru*
boxed 箱に入れて *hako ni irete*
box office 切符売り場 *kippu uriba*
bra, brassiere ブラジャー *burajā*
bracelet ブレスレット *buresuretto*
brakes ブレーキ *burēi*
brake fluid ブレーキ液 *burēki eki*
Brazil ブラジル *Burajiru*
Brazilian (adj.) ブラジルの *Burajiru no*
bread パン *pan*
  French bread フランス・パン *Furansu pan*
to break down 故障する *koshō suru*
breakfast 朝食／朝御飯 *chōshoku/asagohan*
breast 乳房 *chibusa*
bridge 橋 *hashi*
bright はでやかな／明るい *hadeyaka na/akarui*
British イギリスの *Igirisu no*
Britisher イギリス人 *Igirisu jin*
Broadway hits ブロードウェーのヒット *Burōdowē no hitto*
broccoli ブロッコリ *burokkori*
broiled 直火で焼いた *jikabi de yaita*
broken 折れた *oreta*
broken, out of order (mechanical) 故障して／こわれて *koshō shite/kowarete*
brooch ブローチ *burōchi*

brown 茶色い *chairoi*
bruise 打撲傷 *dabokushō*
brunette ブルネット *burunetto*
brushes ブラシ *burashi*
Buddhist temple お寺 *otera*
buffet car ビュッフェ車 *byuffe sha*
building ビル *biru*
(to be) built 建造される *kenzō sareru*
burn やけど *yakedo*
bus バス *basu*
  hotel bus ホテルのバス *hoteru no basu*
  limousine bus リムジン・バス *rimujin basu*
  shuttle bus シャトル・バス *shatoru basu*
bus stop バスの乗り場／バス停 *basu no noriba/basu tei*
business 仕事／ビジネス *shigoto/bijinesu*
business center (hotel) ビジネス・センター *bijinesu sentā*
business district ビジネス街 *bijinesu gai*
business hotel ビジネス・ホテル *bijinesu hoteru*
business operations department 営業部 *eigyō bu*
business trip 仕事の旅行 *shigoto no ryokō*
but けれども／でも *keredomo/demo*
butcher 肉屋 *nikuya*
butter バター *batā*
button ボタン *botan*
to buy 買う *kau*
by (means of) ＿＿で ＿＿ *de*
by the aisle 通路側 *tsūro gawa*
by the hour 時間で *jikan de*
by the way ところで *tokoro de*

by the window 窓ぎわ
madogiwa
Bye. (casual) じゃ。じゃあね。
Jā./Jā ne.

C

cabaret キャバレー *kyabarē*
cabbage キャベツ *kyabetsu*
cable car ケーブル・カー
kēburu kā
caddy キャディー *kyadī*
café 喫茶店／カフェ
kissaten/kafe
cake ケーキ *kēki*
　cheesecake チーズ・ケーキ
　chīzu kēki
　chocolate cake チョコレー
　ト・ケーキ *chokorēto kēki*
calendar カレンダー *karendā*
California rolls カリフォルニ
ア巻 *Kariforunia maki*
to call (telephone) 電話する
denwa suru
camcorder カムコーダー
kamukōdā
camera カメラ *kamera*
camera shop カメラ屋
kameraya
camping キャンプ *kyanpu*
camping site キャンプ場
kyanpu jō
can (n.) かん *kan*
Canada カナダ *Kanada*
Canadian (person) カナダ人
Kanada jin
cancer がん *gan*
candy キャンディー *kyandī*
candy store お菓子屋
okashiya
cane 杖 *tsue*
capital 首都 *shuto*
car 車／自動車 *kuruma/
jidōsha*
　large car 大型車 *ōgata sha*
　medium-sized car 中型車
　chūgata sha

small car 小型車 *kogata
sha*
sports car スポーツ・カー
supōtsu kā
car rental agency レンタカー
の営業所 *rentakā no
eigyōsho*
carburetor キャブレター
kyaburetā
card (business, personal) 名刺
meishi
cardigan カーディガン *kādigan*
cards (playing) トランプ
toranpu
carp 鯉 *koi*
carrots 人参 *ninjin*
carry-on 機内持ち込み品
kinai mochikomi hin
cart カート *kāto*
carved objects 彫刻品
chōkoku hin
to cash 現金化する *genkinka
suru*
cashews カシュー *kashū*
castle お城 *oshiro*
___ castle ＿＿城 *___ jō*
catalog カタログ *katarogu*
cavity 虫歯 *mushiba*
CD シーディー *shīdī*
CD player シーディー・プレ
ーヤー *shīdī purēya*
celery セロリ *serori*
cell phone 携帯電話／携帯
keitai denwa/keitai
center 中央 *chūō*
ceramics 陶磁器 *tōjiki*
ceramics store 瀬戸物屋
setomonoya
cereal シリアル *shiriaru*
chain チェーン／鎖 *chēn/
kusari*
chamber music 室内楽
shitsunaigaku
change (money) おつり
otsuri
to change 変える／代える／
替える／換える *kaeru*

to change (transportation) 乗り換える *norikaeru*

channel (TV) チャンネル *channeru*

chauffeur 運転手 *untenshu*

cheap 安い *yasui*

check, bill 勘定／チェック／会計 *kanjō/chekku/kaikei*

check (personal) 個人用小切手 *kojin yō kogitte*

checks (pattern) チェック／市松模様 *chekku/ichimatsu moyō*

to check (baggage) あずける *azukeru*

to check (examine) 調べる／点検する *shiraberu/tenken suru*

to check in チェック・インする *chekku in suru*

cheek ほほ *hoho*

cheese チーズ *chīzu*

cherries さくらんぼ／チェリー *sakuranbo/cherī*

cherry blossoms 桜 *sakura*

chest 胸 *mune*

chestnuts くり *kuri*

chicken にわとり *niwatori*

chiken skewered and grilled 焼き鳥 *yakitori*

chicken soup チキン・スープ *chikin sūpu*

child (someone else's) お子さん *okosan*

child (your own) 子供 *kodomo*

children 子供 *kodomo*

chill 悪寒 *okan*

china 瀬戸物 *setomono*

China 中国 *Chūgoku*

Chinese (adj.) 中国の *Chūgoku no*

Chinese (lang.) 中国語 *Chūgoku go*

Chinese tile game マージャン *mājan*

mahjong parlor ジャン荘 *jan sō*

mahjong set マージャンのセット *mājan no setto*

chocolate チョコレート *chokorēto*

hot chocolate ココア *kokoa*

chopsticks はし *hashi*

chopstick rest はし置き *hashi oki*

church 教会 *kyōkai*

cigarettes たばこ／タバコ *tabako*

filtered cigarettes フィルター付きのたばこ *firutā tsuki no tabako*

cigarette lighter ライター *raitā*

a pack of cigarettes たばこを一箱 *tabako o hito hako*

cigars 葉巻 *hamaki*

citizen 市民 *shimin*

city 市／都市 *shi/toshi*

big city 都会 *tokai*

clams はまぐり *hamaguri*

classical music クラシック・ミュージック *kurashikku myūjikku*

clean きれいな *kirei na*

to clean (tidy) 片付ける *katazukeru*

cleansing cream クレンジング・クリーム *kurenjingu kurīmu*

clear sky 晴れ *hare*

clerk 店員 *ten-in*

climate 気候 *kikō*

to climb 登る *noboru*

clock 時計 *tokei*

alarm clock 目覚まし時計 *mezamashi dokei*

travel alarm clock 旅行用の目覚まし時計 *ryokō yō no mezamashi dokei*

cloisonné 七宝焼 *shippō yaki*

to close (v.i.) 閉まる *shimaru*

to close (v.t.) 閉める *shimeru*

clothes 洋服 *yōfuku*

clothing store 洋服店 *yōfuku ten*

children's clothing 子供服 *kodomo fuku*

children's clothing store 子供服の店 *kodomo fuku no mise*

men's clothing store 紳士服の店 *shinshi fuku no mise*

women's clothing store 婦人服の店 *fujin fuku no mise*

cloudy 曇り *kumori*

club soda 炭酸／クラブ・ソーダ／プレイン・ソーダ *tansan/kurabu sōda/purein sōda*

clutch (auto) クラッチ *kuratchi*

coast 海岸 *kaigan*

cocktails カクテル *kakuteru*

cocktail lounge カクテル・ラウンジ *kakuteru raunji*

cocoa ココア *kokoa*

codeine コデイン *kodein*

coffee コーヒー *kōhī*

iced coffee アイス・コーヒー *aisu kōhī*

instant coffee インスタント・コーヒー *insutanto kōhī*

coffee shop コーヒー・ショップ *kōhī shoppu*

Japanese coffee shop 喫茶店 *kissaten*

coins 硬貨 *kōka*

cold (weather, climate) 寒い *samui*

cold (food, drink) 冷たい *tsumetai*

cold (head, chest) 風邪 *kaze*

colleague 同僚 *dōryō*

cologne オーデコロン *ōdekoron*

color 色 *iro*

color chart 色の表 *iro no hyō*

color rinse カラー・リンス *karā rinsu*

comb くし *kushi*

to come 来る *kuru*

comedy 喜劇 *kigeki*

company 会社 *kaisha*

company executive 会社の重役 *kaisha no jūyaku*

company president 会社の社長 *kaisha no shachō*

computer room (hotel) コンピュータ・ルーム *konpyūta rūmu*

concert コンサート *konsāto*

concert hall コンサート・ホール *konsāto hōru*

concerto 協奏曲 *kyōsō kyoku*

condom コンドーム *kondōmu*

confectionary お菓子屋 *okashiya*

constipation 便秘 *benpi*

consulate 領事館 *ryōji kan*

contact lenses コンタクト・レンズ *kontakuto renzu*

soft lenses ソフト・コンタクト・レンズ *sofuto kontakuto renzu*

convenient 便利な *benri na*

to cook 料理する *ryōri suru*

cookies クッキー *kukkī*

cooking facilities 料理の施設 *ryōri no shisetsu*

cooking utensils 炊事用具 *suiji yōgu*

cool 涼しい *suzushii*

copying machine コピー機／複写機 *kopī ki/fukusha ki*

corn コーン／とうもろこし *kōn/tōmorokoshi*

corner 角 *kado*

corn flakes コーン・フレーク *kōn furēku*

corn plasters 魚の目膏薬 *uo no me kōyaku*

correct 正しい *tadashii*

correction tape 修正テープ *shūsei tēpu*

cosmetics shop 化粧品店 *keshōhin ten*

cottage 小屋 *koya*

cottage cheese コテッジチーズ *kotejji chīzu*

cotton 脱脂綿 *dasshimen*
cotton (fabric) 木綿 *momen*
cough せき *seki*
cough drops せきどめドロップ *sekidome doroppu*
cough syrup せきどめシロップ *sekidome shiroppu*
counter カウンター *kauntā*
country (nation) 国 *kuni*
country music カントリーミュージック *kantorī myūjikku*
countryside 地方／田舎 *chihō/inaka*
cover charge カバー・チャージ *kabā chāji*
cozy 居心地のいい *igokochi no ii*
crab かに *kani*
crackers クラッカー *kurakkā*
rice crackers おせんべ *osenbe*
crafts 工芸 *kōgei*
craftsperson 工芸家 *kōgeika*
cramp ひきつり *hikitsuri*
cramps (stomach) 腹痛 *fukutsū*
cream ミルク *miruku*
cream rinse クリーム・リンス *kurīmu rinsu*
credit card クレジット・カード *kurejitto kādo*
crib ベビー・ベッド *bebī beddo*
croissant クロワッサン *kurowassan*
to cross 渡る *wataru*
crowded 混んで *konde*
cruise 航海 *kōkai*
cruise ship 遊覧船 *yūran sen*
crutch(es) 松葉杖 *matsubazue*
crystal (watch) ガラスぶた *garasu buta*
cucumber きゅうり *kyūri*
cufflinks カフス・ボタン *kafusu botan*
curfew 門限 *mongen*
curlers カーラー *kārā*
curly 巻き毛／カーリー *makige/kārī*

currency 通貨 *tsūka*
foreign currency 外貨 *gaika*
custard カスタード *kasutādo*
customs 税関 *zeikan*
customs inspection 税関検査 *zeikan kensa*
customs declaration form 税関の申告書 *zeikan no shinkoku sho*
to cut 切る *kiru*

D

daily 毎日の *mainichi no*
dancing おどって *odotte*
Danish pastry デーニッシュ・ペストリー／菓子パン *Dēnisshu pesutorī/kashi pan*
dark 暗い *kurai*
date 日付 *hizuke*
daughter (someone else's) お嬢さん *ojōsan*
daughter (your own) 娘 *musume*
day 日 *hi*
a day 一日 *ichi nichi*
day after tomorrow あさって *asatte*
a few days 数日 *sūjitsu*
a half day 半日 *han nichi*
two days 二日 *futsuka*
by the day 一日ごと(に) *ichi nichi goto (ni)*
per day 一日 *ichi nichi*
decaffeinated coffee カフェインレス／デカフェコーヒー *kafein resu/dekafe kōhī*
December 十二月 *jūnigatsu*
digital camera デジタル・カメラ *dejitaru kamera*
digital tape recorder デジタル テープレコーダー *dejitaru tēpu rekōdā*
delicious おいしい *oishii*
demonstration 実演 *jitsuen*

dentist 歯医者 *haisha*

denture 入れ歯 *ireba*

deodorant デオドラント *deodoranto*

to depart (transportation) 出る *deru*

department store デパート *depāto*

departure 出発 *shuppatsu*

departure gate 出発口 *shuppatsu guchi*

departure time 出発の時間／出発時刻 *shuppatsu no jikan/shuppatsu jikoku*

deposit 保証金 *hoshō kin*

dessert デザート *dezāto*

detective stories 探偵小説 *tantei shōsetsu*

detour 回り道 *mawari michi*

to develop (film) 現像する *genzō suru*

diabetes 糖尿病 *tōnyō byō*

diamond ダイヤ *daiya*

diapers (disposable) 紙おむつ *kamiomutsu*

diarrhea 下痢 *geri*

dictionary 辞書 *jisho*

　English-Japanese dictionary 英和辞典 *eiwa jiten*

　pocket dictionary ポケット版の辞書 *poketto ban no jisho*

diesel (gas) ディーゼル *dīzeru*

diet ダイエット *daietto*

difference 違い *chigai*

different 違う *chigau*

difficult 難しい *muzukashii*

dining car 食堂車 *shokudō sha*

dining room 食堂 *shokudō*

dinner 晩御飯／夕食 *ban gohan/yū shoku*

direct dial ダイヤル直通 *daiyaru chokutsū*

directional signal 方向指示器 *hōkō shiji ki*

director (sports, film) 監督 *kantoku*

director (theater, TV) 演出家 *enshutsuka*

dirty きたない *kitanai*

disabled 障害者 *shōgaisha*

discount 割引き *waribiki*

Disembarkation/Embarkation Card for Foreigner 外国人出入国記録 *gaikoku jin shutsu nyū koku kiroku*

dislocated (medical) 脱臼した *dakkyū shita*

ditch みぞ *mizo*

doctor 医者 *isha*

documents 書類 *shorui*

dollar ドル *doru*

door 戸／ドア *to/doa*

doughnuts ドーナッツ *dōnattsu*

down ＿＿＿の下に ＿＿＿ *no shita ni*

downtown area 繁華街 *hangagai*

draft beer 生ビール *nama bīru*

dress ドレス *doresu*

dressing room 試着室 *shichaku shitsu*

drinking water 飲み水 *nomi mizu*

drinks 飲み物 *nomimono*

drinks (alcoholic) お酒 *osake*

driver 運転手 *untenshu*

to drive 運転する *unten suru*

drugstore ドラッグストア *doraggusutoa*

dry 乾燥している *kansō shite iru*

dry cleaner クリーニング屋 *kurīninguya*

dry cleaning service ドライクリーニングのサービス *doraikurīningu no sābisu*

dubbed (film) 吹き替えられて *fukikaerarete*

dull 鈍い *nibui*

duck あひる *ahiru*

during ＿＿＿ ＿＿＿の間に ＿＿＿no aida ni

Dutch (person) オランダ人 *Oranda jin*
DV camcorder ディービー・カムコーダー *dībī kamukōdā*
DVD ディービーディー *dībīdī*
DVD player ディービーディープレーヤー *dībīdī purēya*

E

ear 耳 *mimi*
ear drops 耳薬 *mimi gusuri*
early 早い *hayai*
earphones イヤフォン *iafon*
earrings イヤリング *iyaringu*
　earrings for pierced ears ピアスのイヤリング *piasu no iyaringu*
earthquake 地震 *jishin*
east 東 *higashi*
easy やさしい *yasashii*
to eat 食べる *taberu*
e-cigarettes 電子タバコ *denshi tabako*
eclair エクレア *ekurea*
eel うなぎ *unagi*
egg たまご *tamago*
eggplant なす *nasu*
elbow ひじ *hiji*
elder brother (someone else's) お兄さん *oniisan*
elder brother (your own) 兄 *ani*
elder sister (someone else's) お姉さん *onēsan*
elder sister (your own) 姉 *ane*
electrical appliance 電気製品 *denki seihin*
electrical appliance store 電気器具店 *denki kigu ten*
electrical transformer 変圧器／トランス *henatsu ki/ toransu*
electricity 電気 *denki*
electric razor 電気カミソリ *denki kamisori*

electronic cigarettes 電子タバコ *denshi tabako*
elevator エレベーター *erebētā*
email イーメール *ī mēru*
email address メールアドレス *mēru adoresu*
embassy 大使館 *taishi kan*
emerald エメラルド *emerarudo*
emergency 緊急事態 *kinkyū jitai*
emery boards 爪やすり *tsume yasuri*
emperor 天皇 *tennō*
engine エンジン *enjin*
engineer エンジニア *enjinia*
England イギリス *Igirisu*
English (lang.) 英語 *eigo*
English-speaking 英語が話せる *eigo ga hanaseru*
to enjoy 楽しむ *tanoshimu*
enlargement 引き伸ばし *hikinobashi*
entertainment 催し物 *moyōshimono*
entrance 入り口 *iriguchi*
envelope 封筒 *fūtō*
eraser 消しゴム *keshigomu*
error 間違い *machigai*
escalator エスカレーター *esukarētā*
estimate 見積もり *mitsumori*
Ethernet イーサネット *Īsanetto*
euro ユーロ *yūro*
European products ヨーロッパ製品 *Yōroppa seihin*
evening 夕方 *yūgata*
to exchange 交換する *kōkan suru*
exchange rate 交換率 *kōkan ritsu*
Excuse me. (forgiveness) ご免なさい。／失礼します。 *Gomennasai./Shitsurei shimasu.*

Excuse me, but ___ (attention getter) すみませんが ___ *Sumimasen ga, ___*

to exhibit 展示する *tenji suru*

exit 出口 *deguchi*

expensive 高い *takai*

to explain 説明する *setsumei suru*

eye 目 *me*

eyebrow pencil まゆずみ *mayuzumi*

eyeglasses 眼鏡 *megane*
  frames わく *waku*
  lenses レンズ *renzu*

eye liner アイ・ライナー *ai rainā*

eye pencil アイ・ペンシル *ai penshiru*

eye shadow アイ・シャドー *ai shadō*

F

fabric 布／生地 *nuno/kiji*

face 顔 *kao*

Facebook フェイスブック *Feisubukku*

face powder おしろい *oshiroi*

FaceTime フェイスタイム *Feisutaimu*

facial フェイシャル *feisharu*

fall 秋 *aki*

family 家族 *kazoku*

famous 有名(な) *yūmei (na)*

fan 扇 *ōgi*

fancy しゃれた *shareta*

far 遠い *tōi*

fare 料金 *ryōkin*

farm 畑 *hatake*

fast, quick 速い *hayai*

fast food ファースト・フード *fāsuto fūdo*

father (someone else's) お父さん *otōsan*

father (your own) 父 *chichi*

fax ファックス *fakkusu*

February 二月 *nigatsu*

female, woman 女の人 *onna no hito*

ferry 連絡船 *renrakusen*

festival お祭り *omatsuri*

fever 熱 *netsu*

few, a little 少し *sukoshi*

fields 野原 *nohara*

filet ヒレ肉 *hire niku*

filet mignon ヒレミニオン *hireminion*

to fill (gas tank) 満タンにする *mantan ni suru*

filling (tooth) 歯のつめもの *ha no tsumemono*
  temporary filling 仮のつめもの *kari no tsumemono*

film フィルム *firumu*

filter (camera) フィルター *firutā*

finance department 経理部 *keiri bu*

fine 元気 *genki*

Fine, thank you. はい、おかげさまで。 *Hai, okagesama de.*

finger 指 *yubi*

to finish (v.i.) 終わる *owaru*
  It's over./I'm finished. 終わりました。 *Owarimashita.*

first-aid kit 救急箱 *kyūkyūbako*

first class 一流の *ichiryū no*

first class (train) グリーン車 *gurīn sha*

first-run film 封切りの映画 *fūkiri no eiga*

first time 初めて *hajimete*

fish 魚 *sakana*
  raw fish (thinly sliced) 刺身 *sashimi*
  raw fish and vinegared rice すし *sushi*

fishing 魚釣り *sakana tsuri*

fishing boat 釣り船 *tsuri bune*

fishing equipment 釣り道具 *tsuri dōgu*

fishing spot 釣り場 *tsuri ba*

fish market 魚屋 *sakanaya*
to fit 合う *au*
to fix 直す *naosu*
fixable 直せる *naoseru*
flashlight 懐中電灯 *kaichū dentō*
flat tire パンク *panku*
flight number 便名 *bin mei*
　connecting flight 乗りつぎ便 *noritsugi bin*
　direct flight 直行便 *chokkō bin*
　nonstop flight ノン・ストップ *non sutoppu*
floor show フロア・ショー *furoa shō*
florist 花屋 *hanaya*
flounder 平目 *hirame*
flower 花 *hana*
flower arrangement 華道／生け花／お花 *kadō/ikebana/ohana*
　headmaster 家元 *iemoto*
flu 流感 *ryūkan*
flying time 飛行時間 *hikō jikan*
focus 焦点 *shōten*
folded たたんで *tatande*
folk art 民芸 *mingei*
folk song フォーク・ソング *fōku songu*
folkware shop 民芸屋 *mingeiya*
food 食べ物 *tabemono*
　Japanese food 日本食品 *Nihon shokuhin*
　Western food 西洋食品 *seiyō shokuhin*
foot (body) 足 *ashi*
football フットボール *futtobōru*
for example 例えば *tatoeba*
forbidden 禁止 *kinshi*
forehead ひたい *hitai*
foreign 外国の *gaikoku no*
foreigner 外国人 *gaikoku jin*
forest 森 *mori*
fork フォーク *fōku*

formal clothing 正装 *seisō*
forward 前の *mae no*
fortress 城塞 *jōsai*
fountain pen 万年筆 *mannenhitsu*
four seasons 四季 *shiki*
fractured 骨が折れた *hone ga oreta*
fragile (goods) こわれもの *kowaremono*
franc フラン *furan*
free (unoccupied) 空いて *aite*
free time 自由時間 *jiyū jikan*
French (adj.) フランスの *Furansu no*
French (lang.) フランス語 *Furansu go*
　French manicure フレンチネイル *Furenchi neiru*
frequency (radio station) 周波数 *shūhasū*
fresh 新鮮な *shinsen na*
Friday 金曜日 *kin-yōbi*
fried (油で)あげた *(abura de) ageta*
friend 友人／友達 *yūjin/tomodachi*
from ___ ___から ___ *kara*
front 前 *mae*
fruit 果物 *kudamono*
fruit compote/cup フルーツ・カップ *furūtsu kappu*
fuel pump ガソリン・ポンプ *gasorin ponpu*
full (I'm full) おなかが、いっぱいです *onaka ga, ippai desu*
furniture 家具 *kagu*

G

garden 庭／庭園 *niwa/teien*
garlic ガーリック／にんにく *gārikku/ninniku*
gas ガス *gasu*

gasoline ガソリン *gasorin*
 unleaded 無鉛ガソリン
 muen gasorin
 regular レギュラー *regyurā*
 super スーパー／ハイオク
 sūpā/haioku
gas station ガソリン・スタンド
 gasorin sutando
gastroenterologist 消化器科の
 医者 *shōkakika no isha*
to gather (v.i.) 集まる
 atsumaru
gauze ガーゼ *gāze*
gay bar ゲイバー *gei bā*
gears ギヤ *giya*
gel ジェル *jeru*
gelato ジェラート *jerāto*
German (adj.) ドイツの
 Doitsu no
German (lang.) ドイツ語
 Doitsu go
Germany ドイツ *Doitsu*
to get off 降りる *oriru*
to get on 乗る *noru*
gift おみやげ *omiyage*
 reciprocal gift おかえし
 okaeshi
gift shop 売店 *baiten*
gin ジン *jin*
ginger しょうが *shōga*
glass グラス *gurasu*
glass (drinking) コップ
 koppu
gloves 手袋 *tebukuro*
glue 接着剤／のり
 setchakuzai/nori
to go 行く *iku*
 Let's go. 行きましょう。
 Ikimashō.
 Shall we go? 行きましょう
 か。*Ikimashō ka.*
gold 金 *kin*
 solid gold 純金 *junkin*
 gold plated 金メッキ(の)
 kin mekki (no)
golf ゴルフ *gorufu*
golf ball ゴルフ・ボール
 gorufu bōru

golf clubs ゴルフ・クラブ
 gorufu kurabu
golf course ゴルフ・コース
 gorufu kōsu
 to play golf ゴルフをする
 gorufu o suru
good, fine いい *ii*
good afternoon こんにちは
 konnichiwa
goodbye さようなら *sayōnara*
good evening こんばんは
 konbanwa
good morning おはようござ
 います *ohayō gozaimasu*
good night おやすみなさい
 oyasuminasai
good quality 上等／上質
 jōtō/jōshitsu
Google+ グーグルプラス
 Gūgurupurasu
grammar 文法 *bunpō*
grammar book 文法の本
 bunpō no hon
grandfather (someone else's)
 おじいさん *ojiisan*
grandfather (your own) 祖父
 sofu
grandmother (someone else's)
 おばあさん *obāsan*
grandmother (your own) 祖母
 sobo
grapefruit グレープ・
 フルーツ *gurēpu furūtsu*
grapes ぶどう *budō*
gray グレイの *gurei no*
Greek (adj.) ギリシャの
 Girisha no
green グリーンの／みどり
 (いろ)の *gurīn no/
 midori (iro) no*
grocery store 食料品店
 shokuryōhin ten
grilled 焼網で焼いた
 yakiami de yaita
groin 股の付け根 *mata no
 tsukene*
ground beef 牛のひき肉
 gyū no hikiniku

guidebook ガイド・ブック
gaido bukku
gym ジム jimu

H

hair 髪の毛 kami no ke
hair color 毛染め ke zome
haircut 散髪 sanpatsu
hair dryer ヘアー・ドライヤー
heā doraiyā
hair salon 美容院 biyōin
hair spray ヘアー・スプレー
heā supurē
ham ハム hamu
hamburger ハンバーガー
hanbāgā
hamburger steak ハンバーグ・
ステーキ hanbāgu sutēki
hammer ハンマー hanmā
hand 手 te
handmade 手作りの／手製の
tezukuri no/te sei no
handicrafts 手工芸品 shu
kōgei hin
handicrafts shop 工芸の店
kōgei no mise
handrail 手すり tesuri
harbor, port 港 minato
hardware store 大工道具屋
daikudōguya
hat 帽子 bōshi
Hawaiian ハワイの Hawai no
hay fever 花粉症 kafun shō
he 彼が kare ga
head 頭 atama
headache 頭痛 zutsū
headlight ヘッド・ライト
heddo raito
headphones ヘッドフォン
heddofon
health club ヘルス・クラブ
herusu kurabu
hearing impaired 難聴
nanchō
heart 心臓 shinzō
heart attack 心臓麻痺
shinzō mahi

heart disease 心臓病 shinzō
byō
heater 暖房 danbō
heavy 重い omoi
heel かかと kakato
height 高さ takasa
hello (telephone/getting
someone's attention)
もしもし moshimoshi
helmet ヘルメット herumetto
to help 助ける tasukeru
Help! 助けて。Tasukete!
hemorrhoids 痔 ji
here ここ koko
high 高い takai
high blood pressure 高血圧
kō ketsuatsu
highchair 子供用の椅子
kodomo yō no isu
highway 高速道路 kōsoku
dōro
hiking ハイキング haikingu
hiking trail ハイキング・コー
ス haikingu kōsu
hill 丘 oka
hire (taxis, limousines)
ハイヤー haiyā
historical drama 時代物
jidaimono
historical sites 旧跡
kyūseki
history 歴史 rekishi
history books 歴史の本
rekishi no hon
horn 警笛 keiteki
horseradish (Japanese)
わさび wasabi
hospital 病院 byōin
hostess ホステス hosutesu
hot (temperature) 暑い atsui
hot (peppery food) からい
karai
hot dog ホットドッグ
hottodoggu
hot springs 温泉 onsen
hotel ホテル hoteru
  business hotel ビジネス・
  ホテル bijinesu hoteru

hotel reservation counter
ホテルの予約カウンター
hoteru no yoyaku kauntā

hotspot ホットスポット
hottosupotto

hour 時間 *jikan*
by the hour 時間で *jikan de*
per hour 一時間で *ichi jikan*

house 家／うち *ie/uchi*

housewares 家庭用品 *katei yōhin*

housewife 主婦 *shufu*

hovercraft ホーバー・クラフト
hōbā kurafuto

how どうやって *dō yatte*

How are you? お元気ですか。
Ogenki desu ka.

How do you do? はじめまし
て。どうぞよろしく。
Hajimemashite. Dōzo yoroshiku.

How do you do? (reply)
はじめまして。こちらこそ、
よろしく。*Hajimemashite.
Kochira koso, yoroshiku.*

How long? どの位 *dono kurai*

How much? どの位 *dono kurai*

How much money? いくら
ikura

humid, damp 湿っている
shimette iru

hungry おなかが、すいていま
す *onaka ga, suite imasu*

husband (someone else's)
御主人 *goshujin*

husband (your own) 主人
shujin

hydrofoil 水中翼船 *suichū yokusen*

I

I 私が *watakushi ga*

ice 氷 *kōri*

ice cream アイスクリーム
aisukurīmu

ice pack 氷のう *hyōnō*

ice water アイス・ウォーター
aisu wōtā

I.D. 身分証明書 *mibun shōmei sho*

ignition 点火装置 *tenka sōchi*

imported 外国の *gaikoku no*

I'm sorry. (apology) ご免なさ
い。／すみません。
Gomennasai./Sumimasen.

in ____に ____に *ni*

in advance 前もって *mae motte*

incense (お)線香 *(o)senkō*

Indian (adj.) インドの
Indo no

indigestion 消化不良 *shōka furyō*

Indonesian (adj.) インドネシ
アの *Indoneshia no*

industrialist 実業家
jitsugyōka

inexpensive 高くない
takakunai

infection 化膿 *kanō*

information center 案内所
annaijo

injection 注射 *chūsha*

injury けが *kega*

insect bite 虫刺され *mushi sasare*

insect repellent 虫よけの薬
mushi yoke no kusuri

inside ____ ____の中に ____
no naka ni

insomnia 不眠症 *fuminshō*

Instagram インスタグラム
Insutaguramu

insulin インシュリン *inshurin*

insurance 保険 *hoken*

intelligent りこうな *rikō na*

interesting, fun おもしろい
omoshiroi

intermission 途中の休憩
tochū no kyūkei

international call 国際電話 *kokusai denwa*

Internet café インターネット・カフェ *intānetto kafe*

interpreter 通訳 *tsūyaku*

intersection 交差点 *kōsaten*

to introduce 紹介する *shōkai suru*

to introduce (oneself) 自己紹介する *jiko shōkai suru*

to invite (polite) お招きする *omaneki suru*

iodine ヨードチンキ *yōdochinki*

iron アイロン *airon*

Is that so? そうですか。*Sō desu ka.*

island 島 *shima*

itchy かゆみ *kayumi*

Italian (adj.) イタリアの *Itaria no*

Italian (lang.) イタリア語 *Itaria go*

Italy イタリア *Itaria*

It doesn't matter. かまいません。*Kamaimasen.*

itemized bill 明細書 *meisai sho*

itinerary 旅行計画 *ryokō keikaku*

It's all right. 大丈夫です。*Daijōbu desu.*

J

jack ジャッキ *jakki*

jacket ジャケット *jaketto*

jade ひすい *hisui*

jam ジャム *jamu*

January 一月 *ichigatsu*

Japan 日本 *Nippon/Nihon*

Japanese (lang.) 日本語 *Nihon go*

Japanese board game 碁 *go*

　go board and stones 碁盤と碁石 *goban to goishi*

Japanese board game 将棋 *shōgi*

shogi board and pieces 将棋盤と駒 *shōgi ban to koma*

Japanese chest of drawers たんす *tansu*

Japanese classical drama 歌舞伎 *kabuki*

　Kabuki runway 花道 *hanamichi*

Japanese classics 日本の古典 *Nihon no koten*

Japanese dolls 日本人形 *Nihon ningyō*

Japanese doll shop 日本人形屋 *Nihon ningyōya*

Japanese folk toys 民芸玩具 *mingei gangu*

Japanese traditional games 日本伝統のゲーム *Nihon dentō no gēmu*

Japanese gardens 日本庭園 *Nihon teien*

Japanese grammar book 日本語の文法の本 *Nihon go no bunpō no hon*

Japanese guest house 民宿 *minshuku*

Japanese martial arts 武術／武道 *bujutsu/budō*

　judo 柔道 *jūdō*

　karate 空手 *karate*

　kendo 剣道 *kendō*

　black belt 黒帯 *kuro obi*

　____ practice ____のけい古 *____ no keiko*

Japanese masked dance-drama 能 *nō*

　Noh masks 能面 *nō men*

Japanese mint しそ *shiso*

Japanese puppet theater 文楽 *bunraku*

　puppets 人形 *ningyō*

Japanese inn 旅館 *ryokan*

Japanese painting 日本画 *Nihon ga*

Japanese pinball パチンコ *pachinko*

　pachinko balls パチンコ玉 *pachinko dama*

pachinko parlor パチンコ屋 *pachinkoya*
prize 景品 *keihin*
Japanese-style 和式の *washiki no*
Japanese swords 日本刀 *Nihon tō*
Japanese sword shop 刀屋 *katanaya*
Japanese traditional music 邦楽 *hōgaku*
Japanese wrestling 相撲 *sumō*
　sumo judge 行司 *gyōji*
　sumo match 取り組み *torikumi*
　sumo ring 土俵 *dohyō*
　sumo tournament 場所 *basho*
　sumo wrestlers 力士 *rikishi*
jazz ジャズ *jazu*
jeans ブルー・ジーン／ジーンズ *burū jīn/jīnzu*
jet ski ジェットスキー *jetto sukī*
jewelry 宝石 *hōseki*
jewelry store 宝石店 *hōseki ten*
jogging ジョギング *jogingu*
jogging path ジョギング・コース *jogingu kōsu*
joint (body) 関節 *kansetsu*
J-POP ジェイポップ *jeipoppu*
juice ジュース *jūsu*
　apple juice リンゴ・ジュース *ringo jūsu*
　grapefruit juice グレープフルーツ・ジュース *gurēpufurūtsu jūsu*
　orange juice オレンジ・ジュース *orenji jūsu*
　pineapple juice パイナップル・ジュース *painappuru jūsu*
　tomato juice トマト・ジュース *tomato jūsu*

July 七月 *shichigatsu*
June 六月 *rokugatsu*

K

karat カラット *karatto*
　14 karats 14金 *jūyon kin*
　18 karats 18金 *jūhakkin*
　22 karats 22金 *nijūni kin*
　24 karats 24金 *nijūyon kin*
　pure gold 純金 *junkin*
ketchup ケチャップ *kechappu*
key 鍵 *kagi*
keyboard キーボード *kībōdo*
key card キーカード *kī kādo*
kilogram キロ *kiro*
　half kilogram 五百グラム *go hyaku guramu*
kimono 着物 *kimono*
kimono store 呉服屋 *gofukuya*
kind (adj.) 親切な *shinsetsu na*
Kindle キンドル *Kindoru*
kite たこ *tako*
knee ひざ *hiza*
knife ナイフ *naifu*
Korea 韓国 *Kankoku*
Korean (adj.) 韓国の *Kankoku no*

L

lacquer bowls うるし塗りのうつわ *urushi nuri no utsuwa*
lacquer trays うるし塗りのお盆 *urushi nuri no obon*
lacquerware 塗り物／漆器 *nurimono/shikki*
ladies' room 女子用のトイレ *joshi yō no toire*
lake 湖 *mizuumi*
lamb 子羊 *kohitsuji*
lamb chop ラム・チョップ *ramu choppu*

lamp ランプ *ranpu*
landline (telephone) 固定電話 *kotei denwa*
landscape 景色 *keshiki*
large (big) 大きい *ōkii*
large (size) エルサイズ *eru saizu*
last train 終電 *shūden*
late おそい *osoi*
later 後で *ato de*
laundromat コイン・ランドリー *koin randorī*
laundry (clothes) 洗濯物 *sentakumono*
laundry (shop) 洗濯屋 *sentakuya*
laundry service 洗濯のサービス *sentaku no sābisu*
lawyer 弁護士 *bengoshi*
laxative 下剤／通じ薬 *gezai/tsūji yaku*
to leak (vi.) もれる *moreru*
leather 皮 *kawa*
left 左 *hidari*
leg 足 *ashi*
lemon レモン *remon*
lemonade レモネード *remonēdo*
lens レンズ *renzu*
lesson レッスン *ressun*
Let's ____. さあ____。 *Sā ____.*
letter 手紙 *tegami*
lettuce レタス *retasu*
library 図書館 *toshokan*
lifeguard 見張り *mihari*
light (shade, color) 明るい *akarui*
light (weight) 軽い *karui*
lightbulb 電球 *denkyū*
limit 制限 *seigen*
line (train) 線 *sen*
LINE (social media) ライン *Rain*
linen 麻／リンネル *asa/rinneru*
LinkedIn リンクトイン *Rinkutoin*

lip 口びる *kuchibiru*
liquor store 酒屋 *sakaya*
list 表／リスト *hyō/risuto*
liter リットル *rittoru*
a little, few 少し *sukoshi*
to live (reside) 住む *sumu*
liver 肝臓／レバー *kanzō/rebā*
lobby ロビー *robī*
lobster ロブスター／伊勢えび *robusutā/Ise ebi*
to lock ロックする *rokku suru*
lodging 宿泊 *shukuhaku*
long 長い *nagai*
long-distance call 長距離電話 *chōkyori denwa*
to look around 見て回る *mite mawaru*
loose (clothes) ゆるい *yurui*
to lose なくす *nakusu*
lost なくした *nakushita*
to be lost 道に迷う *michi ni mayou*
lost and found 遺失物係り *ishitsubutsu gakari*
a lot, many たくさん *takusan*
low 低い *hikui*
lowfat milk ローファット・ミルク／低脂肪の牛乳 *rōfatto miruku/tei shibō no gyūnyū*
luggage 旅行かばん／荷物 *ryokō kaban/nimotsu*
luggage rack 荷物の置き台 *nimotsu no okidai*
lunch (box lunch) （お)弁当 *(o)bentō*

M

magazine 雑誌 *zasshi*
magnificent 立派(な) *rippa (na)*
magnifier 虫めがね *mushi megane*
maid メード *mēdo*
mail 郵便／手紙 *yūbin/tegami*
   airmail 航空便 *kōkū bin*

mail box 郵便ポスト
yūbin posuto

registered mail 書留
kakitome

special delivery 速達
sokutatsu

to mail a letter 手紙を出す
tegami o dasu

to make 作る *tsukuru*

male 男(の人) *otoko (no hito)*

man 男(の人) *otoko (no hito)*

manager マネージャー
manējā

mandarin orange みかん
mikan

mango マンゴー *mangō*

manicure ネイル／マニキュア
neiru/manikyua

manicure design ネイルアート
neiru āto

many, a lot たくさん *takusan*

map 地図 *chizu*

March 三月 *sangatsu*

margarine マーガリン
māgarin

market 市場 *ichiba*

married 結婚して *kekkon shite*

masks お面 *omen*

masseur, masseuse あんまさん
anma san

matches マッチ *matchi*

matinee マチネー *machinē*

May 五月 *gogatsu*

maybe 多分 *tabun*

mayonnaise マヨネーズ
mayonēzu

meal 食事 *shokuji*

light meal 軽い食事／軽食
karui shokuji/keishoku

meal service 食事のサービス
shokuji no sābisu

measurements サイズ *saizu*

meatballs ミートボール／肉
だんご *mītobōru/niku dango*

medicine 薬 *kusuri*

medium (size) 中 *chū*

medium (size) エムサイズ
emu saizu

medium (meat) ミディアム
midiamu

medium rare (meat) ミディ
アム・レア *midiamu rea*

to meet (polite) お会いする
oai suru

melon メロン *meron*

memory card メモリー・カード
memorī kādo

to mend 繕う *tsukurou*

men's clothing 紳士服
shinshi fuku

men's room 男子用のトイレ
danshi yō no toire

menu メニュー *menyū*

message メッセージ *messēji*

metal 金属 *kinzoku*

meter (taxi) メーター *mētā*

Mexican (adj.) メキシコの
Mekishiko no

Mexico メキシコ *Mekishiko*

mezzanine 中二階の(席)
chū nikai no (seki)

microcassette recorder マイ
クロ・カッセット・レコーダー
maikuro kasetto rekōdā

mileage キロ数 *kiro sū*

military (personnel) 軍人
gunjin

milk ミルク／牛乳 *miruku/
gyūnyū*

hot milk 温かい牛乳
atatakai gyūnyū

milkshake ミルクセーキ
miruku sēki

mimosa ミモザ *mimoza*

mind, I don't (permission)
いいですよ／かまいません
ii desu yo/kamaimasen

minimum charge 最低料金
saitei ryōkin

minister 牧師 *bokushi*

mirror 鏡 *kagami*

modem モデム *modemu*

modern モダンな *modan na*

modern dance モダン・ダン
ス *modan dansu*

modern Japanese novels
近代日本小説 *kindai Nihon shōsetsu*

modern music モダン・ミュージック *modan myūjikku*

Monday 月曜日 *getsuyōbi*

money お金 *okane*

money exchange 両替所 *ryōgae jo*

monkey wrench 自在スパナ *jizai supana*

monorail モノレール *monorēru*

month 月 *tsuki*

morning 朝 *asa*

this morning けさ *kesa*

mosque 回教の寺院／モスク *kaikyō no jiin/mosuku*

mother (someone else's) お母さん *okāsan*

mother (your own) 母 *haha*

mountain 山 *yama*

mountain range 山脈 *sanmyaku*

mouse マウス *mausu*

mousse (hair) ムース *mūsu*

movie, film 映画 *eiga*

movie theater 映画館 *eigakan*

Mr./Mrs./Miss/Ms. ＿＿さん *＿＿ san*

MSG (monosodium glutamate) 化学調味料 *kagaku chōmiryō*

mud ぬかるみ *nukarumi*

muscle 筋肉 *kinniku*

museum 博物館 *hakubutsukan*

mushrooms マッシュルーム／シャンピニオン *masshurūmu/shanpinion*

shiitake mushrooms しいたけ *shiitake*

music 音楽 *ongaku*

musical ミュージカル *myūjikaru*

mustache 口ひげ *kuchi hige*

mustard マスタード／からし *masutādo/karashi*

my 私の *watakushi no*

myself 自分で *jibun de*

mystery ミステリー *misuterī*

N

nail ネイル／マニキュア *neiru/manikyua*

nail file 爪やすり *tsume yasuri*

nail polish マニキュア液／エナメル *manikyua eki/enameru*

nail polish remover マニキュア落とし／除光液 *manikyua otoshi/jokō eki*

nail salon ネイルサロン *neiru saron*

name 名前／氏名 *namae/shimei*

napkin ナプキン *napukin*

narrow せまい *semai*

nationality 国籍 *kokuseki*

national park 国立公園 *kokuritsu kōen*

natural (food) 自然(食品) *shizen (shokuhin)*

nausea 吐き気 *hakike*

near 近い *chikai*

nearby ＿＿の近くに *＿＿ no chikaku ni*

nearest 最寄りの *moyori no*

necessary 必要な *hitsuyō na*

neck 首 *kubi*

necklace ネックレス *nekkuresu*

nectarine ネクタリン *nekutarin*

to need いる／必要だ *iru/hitsuyō da*

new 新しい *atarashii*

New Zealand ニュージーランド *Nyūjīrando*

news magazines ニュース関係の雑誌 *nyūsu kankei no zasshi*

newspaper 新聞 *shinbun*

newsstand 新聞売り場 *shinbun uriba*

next 次 *tsugi*
night 夜 *yoru*
nightclub ナイト・クラブ *naito kurabu*
nipple 乳首 *chikubi*
no いいえ *iie*
no chemicals 無農薬 *munōyaku*
No, it isn't. いいえ、違います。 *Iie, chigaimasu.*
noisy やかましい *yakamashii*
noodles (Japanese) うどん／そば／ラーメン *udon/soba/rāmen*
noodle soup ヌードル・スープ *nūdoru sūpu*
noon 昼 *hiru*
north 北 *kita*
nose 鼻 *hana*
no-smoking section 禁煙席 *kin-en seki*
No, thank you. いいえ、けっこうです。 *Iie, kekkō desu.*
notebook ノート *nōto*
notebook computer ノートブック・コンピュータ *nōtobukku konpyūta*
notions 小間物 *komamono*
novel 小説 *shōsetsu*
November 十一月 *jūichigatsu*
now 今 *ima*
number 番号／数 *bangō/kazu*
nurse 看護師 *kangoshi*
nursing 授乳 *ju-nyū*
nuts ナッツ *nattsu*
nylon ナイロン *nairon*

O

oatmeal オートミール *ōtomīru*
occupation 職業 *shokugyō*
ocean 海 *umi*
October 十月 *jūgatsu*
of course もちろん *mochiron*
office オフィス *ofisu*

office worker (male) サラリーマン *sararīman*
office worker (female) オーエル *ōeru*
oil (car) エンジン・オイル *enjin oiru*
oil (food) 油 *abura*
olive oil オリーブ油 *orību yu*
old (people) 年とった *toshi totta*
How old are you? おいくつですか。*Oikutsu desu ka.*
I'm ___ years old. ___歳です。 *___ sai desu.*
old (things) 古い *furui*
old town 旧市街 *kyū shigai*
Olympics オリンピック *Orinpikku*
omelet オムレツ *omuretsu*
on ___ ___ ___の上に *___ no ue ni*
on board (ship) 船に *fune ni*
on foot 歩いて *aruite*
on one's own 自分で *jibun de*
on sale セール *sēru*
on time 時間通りに *jikan dōri ni*
one way 片道 *katamichi*
one-way ticket 片道切符 *katamichi kippu*
onion 玉ねぎ *tamanegi*
onion soup オニオン・スープ *onion sūpu*
onyx しまめのう／オニキス *shima menō/onikisu*
to open (v.i.) 開く *aku*
to open (v.t.) 開ける *akeru*
opera オペラ *opera*
opera house オペラ劇場 *opera gekijō*
optician 眼鏡屋 *meganeya*
or それとも／または／あるいは *soretomo/mata wa/arui wa*
orange オレンジ *orenji*
orchestra 管弦楽団／オーケストラ *kangengaku dan/ōkesutora*

orchestra (theater) 舞台に近い席 *butai ni chikai seki*
order 注文 *chūmon*
to order 注文する *chūmon suru*
organic (food) 有機(食品) *yūki (shokuhin)*
origami paper 折り紙 *origami*
original 元のまま／オリジナル *moto no mama/orijinaru*
other 外の *hoka no*
out of order こわれて *kowarete*
outside ____ ____の外に *____ no soto ni*
outside line (phone) 市内 *shinai*
(It's) over./(I'm) finished. 終わりました。 *Owarimashita.*
oval (nail) オーバルネイル *ōbaru neiru*
overcoat オーバー *ōbā*
overheated オーバー・ヒート *ōbā hīto*
overnight 一晩 *hito ban*
oysters かき *kaki*

P

pacifier おしゃぶり *oshaburi*
package 荷物 *nimotsu*
pain 痛み／苦痛 *itami/kutsū*
to paint (art) 描く *kaku*
painter 画家 *gaka*
palace 宮殿 *kyūden*
pancakes ホット・ケーキ *hotto kēki*
panda パンダ *panda*
pants スラックス *surakkusu*
paper lanterns ちょうちん *chōchin*
paper shop 紙屋／和紙屋 *kamiya/washiya*
papier mâché 張り子細工 *hariko zaiku*
Paralympics パラリンピック *Pararinpikku*

parcel 小包 *kozutsumi*
Pardon me, but ____. すみませんが、____。 *Sumimasen ga, ____.*
parfait パフェー *pafē*
park 公園 *kōen*
to park 駐車する *chūsha suru*
parking fee 駐車料金 *chūsha ryōkin*
parking garage 駐車場 *chūsha jō*
street parking 路上駐車 *rojō chūsha*
pass code/password 暗証 *anshō*
passenger 乗客／旅客 *jōkyaku/ryokyaku*
passport パスポート／旅券 *pasupōto/ryoken*
passport number 旅券番号 *ryoken bangō*
pastry ペストリー *pesutorī*
pastry shop お菓子屋 *okashiya*
paté パテ *pate*
path 道 *michi*
peach 桃 *momo*
peanuts ピーナッツ *pīnattsu*
pear 洋なし *yō nashi*
Japanese pear なし *nashi*
pearls 真珠／パール *shinju/pāru*
cultured pearls 養殖真珠 *yōshoku shinju*
pediatrician 小児科医 *shōnika i*
pedicure ペディキュア *pedikyua*
pencil 鉛筆 *enpitsu*
pencil sharpener 鉛筆削り *enpitsu kezuri*
pendant ペンダント *pendanto*
pepper こしょう *koshō*
green pepper ピーマン *pīman*
performance 上演 *jōen*

performer 出演者 *shutsuensha*

perfume 香水 *kōsui*

permanent wave パーマ *pāma*

per person 一人(当たり) *hitori (atari)*

persimmon 柿 *kaki*

person 人 *hito*

personnel department 人事部 *jinji bu*

pharmacy 薬局／薬屋 *yakkyoku/kusuriya*

  all-night pharmacy 終夜営業の薬局 *shūya eigyō no yakkyoku*

Philippines フィリッピン *Firippin*

photograph, picture 写真 *shashin*

photography shop カメラ屋 *kameraya*

pickles (Japanese) （お)漬け物 *(o) tsukemono*

picture postcards 絵葉書 *ehagaki*

pie パイ *pai*

  apple pie アップル・パイ *appuru pai*

  lemon meringue pie レモン・メレンゲ *remon merenge*

pier 埠頭 *futō*

pillow 枕 *makura*

pin (jewelry) 飾りピン *kazari pin*

pineapple パイナップル *painappuru*

ping pong ピンポン *pinpon*

pink ピンク *pinku*

pipe パイプ *paipu*

  pipe tobacco きざみタバコ *kizami tabako*

plaid 格子じま *kōshi jima*

plants 草 *kusa*

plastic プラスチック／ビニール *purasuchikku/binīru*

plate お皿 *osara*

platinum プラチナ *purachina*

play (theater) 演劇 *engeki*

playground 遊び場 *asobiba*

pleasant 楽しい *tanoshii*

please ___ ___ ___をください／お願いします ___ *o kudasai/onegai shimasu*

please (come in/sit down/begin/have some/go first/etc.) どうぞ *dōzo*

Pleased to meet you. 初めて、おめにかかります。 *Hajimete, ome ni kakarimasu.*

pliers ペンチ *penchi*

plum プラム／すもも *puramu/sumomo*

points of interest 名所 *meisho*

police 警察 *keisatsu*

police officer 警官 *keikan*

to polish みがく *migaku*

politician 政治家 *seijika*

polyester ポリエステル *poriesuteru*

pond 池 *ike*

popcorn ポップコーン *poppukōn*

popular 人気がある *ninki ga aru*

popular songs ポピュラー・ソング *popyurā songu*

porcelain 磁器 *jiki*

pork 豚肉 *buta niku*

pork chop ポーク・チョップ *pōku choppu*

portable component stereo system 携帯コンポステレオ装置 *keitai konpo sutereo sōchi*

portable printer ポータブルプリンター *pōtaburu purintā*

portable radio ポータブル・ラジオ *pōtaburu rajio*

portable scanner ポータブルスキャナー *pōtaburu sukyanā*

porter ポーター *pōtā*

Portuguese (adj.) ポルトガルの
Porutogaru no
postcard 葉書 *hagaki*
post office 郵便局
yūbinkyoku
potato ポテト／じゃがいも
poteto/jagaimo
　baked potato ベークド・ポ
　テト *bēkudo poteto*
　French fries フレンチ・フ
　ライ *Furenchi furai*
　mashed potatoes マッシュ・
　ポテト *masshu poteto*
　sweet potato スイート・
　ポテト／さつまいも *suīto
　poteto/satsuma imo*
potato chips ポテトチップ
poteto chippu
pottery 陶器 *tōki*
pottery shop 瀬戸物屋／陶器
の店 *setomonoya/tōki no
mise*
to pray お祈りする *oinori
suru*
prefectural capital 県庁
所在地 *kenchō shozaichi*
prefecture 県 *ken*
to prefer 好む *konomu*
pregnant 妊娠中 *ninshin chū*
prescription 処方箋
shohōsen
pretty, beautiful きれいな
kirei na
price 値段 *nedan*
priest 神父 *shinpu*
print (pattern) プリント
purinto
print (photo) 焼き付け
yakitsuke
printer プリンター *purintā*
printing paper プリント用紙
purinto yōshi
problem 問題 *mondai*
prosecco プロセッコ *purosekko*
processing fee 取り扱い料金
toriatsukai ryōkin
professor 教授 *kyōju*
program 番組 *bangumi*

prosciutto 生ハム *nama
hamu*
public phone 公衆電話
kōshū denwa
public relations department
渉外部 *shōgai bu*
public transportation 公共
交通機関 *kōkyō kōtsū kikan*
pudding プリン *purin*
　chocolate pudding チョコ
　レート・プリン *chokorēto
　purin*
pulse 脈 *myaku*
purple 紫色の *murasaki iro
no*
purpose 目的 *mokuteki*
purse ハンドバッグ
handobaggu

Q

question 質問 *shitsumon*
quick, fast 速い *hayai*
quiet 静か(な) *shizuka (na)*

R

rabbi ラビ *rabi*
racket ラケット *raketto*
radio ラジオ *rajio*
radio station ラジオ局
rajio kyoku
radish ラディシュ／二十日
大根 *radisshu/hatsuka
daikon*
rain 雨 *ame*
raincoat レイン・コート
rein kōto
rainy season 梅雨 *tsuyu*
raisins 干しぶどう *hoshibudō*
ramp スロープ *surōpu*
rare (meat) レア *rea*
rate 料金 *ryōkin*
raw なま *nama*
razor かみそり *kamisori*
razor blades カミソリの刃
kamisori no ha

to read 読む *yomu*

Really? そうですか／本当 *sō desu ka/hontō*

to the rear うしろの *ushiro no*

receipt レシート *reshīto*

to receive 受け取る *uketoru*

to recommend 推薦する／勧める *suisen suru/susumeru*

to reconfirm 再確認する *sai kakunin suru*

record レコード *rekōdo*

record album レコード・アルバム *rekōdo arubamu*

record player レコード・プレーヤー *rekōdo purēyā*

record store レコード屋 *rekōdoya*

red 赤い *akai*

refund 返金 *henkin*

regular 普通 *futsū*

religious 宗教の *shūkyō no*

religious service 礼拝 *reihai*

to rent 借りる *kariru*

repair 修理 *shūri*

repair tools 修理道具 *shūri dōgu*

to repair 修理する *shūri suru*

repeat it もう一度 *mō ichido*

reputation 評判 *hyōban*

reservation 予約 *yoyaku*

reserved seats (train) 座席指定 *zaseki shitei*

unreserved seats (train) 自由席 *jiyū seki*

restrooms トイレ *toire*

restaurant レストラン *resutoran*

rib ろっ骨 *rokkotsu*

rice (Japanese)
  cooked ご飯 *gohan*
  uncooked 米 *kome*

rice (Western) ライス *raisu*

rice paddy 水田 *suiden*

right (correct) 正しい *tadashii*

right (direction) 右 *migi*

ring (jewelry) 指輪 *yubiwa*

river 川 *kawa*

road 道 *michi*

road map 道路地図 *dōro chizu*

roasted あぶり焼きにした／ローストにした *aburiyaki ni shita/rōsuto ni shita*

robe 化粧着／ローブ *keshō gi/rōbu*

rock'n'roll ロック・ミュージック *rokku myūjikku*

rolls (bread) ロール・パン *rōru pan*

romance (movie) 恋愛物 *ren-ai mono*

room 部屋 *heya*

Japanese room (restaurant) お座敷 *ozashiki*

private room (restaurant) 個室 *koshitsu*

room service ルーム・サービス *rūmu sābisu*

rouge ほお紅 *hoo beni*

round 丸い *marui*

round trip 往復 *ōfuku*

round trip ticket 往復券 *ōfuku ken*

rubber bands 輪ゴム *wa gomu*

ruby ルビー *rubī*

ruler 定規 *jōgi*

rush hour ラッシュ・アワー *rasshu awā*

Russian (adj.) ロシアの *Roshia no*

Russian (lang.) ロシア語 *Roshia go*

S

safe (adj.) 安全な *anzen na*

safe (valuables) 金庫 *kinko*

safey pins 安全ピン *anzen pin*

sailboat ヨット *yotto*

sake bottle とっくり *tokkuri*

sake cup 盃 *sakazuki*
salad サラダ *sarada*
  Caesar salad シーザー・サラダ *shīzā sarada*
salami サラミ・ソーセージ *sarami sōsēji*
sale セール／特売 *sēru／tokubai*
sales department 販売部 *hanbai bu*
salmon さけ *sake*
salt 塩 *shio*
same 同じ *onaji*
sandals サンダル *sandaru*
sandwich サンドイッチ *sandoitchi*
sangria サングリア *sanguria*
sanitary napkins 生理ナプキン *seiri napukin*
sapphire サファイア *safaia*
sardines サーディン／いわし *sādin／iwashi*
Saturday 土曜日 *doyōbi*
saucer 受け皿 *ukezara*
sauna サウナ *sauna*
sausage ソーセージ *sōsēji*
sauteed ソテーにした *sotē ni shita*
scallops 帆立て *hotate*
Scandinavian (adj.) スカンジナビアの *Sukanjinabia no*
scanner スキャナー *sukyanā*
scarf スカーフ *sukāfu*
schedule スケジュール *sukejūru*
school 学校 *gakkō*
science fiction サイエンス・フィクション *saiensu fikushon*
scissors はさみ *hasami*
  cuticle scissors あま皮用のはさみ *amakawa yō no hasami*
scotch (whisky) スコッチ *sukotchi*
Scotch tape セロテープ *serotēpu*
screen スクリーン *sukurīn*

screwdriver ドライバー／ねじ回し *doraibā/neji mawashi*
scroll 掛け軸 *kake jiku*
sculptor 彫刻家 *chōkoku ka*
sculpture 彫刻 *chōkoku*
sea 海 *umi*
seashore 海岸 *kaigan*
seasickness 船酔い *funayoi*
season 季節 *kisetsu*
seat 席 *seki*
seaweed のり *nori*
secretary 秘書 *hisho*
to see 見る *miru*
  Oh, I see. なるほど。 *Naruhodo.*
selfie stick 自分撮りスティック *jibundori sutikku*
to sell 売る *uru*
to send 送る *okuru*
senior citizens シニア／年寄り *shinia/toshiyori*
September 九月 *kugatsu*
service charge サービス料 *sābisu ryō*
service charge 手数料 *tesū ryō*
setting lotion セット・ローション *setto rōshon*
to sew ぬう *nuu*
shampoo シャンプー *shanpū*
sharks さめ *same*
sharp 鋭い *surudoi*
shave ひげそり *higesori*
shaving lotion シェービング・ローション *shēbingu rōshon*
  aftershave lotion アフター シェーブ・ローション *afutāshēbu rōshon*
shave and shampoo ひげそりと洗髪 *higesori to senpatsu*
she 彼女が *kanojo ga*
sherbet シャーベット *shābetto*
  lemon sherbet レモン・シャーベット *remon shābetto*
shingles 帯状疱疹 *taijō hōshin*

Shinto ceremony 神道の儀式
 shintō no gishiki
ship 船 *fune*
shirt ワイシャツ *waishatsu*
shochu 焼酎 *shōchū*
shoes くつ *kutsu*
 to take off one's shoes
 くつをぬぐ *kutsu o nugu*
shoe repair shop くつの
 修理屋 *kutsu no shūriya*
shoe store くつ屋 *kutsuya*
shoelaces くつひも *kutsu
 himo*
shopping ショッピング／
 買い物 *shoppingu/kaimono*
shopping arcade ショッピン
 グ・アーケード *shoppingu
 ākēdo*
shopping area ショッピング街
 shoppingu gai
short 短い *mijikai*
shortcut 近道 *chikamichi*
short story books 短編小説
 tanpen shōsetsu
shorts (briefs) ブリーフ
 burīfu
shoulder 肩 *kata*
show (stage, floor) ショー *shō*
 Broadway show ブロード
 ウェーからのショー
 Burōdowē kara no shō
 first show 最初のショー
 saisho no shō
 last show 最後のショー
 saigo no shō
to show 見せる *miseru*
shower シャワー *shawā*
shrimp えび *ebi*
shrine 神社 *jinja*
sick 病気 *byōki*
sightseeing bus 観光バス
 kankō basu
sightseeing tour 観光旅行
 kankō ryokō
signature 署名 *shomei*
silk 絹／シルク *kinu/shiruku*
silver 銀 *gin*
singer 歌手 *kashu*

singing 歌って *utatte*
single (marital status) 独身
 dokushin
sink (bathroom) 洗面台
 senmen dai
size サイズ *saizu*
skiing スキー *sukī*
skis スキー *sukī*
ski lift リフト *rifuto*
ski poles ストック *sutokku*
ski resort スキー場 *sukī jō*
ski shoes スキーぐつ *sukī
 gutsu*
skim milk スキム・ミルク
 sukimu miruku
skin 肌 *hada*
skin-diving equipment スキ
 ン・ダイビング用具 *sukin
 daibingu yōgu*
skirt スカート *sukāto*
Skype スカイプ *Sukaipu*
to sleep 寝る *neru*
sleeping car 寝台車 *shindai
 sha*
sleeping pills 睡眠薬
 suimin yaku
sleepy ねむい *nemui*
sleeves そで *sode*
 long sleeves 長そで *naga
 sode*
 short sleeves 半そで *han
 sode*
slides スライド *suraido*
slippers スリッパ *surippa*
slow おそい *osoi*
small 小さい *chīsai*
small (size) スモール／小
 sumōru/shō
smart phone スマートフォン／ス
 マホ *sumātofon/sumaho*
to smile 笑う *warau*
to smoke たばこを吸う
 tabako o suu
snack スナック *sunakku*
snack bar スナック・バー
 sunakku bā
Snapchat スナップチャット
 Sunappuchatto

sneakers 運動ぐつ／スニーカー *undō gutsu/sunīkā*

snow 雪 *yuki*

snow board スノー・ボード *sunō bōdo*

soap 石けん *sekken*

soccer サッカー *sakkā*

soccer match サッカーの試合 *sakkā no shiai*

soccer stadium サッカーの競技場 *sakkā no kyōgi jō*

social media ソーシャルメディア *sōsharu media*

socks くつ下／ソックス *kutsushita/sokkusu*

sole くつ底 *kutsuzoko*

solid color 無地 *muji*

some 少し *sukoshi*

somebody, someone 誰か *dareka*

son (someone else's) 息子さん *musuko san*

son (your own) 息子 *musuko*

soon すぐ *sugu*

soup スープ *sūpu*

  bean paste soup みそしる *misoshiru*

  clear soup 吸い物 *suimono*

south 南 *minami*

souvenir おみやげ *omiyage*

souvenir shop おみやげ屋 *omiyageya*

soy sauce しょう油 *shōyu*

spaghetti スパゲッティー *supagettī*

Spain スペイン *Supein*

Spanish (adj.) スペインの *Supein no*

Spanish (lang.) スペイン語 *Supein go*

spark plugs スパーク・プラグ *supāku puragu*

special 特別の *tokubetsu no*

special bargain sale 大安売り *ō yasuuri*

to spend (money) 使う *tsukau*

spinach ほうれん草 *hōrensō*

spine 背骨 *sebone*

spinning スピニング *supiningu*

sponge スポンジ *suponji*

sporting goods store 運道具店 *undōgu ten*

sports wear スポーツウェア *supōtsu wea*

to sprain ねんざする *nenza suru*

spring 春 *haru*

square 四角い *shikakui*

square (nail) スクエアネイル *sukuea neiru*

squid いか *ika*

stainless steel ステンレス *sutenresu*

special class 特等 *tokutō*

stamps 切手 *kitte*

to stand 立つ *tatsu*

stairs 階段 *kaidan*

stapler ホッチキス *hotchikisu*

starched (laundry) のりをきかせて *nori o kikasete*

to start (v.i.) 始まる *hajimaru*

station (train) 駅 *eki*

stationery shop 文房具店 *bunbōgu ten*

to stay 泊まる *tomaru*

steak ステーキ *sutēki*

steering wheel ハンドル *handoru*

step(s) 段差 *dansa*

step (exercise) ステップ *suteppu*

stock exchange 証券取引所 *shōken torihiki jo*

stockings ストッキング *sutokkingu*

stolen 盗まれて *nusumarete*

stomach 胃 *i*

  upset stomach 胃の調子がよくない *i no chōshi ga yoku nai*

stone (jewelry) 宝石 *hōseki*

to stop (v.i.) やめる *yameru*

to stop (transportation) 止まる *tomaru*

store お店 *omise*

story/plot (movie, play) 筋 *suji*

straight (direction) まっすぐ *massugu*

strawberries いちご *ichigo*

stream 小川 *ogawa*

street 通り *tōri*

string ひも *himo*

string beans さやいんげん *sayaingen*

stripes しま模様 *shima moyō*

stroller ベビーカー *bebī kā*

strong 強い *tsuyoi*

student 学生 *gakusei*

stupid ばかな *baka na*

style スタイル *sutairu*

subtitles (film) 字幕 *jimaku*

subway 地下鉄 *chikatetsu*

sudden illness 急病 *kyūbyō*

sugar 砂糖 *satō*

sugar substitute ダイエット甘味料 *daietto kanmiryō*

suit スーツ *sūtsu*

summer 夏 *natsu*

sunburn 日焼け *hiyake*

sundae サンデー *sandē*

Sunday 日曜日 *nichiyōbi*

sunglasses サングラス *sangurasu*

sunscreeen 日焼け止め *hiyakedome*

suntan lotion サンタン・ローション *santan rōshon*

supermarket スーパー *sūpā*

suppositories 座薬 *zayaku*

surfboard サーフ・ボード *sāfu bōdo*

surgeon 外科医 *geka i*

SUV スポーツ多目的車 *supōtsu tamokuteki sha*

sweater セーター *sētā*

sweet 甘い *amai*

to swim 泳ぐ *oyogu*

swimming pool プール *pūru*

Swiss (adj.) スイスの *Suisu no*

swollen はれた *hareta*

swordfish まかじき *makajiki*

symphony シンフォニー *shinfonī*

synagogue ユダヤ教の寺院 *yudaya kyō no jiin*

syrup シロップ *shiroppu*

T

Tabasco タバスコ *Tabasuko*

table テーブル *tēburu*

tablespoon 大さじ *ō saji*

tailor 仕立て屋 *shitateya*

to take a picture 写真をとる *shashin o toru*

talcum powder シッカロール *shikkarōru*

tampons タンポン *tanpon*

tangerine みかん *mikan*

tape measure 巻尺 *makijaku*

tax 税金 *zeikin*

taxi タクシー *takushī*

taxi stand タクシー乗り場 *takushī noriba*

tea 紅茶 *kōcha*

 iced tea アイスティー *aisutī*

 Japanese tea お茶 *ocha*

 Japanese green tea 緑茶 *ryokucha*

 Japanese roasted tea ほうじ茶 *hōjicha*

tea ceremony 茶道 *sadō*

 etiquette of preparing tea 点前 *temae*

tea bowl 茶道のお茶碗／茶碗 *sadō no ochawan/chawan*

teacup 湯飲み茶腕／茶碗 *yunomi jawan/chawan*

teacher 教師／先生 *kyōshi/sensei*

team チーム *chīmu*

teapot 急須／土びん *kyūsu/dobin*

teaspoon 小さじ *ko saji*

tee shirt ティーシャツ *tī shatsu*

telephone 電話 *denwa*

telephone booth 電話ボックス *denwa bokkusu*

public telephone 公衆電話 *kōshū denwa*
telephone call 電話 *denwa*
  local call 市内電話 *shinai denwa*
  long-distance call 長距離電話 *chōkyori denwa*
  English telephone directory 英語の電話帳 *eigo no denwa chō*
telephone card テレフォンカード *terefon kādo*
telephone number 電話番号 *denwa bangō*
  extension number 内線 *naisen*
telephone operator 交換手 *kōkanshu*
television, TV テレビ *terebi*
television set テレビ *terebi*
to tell 教える *oshieru*
temperature, fever 熱 *netsu*
temple お寺 *otera*
tennis テニス *tenisu*
tennis ball テニス・ボール *tenisu bōru*
tennis court テニス・コート *tenisu kōto*
  to play tennis テニスをする *tenisu o suru*
tent テント *tento*
terrace テラス *terasu*
Thai (adj.) タイの *Tai no*
Thai (person) タイ人 *Tai jin*
thank you どうもありがとう *dōmo arigatō*
that/that over there (adj.) その／あの *sono/ano*
that/that over there (n.) それ／あれ *sore/are*
thatch roof わらぶき屋根 *warabuki yane*
theater 劇場 *gekijō*
theft 盗難 *tōnan*
theme テーマ *tēma*
there/over there そこ／あそこ *soko/asoko*

thermometer 体温計 *taion kei*
themostat (car) サーモスタット *sāmosutatto*
they 彼らが *karera ga*
thick 厚い *atsui*
thigh 太もも *futo momo*
thin 薄い *usui*
to think 思う *omou*
I don't think so. そう思いません。*Sō omoimasen.*
I think so. そうだと思います。*So da to omoimasu.*
thirsty のどがかわいています *nodo ga kawaite imasu*
this (adj.) この *kono*
this (n.) これ *kore*
throbbing ズキズキする *zukizuki suru*
thriller, horror movie スリラー *surirā*
throat のど *nodo*
thumb 親指 *oya yubi*
Thursday 木曜日 *mokuyōbi*
ticket チケット／券／切符 *chiketto/ken/kippu*
ticket (air) 航空券 *kōkū ken*
ticket machine (train) 切符の販売機 *kippu no hanbai ki*
ticket window/counter 切符売り場 *kippu uriba*
tie ネクタイ *nekutai*
tight (clothing) きつい *kitsui*
to tighten 締める *shimeru*
time 時間 *jikan*
What time is it? いま何時ですか。*Ima nan ji desu ka.*
timetable 時刻表 *jikoku hyō*
tire タイヤ *taiya*
  tire pressure タイヤの空気圧 *taiya no kūki atsu*
  spare tire スペア・タイヤ *supea taiya*
tired つかれています *tsukarete imasu*
tissues ちり紙／ティッシュー *chirigami/tisshū*
title 題名 *daimei*

to ___ (direction/location)
___ へ／に *e/ni*

toast (bread) トースト *tōsuto*

toast (drinks) 乾杯 *kanpai*

toaster トースター *tōsutā*

tobacco shop たばこ屋
tabakoya

today 今日 *kyō*

  for today 今日の *kyō no*

toddler 幼児 *yōji*

toe 足の指 *ashi no yubi*

together 一緒に *issho ni*

toilet トイレ *toire*

toilet paper トイレット・
ペーパー *toiretto pēpā*

toiletries shop 化粧品店
keshōhin ten

tomato トマト *tomato*

tomorrow あした／あす
ashita/asu

tomorrow night あしたの晩
ashita no ban

tongue 舌 *shita*

tonight 今晩 *konban*

tonsillitis 扁桃腺炎
hentōsen en

tonsils 扁桃腺 *hentōsen*

toothache 歯痛／歯いた
shitsū/ha ita

toothbrush 歯ブラシ *ha
burashi*

toothpaste 練り歯みがき
neri ha migaki

toothpicks ようじ *yōji*

topaz トパーズ *topāzu*

tour ツアー *tsuā*

  group tour グループ・
ツアー *gurūpu tsuā*

  tour guide ツアー・ガイド
tsuā gaido

  guided tour 案内付きの見物
annai tsuki no kenbutsu

  tourist 観光客 *kankō
kyaku*

tourist information center
旅行案内所 *ryokō annai jo*

towels タオル *taoru*

town 町 *machi*

tow truck レッカー車
rekkā sha

toy store おもちゃ屋
omochaya

traditional 伝統的な *dentō
teki na*

train 汽車／列車 *kisha/
ressha*

  commuter train 電車
densha

  express train 快速
kaisoku

  limited express 特急
tokkyū

  local train 普通 *futsū*

  ordinary express 急行
kyūkō

  super express 新幹線
shinkansen

  platform ホーム *hōmu*

  track 線 *sen*

tragedy 悲劇 *higeki*

tranquilizers トランキライザー
torankiraizā

to translate 翻訳する *hon-
yaku suru*

translation 翻訳 *hon-yaku*

transportation 交通機関
kōtsū kikan

travel agency 旅行代理店
ryokō dairi ten

traveler's check 旅行小切手／
トラベラーズ・チェック
*ryokō kogitte/toraberāzu
chekku*

tree 木 *ki*

trip 旅行／旅 *ryokō/tabi*

trout ます *masu*

to try on 試着する *shichaku
suru*

tsunami 津波 *tsunami*

Tuesday 火曜日 *kayōbi*

tuna まぐろ *maguro*

to turn 曲がる *magaru*

turquoise トルコ石 *Toruko
ishi*

tweezers 毛抜き *ke nuki*

Twitter ツイッター *Tsuitta*

type, kind 種類 *shurui*
typhoon 台風 *taifū*
typical 代表的な *daihyō teki na*

U

ugly みにくい *minikui*
uncle (someone else's) おじさん *ojisan*
uncle (your own) おじ *oji*
undershirt アンダーシャツ／肌着 *andā shatsu/hadagi*
to understand わかる *wakaru*
　I understand わかります *wakarimasu*
underwear 下着 *shitagi*
United States アメリカ *Amerika*
university 大学 *daigaku*
up ___ ___の上に ___ *ue ni*
urgent 至急 *shikyū*
urologist 泌尿器科医 *hitsunyōkika i*
to use 使う *tsukau*
user name ユーザーネーム *yuzā nēmu*

V

vacation バケーション／バカンス *bakēshon/bakansu*
valley 谷 *tani*
VCR ビデオ *bideo*
veal 子牛 *koushi*
vegan ビーガン（純菜食主義者）*bīgan (jun saishoku shugi sha)*
vegetables 野菜 *yasai*
vegetarian ベジタリアン *bejitarian*
vending machine 自動販売機 *jidō hanbai ki*
venetian blind ブラインド *buraindo*

very fatty tuna 大とろ *ō toro*
video camera ビデオカメラ *bideo kamera*
video game ビデオ·ゲーム *bideo gēmu*
Vietnamese (adj.) ベトナムの *Betonamu no*
view 眺め *nagame*
village 村 *mura*
vinegar 酢 *su*
vinyl ビニール *binīru*
visually impaired 難視 *nanshi*
vitamins ビタミン剤 *bitamin zai*
vodka ウォッカ *wokka*
volcano 火山 *kazan*
voltage 電圧 *den-atsu*

W

to wait 待つ *matsu*
waiting room 待合い室 *machiai shitsu*
to walk 歩く *aruku*
walker 歩行器 *hokōki*
wallet さいふ *saifu*
walnuts くるみ *kurumi*
to want 欲しい *hoshii*
　I don't want it/any. いりません。／けっこうです。*Irimasen./Kekkō desu.*
warm あたたかい *atatakai*
to wash 洗う *arau*
wash and set シャンプーとセット *shanpū to setto*
watch and clock store 時計屋 *tokeiya*
watch repair shop 時計の修理屋 *tokei no shūriya*
water 水 *mizu*
　water (car) ラジエーターの水 *rajiētā no mizu*
　hot water お湯 *oyu*
　mineral water ミネラル·ウォーター *mineraru wōtā*
　running water 水道 *suidō*

beruto ベルト　*belt*

Betonamu no ベトナムの　*Vietnamese (adj.)*

bīchi parasoru ビーチ・パラソル　*beach umbrella*

bideo ビデオ　*VCR/video*

bideo gēmu ビデオ・ゲーム　*video game*

bideo kamera ビデオカメラ　*video camera*

bideo sōchi no mise ビデオ装置の店　*video equipment shop*

bīfu ビーフ　*beef*

bifuteki ビフテキ　*beefsteak*

bīgan (jun saishoku shugi sha) ビーガン(純菜食主義者)　*vegan*

bijinesu ビジネス　*business*

bijinesu gai ビジネス街　*business district*

bijinesu hoteru ビジネス・ホテル　*business hotel*

bijinesu sentā ビジネス・センター　*business center (hotel)*

bijutsu 美術　*art*

bin mei 便名　*flight number*

bin びん　*bottle*

binīru ビニール　*plastic, vinyl*

binsen 便せん　*writing paper*

biru ビル　*building*

bīru ビール　*beer*

bisuketto ビスケット　*biscuits*

bitamin zai ビタミン剤　*vitamins*

biyōin 美容院　*hair salon*

bodī rōshon ボディー・ローション　*body lotion*

bōi ボーイ　*bellhop*

bokushi 牧師　*minister*

bōru ボール　*bowl*

bōrupen ボールペン　*ballpoint pen*

bōshi 帽子　*hat*

botan ボタン　*button*

bōto ボート　*boat*

budō ぶどう　*grapes*

budō 武道　*Japanese martial arts*

bujutsu 武術　*Japanese martial arts*

bunbōgu ten 文房具店　*stationery shop*

bunpō 文法　*grammar*

bunpō no hon 文法の本　*grammar book*

bunraku 文楽　*Japanese puppet theater*

buraindo ブラインド　*venetian blind*

burajā ブラジャー　*bra, brassiere*

Burajiru ブラジル　*Brazil*

Burajiru no ブラジルの　*Brazilian (adj.)*

burashi ブラシ　*brushes*

burausu ブラウス　*blouse*

burēki ブレーキ　*brakes*

burēki eki ブレーキ液　*brake fluid*

buresuretto ブレスレット　*bracelet*

burīfu ブリーフ　*shorts (briefs)*

burō dorai ブロー・ドライ　*blow dry*

burōchi ブローチ　*brooch*

Burōdowē kara no shō ブロードウェーからのショー　*Broadway show*

Burōdowē no hitto ブロードウェーのヒット　*Broadway hit(s)*

burokkori ブロッコリ　*broccoli*

burondo ブロンド　*blond*

burū jīn ブルー・ジーン　*jeans*

burunetto ブルネット　*brunette*

buta niku 豚肉　*pork*

butai ni chikai seki 舞台に近い席　*orchestra (theater)*

būtsu ブーツ *boots*
byōin 病院 *hospital*
byōki 病気 *sick*
byuffe sha ビュッフェ車 *buffet car*

C

chairoi 茶色い *brown*
chakku チャック *zipper*
channeru チャンネル *channel (TV)*
chawan 茶碗 *teacup, rice bowl*
chekku チェック *bill, check*
chekku チェック *checks (pattern)*
chekku in suru チェック・インする *to check in*
chēn チェーン *chain*
cherī チェリー *cherries*
chi 血 *blood*
chibusa 乳房 *breast*
chichi 父 *father (your own)*
chigai 違い *difference*
chigau 違う *different*
chihō 地方 *countryside*
chiiki 地域 *area*
chikai 近い *near*
chikamichi 近道 *shortcut*
chikatetsu 地下鉄 *subway*
chiketto チケット *ticket*
chikin sūpu チキン・スープ *chicken soup*
chikubi 乳首 *nipple*
chīmu チーム *team*
chirigami ちり紙 *tissues*
chīsai 小さい *small*
chizu 地図 *map*
chīzu チーズ *cheese*
chīzu kēki チーズ・ケーキ *cheesecake*
chōchin ちょうちん *paper lanterns*
chokkō bin 直行便 *direct flight*
chōkoku 彫刻 *sculpture*

chōkoku hin 彫刻品 *carved objects*
chōkoku ka 彫刻家 *sculptor*
chokorēto チョコレート *chocolate*
chokorēto kēki チョコレート・ケーキ *chocolate cake*
chokorēto purin チョコレート・プリン *chocolate pudding*
chōkyori denwa 長距離電話 *long-distance call*
chosha 著者 *author*
chōshoku 朝食 *breakfast*
chū 中 *medium (size)*
chū bin 中びん *medium-size bottle*
chū nikai no (seki) 中二階の (席) *mezzanine*
chūgata sha 中型車 *medium-sized car*
Chūgoku 中国 *China*
Chūgoku go 中国語 *Chinese (lang.)*
Chūgoku no 中国の *Chinese (adj.)*
chūmon 注文 *order*
chūmon suru 注文する *to order*
chūō 中央 *center*
chūsha 注射 *injection*
chūsha jō 駐車場 *parking garage*
chūsha ryōkin 駐車料金 *parking fee*
chūsha suru 駐車する *to park*

D

dabokushō 打撲傷 *bruise*
daietto ダイエット *diet*
daietto kanmiryō ダイエット甘味料 *sugar substitute*
daigaku 大学 *university*
daihyō teki na 代表的な *typical*
Daijōbu desu. 大丈夫です。 *It's all right.*

daikudōguya 大工道具屋 *hardware store*

daimei 題名 *title*

daiya ダイヤ *diamond*

daiyaru chokutsū ダイヤル直通 *direct dial*

dakkyū shita 脱臼した *dislocated (medical)*

danbō 暖房 *heater*

dansa 段差 *step(s)*

danshi yō no toire 男子用のトイレ *men's room*

dare 誰 *who*

dareka 誰か *somebody, someone*

dasshimen 脱脂綿 *cotton*

___ de ___で *at*

___ de ___で *by (means of)*

deguchi 出口 *exit*

dekafe kōhī デカフェコーヒー *decaffeinated coffee*

dejitaru kamera デジタル・カメラ *digital camera*

dejitaru no tokei デジタルの時計 *digital watch*

dejitaru tēpu rekōdā デジタル・テープレコーダー *digital tape recorder*

demo でも *but*

den-atsu 電圧 *voltage*

denchi 電池 *battery*

Dēnisshu pesutorī デーニッシュ・ペストリー *Danish pastry*

denki 電気 *electricity*

denki kamisori 電気カミソリ *electric razor*

denki kigu ten 電気器具店 *electrical appliance store*

denki seihin 電気製品 *electrical appliance*

denkyū 電球 *lightbulb*

densha 電車 *commuter train*

denshi tabako 電子タバコ *electronic cigarettes, e-cigarettes*

denshin sōkin 電信送金 *wire transfer*

dentō teki na 伝統的な *traditional*

denwa 電話 *telephone, telephone call*

denwa bangō 電話番号 *telephone number*

denwa bokkusu 電話ボックス *telephone booth*

denwa suru 電話する *to call (telephone)*

deodoranto デオドラント *deodorant*

depāto デパート *department store*

deru 出る *to depart (transportation)*

dezāto デザート *dessert*

dībī kamukōdā ディービー・カムコーダー *DV camcorder*

dībīdī ディービーディー *DVD*

dībīdī purēyā ディービーディー・プレーヤー *DVD player*

dīzeru ディーゼル *diesel (gas)*

dō shite どうして *why*

dō yatte どうやって *how*

doa ドア *door*

dobin どびん *teapot*

dōbutsu en 動物園 *zoo*

dochira どちら *which*

dohyō 土俵 *sumo ring*

Doitsu ドイツ *Germany*

Doitsu go ドイツ語 *German (lang.)*

Doitsu no ドイツの *German (adj.)*

doko どこ *where*

dokushin 独身 *single (marital status)*

dōmo arigatō どうもありがとう *thank you*

donata どなた *who*

dōnattsu ドーナッツ *doughnuts*

dono kurai どの位 *How long?*

dono kurai どの位 *How much?*

doraggusutoa ドラッグストア *drugstore*

doraibā ドライバー
screwdriver

doraikurīningu no sābisu
ドライクリーニングのサービス
dry cleaning service

dore どれ *which*

doresu ドレス *dress*

dōro chizu 道路地図 *road
map*

doru ドル *dollar*

dōryō 同僚 *colleague*

doyōbi 土曜日 *Saturday*

dōzo どうぞ *please (come
in/sit down/begin/have
some/go first, etc.)*

E

_____ e _____ へ *to
(direction/location)*

ē ええ *yes*

earobikkusu エアロビックス
aerobics

ebi えび *shrimp*

ehagaki 絵葉書 *picture
postcards*

eiga 映画 *movie, film*

eigakan 映画館 *movie
theater*

eigo 英語 *English (lang.)*

eigo ga hanaseru 英語が
話せる *English-speaking*

eigo no denwa chō 英語の
電話帳 *English telephone
directory*

eigyō bu 営業部 *business
operations department*

eiwa jiten 英和辞典
English-Japanese dictionary

eki 駅 *station (train)*

ekurea エクレア *eclair*

emerarudo エメラルド
emerald

emu saizu エムサイズ
medium (size)

en 円 *yen*

enameru エナメル *nail polish*

engeki 演劇 *play (theater)*

enjin oiru エンジン・オイル
oil (car)

enjin エンジン *engine*

enjinia エンジニア *engineer*

enpitsu 鉛筆 *pencil*

enpitsu kezuri 鉛筆削り
pencil sharpener

enshutsuka 演出家
director (theater, TV)

erebētā エレベーター *elevator*

eru saizu エルサイズ *large
(size)*

ēru エール *ale*

esukarētā エスカレーター
escalator

ē tī emu エーティーエム *ATM*

F

fakkusu ファックス *fax*

fāsuto fūdo ファースト・フード
fast food

feisharu フェイシャル *facial*

Feisubukku フェイスブック
Facebook

Feisutaimu フェイスタイム
FaceTime

Firippin フィリッピン
Philippines

firumu フィルム *film*

firutā フィルター *filter*

firutā tsuki no tabako
フィルター付きのたばこ
filtered cigarettes

fōku フォーク *fork*

fōku songu フォーク・ソング
folk song

fujin fuku 婦人服 *women's
clothing*

fujin fuku no mise 婦人服の
店 *women's clothing store*

fukikaerarete 吹き替えら
れて *dubbed (film)*

fūkiri no eiga 封切りの映画
first-run film

fuku ふく *to wipe*

fukusha ki 複写機 *copying machine*

fukutsū 腹痛 *cramps (stomach)*

fuminshō 不眠症 *insomnia*

fun-iki 雰囲気 *atmosphere*

funayoi 船酔い *seasickness*

fune 船 *ship*

fune ni 船に *on board (ship)*

Furansu go フランス語 *French (lang.)*

Furansu no フランスの *French (adj.)*

Furansu pan フランス・パン *French bread*

Furenchi furai フレンチ・フライ *French fries*

Furenchi neiru フレンチネイル *French manicure*

furo 風呂 *bath, bathtub*

furoa shō フロア・ショー *floor show*

furonto garasu フロント・ガラス *windshield*

furui 古い *old (things)*

furūtsu kappu フルーツ・カップ *fruit compote/cup*

futo momo 太もも *thigh*

futō 埠頭 *pier*

fūtō 封筒 *envelope*

futsū 普通 *local train*

futsū 普通 *regular (not special)*

futsuka 二日 *two days/the second day*

futtobōru フットボール *football*

fuyu 冬 *winter*

G

gaido bukku ガイド・ブック *guidebook*

gaika 外貨 *foreign currency*

gaikoku jin 外国人 *foreigner*

gaikoku jin shutsu nyū koku kiroku 外国人出入国記録 *Disembarkation/Embarkation Card for Foreigner*

gaikoku no 外国の *foreign*

gaikoku no 外国の *imported*

gaka 画家 *painter*

gakkō 学校 *school*

gakudan 楽団 *band*

gakusei 学生 *student*

gan がん *cancer*

gankin 元金 *principal*

garasu buta ガラスぶた *crystal (watch)*

gārikku ガーリック *garlic*

garō 画廊 *art gallery*

gasorin ガソリン *gasoline*

gasorin ponpu ガソリン・ポンプ *fuel pump*

gasorin sutando ガソリン・スタンド *gas station*

gasu ガス *gas*

gāze ガーゼ *gauze*

gei bā ゲイバー *gay bar*

geijutsuka 芸術家 *artist*

geka i 外科医 *surgeon*

gekijō 劇場 *theater*

genki 元気 *fine*

genkinka suru 現金化する *to cash*

genzō suru 現像する *to develop (film)*

geri 下痢 *diarrhea*

getsuyōbi 月曜日 *Monday*

gezai 下剤 *laxative*

gin 銀 *silver*

ginkō 銀行 *bank*

Girisha no ギリシャの *Greek (adj.)*

giya ギヤ *gears*

go 碁 *Japanese board game*

go hyaku guramu 五百グラム *half kilogram (500 grams)*

goban to goishi 碁盤と碁石 *go board and stones*

gofukuya 呉服屋 *kimono store*

gogatsu 五月 *May*

gogo 午後 *afternoon*

gohan ご飯 *cooked rice/meal*

Gomennasai. ご免なさい。 *Excuse me. (forgiveness)*

___ **goro** ___ 頃 *around
(approximate time)*

gorufu ゴルフ *golf*

gorufu bōru ゴルフ・ボール
golf ball

gorufu kōsu ゴルフ・コース
golf course

gorufu kurabu ゴルフ・
クラブ *golf clubs*

gorufu o suru ゴルフをする
to play golf

goshujin 御主人 *husband
(someone else's)*

Gūgurupurasu グーグルプラス
Google+

gunjin 軍人 *military
(personnel)*

gurasu グラス *glass*

gurei no グレイの *gray*

gurēpufurūtsu グレープ
フルーツ *grapefruit*

gurēpufurūtsu jūsu グレープ
フルーツ・ジュース
grapefruit juice

gurīn no グリーンの *green*

gurīn sha グリーン車 *first
class (train)*

gurūpu tsuā グループ・
ツアー *group tour*

gyōji 行司 *sumo judge*

gyū no hikiniku 牛のひき肉
ground beef

gyūniku 牛肉 *beef*

gyūnyū 牛乳 *milk*

H

ha burashi 歯ブラシ
toothbrush

ha ita 歯いた *toothache*

ha no tsumemono 歯のつめ
もの *filling (tooth)*

hachigatsu 八月 *August*

hada 肌 *skin*

hadagi 肌着 *undershirt*

hadeyaka na はでやかな
bright

hagaki 葉書 *postcard*

haha 母 *mother (your own)*

hai はい *yes*

Hai, okagesama de. はい、お
かげさまで。*Fine, thank you.*

Hai, sō desu. はい、そうです。
Yes, it is.

haikingu ハイキング *hiking*

haikingu kōsu ハイキング・
コース *hiking trail*

haioku ハイオク *high
octane (gas)*

haisha 歯医者 *dentist*

haiyā ハイヤー *hire (taxis,
limousines)*

hajimaru 始まる *to start
(v.i.)*

**Hajimemashite. Dōzo
yoroshiku.** はじめまして。ど
うぞよろしく。*How do you do?*

**Hajimemashite. Kochira
koso yoroshiku.** はじめま
して。こちらこそよろしく。
How do you do? (reply)

hajimete 初めて *first time*

Hajimete, ome ni kakarimasu.
初めて、おめにかかります。
Pleased to meet you.

hakike 吐き気 *nausea*

hako ni irete 箱に入れて
boxed

hakubutsukan 博物館
museum

hamaguri はまぐり *clams*

hamaki 葉巻 *cigars*

hamu ハム *ham*

han nichi 半日 *a half day*

han sode 半そで *short sleeves*

hana 鼻 *nose*

hana 花 *flower*

hanamichi 花道 *Kabuki
runway*

hanaya 花屋 *florist*

hanbāgā ハンバーガー
hamburger

hanbāgu sutēki ハンバーグ・
ステーキ *hamburger steak*

hanbai bu 販売部 *sales
department*

handobaggu ハンドバッグ
purse
handoru ハンドル *steering
wheel*
hangaya 版画屋 *woodblock
print shop*
hankagai 繁華街 *downtown
area*
hanmā ハンマー *hammer*
hare 晴れ *clear sky*
hareta はれた *swollen*
hari ryōji 針療治
acupuncture
hari no ryōjishi 針の療治師
acupuncturist
hariko zaiku 張り子細工
papier mâché
haru 春 *spring*
hasami はさみ *scissors*
hashi 橋 *bridge*
hashi はし *chopsticks*
hashi oki はし置き
chopstick rest
hatake 畑 *farm*
hatsuka daikon 二十日大根
radish
Hawai no ハワイの
Hawaiian
hayai 速い *fast, quick*
hayai 早い *early*
heā doraiyā ヘアー・ドライ
ヤー *hair dryer*
heā pin ヘアー・ピン
bobby pins
heā supurē ヘアー・スプレー
hair spray
heddo raito ヘッド・ライト
headlight
heddofon ヘッドフォン
headphones
hen-atsu ki 変圧器
electrical transformer
henkin 返金 *refund*
hentōsen 扁桃腺 *tonsils*
hentōsen en 扁桃腺炎
tonsillitis
herumetto ヘルメット
helmet

herusu kurabu ヘルス・
クラブ *health club*
heya 部屋 *room*
hi 日 *day*
hidari 左 *left*
higashi 東 *east*
higeki 悲劇 *tragedy*
higesori ひげそり *shave*
higesori to senpatsu ひげそ
りと洗髪 *shave and
shampoo*
hiji ひじ *elbow*
hikidasu 引き出す *to
withdraw*
hikinobashi 引き伸ばし
enlargement
hikitsuri ひきつり *cramp*
hikki yōshi 筆記用紙
writing pad
hikō jikan 飛行時間 *flying
time*
hikōjō 飛行場 *airport*
hikōki 飛行機 *airplane*
hikui ひくい *low*
himo ひも *string*
hirame 平目 *flounder*
hire niku ヒレ肉 *filet*
hireminion ヒレミニオン
filet mignon
hiroi 広い *wide*
hiru 昼 *noon*
hisho 秘書 *secretary*
hisui ひすい *jade*
hitai ひたい *forehead*
hito 人 *person*
hito ban 一晩 *overnight*
hitori ひとり *alone*
hitori (atari) 一人(当たり)
per person
hitsunyōkika i 泌尿器科医
urologist
hitsuyō da 必要だ *to need*
hitsuyō na 必要な *necessary*
hiyake 日焼け *sunburn*
hiyakedome 日焼け止め
sunscreeen
hiza ひざ *knee*
hizuke 日付 *date*

hōbā kurafuto ホーバー・クラフト *hovercraft*

hōgaku 邦楽 *Japanese traditional music*

hoho ほほ *cheek*

hōjicha ほうじ茶 *Japanese roasted tea*

hoka no 外の *another*

hoka no 外の *other*

hoken 保険 *insurance*

hokōki 歩行器 *walker*

hōkō shiji ki 方向指示器 *directional signal*

hōmu ホーム *platform*

hon 本 *book*

hontō 本当 *Really?*

hon-ya 本屋 *bookstore*

hon-yaku 翻訳 *translation*

hon-yaku suru 翻訳する *to translate*

hone 骨 *bone*

hone ga oreta 骨が折れた *fractured*

honyū bin 哺乳ビン *baby bottle*

hoo beni ほお紅 *rouge*

hōrensō ほうれん草 *spinach*

hōseki 宝石 *jewelry, stone (jewelry)*

hōseki ten 宝石店 *jewelry store*

hoshibudō 干しぶどう *raisins*

hoshii 欲しい *to want*

hoshō kin 保証金 *deposit*

hōsō yōshi 包装用紙 *wrapping paper*

hosutesu ホステス *hostess*

hōtai 包帯 *bandages*

hotate 帆立て *scallops*

hotchikisu ホッチキス *stapler*

hoteru ホテル *hotel*

hoteru no basu ホテルのバス *hotel bus*

hoteru no yoyaku kauntā ホテルの予約カウンター *hotel reservation counter*

hotto kēki ホット・ケーキ *pancakes*

hottodoggu ホットドッグ *hot dog*

hottosupotto ホットスポット *hotspot*

howaito wain ホワイト・ワイン *white wine*

hyō 表 *list*

hyōban 評判 *reputation*

hyōnō 氷のう *ice pack*

I

i 胃 *stomach*

iafon イヤフォン *earphones*

i no chōshi ga yoku nai 胃の調子がよくない *upset stomach*

ichi jikan 一時間 *per hour*

ichi nichi 一日 *a day/per day*

ichi nichi goto (ni) 一日ごと (に) *by the day*

ichiba 市場 *market*

ichigatsu 一月 *January*

ichigo いちご *strawberries*

ichimatsu moyō 市松模様 *checks (pattern)*

ichiryū no 一流の *first class*

ie 家 *house*

iemoto 家元 *headmaster*

Igirisu イギリス *England*

Igirisu jin イギリス人 *Britisher*

Igirisu no イギリスの *British*

igokochi no ii 居心地のいい *cozy*

ii desu yo いいですよ *I don't mind. (permission)*

ii いい *good, fine*

iie いいえ *no*

Iie, chigaimasu. いいえ、違います。 *No, it isn't.*

Iie, dō itashimashite. いいえ、どういたしまして。 *You're welcome.*

Iie, kekkō desu. いいえ、けっこうです。 *No thank you.*

ika いか *squid*

ike 池 *pond*

ikebana 生け花 *flower arrangement*
Ikimashō. 行きましょう。 *Let's go.*
Ikimashō ka. 行きましょうか。 *Shall we go?*
iku 行く *to go*
ikura いくら *How much money?*
inaka 田舎 *countryside*
ima 今 *now*
Ima nan ji desu ka. いま何時ですか。 *What time is it?*
ī mēru イーメール *email*
imōto 妹 *younger sister (your own)*
imōto san 妹さん *younger sister (someone else's)*
Indo no インドの *Indian (adj.)*
Indoneshia no インドネシアの *Indonesian (adj.)*
inshurin インシュリン *insulin*
Insutaguramu インスタグラム *Instragram*
insutanto kōhī インスタント・コーヒー *instant coffee*
intānetto kafe インターネット・カフェ *Internet café*
ireba 入れ歯 *denture*
iriguchi 入り口 *entrance*
Irimasen. いりません。 *I don't want it/any.*
iro 色 *color*
iro no hyō 色の表 *color chart*
iru いる *to need*
isan 胃散 *antacid*
Īsanetto イーサネット *Ethernet*
ise ebi 伊勢エビ *lobster*
isha 医者 *doctor*
ishitsubutsu gakari 遺失物係り *lost and found*
issho ni 一緒に *together*
itami 痛み *pain*
Itaria イタリア *Italy*
Itaria go イタリア語 *Italian (lang.)*

Itaria no イタリアの *Italian (adj.)*
itsu いつ *when*
itsumo いつも *always*
iwashi いわし *sardines*
iyaringu イヤリング *earrings*

J

Jā./Jā ne. じゃ。じゃあね。 *Bye (casual).*
jagaimo じゃがいも *potato*
jaketto ジャケット *jacket*
jakki ジャッキ *jack*
jamu ジャム *jam*
jan sō ジャン荘 *mahjong parlor*
jazu ジャズ *jazz*
Jeipoppu ジェイポップ *J-POP*
jerāto ジェラート *gelato*
jeru ジェル *gel*
jetto sukī ジェットスキー *jet ski*
ji 痔 *hemorrhoids*
jibun de 自分で *oneself/on one's own*
jibundori sutikku 自分撮りスティック *selfie stick*
jidaimono 時代物 *historical drama*
jidō hanbai ki 自動販売機 *vending machine*
jidō hensoku 自動変速 *automatic transmission*
jidōsha 自動車 *car*
jikabi de yaita 直火で焼いた *broiled*
jikan 時間 *hour, time*
jikan de 時間で *by the hour*
jikan dōri ni 時間通りに *on time*
jiki 磁器 *porcelain*
jiko 事故 *accident*
jiko shōkai suru 自己紹介する *to introduce (oneself)*
jikoku hyō 時刻表 *timetable*
jimaku 字幕 *subtitles (film)*
jimu ジム *gym*

jin ジン *gin*
jinja 神社 *shrine*
jinji bu 人事部 *personnel department*
jinkō kanmiryō 人工甘味料 *artificial sweetener*
jīnzu ジーンズ *jeans*
jishin 地震 *earthquake*
jisho 辞書 *dictionary*
jitensha 自転車 *bicycle, bike*
jitsuen 実演 *demonstration*
jitsugyōka 実業家 *industrialist*
jiyū seki 自由席 *unreserved seats (train)*
jiyū jikan 自由時間 *free time*
jizai supana 自在スパナ *monkey wrench*
___ jō ___城 ___ *castle*
jōen 上演 *performance*
jōgi 定規 *ruler*
jogingu ジョギング *jogging*
jogingu kōsu ジョギング・コース *jogging path*
jokō eki 除光液 *nail polish remover*
jōkyaku 乗客 *passenger*
jōriku suru 上陸する *to go ashore*
jōsai 城塞 *fortress*
josei 女性 *female, woman*
joshi yō no toire 女子用のトイレ *ladies' room*
jōtō/jōshitsu 上等/上質 *good quality*
jūgatsu 十月 *October*
jūdō 柔道 *judo*
jūhakkin 18金 *18 karats*
jūichigatsu 十一月 *November*
jūnigatsu 十二月 *December*
junkin 純金 *pure gold, solid gold*
ju-nyū 授乳 *nursing*
jūsho 住所 *address*
jūsu ジュース *juice*
jūyon kin 14金 *14 karats*

K

kabā chāji カバー・チャージ *cover charge*
kabuki 歌舞伎 *Japanese classical drama*
kādigan カーディガン *cardigan*
kado 角 *corner*
kadō 華道 *flower arrangement*
kaeru 変える／代える／替える／換える *to change*
kafe カフェ *café*
kafein resu kōhī カフェインレスコーヒー *decaffeinated coffee*
kafun shō 花粉症 *hay fever*
kafusu botan カフス・ボタン *cufflinks*
kagaku chōmiryō 化学調味料 *MSG (monosodium glutamate)*
kagami 鏡 *mirror*
kagi 鍵 *key*
kago かご *basket*
kagu 家具 *furniture*
kaichū dentō 懐中電灯 *flashlight*
kaidan 階段 *stairs*
kaigan 海岸 *beach, coast, seashore*
kaikei 会計 *bill, check*
kaikyō no jiin 回教の寺院 *mosque*
kaimono 買い物 *shopping*
kaisha 会社 *company*
kaisha no jūyaku 会社の重役 *company executive*
kaisha no shachō 会社の社長 *company president*
kaisoku 快速 *express train*
kakato かかと *heel*
kake jiku 掛け軸 *scroll*
kaki 柿 *persimmon*
kaki かき *oysters*
kakitome 書留 *registered mail*

kaku 書く *to write*
kaku 描く *to paint (art)*
kakuteru カクテル *cocktails*
kakuteru raunji カクテル・ラウンジ *cocktail lounge*
Kamaimasen. かまいません。 *I don't mind./It doesn't matter.*
kamera カメラ *camera*
kameraya カメラ屋 *camera shop, photography shop*
kami no ke 髪の毛 *hair*
kamiomutsu 紙おむつ *diapers (disposable)*
kamisori かみそり *razor*
kamisori no ha カミソリの刃 *razor blades*
kamiya 紙屋 *paper shop*
kamukōdā カムコーダー *camcorder*
kan かん *can*
Kanada カナダ *Canada*
Kanada jin カナダ人 *Canadian (person)*
kanai 家内 *wife (your own)*
kangei suru 歓迎する *to welcome*
kangengaku dan 管弦楽団 *orchestra*
kangoshi 看護師 *nurse*
kani かに *crab*
kanjō 勘定 *bill, check*
kankō basu 観光バス *sightseeing bus*
kankō ryokō 観光旅行 *sightseeing tour*
kankō kyaku 観光客 *tourist*
Kankoku 韓国 *Korea*
Kankoku no 韓国の *Korean (adj.)*
kanō 化膿 *infection*
kanojo ga 彼女が *she*
kanpai 乾杯 *toast (drinks)*
kansetsu 関節 *joint (body)*
kansetsu en 関節炎 *arthritis*
kansō shite iru 乾燥している *dry*

kantoku 監督 *director (sports, film)*
kantorī myūjikku カントリーミュージック *country music*
kanzō 肝臓 *liver*
kao 顔 *face*
____ kara ____ から *from ____*
karā rinsu カラー・リンス *color rinse*
kārā カーラー *curlers*
karada 体 *body*
karai からい *hot (peppery food)*
karashi からし *mustard*
karate 空手 *karate*
karatto カラット *karat*
kare ga 彼が *he*
karendā カレンダー *calendar*
karera ga 彼らが *they*
kārī カーリー *curly*
kari no tsumemono 仮のつめもの *temporary filling*
Kariforunia maki カリフォルニア巻 *California rolls*
kariru 借りる *to rent*
karui shokuji 軽い食事 *light meal*
karui 軽い *light (weight)*
kasetto カセット *cassette*
kashi pan 菓子パン *Danish pastry/sweet roll*
kashu 歌手 *singer*
kasutādo カスタード *custard*
kata 肩 *shoulder*
katamichi 片道 *one way*
katamichi kippu 片道切符 *one-way ticket*
katanaya 刀屋 *Japanese sword shop*
katarogu カタログ *catalog*
katazukeru 片付ける *to clean (tidy)*
katei yōhin 家庭用品 *housewares*
kau 買う *to buy*
kauntā カウンター *counter*
kawa 皮 *leather*
kawa 川 *river*

kayōbi 火曜日 *Tuesday*
kayumi かゆみ *itchy*
kazan 火山 *volcano*
kazari pin 飾りピン *pin (jewelry)*
kaze 風邪 *cold (head, chest)*
kaze 風 *wind*
kazoku 家族 *family*
kazu 数 *number*
ke zome 毛染め *hair color*
ke nuki 毛抜き *tweezers*
kēburu kā ケーブル・カー *cable car*
kechappu ケチャップ *ketchup*
kega けが *injury*
keihin 景品 *prize*
keikan 警官 *police officer*
keiri bu 経理部 *finance department*
keisatsu 警察 *police*
keishoku 軽食 *light meal*
keitai 携帯 *cell phone*
keitai denwa 携帯電話 *cell phone*
keitai konpo sutereo sōchi 携帯コンポステレオ装置 *portable component stereo system*
keiteki 警笛 *horn*
kēki ケーキ *cake*
Kekkō desu. けっこうです。*I don't want it/any.*
kekkon shite 結婚して *married*
ken 県 *prefecture*
ken 券 *ticket*
kenchiku 建築 *architecture*
kenchikuka 建築家 *architect*
kenchō shozaichi 県庁所在地 *prefectural capital*
kendō 剣道 *kendo (martial art)*
kenzō sareru 建造される *(to be) built*
keredomo けれども *but*
kesa けさ *this morning*
keshigomu 消しゴム *eraser*

keshiki 景色 *landscape*
keshō gi 化粧着 *robe*
keshōhin ten 化粧品店 *cosmetics shop, toiletries shop*
ketsuatsu 血圧 *blood pressure*
ki 木 *tree, wood*
kībōdo キーボード *keyboard*
kigeki 喜劇 *comedy*
kiiroi 黄色い *yellow*
kiji 生地 *fabric*
kī kādo キーカード *key card*
kikō 気候 *climate*
kimono 着物 *kimono*
kin 金 *gold*
kin mekki (no) 金メッキ(の) *gold plated*
kin-en seki 禁煙席 *no-smoking section*
kin-yōbi 金曜日 *Friday*
kinai mochikomi hin 機内持ち込み品 *carry-on*
kindai Nihon shōsetsu 近代日本小説 *modern Japanese novels*
Kindoru キンドル *Kindle*
kinko 金庫 *safe (valuables)*
kinkyū jitai 緊急事態 *emergency*
kinniku 筋肉 *muscle*
kinshi 禁止 *forbidden*
kinu 絹 *silk*
kinzoku 金属 *metal*
kippu 切符 *ticket*
kippu no hanbai ki 切符の販売機 *ticket machine (train)*
kippu uriba 切符売り場 *box office*
kippu uriba 切符売り場 *ticket window/counter*
kirei (na) きれいな *clean, pretty, beautiful*
kiro sū キロ数 *mileage*
kiro キロ *kilogram*
kiru 切る *to cut*
kiru 着る *to wear*

kisetsu 季節 *season*
kisha 汽車 *train*
kissaten 喫茶店 *Japanese coffee shop*
kita 北 *north*
kitanai きたない *dirty*
kitsui きつい *tight (clothing)*
kitte 切手 *stamps*
kizami tabako きざみタバコ *pipe tobacco*
ko bin 小びん *small bottle*
kō ketsuatsu 高血圧 *high blood pressure*
ko saji 小さじ *teaspoon*
kōcha 紅茶 *tea*
kodein コデイン *codeine*
kodomo 子供 *child (your own)*
kodomo 子供 *children*
kodomo fuku 子供服 *children's clothing*
kodomo fuku no mise 子供服の店 *children's clothing store*
kodomo yō no isu 子供用の椅子 *highchair*
kōen 公園 *park*
kogata sha 小型車 *small car*
kōgei 工芸 *crafts*
kōgei no mise 工芸の店 *handicrafts shop*
kōgeika 工芸家 *craftsperson*
kōhī コーヒー *coffee*
kōhī shoppu コーヒー・ショップ *coffee shop*
kohitsuji 子羊 *lamb*
koi 鯉 *carp*
koin randorī コイン・ランドリー *laundromat*
kojin yō kogitte 個人用小切手 *check (personal)*
kōka 硬貨 *coins*
kōkai 航海 *cruise*
kōkan ritsu 交換率 *exchange rate*
kōkan suru 交換する *to exchange*
koko ここ *here*

kokoa ココア *cocoa, hot chocolate*
kōkoku 広告 *ad*
kōkū bin 航空便 *airmail*
kōkū ken 航空券 *ticket (air)*
kōkū shokan 航空書簡 *aerogram*
kokuritsu kōen 国立公園 *national park*
kokusai denwa 国際電話 *international call*
kokuseki 国籍 *nationality*
kōkyō kōtsū kikan 公共交通機関 *public transportation*
komamono 小間物 *notions*
kome 米 *uncooked rice*
komori 子守 *baby-sitter*
kōn コーン *corn*
kōn furēku コーン・フレーク *corn flakes*
konban 今晩 *tonight*
konbanwa こんばんは *good evening*
konde 混んで *crowded*
kondōmu コンドーム *condom*
konnichiwa こんにちは *good afternoon*
kono この *this (adj.)*
konomu 好む *to prefer*
konpyūta rūmu コンピューター・ルーム *computer room (hotel)*
konsāto コンサート *concert*
konsāto hōru コンサート・ホール *concert hall*
konshū 今週 *this week*
kontakuto renzu コンタクト・レンズ *contact lenses*
kopī ki コピー機 *copying machine*
koppu コップ *glass (drinking)*
kore これ *this (n.)*
kōri 氷 *ice*
kōsaten 交差点 *intersection*
kōsei busshitsu 抗生物質 *antibiotics*
kōshi jima 格子じま *plaid*

koshitsu 個室 *private room (restaurant)*

koshō こしょう *pepper*

koshō shite 故障して *broken, out of order*

koshō suru 故障する *to break down*

kōshū denwa 公衆電話 *public telephone*

kōsoku dōro 高速道路 *highway*

kōsui 香水 *perfume*

kotei denwa 固定電話 *landline (telephone)*

kotejji chīzu コテッジチーズ *cottage cheese*

koten barē 古典バレー *classical ballet*

kōtsū kikan 交通機関 *transportation*

kottō hin 骨董品 *antiques*

koushi 子牛 *veal*

kowaremono こわれもの *fragile (goods)*

kowarete こわれて *broken, out of order*

koya 小屋 *cottage*

kōyō 紅葉 *autumn leaves*

kozutsumi 小包 *parcel*

kubi 首 *neck*

kuchi hige 口ひげ *mustache*

kuchibiru 口びる *lip*

kuchibuki garasu 口吹きガラス *blown glass*

kudamono 果物 *fruit*

kugatsu 九月 *September*

kukkī クッキー *cookies*

kūkō 空港 *airport*

kumori 曇り *cloudy*

kuni 国 *country (nation)*

kuōtsu no tokei クォーツの時計 *quartz watch*

kurabu sōda クラブ・ソーダ *club soda*

kurai 暗い *dark*

kurakka クラッカー *crackers*

kurashikku myūjikku クラシック・ミュージック *classical music*

kuratchi クラッチ *clutch (auto)*

kurejitto kādo クレジット・カード *credit card*

kurenjingu kurīmu クレンジング・クリーム *cleansing cream*

kuri くり *chestnuts*

kurīmu rinsu クリーム・リンス *cream rinse*

kurīninguya クリーニング屋 *dry cleaner*

kuroi 黒い *black*

kuro obi 黒帯 *black belt*

kurowassan クロワッサン *croissant*

kuru 来る *to come*

kuruma no seibishi 車の整備士 *auto mechanic*

kuruma 車 *car*

kuruma isu 車椅子 *wheelchair*

kurumi くるみ *walnut*

kusa 草 *plant*

kusari 鎖 *chain*

kushi くし *comb*

kusuri 薬 *medicine*

kusuriya 薬屋 *pharmacy*

kutsu くつ *shoes*

kutsū 苦痛 *pain*

kutsu himo くつひも *shoelaces*

kutsu no shūriya くつの修理屋 *shoe repair shop*

kutsu o nugu くつをぬぐ *to take off one's shoes*

kutsushita くつ下 *socks*

kutsuya くつ屋 *shoe store*

kutsuzoko くつ底 *sole*

kyabarē キャバレー *cabaret*

kyabetsu キャベツ *cabbage*

kyaburetā キャブレター *carburetor*

kyadī キャディー *caddy*

kyandī キャンディー *candy*

kyanpu キャンプ *camping*

kyanpu jō キャンプ場 *camping site*

kyō 今日 *today*

kyō no 今日の *for today*

kyōju 教授 *professor*

kyōkai 教会 *church*

kyōshi 教師 *teacher*

kyōsō kyoku 協奏曲 *concerto*

kyū shigai 旧市街 *old town*

kyūbyō 急病 *sudden illness*

kyūden 宮殿 *palace*

kyūkō 急行 *ordinary express*

kyūkyūbako 救急箱 *first-aid kit*

kyūkyūsha 救急車 *ambulance*

kyūri きゅうり *cucumber*

kyūseki 旧跡 *historical sites*

kyūsu 急須 *teapot*

M

machi 町 *town*

machiai shitsu 待合い室 *waiting room*

machigai 間違い *error*

machigatta 間違った *wrong*

machinē マチネー *matinee*

mado 窓 *window*

madogawa 窓がわ *by the window*

mae 前 *front*

mae motte 前もって *in advance*

mae no 前の *forward*

maegami 前髪 *bangs*

māgarin マーガリン *margarine*

magaru 曲がる *to turn*

maguro まぐろ *tuna*

maikuro kasetto rekōdā マイクロ・カセット・レコーダー *microcassette recorder*

mainichi no 毎日の *daily*

mājan マージャン *Chinese tile game (mahjong)*

mājan no setto マージャンの セット *mahjong set*

makajiki まかじき *swordfish*

makige 巻き毛 *curly*

makijaku 巻尺 *tape measure*

makura 枕 *pillow*

manējā マネージャー *manager*

mangō マンゴー *mango*

manikyua マニキュア *manicure*

manikyua eki マニキュア液 *nail polish*

manikyua otoshii マニキュア 落とし *nail polish remover*

mannenhitsu 万年筆 *fountain pen*

mantan ni suru 満タンにする *to fill (gas tank)*

marui 丸い *round*

masshu poteto マッシュ・ポ テト *mashed potatoes*

masshurūmu マッシュルーム *mushrooms*

massugu まっすぐ *straight (direction)*

masu ます *trout*

masutādo マスタード *mustard*

mata また *also*

mata no tsukene 股の付け根 *groin*

mata wa または *or*

matchi マッチ *matches*

matsu 待つ *to wait*

matsubazue 松葉杖 *crutch(es)*

mausu マウス *mouse*

mawari michi 回り道 *detour*

mayonēzu マヨネーズ *mayonnaise*

mayuzumi まゆずみ *eyebrow pencil*

mazui まずい *awful-tasting*

me 目 *eye*

mēdo メード *maid*

megane 眼鏡 *eyeglasses*

meganeya 眼鏡屋 *optician*

meisai sho 明細書 *itemized bill*

meishi 名刺 *card (business, personal)*

meisho 名所 *points of interest*

Mekishiko メキシコ *Mexico*

Mekishiko no メキシコの *Mexican (adj.)*

memorī kādo メモリー・カード *memory card*

menyū メニュー *menu*

meron メロン *melon*

mēru adoresu メールアドレス *email address*

messēji メッセージ *message*

mētā メーター *meter (taxi)*

mezamashi dokei 目覚まし時計 *alarm clock*

mibun shōmei sho 身分証明書 *I.D.*

michi 道 *road, path*

michi ni mayou 道に迷う *to be lost*

midiamu ミディアム *medium (meat)*

midiamu rea ミディアム・レア *medium rare (meat)*

midori iro no みどりいろの *green*

migaku みがく *to polish*

migi 右 *right (direction)*

mihari 見張り *lifeguard*

mijikai 短い *short*

mikan みかん *mandarin orange/tangerine*

mikisā ミキサー *blender*

mikkusu sando ミックスサンド *assorted sandwiches*

mimi 耳 *ear*

mimi gusuri 耳薬 *ear drops*

mimono みもの *attractions*

mimoza ミモザ *mimosa*

minami 南 *south*

minato 港 *harbor, port*

mineraru wōtā ミネラル・ウォーター *mineral water*

mingei 民芸 *folk art*

mingei gangu 民芸玩具 *Japanese folk toys*

mingeiya 民芸屋 *folkware shop*

minikui みにくい *ugly*

minshuku 民宿 *Japanese guest house*

miru 見る *to see*

miruku ミルク *cream/milk*

miruku sēki ミルクセーキ *milkshake*

miseru 見せる *to show*

misoshiru みそしる *bean paste soup*

misuterī ミステリー *mystery*

mite mawaru 見て回る *to look around*

mītobōru ミートボール *meatballs*

mitsumori 見積もり *estimate*

mizo みぞ *ditch*

mizu 水 *water*

mizu nomiba 水飲み場 *water fountain*

mizugi 水着 *bathing suit*

mizuumi 湖 *lake*

mo も *also*

mō ichido もう一度 *again, repeat it*

mochiron もちろん *of course*

mōchō en 盲腸炎 *appendicitis*

modan barē モダン・バレー *modern ballet*

modan dansu モダン・ダンス *modern dance*

modan myūjikku モダン・ミュージック *modern music*

modan na モダンな *modern*

modemu モデム *modem*

mōfu 毛布 *blanket*

mokuhanga 木版画 *woodblock prints*

mokusei no 木製の *wooden*

mokuteki 目的 *purpose*

mokuyōbi 木曜日 *Thursday*

momen 木綿 *cotton (fabric)*

momo 桃 *peach*

mondai 問題 *problem*

mongen 門限 *curfew*

monorēru モノレール *monorail*

moreru もれる *to leak (v.i.)*

mori 森 *forest*

moriawase 盛り合わせ *assorted food*

moshimoshi もしもし *hello (telephone/getting someone's attention)*

mosuku モスク *mosque*

moto no mama 元のまま *original*

motto ii もっといい *better*

moyori no 最寄りの *nearest*

moyōshimono 催し物 *entertainment*

muen gasorin 無鉛ガソリン *unleaded (gasoline)*

muji 無地 *solid color*

mune 胸 *chest*

munōyaku 無農薬 *no chemicals*

mura 村 *village*

murasaki iro no 紫色の *purple*

musen ran 無線LAN *Wi-Fi*

mushi megane 虫めがね *magnifier*

mushi sasare 虫刺され *insect bite*

mushi yoke no kusuri 虫よけの薬 *insect repellent*

mushiba 虫歯 *cavity*

mūsu ムース *mousse*

musuko 息子 *son (your own)*

musuko san 息子さん *son (someone else's)*

musume 娘 *daughter (your own)*

muzukashii 難しい *difficult*

myaku 脈 *pulse*

myūjikaru ミュージカル *musical*

N

naga sode 長そで *long sleeves*

nagai 長い *long*

nagame 眺め *view*

naifu ナイフ *knife*

nairon ナイロン *nylon*

naisen 内線 *extension number*

naito kurabu ナイト・クラブ *nightclub*

nakushita なくした *lost*

nakusu なくす *to lose*

nama なま *raw*

nama bīru 生ビール *draft beer*

nama hamu 生ハム *prosciutto*

namae 名前 *name*

nami 波 *waves (water)*

nanchō 難聴 *hearing impaired*

nan ji 何時 *what time*

nani 何 *what*

nanshi 難視 *visually impaired*

naoseru 直せる *fixable*

naosu 直す *to alter (clothing), to fix*

napukin ナプキン *napkin*

Naruhodo. なるほど。*Oh, I see.*

nashi なし *Japanese pear*

nasu なす *eggplant*

natsu 夏 *summer*

nattsu ナッツ *nuts*

naya 納屋 *barn*

naze なぜ *why*

nedan 値段 *price*

neiru ネイル *manicure*

neiru āto ネイルアート *manicure design*

neiru saron ネイルサロン *nail salon*

neji mawashi ねじ回し *screwdriver*

nekkuresu ネックレス *necklace*

nekutai ネクタイ *tie*

nekutarin ネクタリン *nectarine*

nemui ねむい *sleepy*

nenrei seigen 年齢制限 *age limit*

nenza suru ねんざする *to sprain*

neri ha migaki 練り歯みがき *toothpaste*

neru 寝る *to sleep*
netsu 熱 *fever, temperature*
____ **ni** ____ に *in* ____
____ **ni** ____ に *to* ____
　(*direction/location*)
nibui 鈍い *dull*
nichiyōbi 日曜日 *Sunday*
nigatsu 二月 *February*
Nihon dentō no gēmu 日本伝
　統のゲーム *Japanese*
　traditional games
Nihon ga 日本画 *Japanese*
　painting
Nihon go 日本語 *Japanese*
　(*lang.*)
Nihon go no bunpō no hon
　日本語の文法の本 *Japanese*
　grammar book
Nihon ningyō 日本人形
　Japanese dolls
Nihon ningyōya 日本人形屋
　Japanese doll shop
Nihon no koten 日本の古典
　Japanese classics
Nihon shokuhin 日本食品
　Japanese food
Nihon teien 日本庭園
　Japanese gardens
Nihon tō 日本刀 *Japanese*
　swords
nijūni kin 22金 *22 karats*
nijūyon kin 24金 *24 karats*
nikai no shōmen (no seki)
　二階の正面(の席) *balcony*
　(*theater*)
niku dango 肉だんご *meatballs*
nikuya 肉屋 *butcher*
nimotsu 荷物 *baggage,*
　package, luggage
nimotsu no okidai 荷物の置
　き台 *luggage rack*
ningyō 人形 *puppets*
ninjin 人参 *carrots*
ninki ga aru 人気がある
　popular
ninniku にんにく *garlic*
ninshin chū 妊娠中 *pregnant*
Nippon/Nihon 日本 *Japan*

nishi 西 *west*
nita 煮た *boiled*
niwa 庭 *garden*
niwatori にわとり *chicken*
____ **no ue ni** ____の上に
　on ____
____ **no keiko** ____のけい古
　____ *practice*
____ **no aida ni** ____の間に
　during
____ **no chikaku ni** ____の近
　くに *nearby*
____ **no ato de** ____のあとで
　after ____
____ **no ue ni** ____の上に
　up ____
____ **no mae ni** ____の前に
　before
____ **no naka ni** ____の中に
　inside
____ **no shita ni** ____ の下に
　down
____ **no soto ni** ____の外に
　outside ____
nō 能 *Japanese masked*
　dance-drama
nō men 能面 *Noh masks*
noboru 登る *to climb*
nodo のど *throat*
nodo ga kawaite imasu
　のどがかわいています *thirsty*
nohara 野原 *fields*
nomi mizu 飲み水 *drinking*
　water
nomimono 飲み物 *drinks*
nomu 飲む *to drink*
non sutoppu ノン・ストップ
　nonstop flight
nori のり *glue*
nori のり *seaweed*
nori o kikasete のりをきかせ
　て *starched (laundry)*
norikaeru 乗り換える *to*
　change (transportation)
noritsugi bin 乗りつぎ便
　connecting flight
noru 乗る *to get on*
nōto ノート *notebook*

nōtobukku konpyūta ノートブック・コンピュータ notebook computer

nūdoru sūpu ヌードル・スープ noodle soup

nukarumi ぬかるみ mud

nuno 布 fabric

nurimono 塗り物 lacquerware

nusumarete 盗まれて stolen

nuu ぬう to sew

Nyūjīrando ニュージーランド New Zealand

nyūjō ryō 入場料 admission fee

nyūsu kankei no zasshi ニュース関係の雑誌 news magazines

O

ō bin 大びん large bottle

____ o kudasai ____をください _(n.)_ , please.

____ o onegai shimasu ____をお願いします _(n.)_ , please.

ō saji 大さじ tablespoon

ō toro 大とろ very fatty tuna

ō yasuuri 大安売り special bargain sale

oai suru お会いする to meet (polite)

oba おば aunt (your own)

ōbā オーバー overcoat

ōbā hīto オーバー・ヒート overheated

ōbaru neiru オーバルネイル oval (nail)

obasan おばさん aunt (someone else's)

obāsan おばあさん grandmother (someone else's)

obenjo お便所 bathroom

obentō お弁当 lunch box (box lunch)

ocha お茶 Japanese tea

ōdekoron オーデコロン cologne

odotte おどって dancing

ōeru オーエル office worker (female)

ofisu オフィス office

ōfuku 往復 round trip

ōfuku ken 往復券 round trip ticket

ofuro お風呂 bath, bathtub

ōgata sha 大型車 large car

ogawa 小川 stream

Ogenki desu ka. お元気ですか。How are you?

ōgi 扇 fan

ohana お花 flower arrangement

ohayō gozaimasu おはようございます good morning

Oikutsu desu ka. おいくつですか。How old are you?

oinori suru お祈りする to pray

oishii おいしい delicious

oji おじ uncle (your own)

ojigi おじぎ bow (n.)

ojigi suru おじぎする to bow

ojisan おじさん uncle (someone else's)

ojiisan おじいさん grandfather (someone else's)

ojōsan お嬢さん daughter (someone else's)

oka 丘 hill

okaeshi おかえし return gift

okan 悪寒 chill

okane お金 money

okāsan お母さん mother (someone else's)

okashiya お菓子屋 candy store, confectionary, pastry shop

ōkesutora オーケストラ orchestra

ōkii 大きい big, large

okosan お子さん child (someone else's)

okuru 送る to send

okusan 奥さん *wife (someone else's)*

omaneki suru お招きする *to invite (polite)*

omatsuri お祭り *festival*

omen お面 *masks*

omise お店 *store*

omiyage おみやげ *gift, souvenir*

omiyageya おみやげ屋 *souvenir shop*

omo na mimono 主なみもの *main attractions*

omochaya おもちゃ屋 *toy store*

omoi 重い *heavy*

omoshiroi おもしろい *interesting, fun*

omou 思う *to think*

omuretsu オムレツ *omelet*

onaji 同じ *same*

onaka おなか *abdomen*

onaka ga, ippai desu おなかが、いっぱいです *full (I'm full)*

onaka ga, suite imasu おなかが、すいています *hungry*

onēsan お姉さん *elder sister (someone else's)*

ongaku 音楽 *music*

oniisan お兄さん *elder brother (someone else's)*

onikisu オニキス *onyx*

onion sūpu オニオン・スープ *onion soup*

onna 女 *female, woman*

onna no hito 女の人 *female, woman*

onsen 温泉 *hot springs*

opera オペラ *opera*

opera gekijō オペラ劇場 *opera house*

Oranda jin オランダ人 *Dutch (person)*

orenji オレンジ *orange*

orenji jūsu オレンジ・ジュース *orange juice*

oreta 折れた *broken*

orību yu オリーブ油 *olive oil*

origami 折り紙 *origami paper*

orijinaru オリジナル *original*

Orinpikku オリンピック *Olympics*

oriru 降りる *to get off*

osake お酒 *drinks (alcoholic)*

osake お酒 *Japanese rice wine*

osara お皿 *plate*

osatsu お札 *bills (currency)*

osenbe おせんべ *rice crackers*

osenkō お線香 *incense*

oshaburi おしゃぶり *pacifier*

oshieru 教える *to tell*

oshime おしめ *diapers*

oshiri fuki おしりふき *baby wipes*

oshiro お城 *castle*

oshiroi おしろい *face powder*

osoi おそい *late, slow*

Ōsutoraria オーストラリア *Australia*

otearai お手洗い *bathroom*

otera お寺 *Buddhist temple, temple*

otoko (no hito) 男(の人) *male, man*

ōtomachikku オートマチック *automatic transmission*

ōtomīru オートミール *oatmeal*

otōsan お父さん *father (someone else's)*

otōto 弟 *younger brother (your own)*

otōto san 弟さん *younger brother (someone else's)*

otsukemono お漬け物 *pickles*

otsuri おつり *change (money)*

Owarimashita. 終わりました。*It's over./I'm finished.*

owaru 終わる *to finish (v.i.)*

oya yubi 親指 *thumb*

oyasuminasai おやすみなさい *good night*

oyogu 泳ぐ *to swim*

oyu お湯 *hot water*
ozashiki お座敷 *Japanese room (restaurant)*

P

pachinko パチンコ *Japanese pinball*
pachinko dama パチンコ玉 *pachinko balls*
pachinkoya パチンコ屋 *pachinko parlor*
pafē パフェー *parfait*
pai パイ *pie*
painappuru パイナップル *pineapple*
painappuru jūsu パイナップル・ジュース *pineapple juice*
paipu パイプ *pipe*
pāma パーマ *permanent wave*
pan パン *bread*
pan-ya パン屋 *bakery*
panda パンダ *panda*
panku パンク *flat tire*
Pararinpikku パラリンピック *Paralympics*
pāru パール *pearls*
pasupōto パスポート *passport*
pate パテ *paté*
pedikyua ペディキュア *pedicure*
penchi ペンチ *pliers*
pendanto ペンダント *pendant*
piasu no iyaringu ピアスのイヤリング *earrings for pierced ears*
pīman ピーマン *green pepper*
pīnattsu ピーナッツ *peanuts*
pinku ピンク *pink*
pinpon ピンポン *ping pong*
poketto ban no jisho ポケット版の辞書 *pocket dictionary*
pōku choppu ポーク・チョップ *pork chop*
poppukōn ポップコーン *popcorn*
popyurā songu ポピュラー・ソング *popular songs*

poriesuteru ポリエステル *polyester*
Porutogaru no ポルトガルの *Portuguese (adj.)*
pōtā ポーター *porter*
pōtaburu purintā ポータブルプリンター *portable printer*
pōtaburu rajio ポータブル・ラジオ *portable radio*
pōtaburu sukyanā ポータブルスキャナー *portable scanner*
poteto ポテト *potato*
potetochippu ポテトチップ *potato chips*
purachina プラチナ *platinum*
puragu no adaputā プラグのアダプター *adapter plug*
puramu プラム *plum*
purasuchikku プラスチック *plastic*
purein sōda プレイン・ソーダ *club soda*
purin プリン *pudding*
purintā プリンター *printer*
purinto プリント *print (pattern)*
purinto yōshi プリント用紙 *printing paper*
purosekko プロセッコ *prosecco*
puro yakyū プロ野球 *professional baseball*
pūru プール *swimming pool*

R

rabi ラビ *rabbi*
radisshu ラディシュ *radish*
Rain ライン *LINE (social media)*
raisu ライス *rice (Western)*
raitā ライター *cigarette lighter*
rajio ラジオ *radio*
rajio kyoku ラジオ局 *radio station*
raketto ラケット *racket*

rāmen ラーメン *Chinese-style noodles*

ramu choppu ラム・チョップ *lamb chop*

ranpu ランプ *lamp*

rasshu awā ラッシュ・アワー *rush hour*

rea レア *rare (meat)*

rebā レバー *liver*

reddo wain レッド・ワイン *red wine*

regyurā レギュラー *regular (gas)*

reibō 冷房 *air conditioner*

reihai 礼拝 *religious service*

rein kōto レイン・コート *raincoat*

rekishi 歴史 *history*

rekishi no hon 歴史の本 *history books*

rekkā sha レッカー車 *tow truck*

rekōdo レコード *record*

rekōdo arubamu レコード・アルバム *record album*

rekōdo purēyā レコード・プレーヤー *record player*

rekōdoya レコード屋 *record store*

remon レモン *lemon*

remon merenge レモン・メレンゲ *lemon meringue pie*

remon shābetto レモン・シャーベット *lemon sherbet*

remonēdo レモネード *lemonade*

ren-ai mono 恋愛物 *romance (movie)*

renrakusen 連絡船 *ferry*

rentakā no eigyōsho レンタカーの営業所 *car rental agency*

rentogen レントゲン *X-ray*

renzu レンズ *lens, lenses*

reshīto レシート *receipt*

ressha 列車 *train*

ressun レッスン *lesson*

resutoran レストラン *restaurant*

retasu レタス *lettuce*

rifuto リフト *ski lift*

rikishi 力士 *sumo wrestlers*

rikō na りこうな *intelligent*

rimujin basu リムジン・バス *limousine bus*

ringo りんご *apple*

ringo jūsu リンゴ・ジュース *apple juice*

Rinkutoin リンクトイン *LinkedIn*

rinneru リンネル *linen*

rippa (na) 立派(な) *magnificent*

risuto リスト *list*

rittoru リットル *liter*

robī ロビー *lobby*

rōbu ローブ *robe*

robusutā ロブスター *lobster*

rōfatto miruku ローファット・ミルク *lowfat milk*

rojō chūsha 路上駐車 *street parking*

rokkotsu ろっ骨 *rib*

rokku myūjikku ロック・ミュージック *rock'n'roll*

rokku suru ロックする *to lock*

rokugatsu 六月 *June*

rōru pan ロール・パン *rolls (bread)*

Roshia go ロシア語 *Russian (lang.)*

Roshia no ロシアの *Russian (adj.)*

rōsuto bīfu ロースト・ビーフ *roast beef*

rōsuto ni shita ローストにした *roasted*

rubī ルビー *ruby*

rūmu sābisu ルーム・サービス *room service*

ryōgae jo 両替所 *money exchange*

ryōji kan 領事館 *consulate*

ryokan 旅館 *Japanese inn*

ryoken 旅券 *passport*

ryoken bangō 旅券番号 *passport number*
ryōkin 料金 *fare, rate*
ryokō 旅行 *trip*
ryokō annai jo 旅行案内所 *tourist information center*
ryokō dairi ten 旅行代理店 *travel agency*
ryokō kaban 旅行かばん *luggage*
ryokō keikaku 旅行計画 *itinerary*
ryokō kogitte 旅行小切手 *traveler's check*
ryokō yō no mezamashi dokei 旅行用の目覚まし時計 *travel alarm clock*
ryokucha 緑茶 *Japanese green tea*
ryokyaku 旅客 *passenger*
ryōri suru 料理する *to cook*
ryōri no shisetsu 料理の施設 *cooking facilities*
ryōshūsho 領収書 *receipt*
ryūkan 流感 *flu*

S

Sā ___ さあ___ *Let's ___*
sābisu ryō サービス料 *service charge*
sādin サーディン *sardines*
sadō 茶道 *tea ceremony*
sadō no ochawan/chawan 茶道のお茶碗／茶碗 *tea bowl*
safaia サファイア *sapphire*
sāfu bōdo サーフ・ボード *surf board*
sai kakunin suru 再確認する *to reconfirm*
___ sai desu. ___歳です。 *I'm ___ years old.*
saiensu fikushon サイエンス・フィクション *science fiction*
saifu さいふ *wallet*

saigo no shō 最後のショー *last show*
saikuringu サイクリング *bicycling*
saikuringu kōsu サイクリング・コース *bicycling course*
saisho no shō 最初のショー *first show*
saitei ryōkin 最低料金 *minimum charge*
saizu サイズ *measurements, size*
sakana 魚 *fish*
sakana tsuri 魚釣り *fishing*
sakanaya 魚屋 *fish market*
sakaya 酒屋 *liquor store*
sakazuki 盃 *sake cup*
sake さけ *salmon*
sake 酒 *Japanese rice wine*
sakka 作家 *writer*
sakkā サッカー *soccer*
sakkā no kyōgi jō サッカーの競技場 *soccer stadium*
sakkā no shiai サッカーの試合 *soccer match*
sakura 桜 *cherry blossoms*
sakuranbo さくらんぼ *cherries*
same さめ *sharks*
sāmosutatto サーモスタット *thermostat (car)*
samui 寒い *cold (weather, climate)*
___ san ___さん *Mr./Mrs./Miss/Ms.*
sandaru サンダル *sandals*
sandē サンデー *sundae*
sandoitchi サンドイッチ *sandwich*
sangatsu 三月 *March*
sanguria サングリア *sangria*
sangurasu サングラス *sunglasses*
sanmyaku 山脈 *mountain range*
sanpatsu 散髪 *haircut*
santan rōshon サンタン・ローション *suntan lotion*
sarada サラダ *salad*

sarami sōsēji サラミ・ソーセージ *salami*

sararīman サラリーマン *office worker (male)*

sashimi 刺身 *raw fish (thinly sliced)*

satō 砂糖 *sugar*

satsuma imo さつまいも *sweet potato*

sauna サウナ *sauna*

sayaingen さやいんげん *string beans*

sayōnara さようなら *goodbye*

sebone 背骨 *spine*

seibu geki 西部劇 *western (film)*

seigen 制限 *limit*

seijika 政治家 *politician*

seinen gappi 生年月日 *birthdate*

seiri napukin 生理ナプキン *sanitary napkins*

seisō 正装 *formal clothing*

seiyō shokuhin 西洋食品 *Western food*

seki せき *cough*

seki 席 *seat*

sekidome doroppu せきどめドロップ *cough drops*

sekidome shiroppu せきどめシロップ *cough syrup*

sekken 石けん *soap*

semai せまい *narrow*

sen 線 *line, track (train)*

senaka 背中 *back (body)*

senkō 線香 *incense*

senmen dai 洗面台 *bathroom sink*

sensei 先生 *teacher*

sentaku no sābisu 洗濯のサービス *laundry service*

sentakumono 洗濯物 *laundry (clothes)*

sentakuya 洗濯屋 *laundry (shop)*

serori セロリ *celery*

serotēpu セロテープ *Scotch tape*

sēru セール *on sale*

sētā セーター *sweater*

setchakuzai 接着剤 *glue*

setomono 瀬戸物 *china*

setomonoya 瀬戸物屋 *ceramics store/shop*

setsumei suru 説明する *to explain*

setto rōshon セット・ローション *setting lotion*

shābetto シャーベット *sherbet*

shabu shabu しゃぶしゃぶ *beef cooked in broth*

shanpinion シャンピニオン *mushrooms*

shanpū シャンプー *shampoo*

shareta しゃれた *fancy*

shashin 写真 *photograph, picture*

shashin o toru 写真をとる *to take a picture*

shatoru basu シャトル・バス *shuttle bus*

shawā シャワー *shower*

shēbingu rōshon シェービング・ローション *shaving lotion*

shi 市 *city*

shiai 試合 *ball game*

shiatsu 指圧 *acupressure*

shiatsu shi 指圧師 *acupressurist*

shichaku shitsu 試着室 *dressing room*

shichaku suru 試着する *to try on*

shichigatsu 七月 *July*

shīdī シーディー *CD*

shīdī purēyā シーディー・プレーヤー *CD player*

shigatsu 四月 *April*

shigoto 仕事 *business*

shigoto no ryokō 仕事の旅行 *business trip*

shiitake しいたけ *shiitake mushrooms*

shikakui 四角い *square*

shiki 四季 *four seasons*

shikkarōru シッカロール
talcum powder

shikki 漆器 *lacquerware*

shikyū 至急 *urgent*

shima 島 *island*

shima menō しまめのう *onyx*

shima moyō しま模様 *stripes*

shimaru 閉まる *to close (v.i.)*

shimei 氏名 *name*

shimeru 締める *to tighten*

shimeru 閉める *to close (v.t.)*

shimette iru 湿っている
humid, damp

shimin 市民 *citizen*

shinai 市内 *outside line
(phone)*

shinai denwa 市内電話 *local
call*

shinbun 新聞 *newspaper*

shinbun uriba 新聞売り場
newsstand

shindai sha 寝台車
sleeping car

shinfonī シンフォニー
symphony

shinju 真珠 *pearls*

shinia シニア *senior citizens*

shinkansen 新幹線 *super
express train*

shinpu 神父 *priest*

shinsen na 新鮮な *fresh*

shinsetsu na 親切な *kind
(adj.)*

shinshi fuku 紳士服 *men's
clothing*

shinshi fuku no mise 紳士服
の店 *men's clothing store*

shintō no gishiki 神道の儀式
Shinto ceremony

shinzō 心臓 *heart*

shinzō byō 心臓病 *heart
disease*

shinzō mahi 心臓麻痺 *heart
attack*

shio 塩 *salt*

shippō yaki 七宝焼 *cloisonné*

shiraberu 調べる *to check
(examine)*

shiriaru シリアル *cereal*

shiro kuro (no) 白黒(の)
black-and-white

shiroi 白い *white*

shiroppu シロップ *syrup*

shiruku シルク *silk*

shiso しそ *Japanese mint*

shita 舌 *tongue*

shitagi 下着 *underwear*

shitateya 仕立て屋 *tailor*

shitsū 歯痛 *toothache*

shitsumon 質問 *question*

shitsunaigaku 室内楽
chamber music

Shitsurei shimasu. 失礼します。
Excuse me. (forgiveness)

shīzā sarada シーザー・サラダ
Caesar salad

shizen (shokuhin) 自然(食品)
natural (food)

shizuka (na) 静か(な) *quiet*

shō ショー *show (stage, floor)*

shō 小 *small (size)*

shōchū 焼酎 *shochu*

shōdokuyaku 消毒薬
antiseptic

shōga しょうが *ginger*

shōgai bu 渉外部 *public
relations department*

shōgaisha 障害者 *disabled*

shōgi 将棋 *Japanese board
game*

shōgi ban to koma 将棋盤と
駒 *shogi board and pieces*

shohōsen 処方箋
prescription

shōka furyō 消化不良
indigestion

shōkai suru 紹介する *to
introduce*

shōkakika no isha 消化器科の
医者 *gastroenterologist*

shōken torihiki jo 証券取引所
stock exchange

shokudō 食堂 *dining room*

shokudō sha 食堂車 *dining
car*

shokugyō 職業 *occupation*

shokuji 食事 *meal*

shokuji no sābisu 食事のサービス *meal service*

shokuryōhin ten 食料品店 *grocery store*

shomei 署名 *signature*

shōnika i 小児科医 *pediatrician*

shoppingu ショッピング *shopping*

shoppingu ākēdo ショッピング・アーケード *shopping arcade*

shoppingu gai ショッピング街 *shopping area*

shorui 書類 *documents*

shōsetsu 小説 *novel*

shoshinsha 初心者 *beginner*

shōten 焦点 *focus*

shōyu しょう油 *soy sauce*

shū 週 *week*

shu kōgei hin 手工芸品 *handicrafts*

shūden 終電 *last train*

shufu 主婦 *housewife*

shūhasū 周波数 *frequency (radio station)*

shujin 主人 *husband (your own)*

shukuhaku 宿泊 *lodging*

shūkyō no 宗教の *religious*

shūmatsu 週末 *weekend*

shuppatsu 出発 *departure*

shuppatsu guchi 出発口 *departure gate*

shuppatsu jikoku 出発時刻 *departure time*

shuppatsu no jikan 出発の時間 *departure time*

shūri 修理 *repair*

shūri dōgu 修理道具 *repair tools*

shūri kōjō 修理工場 *auto repair shop*

shūri suru 修理する *to repair*

shurui 種類 *type, kind*

shūsei tēpu 修正テープ *correction tape*

shuto 首都 *capital*

shutsuensha 出演者 *performer*

shūya eigyō no yakkyoku 終夜営業の薬局 *all-night pharmacy*

Sō desu ka そうですか *Really?*

Sō da to omoimasu. そうだと思います。*I think so.*

Sō desu ka. そうですか。*Is that so?*

Sō omoimasen. そう思いません。*I don't think so.*

soba そば *buckwheat noodles*

sobo 祖母 *grandmother (your own)*

sode そで *sleeves*

sofu 祖父 *grandfather (your own)*

sofuto kontakuto renzu ソフト・コンタクトレンズ *soft contact lenses*

soko そこ *there*

sokkusu ソックス *socks*

sokutatsu 速達 *special delivery*

sono その *that (adj.)*

sore それ *that (n.)*

soretomo それとも *or*

sōsēji ソーセージ *sausage*

sōsharu media ソーシャルメディア *social media*

soshite そして *and (between sentences)*

sotē ni shita ソテーにした *sauteed*

su 酢 *vinegar*

subarashii 素晴らしい *wonderful*

sugu すぐ *soon*

suichū yokusen 水中翼船 *hydrofoil*

suiden 水田 *rice paddy*

suidō 水道 *running water*

suiji yōgu 炊事用具 *cooking utensils*

suijō sukī 水上スキー *water skis*

suika 西瓜 *watermelon*

suimin yaku 睡眠薬 *sleeping pills*

suimono 吸い物 *clear soup*

suisen suru 推薦する *to recommend*

Suisu no スイスの *Swiss (adj.)*

suīto poteto スイート・ポテト *sweet potato*

suiyōbi 水曜日 *Wednesday*

suizokukan 水族館 *aquarium*

suji 筋 *plot (movie, play)*

sūjitsu 数日 *a few days*

sukāfu スカーフ *scarf*

Sukaipu スカイプ *Skype*

Sukanjinabia no スカンジナビアの *Scandinavian (adj.)*

sukāto スカート *skirt*

sukejūru スケジュール *schedule*

sukī スキー *skiing, skis*

sukī gutsu スキーぐつ *ski shoes*

sukī jō スキー場 *ski resort*

sukimu miruku スキム・ミルク *skim milk*

sukin daibingu yōgu スキン・ダイビング用具 *skin-diving equipment*

sukiyaki すき焼き *beef cooked in seasoned broth*

sukoshi 少し *a little, few, some*

sukotchi スコッチ *scotch (whisky)*

sukuea neiru スクエアネイル *square (nail)*

sukurīn スクリーン *screen*

sukyanā スキャナー *scanner*

sumaho スマホ *smart phone*

sumātofon スマートフォン *smart phone*

Sumimasen. すみません。 *I'm sorry. (apology)*

Sumimasen ga, ____. すみませんが____。*Pardon me, but ____.*

sumō 相撲 *Japanese wrestling*

sumomo すもも *plum*

sumōru スモール *small (size)*

sumu 住む *to live (reside)*

sunakku スナック *snack*

sunakku bā スナック・バー *snack bar*

Sunappuchatto スナップチャット *Snapchat*

sunīkā スニーカー *sneakers*

sunō bōdo スノー・ボード *snow board*

sūpā スーパー *supermarket/ super (gas)*

supagettī スパゲッティー *spaghetti*

supāku puragu スパーク・プラグ *spark plugs*

supea taiya スペア・タイヤ *spare tire*

Supein スペイン *Spain*

Supein go スペイン語 *Spanish (lang.)*

Supein no スペインの *Spanish (adj.)*

supiningu スピニング *spinning*

suponji スポンジ *sponge*

supōtsu kā スポーツ・カー *sports car*

supōtsu tamokuteki sha スポーツ多目的車 *SUV*

supōtsu wea スポーツウェア *sports wear*

sūpu スープ *soup*

suraido スライド *slides*

surakkusu スラックス *pants*

surippa スリッパ *slippers*

surippu スリップ *slip*

surirā スリラー *thriller, horror movie*

surōpu スロープ *ramp*

surudoi 鋭い *sharp*

sushi すし *raw fish and vinegared rice*

susumeru 勧める *to recommend*

sutairu スタイル *style*

sutēki ステーキ *steak*
sutenresu ステンレス *stainless steel*
suteppu ステップ *step (exercise)*
sutokkingu ストッキング *stockings*
sutokku ストック *ski poles*
sūtsu スーツ *suit*
suzushii 涼しい *cool*

T

tabako たばこ／タバコ *cigarettes*
tabako o hito hako たばこを一箱 *a pack of cigarettes*
tabako o suu たばこを吸う *to smoke*
tabakoya たばこ屋 *tobacco shop*
Tabasuko タバスコ *Tabasco*
tabemono 食べ物 *food*
taberu 食べる *to eat*
tabi 旅 *trip*
tabun 多分 *maybe*
tadashii 正しい *correct, right*
Tai jin タイ人 *Thai (person)*
Tai no タイの *Thai (adj.)*
taifū 台風 *typhoon*
taijō hōshin 帯状疱疹 *shingles*
taion kei 体温計 *thermometer*
taishi kan 大使館 *embassy*
taiya タイヤ *tire*
taiya no kūki atsu タイヤの空気圧 *tire pressure*
takai 高い *expensive/high/tall*
takakunai 高くない *inexpensive*
takasa 高さ *height*
take 竹 *bamboo*
take no kago 竹のかご *bamboo basket*
takezaiku no mise 竹細工の店 *bamboo craft shop*
taki 滝 *waterfall*
tako たこ *kite*
takusan たくさん *a lot, many*

takushī タクシー *taxi*
takushī noriba タクシー乗り場 *taxi stand*
tamago たまご *egg*
tamanegi 玉ねぎ *onion*
tani 谷 *valley*
tanoshii 楽しい *pleasant*
tanoshimu 楽しむ *to enjoy*
tanpen shōsetsu 短編小説 *short story books*
tanpon タンポン *tampons*
tansan 炭酸 *club soda*
tansu たんす *Japanese chest of drawers*
tantei shōsetsu 探偵小説 *detective stories*
taoru タオル *towels*
tasukeru 助ける *to help*
Tasukete! 助けて。*Help!*
tatande たたんで *folded*
tatoeba 例えば *for example*
tatsu 立つ *to stand*
te 手 *hand*
tebukuro 手袋 *gloves*
tēburu テーブル *table*
tegami 手紙 *letter, mail*
tegami o dasu 手紙を出す *to mail a letter*
tei shibō no gyūnyū 低脂肪の牛乳 *lowfat milk*
teien 庭園 *garden*
tekubi 手首 *wrist*
tēma テーマ *theme*
temae 点前 *etiquette of preparing tea*
ten-in 店員 *clerk*
tenisu テニス *tennis*
tenisu bōru テニス・ボール *tennis ball*
tenisu kōto テニス・コート *tennis court*
tenisu o suru テニスをする *to play tennis*
tenji suru 展示する *to exhibit*
tenka sōchi 点火装置 *ignition*
tenken suru 点検する *to check (examine)*
tenki 天気 *weather*

tenki yohō 天気予報 *weather forecast*

tennō 天皇 *emperor*

tenpi de yaita 天火で焼いた *baked*

tenpura 天ぷら *batter-fried food*

tento テント *tent*

terasu テラス *terrace*

terebi テレビ *television, television set, TV*

terefon kādo テレフォンカード *prepaid telephone card*

te sei no 手製の *handmade*

tesuri 手すり *handrail*

tesū ryō 手数料 *service charge*

tezukuri no 手作りの *handmade*

tī shatsu ティーシャツ *tee shirt*

tisshū ティッシュー *tissues*

to 戸 *door*

to と *and (between nouns)*

tōchaku 到着 *arrival*

tōchaku no jikan 到着の時間 *arrival time*

tochū no kyūkei 途中の休憩 *intermission*

tōfu 豆腐 *bean curd*

tōi 遠い *far*

toire トイレ *bathroom, restroom, toilet*

toiretto pēpā トイレット・ペーパー *toilet paper*

tōjiki 陶磁器 *ceramics*

tokai 都会 *big city*

tokei 時計 *clock*

tokei no shūriya 時計の修理屋 *watch repair shop*

tokeiya 時計屋 *watch and clock store*

tōki 陶器 *pottery*

tōki no mise 陶器の店 *pottery shop*

tokkuri とっくり *sake bottle*

tokkyū 特急 *limited express*

tokoro de ところで *by the way*

tokoya 床屋 *barbershop*

tokubai 特売 *bargain sale*

tokubetsu no 特別の *special*

tokutō 特等 *special class*

tomaru 泊まる *to stay*

tomaru 止まる *to stop (transportation)*

tomato トマト *tomato*

tomato jūsu トマト・ジュース *tomato juice*

tomodachi 友達 *friend*

tōmorokoshi とうもろこし *corn*

tōnan 盗難 *theft*

tōnyōbyō 糖尿病 *diabetes*

topāzu トパーズ *topaz*

toraberāzu chekku トラベラーズ・チェック *traveler's check*

torankiraizā トランキライザー *tranquilizers*

toranpu トランプ *cards (playing)*

toransu トランス *electrical transformer*

tori 鳥 *bird*

tōri 通り *street*

toriatsukai ryōkin 取り扱い料金 *processing fee*

torikumi 取り組み *sumo match*

Toruko ishi トルコ石 *turquoise*

toshi 都市 *city*

toshi totta 年とった *old (people)*

toshiyori 年寄り *senior citizens*

toshokan 図書館 *library*

tōsutā トースター *toaster*

tōsuto トースト *toast (bread)*

tsuā ツアー *tour*

tsuā gaido ツアー・ガイド *tour guide*

tsue 杖 *cane*

tsugi 次 *next*

Tsuitta ツイッター *Twitter*

tsūji yaku 通じ薬 *laxative*

tsūka 通貨 *currency*

tsukarete imasu つかれてい
ます *tired*
tsukau 使う *to spend
(money)/to use*
tsukemono 漬け物 *pickles*
tsuki 月 *month*
tsuku 着く *to arrive*
tsukurou 繕う *to mend*
tsukuru 作る *to make*
tsumami つまみ *appetizers*
tsume yasuri 爪やすり
emery boards, nail file
tsumetai 冷たい *cold (food,
drink)*
tsuri ba 釣り場 *fishing spot*
tsuri bune 釣り船 *fishing
boat*
tsuri dōgu 釣り道具 *fishing
equipment*
tsūro 通路 *aisle*
tsūro gawa 通路側 *by the
aisle*
tsūyaku 通訳 *interpreter*
tsuyoi 強い *strong*
tsuyu 梅雨 *rainy season*

U

uchi うち *house*
ude 腕 *arm*
ude dokei 腕時計 *wristwatch*
udon うどん *wheat noodles*
uisukī ウイスキー *whiskey*
uketoru 受け取る *to receive*
ukezara 受け皿 *saucer*
umi 海 *ocean, sea*
unagi うなぎ *eel*
undō gutsu 運動ぐつ *sneakers*
undōgu ten 運動具店
sporting goods store
untenshu 運転手 *driver,
chauffeur*
unten suru 運転する *to drive*
uo no me kōyaku 魚の目膏薬
corn plasters
uru 売る *to sell*
ūru ウール *wool*
urushi nuri no obon うるし
塗りのお盆 *lacquer trays*

urushi nuri no utsuwa うるし
塗りのうつわ *lacquer bowls*
ushiro うしろ *back (location)*
ushiro no うしろの *to the
rear*
usui 薄い *thin*
utatte 歌って *singing*

W

wa gomu 輪ゴム *rubber bands*
waifai ワイファイ *Wi-Fi*
wain ワイン *wine*
wain bā ワインバー *wine bar*
waipā ワイパー *windshield
wiper*
waishatsu ワイシャツ *shirt*
wakai 若い *young*
wakai hito 若い人 *young
people*
wakarimasu わかります *I
understand*
wakaru わかる *to understand*
waku わく *frames*
wan 湾 *bay*
warabuki yane わらぶき屋根
thatch roof
warau 笑う *to smile*
waribiki 割引き *discount*
warui 悪い *bad, wrong*
wasabi わさび *horseradish
(Japanese)*
washiki no 和式の
Japanese-style
washiya 和紙屋 *paper shop*
watakushi ga 私が *I*
watakushi no 私の *my*
watakushi tachi ga 私たちが
we
wataru 渡る *to cross*
wēbu ウェーブ *waves (hair)*
weru dān ウェルダーン
well-done (meat)
windō shoppingu o suru ウィ
ンドー・ショッピングをする
to window shop
wokka ウォッカ *vodka*

Y

yakamashii やかましい *noisy*

yakedo やけど *burn*

yakiami de yaita 焼網で焼いた *grilled*

yakitori 焼き鳥 *chicken skewered and grilled*

yakitsuke 焼き付け *print (photo)*

yakkyoku 薬局 *pharmacy*

yakyū 野球 *baseball*

yakyūjō 野球場 *ballpark*

yama 山 *mountain*

yameru やめる *to stop (v.i.)*

yasai 野菜 *vegetables*

yasashii やさしい *easy*

yasui 安い *cheap*

yō nashi 洋なし *pear*

yōdochinki ヨードチンキ *iodine*

yōfuku 洋服 *clothes*

yōfuku ten 洋服店 *clothing store*

yōguruto ヨーグルト *yogurt*

yōji ようじ *toothpicks*

yōji 幼児 *toddler*

yokushitsu 浴室 *bathroom*

yokusō 浴そう *bathtub*

yoku yaketa よく焼けた *well-done (meat)*

yomu 読む *to read*

yorokonde 喜んで *with pleasure*

Yōroppa seihin ヨーロッパ製品 *European products*

yoru 夜 *night*

yōshiki no 洋式の *Western-style*

yōshoku shinju 養殖真珠 *cultured pearls*

yotto ヨット *sailboat*

yowai 弱い *weak*

yoyaku 予約 *appointment, reservation*

yubi 指 *finger*

yūbin 郵便 *mail*

yūbin posuto 郵便ポスト *mail box*

yūbinkyoku 郵便局 *post office*

yubiwa 指輪 *ring (jewelry)*

yudaya kyō no jiin ユダヤ教の寺院 *synagogue*

yudeta ゆでた *boiled*

yūgata 夕方 *evening*

yūjin 友人 *friend*

yuki 雪 *snow*

yūki (shokuhin) 有機(食品) *organic (food)*

yūmei (na) 有名(な) *famous*

yunomi jawan 湯飲み茶腕 *teacup*

yūran sen 遊覧船 *cruise ship*

yūro ユーロ *euro*

yurui ゆるい *loose (clothes)*

yūshoku 夕食 *dinner*

yūzā nēmu ユーザーネーム *user name*

Z

zaseki shitei 座席指定 *reserved seats (train)*

zasshi 雑誌 *magazine*

zayaku 座薬 *suppositories*

zeikan 税関 *customs*

zeikan kensa 税関検査 *customs inspection*

zeikan no shinkoku sho 税関の申告書 *customs declaration*

zeikin 税金 *tax*

zenbu de 全部で *altogether*

zensai 前菜 *appetizers*

zensoku ぜんそく *asthma*

zukizuki suru ズキズキする *throbbing*

zukkīni ズッキーニ *zucchini*

zutsū 頭痛 *headache*

DIALOGUES

THE BASICS

Speaker 1:　すみませんが。 *Sumimasen ga.*	Excuse me.
Speaker 2:　はい、何ですか。 *Hai, nan desu ka.*	Yes, what is it?
1:　ちょっと、助けてもらえますか。 *Chotto, tasukete moraemasu ka.*	Can you help me?
2:　ええ、もちろん。 *Ē, mochiron.*	Yes, of course.
1:　道に迷ってしまいました。 *Michi ni mayotte shimaimashita.*	I've lost my way.
2:　どこに行きたいですか。 *Doko ni ikitai desu ka.*	Where do you want to go?
1:　本屋をさがしています。 *Hon-ya o sagashite imasu.*	I'm looking for the bookstore.
2:　ああ、それはここの近くです。連れていってあげましょう。 *Ā, sore wa koko no chikaku desu. Tsurete itte agemashō.*	Oh, it's near here. I'll take you.
1:　どうもすみません。 *Dōmo sumimasen.*	Sorry to bother you.
2:　いいえ。それは、私の店です。 *Iie, sore wa, watakushi no mise desu.*	No, not at all. It's my store.

THE LAND AND PEOPLE

Speaker 1:　こんにちは。 *Konnichiwa.*	Good afternoon.
Speaker 2:　こんにちは。 *Konnichiwa.*	Good afternoon.
1:　いい天気ですねえ。 *Ii tenki desu nē.*	It's nice weather, isn't it?
2:　ええ、本当に。 *Ē, hontō ni.*	Yes, indeed.

1: ところで、私の名前はメリー・ジャクソンです。どうぞ、よろしく。
Tokorode, watakushi no namae wa, Merī Jakuson desu. Dōzo, yoroshiku.

By the way, my name is Mary Jackson. How do you do?

2: 私の名前は、鈴木武雄です。こちらこそよろしく。*Watakushi no namae wa, Suzuki Takeo desu. Kochira koso yoroshiku.*

My name is Takeo Suzuki. How do you do?

2: 日本は、初めてですか。*Nihon wa, hajimete desu ka.*

Is this your first visit to Japan?

1: はい、初めてです。*Hai, hajimete desu.*

Yes, it is.

2: 日本の食べ物は、大丈夫ですか。*Nihon no tabemono wa, daijōbu desu ka.*

Are you okay with Japanese food?

1: はい、大好きです。けれども、納豆はだめです。*Hai, daisuki desu. Keredomo, nattō wa dame desu.*

Yes, I like it very much. But I don't like fermented soy beans.

WHEN YOU ARRIVE

Speaker 1: 赤坂の_____ホテルまで行きたいのですが。タクシーは、いくらかかりますか。*Akasaka no _____ Hoteru made ikitai no desu ga. Takushī wa, ikura kakarimasu ka.*

I want to go to _____ Hotel in Akasaka. How much will a taxi cost?

Speaker 2: 二万八千円ぐらいだと思います。*Ni man hassen en gurai da to omoimasu.*

I think it will cost about 28,000 yen.

1: それはドルだといくらですか。*Sore wa doru da to ikura desu ka.*

How much is that in dollars?

2: 約二百八十ドルです。*Yaku ni hyaku hachi jū doru desu.*

It's about 280 dollars.

1: ああ、八十ドル。まあまあですね。*Ā, hachi jū doru. Māmā desu ne.*

Oh, eighty dollars. That's quite reasonable.

2: いいえ、八十ではなくて、二百八十
です。 *Iie, hachi jū dewa nakute, ni
hyaku hachi jū desu.*

No, not eighty—
it's two hundred
eighty.

1: 二百八十ドル！ずいぶん高いですね。
*Ni hyaku hachi jū doru! Zuibun
takai desu ne.*

Two hundred eighty
dollars! That's
very expensive.

2: ホテルまで行く、リムジン・バスがあ
りますよ。 *Hoteru made iku, rimujin
basu ga arimasu yo. Yasukute benri
desu.*

There's a
limousine bus that
goes to the Hotel.
It's convenient and
inexpensive.

1: それは、いくらかかりますか。
Sore wa, ikura kakarimasu ka.

How much will it
cost?

2. 三千百円。ほんの三十一ドルです。
*San zen hyaku en. Hon no san jū
ichi doru desu.*

It's 3,100 yen. That's
only thirty-one
dollars.

BANKING AND MONEY MATTERS

Speaker 1: 個人用小切手が使えますか。
Kojin yō kogitte ga tsukaemasu ka.

Can I use a personal
check?

Speaker 2:申し訳ありませんが、使え
ません。*Mōshiwake arimasen ga,
tsukaemasen.*

I'm sorry, but you
can't.

1: ドルで払えますか。*Doru de
haraemasu ka.*

Can I pay with
dollars?

2: いいえ、円でお願いします。*Iie,
en de onegai shimasu.*

No. Please pay with
yen.

1: 円が足りません。近くで、ドルを
円に交換できますか。*En ga
tarimasen. Chikaku de, doru o en ni
kōkan dekimasu ka.*

I don't have enough
yen. Can I exchange
dollars to yen near
here?

2: はい、できます。駅前の銀行に行
ってください。*Hai, dekimasu. Eki
mae no ginkō ni itte kudasai.*

Yes, you can. Go to
the bank in front of
the train station.

1: そこの交換率は、いいですか。
Soko no kōkan ritsu wa, ii desu ka.

Do they give you a good exchange rate?

2: ええ、多分。*Ē, tabun.*

Yes, maybe.

1: 分かりました。すぐ、戻ってきます。*Wakarimashita. Sugu, modotte kimasu.*

I understand. I'll be right back.

2: どうぞ、ごゆっくり。*Dōzo, goyukkuri.*

Please, take your time.

AT THE HOTEL

Speaker 1: もしもし、フロント・デスクですか。*Moshi moshi, furonto desuku desu ka.*

Hello, is this the front desk?

Speaker 2: はい。何かご用ですか。*Hai. Nanika goyō desu ka.*

Yes. May I help you?

1: 五百号室のエド・ペリーですが。メッセージがありますか。*Go hyaku gō shitsu no Edo Perī desu ga. Messēji ga arimasu ka.*

I'm Ed Perry in Room 500. Are there any messages for me?

2: はい。田辺さんからお電話がありました。*Hai. Tanabe san kara odenwa ga arimashita.*

Yes. There was a telephone call from Mr. Tanabe.

1: それで、メッセージは。*Sore de, messēji wa.*

And the message?

2: あすの朝九時に、オフィスに来てくださいとのことでした。*Asu no asa ku ji ni, ofisu ni kite kudasai to no koto deshita.*

He said please come to his office at 9 o'clock tomorrow morning.

1: 分かりました。丸の内まで、どのくらい時間がかかりますか。*Wakarimashita. Marunouchi made, dono kurai jikan ga kakarimasu ka.*

I see. How long does it take to get to Marunouchi?

2: 地下鉄で三十分、タクシーで
一時間かかります。*Chikatetsu de
san juppun, takushī de ichi jikan
kakarimasu.*

It takes thirty
minutes by subway,
one hour by taxi.

1: タクシーは、地下鉄の倍かかる
のですか。*Takushī wa, chikatetsu
no bai kakaru no desu ka.*

A taxi takes twice as
long as the subway?

2: ラッシュ・アワーでは、かかり ます。
Rasshu awā dewa kakarimasu.

In rush hour it does.

GETTING AROUND TOWN

Speaker 1: 赤坂に行きたいのですが。
どの切符の販売機を使ったらいいで
すか。*Akasaka ni ikitai no desu ga.
Dono kippu no hanbai ki o
tsukattara ii desu ka.*

I'd like to go to
Akasaka. Which
ticket machine
should I use?

Speaker 2: この販売機を使います。
Kono hanbai ki o tsukaimasu.

You use this
machine.

1: いくら入れますか。*Ikura
iremasu ka.*

How much do I put
in?

2: 二百八十円入れます。*Ni hyaku
hachi jū en iremasu.*

280 yen.

1: 乗り換えがありますか。*Norikae
ga arimasu ka.*

Do I have to change
trains?

2: はい。霞ヶ関で、丸の内線に乗り
換えです。*Hai. Kasumigaseki de,
Marunouchi sen ni norikae desu.*

Yes. You change to
the Marunouchi line
at Kasumigaseki.

1: どうやって、霞ヶ関が分かりま
すか。*Dō yatte, Kasumigaseki ga
wakarimasu ka.*

How will I recognize
Kasumigaseki?

2: 車内放送があるから、大丈夫です。
*Shanai hōsō ga aru kara daijōbu
desu.*

It's okay. There are
announcements on
the train.

1: 赤坂行きのホームは、見つかるで
しょうか。*Akasaka yuki no hōmu
wa, mitsukaru deshō ka.*

Can I find the
platform for the
train to Akasaka?

2: ローマ字の色別のサインがあるから、子供でも見つかります。*Rōma ji no iro betsu no sain ga aru kara, kodomo demo mitsukarimasu.*

There are color coded signs with Roman characters. Even a child can find it.

PLANNING A TRIP

Speaker 1: 仕事が済んだら、少し見物をしたいのですが。どこに行ったらいいですか。*Shigoto ga sundara, sukoshi kenbutsu o shitai no desu ga. Doko ni ittara ii desu ka.*

I'd like to do some sightseeing after finishing business. Where shall I go?

Speaker 2: どのくらい、時間がありますか。*Dono kurai, jikan ga arimasu ka.*

How much time do you have?

1: 三日、あります。*Mikka, arimasu.*

I have three days.

2: そうですねえ。箱根に一泊旅行、その後日光に日帰りの旅行はいかがですか。*Sō desu nē. Hakone ni ippaku ryokō, sono ato Nikkō ni higaeri no ryokō wa ikaga desu ka.*

Let me see. How about an overnight trip to Hakone, then a day trip to Nikko?

1: どうやって行きますか。*Dō yatte ikimasu ka.*

How do I get there?

2: 電車も、観光バスもあります。*Densha mo, kankō basu mo arimasu.*

There are trains and sightseeing buses, too.

1: 予約の必要が、ありますか。*Yoyaku no hitsuyō ga arimasu ka.*

Do I need to make reservations?

2: 旅行代理店が、全部アレンジしてくれます。*Ryokō dairi ten ga, zenbu arenji shite kuremasu.*

A travel agency can arrange everything for you.

1: 箱根では、温泉のある旅館に泊まれますか。*Hakone dewa, onsen no aru ryokan ni tomaremasu ka.*

Can I stay at a Japanese inn with hot springs?

2:　はい。よければ、大浴場を試した
らいかがですか。いい気持ちですよ。
*Hai. Yokereba, dai yokujō o
tameshitara ikaga desu ka. Ii
kimochi desu yo.*

Yes. If you like, try a big communal bath. It feels good.

ENTERTAINMENT

Speaker 1:　いま、何か面白い催し物
をやっていますか。*Ima, nanika
omoshiroi moyōshimono o yatte
imasu ka.*

Is there any interesting entertainment in town now?

Speaker 2:　どんなものを見たいで
すか。*Donna mono o mitai desu ka.*

What kind of event do you want to see?

1:　映画や音楽より、舞台に興味があ
ります。*Eiga ya ongaku yori, butai
ni kyōmi ga arimasu.*

I'm more interested in the theater than movies and music.

2:　伝統的なものですか、現代物で
すか。*Dentō teki na mono desu ka,
gendai mono desu ka.*

Traditional performances or contemporary ones?

1:　歌舞伎とか、文楽とか、能とか、、、
*Kabuki toka Bunraku toka, Nō toka
. . . . .*

Kabuki, Bunraku, and Noh......

2:　今、文楽と能はやっていません。
けれども、歌舞伎は見られますよ。
*Ima, Bunraku to Nō wa yatte imasen.
Keredomo, Kabuki wa miraremasu
yo.*

There are no Bunraku or Noh performances right now. But you can see Kabuki.

1:　券は、どこで買えますか。*Ken wa,
doko de kaemasu ka.*

Where can I buy a ticket?

2:　プレイ・ガイドで買えます。*Purei
Gaido de kaemasu.*

You can buy one at a Play Guide.

1:　相撲も見たいのですが。*Sumō mo
mitai no desu ga.*

I'd like to see Sumo, too.

2: いい券を買うのは、難しいですよ。
テレビで見たらいかがですか。 *Ii ken
o kau no wa, muzukashii desu yo.
Terebi de mitara ikaga desu ka.*

It's difficult to buy
good tickets for
Sumo. Why don't
you watch it on TV?

FOOD AND DRINK

Speaker 2: 和食は好きですか。
Washoku wa suki desu ka.

Do you like
Japanese food?

Speaker 1: はい。昨日の晩はすき
焼き、おとといの晩は天ぷらを食べ
ました。 *Hai, kinō no ban wa
sukiyaki, ototoi no ban wa tenpura o
tabemashita.*

Yes. Last night I had
sukiyaki, and the
night before I had
tempura.

2: 毎晩、和食ですか。 *Maiban,
washoku desu ka.*

Are you eating
Japanese food every
night?

1: はい。今晩は、すしが食べたい
です。いいおすし屋をご存じですか。
*Hai, konban wa, sushi ga tabetai
desu. Ii osushiya o gozonji desu ka.*

Yes. I'd like to have
sushi tonight. Do
you know a good
sushi shop?

2: ええ。行きましょう。何でも食べ
られますか。 *Ē. Ikimashō. Nandemo
taberaremasu ka.*

Sure. Let's go. Can
you eat everything?

1: 何でもって、どういう意味ですか。
Nandemotte, dō iu imi desu ka.

What do you mean
by everything?

2: 甘えびはどうですか。 *Ama ebi
wa dō desu ka.*

How about raw
shrimp?

1: ええ、多分。 *Ē, tabun.*

Well, maybe.

2: 生きたえびは。 *Ikita ebi wa.*

And live shrimp?

1: 急に、食欲がなくなりました。
*Kyū ni, shokuyoku ga
nakunarimashita.*

I just lost my
appetite!

MEETING PEOPLE

1: ここは、素晴らしい所ですねえ。
何から何まで、楽しんでいます。
*Koko wa, subarashii tokoro
desu nē. Nani kara nani made,
tanoshinde imasu.*

This is a wonderful
place. I've been
enjoying everything
here.

2: ありがとうございます。*Arigatō
gozaimasu.*

Thank you very
much.

1: ここにお住まいですか。*Koko ni
osumai desu ka.*

Do you live here?

2: はい、住んでいます。*Hai, sunde
imasu.*

Yes, I do.

1: 私は、今まで _____ と、_____
に 行きました。*Watakushi wa, ima
made _____ to, _____ ni
ikimashita.*

I've been to _____
and _____ .

2: _____ も、面白いですよ。*_____
mo, omoshiroi desu yo.*

_____ is interesting,
too.

1: あした、行ってみます。ところで、
私は、マイク・テーラーです。どうぞ、
よろしく。*Ashita, itte mimasu.
Tokoro de, watakushi wa, Maiku
Tērā desu. Dōzo, yoroshiku.*

I'll go there
tomorrow. By the
way, I'm Mike
Taylor. How do you
do?

2: 私は、鈴木文子です。こちらこそ、
よろしく。*Watakushi wa, Suzuki
Fumiko desu. Kochira koso,
yoroshiku.*

I'm Fumiko Suzuki.
How do you do?

1: また、お目にかかれますか。
Mata, omne ni kakaremasu ka.

Can I see you again?

2: はい、電話をください。夫も、
きっと一緒に来たがると思います。
*Hai, denwa o kudasai. Otto mo,
kitto issho ni kitagaru to omoimasu.*

Yes, give me a call.
And I'm sure my
husband would love
to join us, too.

SHOPPING 1

Speaker 1: おみやげの買い物が、たくさんあります。*Omiyage no kaimono ga, takusan arimasu.*

I have a lot of souvenir shopping to do.

Speaker 2: どんなものが、買いたいですか。*Donna mono ga, kaitai desu ka.*

What kind of things do you want to buy?

1: 代表的な、日本のものが欲しいんです。*Daihyō teki na Nihon no mono ga hoshiin desu.*

I want typical Japanese items.

2: 例えば、、、、*Tatoeba, ...*

For example?

1: オーディオ装置とか、多分カメラ。*Ōdio sōchi toka, tabun kamera.*

Audio equipment, maybe a camera.

2: それなら、秋葉原に行くといいですよ。他には。*Sore nara, Akihabara ni iku to ii desu yo. Hoka niwa.*

Go to Akihabara for that. Anything else?

1: 台所用品、着物、版画のようなものです。*Daidokoro yōhin, kimono, hanga no yō na mono desu.*

Things like kitchen utensils, kimono, and woodblock prints.

2: 銀座や、新宿や、池袋に行ってみるといいですよ。デパートがたくさんあります。*Ginza ya, Shinjuku ya, Ikebukuro ni itte miru to ii desu yo. Depāto ga takusan arimasu.*

Try Ginza, Shinjuku, or Ikebukuro. There are many department stores.

1: 値段のかけ引きが、できますか。*Nedan no kakehiki ga, dekimasu ka.*

Can you bargain?

2: 秋葉原だけです。ほかでは、できません。*Akihabara dake desu. Hoka dewa, dekimasen.*

Only at Ahihabara. Nowhere else.

SHOPPING 2

Speaker 2:　いらっしゃいませ。
Irasshai mase.

Welcome.

Speaker 1:　こんにちは。*Konnichiwa.*

Good afternoon.

2:　特に何か、おさがしですか。*Toku ni, nanika osagashi desu ka.*

Are you looking for anything particular?

1:　ブラウスをさがしています。
Burausu o sagashite imasu.

I'm looking for a blouse.

2:　贈り物ですか。*Okurimono desu ka.*

Is it a gift?

1:　はい、妻へのプレゼントです。
Hai, tsuma e no purezento desu.

Yes. It's a present for my wife.

2:　奥様のサイズは。*Okusama no saizu wa.*

What's your wife's size?

1:　アメリカサイズの六です。
Amerika saizu no roku desu.

American size 6.

2:　日本のサイズだと七ですね。この黒い絹のは、いかがですか。*Nihon no saizu da to, nana desu ne. Kono kuroi kinu no wa, ikaga desu ka.*

That'll be Japanese size 7. How about this black silk one?

1:　素晴らしいですね。いくらですか。*Subarashii desu ne. Ikura desu ka.*

It's wonderful. How much is it?

2:　三万五千円です。よろしければ、クレジット・カードが使えますよ。
San man go sen en desu. Yoroshikereba, kurejitto kādo ga tsukaemasu yo.

It's 35,000 yen. If you like, you can use a credit card.

HEALTH AND MEDICAL CARE

Speaker 1:　おなかが痛いんです。夕べは、よく眠れませんでした。
Onaka ga itain desu. Yūbe wa, yoku nemuremasen deshita.

I have a stomach ache. I couldn't sleep well last night.

Speaker 2: どこが痛いですか。*Doko ga itai desu ka.*

Where does it hurt?

1: ここです。*Koko desu.*

Right here.

2: 鋭い痛みですか。*Surudoi itami desu ka.*

Is it a sharp pain?

1: いいえ、鈍い痛みです。*Iie, nibui itami desu.*

No, it's a dull pain.

2: 熱と血圧を、測ります。*Netsu to ketsuatsu o, hakarimasu.*

I'm going to take your temperature and blood pressure.

1: 先生、どうですか。*Sensei, dō desu ka.*

Doctor, how am I?

2: 熱も血圧も、平常です。症状を和らげるために、薬をあげましょう。*Netsu mo ketsuatsu mo, heijō desu. Shōjō o yawarageru tame ni, kusuri o agemashō.*

Both your temperature and blood pressure are normal. I'm giving you some medicine to relieve your symptoms.

1: 病気ですか。*Byōki desu ka.*

Am I sick?

2: いいえ、心配はいりません。単なる、時差ボケと食べ過ぎのコンビネーションに過ぎません。*Iie, shinpai wa irimasen. Tan naru, jisa boke to tabesugi no konbinēshon ni sugimasen.*

No, don't worry. It's just a combination of jet lag and overeating.

COMMUNICATIONS

Speaker 1: 電話をかけるのに、硬貨がいるんですが。千円札をくずしてもらえますか。*Denwa o kakeru no ni, kōka ga irun desu ga. Sen en satsu o kuzushite moraemasu ka.*

I need some coins for telephone calls. Can you change a 1,000-yen bill?

Speaker 2: いいですよ。けれども、テレフォン・カードを買うと便利ですよ。*Ii desu yo. Keredomo, terefon kādo o kau to benri desu yo.*

Sure. But if you buy a telephone card, it's convenient.

1: 使い方は。*Tsukaikata wa.*

How do I use it?

2: 簡単です。差し込み口に入れるだけで、終わったら、カードは戻ってきます。*Kantan desu. Sashikimiguchi ni ireru dake de, owattara, kādo wa modotte kimasu.*

Simple. Just insert it into a slot. When you finish, it'll be returned.

1: いくらですか。*Ikura desu ka.*

How much is it?

2: 千円です。*Sen en desu.*

It's 1,000 yen.

1: はい、それをいただきます。 *Hai, sore o itadakimasu.*

Yes, I'll take it.

2: 日本のどこでも、使えますよ。*Nihon no doko demo, tsukaemasu yo.*

You can use it anywhere in Japan.

1: 今度の旅行で、千円を全部使わなかったら。*Kondo no ryokō de, sen en o zenbu tsukawanakattara.*

What if I don't use up the 1,000 yen on this trip?

2: その時は、また日本へ戻ってこなければなりません。*Sono toki wa, mata Nihon e modotte konakereba narimasen.*

Then you have to come back to Japan!

DRIVING A CAR

Speaker 1: 車を借りたいのですが。*Kuruma o karitai no desu ga.*

I'd like to rent a car.

Speaker 2: 日本で、運転したことがありますか。左側通行ですよ。*Nihon de, unten shita koto ga arimasu ka. Hidarigawa tsūkō desu yo.*

Have you driven in Japan? You drive on the left side of the road.

1: いいえ。でも、イギリスで運転した ことがあるから大丈夫です。*Iie. Demo, Igirisu de unten shita koto ga aru kara daijōbu desu.*

No. But I'll be okay. I have driven in England.

2: 日本語のサインは、読めますか。 *Nihon go no sain wa, yomemasu ka.*

Can you read signs in Japanese?

1: まあ、何とかなるでしょう。*Mā, nantoka naru deshō.*

Somehow I'll manage.

2: どこまで、行くんですか。*Doko made, ikun desu ka.*

Where are you going?

1: 九州まで。*Kyūshū made.*

To Kyushu.

2: 長距離のドライブですよ。*Chō kyori no doraibu desu yo.*

That's a long drive.

1: 分かっています。でも、時間は そんなにかかりません。高速運転が 得意ですから。*Wakatte imasu. Demo, jikan wa sonna ni kakarimasen. Kōsoku unten ga tokui desu kara.*

I know. But it won't take long. I drive fast.

2: それでは、保険をたくさんかけた 方がいいでしょう。ご幸運をお祈り します。*Soredewa, hoken o takusan kaketa hō ga ii deshō. Go kōun o oinori shimasu.*

Well then, you'd better get a lot of insurance. And good luck!

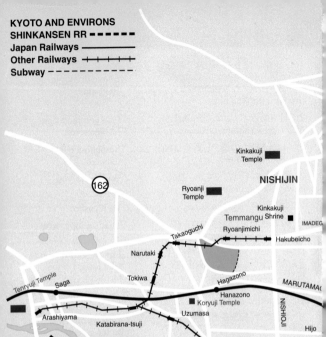
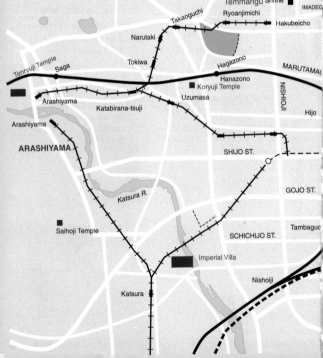